Pie Tra,

To DAVID CHRISTOFFERSON

ONE OF THE NICEST MEN IT HAS

EVER BEEN MY PLEASURE to KNOW.

THANK YOU FOR BEING MY COMPUTER

COACH AND FOR BEING MY CRIBBAGE FOIL.

ALL THE VERY BEST to YOU.

David Proctor

PIE TRAYNOR

A Baseball Biography

James Forr *and*
David Proctor

McFarland & Company, Inc., Publishers
Jefferson, North Carolina, and London

LIBRARY OF CONGRESS CATALOGUING-IN-PUBLICATION DATA

Forr, James, 1972–
    Pie Traynor : a baseball biography / James Forr and
David Proctor.
        p.   cm.
    Includes bibliographical references and index.

    ISBN 978-0-7864-4385-7
    softcover : 50# alkaline paper ∞

    1. Traynor, Pie, 1898–1972.   2. Baseball players— United
States— Biography.   3. Pittsburgh Pirates (Baseball team)
I. Proctor, David, 1944–   II. Title.
GV865.T695F67   2010
796.357092 — dc22 [B]   2009049168

British Library cataloguing data are available

On the cover: Pie and little boy on dugout
(©*Pittsburgh Post-Gazette*)

Manufactured in the United States of America

*McFarland & Company, Inc., Publishers
    Box 611, Jefferson, North Carolina 28640
    www.mcfarlandpub.com*

To John Garner, the Cape Cod League's
director of public relations and broadcasting,
who made our collaboration possible.

In memory of James' son,
Arthur Solomon Forr
(April 20, 2009–April 20, 2009)

Table of Contents

Acknowledgments

Anyone who is cynical about human nature should be required to research a book. So many people were willing, even eager, to help us and we are indebted to them for their cooperation. With apologies to those we inadvertently omit, and in no logical order, we wish to say thank you to the following people.

We begin with John Garner, director of public relations and broadcasting for the Cape Cod League, who first put James and David in touch with one another. Elsewhere in New England, thanks to Fred Wallace, Framingham, Massachusetts, town historian; Mary Cerato of the Somerville, Massachusetts, Public School Department; Professor Sol Gittleman of Tufts University, a scholar and gentleman in the truest sense of those words; Stephanie Lucarelli of the Arlington, Massachusetts, Town Hall; Joyce Brothers from the Narragansett, Rhode Island, Public Library; Al Irish of the Falmouth, Massachusetts, Historical Society and historian of the Cape Cod Baseball Hall of Fame and Museum; Ken Bowes of the Martha's Vineyard Public Library; Arthur Pollock of the *Boston Herald*; Aaron Schmidt and Henry Scannell of the Boston Public Library; Ron Castile, Maura Copeland, and especially Kevin O'Kelly of the Somerville, Massachusetts, Public Library; Anna Duprey, Kate Deviny, and Jan Gryskiewicz of the Westfield, Massachusetts, Athanaeum; Elaine Ardia of the Edmund S. Muskie Archives and Special Collections Library of Bates College in Lewiston, Maine; and Jon Litchfield from Northeastern University's Sports Information Department.

In Pittsburgh, we are indebted to Jerry Boscia from Past Unpuzzlers, who knows, literally and figuratively, where the bodies are buried around the city. Bill Cardille, Traynor's friend from his television days, was always happy to answer whatever questions we had. John Mehno helped get the ball rolling, giving us a number of leads and ideas for people to speak with. Thanks also to Sally O'Leary, Dan Hart, and Dave Arrigo from the Pittsburgh Pirates; Eric Estes from the Pittsburgh Steelers; Eric Hotchkiss from the University of Pittsburgh Sports Information Department; from the *Pittsburgh Post-Gazette* Angelika Kane and Shari Smedley; Bob Dickey from KQV Radio; and John Buriak, who runs the website ChillerTheaterMemories.com.

A tip of the hat also to Carole Fure from the Burnett County, Wisconsin, Historical Society; Julie Schlesselman-Stambaugh from the Whitewater Valley, Indiana, Community Library District; Jeremy Jones, John Horne and the rest of the good folks at the National Baseball Hall of Fame Library in Cooperstown, New York, who work so hard to keep the history of the game of baseball alive; Joanie Gearin from the National Archives and Records Administration; Elizabeth Yura from the Associated Press; Norman Currie from Corbis; and Gary Shutlock of the Public Archives of Nova Scotia.

Also a tip of the hat to Tony and Donna Alibrandi, Tony Bartirome, Jan Beaujon, Bill Christine, Bob Correia, Jewel Ens, Joan Estienne, Jim Farmer, Bob Golub, Mike Helmer, Ralphie Hill, Martha Shea, Karl Lindholm, Brooks Robinson, Jim Sandoval, and Bill Wintz for their help and contributions.

And of course, our cohorts from the Society for American Baseball Research were invaluable with their support and responses to our cries for help. Specifically, we would like to thank the late Dick Thompson, Jerry Casway, Kit Crissey, Thomas Garrett, Bill Nowlin, Ronald Selter, and Nick Wilson. Also Eileen Canepari from the SABR Lending Library deserves a tip of the cap for shipping us a couple of articles on rather short notice.

Also we are grateful for the cooperation of members of the Traynor family, all of whom it was a pleasure to meet and work with — Marilyn Traynor Lenick; Bobby Jr., David, and Hal Traynor; Paul N. and Marybeth Traynor; Sharon Traynor; and Mary Lou Traynor Fisher.

David wishes to extend special appreciation to his cribbage buddies; Bob Arnold for his tireless and diligent proofreading; James Alan Russell for his financial support; attorney Debbie Basile of the law firm of Doherty, Wallace, Pillsbury & Murphy, PC, Springfield, Massachusetts; his friend and co-worker Don Marsh, the best Nixie clerk in the entire U.S. Postal Service; and Mary Indomenico, David's personal typist, whose work is absolutely "perfect in print."

Lastly, and most gratefully, David wishes to thank his wife, Vivian Proctor, for her sacrifice of family time and her endless patience and encouragement.

James extends special appreciation to his wife, Cheryl Hill, who was content to sit on the sofa while her husband spent romantic evenings with baseball-reference.com; to Baxter the Hound for his comic relief; and to two people who are no longer with us but who serve as ongoing sources of inspiration — his dad, Jim, and son, Arthur.

Preface

It seems strange to both of us that it took this long, nearly 40 years after his death, for someone to write the life story of Pie Traynor. Until now, Traynor was perhaps the most prominent member of the Baseball Hall of Fame who had not been the subject of a biography. Perhaps it is because some historians assumed that Traynor's life story was not very compelling. There is, after all, an old canard that nice guys make for boring biographies, and Traynor was about as nice a guy as anyone could hope to meet.

Or possibly an apparent dearth of readily available background information warned some people off. Although Traynor could strike up a conversation with a fence post, he was a modest man who was somewhat uncomfortable discussing his accomplishments—and exceedingly uncomfortable discussing his life. We often mentioned to each other that if we could have brought Traynor back from the dead and spent even 30 minutes with him, we could have made this a much better book. We did the best we could with what we had to work with, but he took a lot of memories and rich insights with him.

A final hypothesis is that maybe a lot fewer people know about (or care about) Traynor today. For decades people spoke of him as the greatest third baseman in history. But when modern baseball fans or members of the media debate the all-time greatest at the position, his name seldom enters the discussion. And to some extent that is understandable.

In light of this, we find it to be a stroke of good fortune that we both began working on biographies of Traynor independently, at roughly the same time, albeit completely unbeknownst to one another.

We came to this project via two very different routes. David's original connection to Traynor was more personal and direct. On a fall New England evening in 2000, a drop-dead handsome young man knocked on his front door. "Hi! I'm Jim Traynor and I'm here to take your daughter out." Like most loving dads, David wanted to know a little something about this young stranger who was there to see his daughter. He was curious about Jim's personality, background, interests and, certainly, his plans for the evening. But most of all, David, a member of the Society for American Baseball Research, was fixated on that last name. He got right to the point and blurted out, "Are you related to Pie Traynor?"

In his thick New Jersey accent, Jim replied, "Yeah, I'm his great nephew."

As we would later learn, that actually wasn't quite accurate; but, in another way, it was exactly the right answer. As far as David was concerned, the kid was okay. On November 16, 2001, Jim Traynor married David's daughter, Krista. They are now proud parents of a beautiful daughter, Nicole.

David never intended to write a book about Pie Traynor; he would have been content just to read one. Long a student of baseball's so-called Golden Era, he knew a little about Traynor but now had a compelling reason to learn more. But he was astonished to find there wasn't a whole lot out there. What he did uncover suggested to him that Traynor was a man whose story needed to be told, not just because of the kind of player he was, but also because David was captivated by the kind of person Traynor was and what he meant to the city of Pittsburgh for nearly a half-century. So David embarked upon the quest to write the definitive Traynor biography.

For James, the first seed for this book probably was planted somewhere in the dark, unconscious recesses of his mind about 30 years ago. He was adopted and raised by his grandparents and grew particularly close to his grandfather, who, to him, was always "Dad."

James and his grandfather bonded over sports, baseball in particular. They would pass hot Sunday afternoons or sticky weeknights on the back porch — Dad on his lounge chair taking drags from a Salem, James scurrying around underfoot — listening to the Pittsburgh Pirates on the radio. Now and then, when he wasn't busy grunting obscenities at Dave Parker or Dale Berra, the old man would weave stories about the heroes from his youth, a far away, sepia-toned time that to his grandson seemed almost unimaginable.

When his grandfather took James on these little excursions back to the Paleozoic era, he often would rave about Pie Traynor. But for many years, Traynor remained an empty vessel for James, really nothing more than a peculiar name belonging to a great player who lived in a hazy corner of an elderly man's memory.

Many years later James stumbled upon a couple of things about Traynor that began to bring the man to life. First was a newspaper column that mentioned, in passing, Traynor's daily habit of walking the streets of Pittsburgh, greeting people along the way. There was another column in which the writer reminisced about watching Traynor on local broadcasts of professional wrestling. Wrestling, of all things? James was intrigued.

Those little morsels James picked up inspired him to write a short piece on Traynor for the Society of American Baseball Research's Bio Project. That article, in turn, prompted a response from the late Dick Thompson, a longtime SABR member who suggested turning the piece into a full-length biography.

Our paths crossed thanks to John Garner, director of public relations and broadcasting for the Cape Cod League, who put us in touch. We got together in Springfield, Massachusetts, at the Basketball Hall of Fame, one afternoon and concluded that a collaboration made a lot of sense. David lives in Massachusetts and had done a lot of digging into Traynor's early life in the Boston area. James, who lived in Pennsylvania at the time, had been working the other end of Traynor's life, his retirement years in Pittsburgh. It seemed like a perfect fit. Working separately, our books would have taken much longer to complete and probably would not have been nearly as thorough as what we pulled together in this combined effort.

We strove to make this biography more than a dry summary of box scores culled from yellowed newspapers, although at times we felt it was useful to bop along with the day-by-day rhythm of a baseball season. But if the most memorable thing readers take away from this book is, for example, that Pie Traynor had a really good World Series in 1925, then we've flopped. We want readers to feel what it was like for Traynor as an ambitious boy of meager means trying to make a name for himself. We want readers to see a master craftsman learning and plying his trade at third base. We want readers to taste the bitter disappointment of a pennant that got away. We want readers to hear the voices of people who knew him as a man, not only as a ballplayer.

Pie Traynor was a gifted athlete and a remarkably kind and giving person, but he was no deity, of course. He had failures, insecurities, quirks, and moments of pettiness just like we all do. We will address his flaws and mistakes openly and honestly. Our purpose in doing so is not to denigrate the man — quite the contrary, actually. It is, after all, the intermingling of imperfections and virtues that makes a person unique and genuine. All of us probably can see many of our own frailties and shortcomings reflected in Traynor, but maybe we also can see in him the better side of human nature and perhaps a little of what we aspire to be.

So in the words of legendary broadcaster Vin Scully, we urge you to pull up a chair, stick around a while, and learn a little about one of baseball's forgotten stars.

1

From Canada to Somerville

It is ingrained in our collective unconscious to think about our lives as a journey. We see the metaphor everywhere, although we seldom actively think about it.

Certainly artists and other creative people are in tune with the journey metaphor. In Robert Frost's poem "The Road Not Taken," the narrator uses the metaphor of a fork in the road to represent his decision to live boldly rather than follow the crowd. In *The Wizard of Oz*, Dorothy and her friends grow and evolve as they travel the Yellow Brick Road. For the Beatles, "The Long and Winding Road" symbolized the vicissitudes and travails of life.

But the journey-of-life metaphor is not the exclusive domain of so-called right-brained thinkers or of ethereal beings like Robert Frost and Paul McCartney. We all use the metaphor to make sense of how time passes before us. The United States Department of Health and Human Services has a program for low-income children called "Head Start." We stress the importance of "staying on track" as we progress toward our life goals. Many of us hope to "climb the ladder" of success so that we can "move up" in life. We urge our favorite team to part ways with an aging athlete who is reaching "the end of the line."

Pie Traynor was not a man prone to waxing deeply philosophical about his own life; he was too busy living that life. But surely there were times when he ripped open a pack of smokes, lit one up, leaned back in his chair and reflected on his journey — usually with pride at how far he had come, now and then with disappointment at how much ground he had lost. It is a natural process we all go through as we seek the answer to the complicated but elemental question of "How did I get here?"

For better and for worse, Traynor seemed never to forget where his journey began. From a young man in deep poverty with barely a grammar school education, Traynor scaled the heights of his chosen profession, acquiring all of the attendant wealth, public adoration and social connections. The insecurities and fears that can accompany economic hardship stayed with him, motivating Traynor to work extremely hard. They also drove him to distraction when things weren't going well. Only after he left baseball did he seem to grow completely at peace with himself.

At the same time, Traynor's awareness of his humble beginnings kept him grounded. Here was a man who could hobnob with wealthy industrialists in the afternoon, mesmerize a group of Little Leaguers in the evening, and then on his way home plop down on a barstool and share a beer with a steel-worker.

Although much of Traynor's path through life is well documented, some of his earliest footprints are rather faint. Time has washed away many details; anyone who knew him as a youngster, of course, is long since dead. However, Traynor did a decent job of covering his own tracks, too. He could keep an audience enthralled for hours with his infinite mental library of stories, but one of his least favorite topics was himself. He recalled statistics with almost photographic precision, but that amazing memory could conveniently fail when asked to summon details of his youth or personal life. Traynor was a contradiction — a man who cherished the public spotlight but who simultaneously kept important parts of himself hidden deep in the shadows offstage.

Pie Traynor's road wended out of the United Kingdom, through the Maritime Provinces of eastern Canada, and then into Massachusetts. His father, James Henry Traynor, was born in Halifax, Nova Scotia, on January 20, 1876.[1] He was a first-generation Canadian, the son of an Irish dock worker also named James Traynor, and his English wife Elizabeth (Peach) Traynor.[2]

Pie's maternal grandmother, Eliza Matthews, also relocated from Great Britain to Canada, where she met her husband, Joseph Matthews, in St. John's, Newfoundland.[3] They had five children. Lydia Maud Matthews, Pie's mother, was the fourth, born in St. John's, on June 30, 1881. Sometime after Maud's birth, the family relocated to Halifax, where she met James Traynor.

Maud grew up fast. At age 16, she and 21-year-old James were married by a Methodist minister in a courthouse civil ceremony on August 26, 1897.[4] Less than three months later, they welcomed their first child into the family — son James Edward Traynor (known as Eddie), born in Halifax on November 17, 1897.

Shortly thereafter, the Traynors departed Canada and relocated to Massachusetts, though it is unclear exactly when or how that happened. Their names appear to be absent from any immigration records. U.S. Census documents do not help much, either; it seems the Traynors told a different version of their story every time a census taker knocked on the door. On some census forms, it appears that James came to the States first and then sent for his wife and son later, which is how many immigrant families established themselves in the U.S. However, other census records seem to suggest they arrived together. And their stated years of arrival vary from one census to the next,[5] making the truth hard to determine.

It is not inconceivable that they entered the country illegally. On maps the border between New England and Canada is well defined but in reality that line was quite blurry at the time. Beginning in the mid–1800s, throngs of Canadians from the Maritime region ventured back and forth to work on American fishing vessels or in American shipyards and lumber camps. For decades immigration authorities turned a blind eye.

By the time the Traynors arrived in Massachusetts, the U.S. Government was trying to establish some semblance of control over border traffic, but as the Bureau of Immigration admitted, "Anyone who really wanted to go to America could scarcely be kept out, no matter how vigilant the United States authorities may be."[6] The Maritime Provinces suffered a significant talent drain from 1875 to 1900, as many of their most ambitious young people, both blue collar and white collar, poured into New England seeking better opportunities.

Major league baseball was one of the industries that was better for it. Along with Pie Traynor, other stars of the early 1900s who could trace their lineage to the Maritimes include Cubs Hall of Fame catcher Gabby Hartnett and Stuffy McInnis, part of the Philadelphia Athletics $100,000 infield in the early teens. In fact, McInnis returned to Canada following World War II to coach a community baseball team.[7]

Whatever the circumstances of their arrival, the three members of the Traynor clan made their first home in America in a multiple-unit rooming house at 96 Clark Street in the industrial south end of Framingham, Massachusetts, about 20 miles west of Boston.[8] James, a printer by trade, secured a position at the Dennison Manufacturing Company, which was within walking distance of his house. Dennison, whose claim to fame was the production of luggage tags reinforced with paper washers, was founded in Maine but consolidated all of its operations in Framingham in 1897.[9] The company remained in the same location, just north of the Chesapeake railroad tracks, for nearly 100 years.

Life was hard and disillusioning for many immigrants who came to the United States from Europe expecting to find streets paved with gold. Rather than riches, they regularly encountered overt discrimination, formidable language and cultural barriers, subsistence-level pay, and miserable working conditions. By contrast, the Traynors' adjustment appeared reasonably smooth. As Canadians, they spoke English with hardly any discernable accent, which blunted a lot of the discrimination they might have faced. And although their Irish descent might have created headaches at one time, it wasn't as big a deal by the late 1890s. "By the turn of the 20th century, the Irish had pretty much assimilated into mainstream American culture," said professor Sol Gittleman of Tufts University near Boston.[10] "They had endured the stereotypes of lazy, dirty, and up to no good; and [also had overcome] religious persecution because they were Catholic living in a Protestant culture."[11]

The Irish actually were thriving in the Boston area. The city of Somerville, where the Traynors eventually relocated, elected its first Irish mayor in 1880. John "Honey Fitz" Fitzgerald, patriarch of the Kennedy family, had begun his political ascent and would be elected mayor of Boston in 1906. There were sports heroes like the Boston Beaneaters' Mike "King" Kelly and the great Red Sox and Beaneater third baseman Jimmy Collins who served as role models and helped to shatter ethnic stereotypes. When the Traynors arrived on the scene, Italians already had replaced the Irish on the lower rungs of the American caste system.

James also was fortunate to land a job with a relatively benign employer. It's not as if Dennison was a land of milk and honey; James, a staunch and active union man, went on strike with his colleagues in 1903 in pursuit of higher wages.[12] But all in all, the company treated its people well. Dennison was a pioneer in providing unemployment insurance for laid off workers.[13] It also offered an on-site medical clinic, a lunchroom, recreational facilities, and a circulating library, all of which were highly progressive concepts in the early twentieth century.[14]

The Traynors' hardscrabble rooming house on Clark Street was where Harold Joseph Traynor, whom the world came to know as "Pie," was born on November 11, 1898. He was the second of their seven children. Baseball record books and even Traynor's gravestone inaccurately list his year of birth as 1899. But Traynor's birth certificate, his World War I draft registration card, his official application for wartime work in Boston, and United States Census

Above and opposite: Like many players of his era, Traynor shaved a year off his age so that he seemed younger, and thus a more attractive prospect, to major league scouts. Even his headstone at Homewood Cemetery in Pittsburgh lists his year of birth as 1899, but the transcript of his birth certificate (opposite) and other primary sources tell the real story (headstone photograph by Susan Kane).

Commonwealth of Massachusetts
United States of America
Town of Framingham

Certificate of Birth

From the Records of Births in the Town of Framingham, Massachusetts, U.S.A.

Name:	**Harold Joseph Traynor**
Date of Birth:	**November 11, 1898**
Place of Birth:	**Framingham, MA**
Sex, and if Twin:	**Male**
Maiden Name of Mother:	**Lydia Matthews**
Birthplace of Mother:	**Halifax, N.S.**
Name of Father:	**James H. Traynor**
Occupation of Father:	**Compositor**
Birthplace of Father:	**Halifax, N.S.**
Residence:	**Framingham, MA**
Date of Record:	**February 1899**

I, Valerie Mulvey, depose and say that I hold the office of Town Clerk of the Town of Framingham, County of Middlesex, and Commonwealth of Massachusetts; that the records of births required by law to be kept in said Town are in my custody, and that the above is a true copy from the records of births in said Town, as certified by me.

Witness my hand and seal of said Town on August 10, 2005

Valerie Mulvey, Town Clerk

records all indicate he was born in 1898.[15] It looks like shortly after World War I, when he was 20 and beginning to think more seriously about a career in professional baseball, Traynor quietly lopped a year off his age. It was not an uncommon practice at the time among players concerned they might appear a little too old for prospect status. For whatever reason, he stuck to his little white lie long after he became a star and long after his age would have mattered to anyone.

The details of how young Harold interacted with his parents are sketchy, but the relationship seems to have been relatively pleasant and free of any significant conflict. While some other stars of baseball's early days—Babe Ruth, Ty Cobb, and John McGraw, to name a few—were shaped by abusive, neglectful, or otherwise emotionally unhealthy home environments, that does not appear to have been the case for Traynor.

His father resembled the kind of man Pie eventually became—sociable, funny, a classic extrovert who was energized by spending time around people. His mother, Maud, on the other hand, preferred a lower profile. She came off as articulate, but very reserved and soft-spoken. As a younger woman she maintained a dowdy and plain appearance, but the windfall from Pie's baseball earnings allowed her to modernize her wardrobe somewhat. Maud, who seems to have been the family disciplinarian, also was a compulsive neat freak obsessed with keeping her home clean and her kids germ-free.

It doesn't seem that organized religion played a particularly influential role in the Traynor home, at least not for Pie. James was raised Roman Catholic, Maud grew up Methodist; Pie, as an adult, called himself an Episcopalian, married in a Presbyterian church, and had his eulogy read by a rabbi.[16] As for Pie's budding baseball career, James and Maud, at least initially, were indifferent— they neither encouraged it nor discouraged it.[17]

The Traynors were itinerant renters during their early years in Massachusetts. They changed addresses twice during their time in Framingham, in 1900 and again in 1902. In the fall of 1904, just two months after five-year-old Pie had begun classes at Lincoln Elementary School, James Traynor moved his family out of town.[18] He accepted a job as a typesetter at the *Boston Transcript* newspaper, where it is believed he remained for the rest of his working life. The new post meant relocating to Somerville, Massachusetts, a crowded working-class suburb just outside of Boston, about three miles north of the Charles River, nestled between Cambridge and Charlestown.

The Traynors were part of a huge influx into Somerville. In 1880, the city's population stood at 25,000. By 1910, it had nearly tripled, to more than 77,000. Ten years later, when Pie left town to begin his professional baseball career, 93,090 people were squeezed into a town whose boundaries encompassed just 4.22 square miles, making it one of the most densely populated cities in the United States.

By the turn of the twentieth century, the eastern one-third of Somerville had been built up for some time, but the rest of the city was transforming by the day. The central and western part of town had consisted mostly of rangeland used for cattle grazing or growing small crops before the ranchers sold to developers, who carved streets and city blocks out of the pasture. Between 1897 and 1907, an average of nearly four houses a week popped up on this land where there used to be little other than grass and cows.[19] With no zoning ordinances, it was common to find private homes mingling on the same block with factories and shops.

The earliest known photograph of Traynor, shot in front of his home in Somerville, Massachusetts, around 1906, when he would have been seven or eight years old. *Left to right*: older brother Eddie, younger brothers Art and Bobby, and Pie (Marilyn Lenick).

Somerville was an important railroad hub but meatpacking was its biggest industry, which is how it earned the name "the Chicago of New England." The rapid urban growth also was a boon for the building trades, with carpenters, lumber yards, brick makers, and metal and glass works thriving. Somerville's population consisted mostly of native-born Americans of English and Irish descent. About one-third of the total population consisted of immigrants, more than half of whom came from Ireland or, like Pie's parents, from Canada. Italians were becoming increasingly prominent as well. A sprinkling of Germans, Polish, and Portuguese could be found. African Americans were almost non-existent.

This was a period in which American society experienced change at a dizzying pace. Life in Somerville in 1905, as in the rest of the United States, was crude and difficult in comparison to what it would become just two decades later. Wages for the average American worker totaled about $500 a year. Around ten percent of the population was illiterate. Only about 78,000 motorized vehicles traveled American roads, but that was nearly a tenfold increase from five years earlier. (In Somerville, livery stables doubled as engine repair shops and people who purchased new cars were recognized in the newspapers.) Most births took place in the home. Tuberculosis, pneumonia and influenza were the leading causes of death. Average life expectancy was just 47 years.

James and his family settled in a rented flat at 47 Alpine Street in the central part of Somerville, where most of the city's Irish population resided, a stone's throw from Tufts College. The neighborhood is known as Magoun Square, an area that consisted of four large city blocks bisected by railroad tracks. Most of the people living in that area were, like the Traynors, just trying to get by. They included both blue-collar laborers and white-collar working stiffs like teachers, clerks, and small businessmen.[20]

The Traynors' home was similar to many in the area. It was a two-story dwelling, intended to be occupied by an owner on one floor and a renter and his family on the other. The houses in Magoun Square were packed closely together, with only about seven feet between each house and little in the way of either a front or backyard. Renters like the Traynors typically paid about $25 to 35 each month.[21]

Pie immediately enrolled at now-demolished Bingham Grammar School on Lowell Street and Wilton Avenue in Somerville. After classes he and his buddies would troop across the railroad tracks to the corner of Lowell and Albion streets, where they would choose up sides for a game of baseball. At first, the older boys decided Traynor, in spite of his relentless nagging, was too young to play and relegated him to the chore of retrieving foul balls. Eventually the squeaky wheel got some grease. As the story goes, the boys, needing a catcher one day, shoved Pie behind the plate, partly as a gag. Traynor claimed he stood in there without a mask, got smacked in the mouth, and lost two of his teeth. "That was the first game I ever played that left an imprint on my memory," he said.[22]

As Traynor grew up, he became a regular part of this group of kids who represented the Bingham School on the local playgrounds. It was not organized baseball — no standings, no uniforms, no scoreboards — but it was where Traynor received his first real taste of the game, waging battle with the rival Proctor School Panthers and the Winter Hill Wildcats from the Forster School.[23] As teenagers, many of Traynor's Bingham teammates went on to play at Somerville High School or joined Traynor on the Boston-area sandlots. Classmate Frank Kelliher had a major league career consisting of one at-bat with the Washington Senators in 1919. Another of his Bingham friends, Dick Trum, was a decorated war hero who died in combat during World War I. Somerville's largest ball field, City Field, was renamed in his honor in 1923.[24]

During this period young Harold picked up the distinctive and memorable nickname that would stick with him for the rest of his life. There is a certain mythology around how Harold became "Pie." Over the years sportswriters offered at least three different explanations. For his part, Traynor enjoyed keeping things a little mysterious. "I guess it was a little bit of each," he winked.[25]

One tale has young Harold playing in the dirt one evening when his father got home from work. James spied his grubby son and laughed, "You look like pied type," which is a printer's term for jumbled text.[26]

Traynor with his namesake in 1933 (Boston Public Library, Print Department).

The explanation that Traynor gave most frequently (and the one that seems the most plausible) is that the name simply evolved from his love of pie. But even here there are slightly different twists on the story. According to one version, Traynor got the nickname from an older kid in the neighborhood named Ben Nangle, who worked at his family's variety store. Every week, Harold's mother would send him on a shopping trip. Inevitably the last item on the grocery list was pie, which became a running joke between the two boys. "Ben eventually started calling Harold 'Pieface,' which was later shortened by his friends on the playground to 'Pie.'"[27]

A variation of that anecdote focuses on an unnamed parish priest who had played baseball in college and organized and umpired pickup games for the boys in the neighborhood. "After the games, the priest would treat the youngsters to anything they wanted. Most of them would request ice cream — but not Harold Traynor. His inevitable response was, 'I'll have pie, Father.' So the priest began calling him Pie."[28]

The truth is probably a combination of the latter two yarns. There was, indeed, a kid named Bernard Nangle working at a store in Traynor's neighborhood. Presumably, somewhere along the way he began calling himself Ben, which was a common nickname for Bernard. The boy's family owned and operated a variety store on Albion Street, just down the road from where Traynor and his Bingham School chums played ball.[29] Traynor said the store was a popular hangout not only for the local children, but also for some of the adults in the neighborhood.[30]

Young Ben was about five years old when his father died in 1898, but it seems that he began to help his mother, Susan, mind the store when he grew old enough. He liked baseball, so one could imagine he might have gone down the street as a teenager, umpired the younger children's games, and then paraded them back to his family's store for a post-game snack.

Eventually a higher duty called. In 1910 Ben Nangle enrolled at St. Bonaventure College and Seminary (now St. Bonaventure University) in Olean, New York, where he suited up at catcher for his intramural baseball team.[31] He was ordained in 1917 and later became attached to parishes around the state of New York, including several in New York City. He stayed in touch with Traynor through the years, even tipping him off from time to time when he caught wind of a young ballplayer the Pirates might be interested in.[32] Nangle was pastor of St. John's Roman Catholic Church in West Hurley, New York, when he died on April 24, 1945.[33]

Traynor's nickname became a central part of his identity; it fit perfectly with his affable personality and childlike on-field exuberance. It also spawned countless bad puns and corny metaphors (witness a series of get-to-know-him articles titled, "Cut Yourself a Piece of Pie" in the *Pittsburgh Press* after he was named manager). Throughout Traynor's baseball career civic organizations and groups of fans were always honoring him for one reason or another. In doing so, they inevitably shoved a humongous pie under his nose. He ate so much pie over the years that he grew to dislike it.[34]

Meanwhile, the Traynor family was expanding rapidly. Maud had given birth to her third and fourth sons before leaving Framingham — Robert in 1900 and Arthur, who had the distinction of being the first baby born in Framingham, in 1903. Daughter Mary was born in Somerville in 1909, followed by sons Charles in 1912 and John in 1913. After John was born, the Traynors left their home on Alpine Street for similar digs (but perhaps lower rent) about a block north at 48 Princeton Street.

Naturally, raising seven children takes a lot of money, and James Traynor's salary only went so far. As was often the case in large working-class families, it fell to the older sons to pick up the slack. In 1912, after completing seventh grade, Pie followed in the footsteps of his older brother, Eddie, and dropped out of school to help support the family. From then until he began his professional baseball career eight years later, Pie held an assortment of low-paying jobs to help his father keep a roof overhead and food on the table. It is believed his first position was as a messenger boy, possibly at the Derby Desk Company, a manufacturer of office furniture located just a couple of blocks from the Traynor home. At other times during his youth, he worked for a bakery and as an ironworker at a factory that manufactured tractors.[35]

In June 1913, the Massachusetts Legislature passed two laws to crack down on truancy and limit the kinds of jobs and hours minors could work. The state began to require kids with jobs to possess a work permit, and local school

Some members of Pie Traynor's family around 1920. *Left to right, back row*: Pie's brother Bobby, mother Maud, brother Eddie, unknown. *Middle row:* Father James, sister Lulu. *Front row:* brother Charley, brother John, unknown (Marilyn Lenick).

officials were free to inspect the names and ages of all working minors. Perhaps it was just coincidence, but shortly after the passage of these bills, Traynor returned to school to complete the mandatory eight years of education. He graduated from Bingham School in January 1915, alongside his younger brother, Bobby.[36] Pie entered Somerville High School on January 26, but he didn't last two months, withdrawing on March 19. His high school transcript reads, "Necessary to leave school in order to go to work."[37] He never returned.

Had his family been doing a little better financially, Traynor almost certainly would have remained in school. According to a 1923 article in the *Boston Globe*, he assumed it would be difficult to attract the attention of scouts if he wasn't playing high school baseball, and thus feared he was throwing away any chance of a career in the sport.[38] He also recognized that, baseball ambitions aside, education could open a pathway to a decent life, one in which he wasn't living hand-to-mouth. In the early days of his major league career, he set his sights on winning admission to Boston University so he could take classes in the offseason. As an older man he probably spoke to hundreds of youth organizations, and a staple of those speeches was a plea to the kids to get a good education. Traynor might have been a little self-conscious about dropping out, too. He seemed to have a proclivity for telling probing reporters that he played baseball at Somerville High School, which was pure baloney.

Even though life circumstances relegated school to the back burner, Traynor, as it turned out, had plenty of time for baseball. By the end of seventh grade he had long since outgrown the Bingham School nine. Beginning at age 11, he joined the more advanced Highland Athletic Club team, where he had the thrill of wearing a baseball uniform for the first time.[39] "He was a natural from the very beginning," according to Highland teammate Oliver Emery.[40]

Somerville had a proud local baseball heritage. As far back as 1906, Somerville High School captured the Greater Boston Interscholastic League championship. A local sportswriter declared them the best team in the state; his not-so-rigorous criteria was that he couldn't imagine how any other team in Massachusetts could be any better. Somerville High was almost as good the following year, but they finished second in the league after forfeiting a game for using an ineligible player. A star of those Somerville High teams was Art Graham, whose son, Skinny Graham, played briefly for the Boston Red Sox in 1934 and '35.

For the first three decades of the twentieth century, Somerville produced a steady flow of excellent baseball players; at one point in the 1920s, Somerville High had three future major leaguers on its roster. The city's first major leaguer was pitcher Walt Whittaker, who was about four years older than Traynor. He was credited with eight of Somerville High's 15 victories in 1911. He worked two innings of relief for the Philadelphia Athletics in 1916 before he returned home to wrap up his studies at Tufts College and become a dentist.

A man who enjoyed a much more productive big league career was Horace

Traynor (*seated*), age 12, with some of his Highland Athletic Club teammates in Somerville, Massachusetts, in 1911 (Marilyn Lenick).

"Hod" Ford. He was one year older than Traynor; the two men would have been high school teammates had Traynor remained in school. Ford started at shortstop for Somerville High and led the baseball team to consecutive league titles in 1914 and 1915. He went on to play ball at Tufts, where he graduated with a degree in mechanical engineering, and then broke into the majors with the Boston Braves in September 1919. Ford had a nomadic career, spending time with the Braves, Phillies, Dodgers, Reds, and Cardinals during his 15 seasons in the bigs. He was a starter for much of that time, shuttling back and forth between shortstop and second base over the years. He never hit much, but was a first-rate glove man.

Somerville's sandlot and semipro teams sprung up in association with churches, businesses, or organizations like the local Y.M.C.A. Among the premier teams were the Somerville Base Ball Club, established in 1911, and Hod Ford's curiously named Brown Class team, sponsored by the West Somerville Congregational Church. That club also featured Lester Bangs, who went on to a 13-year minor league career and also played an important role in helping Traynor break into the professional ranks.

Teams scrounged for games by taking out ads in the *Boston Globe*. Sometimes the ads called out specific clubs, challenging them to step forward.

> Ball Square A.A. of West Somerville has a few open dates and would like to hear
> from teams of the class of Lindon, St. Ambrose, Everett, Mead, Morrison, Ded-
> ham, Weymouth, Norwood, or Winthrop. Frank Emmett, 53 Lowden Ave.,
> Somerville, or telephone 2016-M or 5585-M.[41]

Other ads spotlighted a team's top players—often local high school legends,
college standouts or, once in a while, an ex-major leaguer—to entice opponents eager to pit themselves against the best.

> The Converse Rubber Shoe Company of Malden is seeking to schedule games
> away from home. The players include Johnny Murphy, captain of Dartmouth, ss;
> Ballou of Holy Cross, 2b; Dempsey and Morrisey of Boston College and Gilligan
> of St. Anselm's. Chester Emerson played with the Athletics for a year after
> finishing at Dartmouth.... Write to E.J. Dempsey, care of Converse Rubber Shoe
> Company, Malden or call Malden 1600 between 8:30 and 5.[42]

Sometimes an ad dripped with youthful swagger and bravado.

> Claiming the 14–15 year old championship of the state, the Dorchester Boys'
> club is willing to take on any club that questions the claim. Address: S. Stein-
> berg, 37 Greenock Street, Dorchester.[43]

Two newspapers, the *Journal* and the *Press*, served Somerville at that time.
The papers published only once a week and therefore reserved most of their
local baseball coverage for the top-shelf teams, which meant Traynor's earliest
performances on the sandlots went almost completely undocumented. From
what can be determined, his name first appeared in print on May 23, 1913,
when he was 14 years old. A summary of a Highland Athletic Club game against
the Rotary Athletic Club of South Boston included a vague blurb, noting, "The
features of the game [included] the playing of Traynor at short stop."[44] That
was just about all that was heard from Traynor for another couple of years. During the summers of 1914 and 1915, he evidently continued to play on youth
teams around the Boston area—including a team of 15–17-year-olds in Arlington, Massachusetts—while awaiting an opportunity with one of the high-profile
Somerville clubs.

By early 1916 it looks as if Traynor, who had recently turned 17, was beginning to take measure of his life. His major league ambitions still appeared to
be little more than a fantasy. Although he was a promising young athlete, there
was no shortage of excellent high school- and college-age ballplayers in and
around Boston to keep big league scouts occupied. Traynor was playing in
obscurity, and at that point it's likely few, if any, scouts even knew he existed.
On top of it, not playing for a high school or college team made it that much
harder for someone to discover him down the road. He certainly had a chance,
but somewhere along the line he would have to catch a break or two.

What's more, if no break ever came, Traynor's job prospects and earning
capacity were going to be limited without a high school diploma. As a result,
by 1916 he was prepared to veer in a different direction. On February 1 of that

year, as Traynor told it, he and brother Eddie went to a recruiting station with plans to enlist in the army.[45]

To his disappointment, Pie learned that he was about nine months too young; the army sent him back home. But Uncle Sam was more than happy to take his brother.[46] Upon the entry of the United States into World War I, Eddie, who had been serving at the Mexican border, shipped off to Europe with Company K of the 104th Infantry Battalion. He was severely injured at the Battle of Belleau Wood near the Marne River in France in June 1918. Belleau Wood was one of the bloodiest battles American forces fought during the war, with more than 1,800 U.S. servicemen killed and nearly 8,000 more wounded.

Eddie was felled by a bullet that went through his arm and penetrated his chest before fragmenting. He survived, yet barely. According to family lore, two military policemen arrived at the Traynor front door to inform them that their son was dead. Only after the family had begun collecting Eddie's military death benefits did they learn he was still alive.[47]

Eddie was awarded the World War I Victory Medal and Bronze Victory Button, but he never fully recovered from his wounds.[48] He was in and out of hospitals for the rest of his life and found it difficult to hold down a full-time job.[49] He lived at home with his parents and siblings until 1930 when, at age 32, he married Ann Ryan, a bold, strong-minded woman several years his senior. Because of Eddie's physical maladies, Ann was forced to become her family's primary breadwinner. She worked for years at the William Underwood Company in Watertown, Massachusetts, best known for making a canned meat spread called Underwood Deviled Ham. Their only child, Jimmy, served in the Marines during the Korean War and became an accomplished Golden Gloves boxer — a tremendous source of pride for Uncle Pie, a boxing nut.[50] Eddie died in 1975 at the age of 77.[51] Ann made it to age 101 before she died in 1994.[52]

His military ambitions thwarted, Pie finally found a permanent spot on an upper level Somerville sandlot team during the summer of 1916. Local newspapers gave his Ball Square Athletic Club team almost no coverage until August 4, by which time they had earned some ink with an 11–0 record. About a week later, the team ran its winning streak to 14 with a 12–7 victory over the Covington All-Stars of South Boston. "[T]he hitting of Coffey and Trainor [sic] was the feature of the game."[53] Traynor doubled, tripled, and scored two runs. Ball Square's streak finally came to an end in September when they dropped a 1–0 game to the Roxbury White Sox, reportedly the only team to defeat Ball Square in two years.[54]

In the seven Ball Square games from that summer for which box scores are available, Traynor batted .448, with 13 hits (including four doubles and a triple) in 29 at-bats. Though it is dangerous to draw any conclusions based on seven games, it looks like Traynor had some idea of what he was doing with the glove, too. He was charged with just two errors in 46 chances at shortstop.

Traynor was back with Ball Square in 1917. Press coverage was even more sporadic than it had been the previous year; only five box scores appeared in the two Somerville newspapers. The most notable aspect of the coverage that season was the papers began referring to Traynor as "Pie" for the first time, although they continued to bungle the spelling of his last name.

Traynor's success with Ball Square represented some progress in his baseball career, but he was going to turn 19 years old in November. If he was going to make baseball his livelihood, he would have to attract the attention of a professional team before too much longer. But first came the small matter of helping his country win a war.

2

Discovered on Cape Cod

Somerville was a cold, dark, hungry place in the winter of 1917-18. In the midst of a punishing winter, a coal shortage closed Somerville schools in December and January. The government ordered all lights in the city, except those required for public safety, to be dimmed in order to save energy. For the same reason, businesses were limited to operating from 9:00 A.M. to 5:00 P.M. Like people all across America during this time of war, city residents dealt with wheatless Mondays, meatless Tuesdays, and porkless Thursdays as a part of the government's voluntary plan to conserve food.

Everyone in Somerville had it rough, but for the Traynor family, these were acutely trying times. They might not have been dirt poor, but they weren't far from it. James Traynor's wallet was getting crunched from every angle — spiraling rents, inflation, a large family (even with Eddie in the service), and an income that couldn't keep pace with it all. His job at the *Boston Transcript*'s printing press was a solid, steady position, but hardly lucrative. In 1917 he swallowed hard and surrendered the flat on Princeton Street and signed a lease on a mid-nineteenth century hovel located at 20 Woodbine Street. The timeworn cottage-style house bunched the entire family into just two rooms. It was a clear step backward.

It seems Pie began to live apart from his family at this point. On his application for wartime work, he listed his address at 15 Woodbine, across the street from his parents and siblings.[1] His reasons for renting his own place are uncertain. As would become evident within a few years, Traynor was an ambitious young man who felt compelled to make something of himself. Given that he apparently tried to sign up for the army in 1916, and that he left Massachusetts later in 1918 to take a wartime job, it seems reasonable to speculate that at age 19 he was itchy to assert his independence and strike out on his own. Or it could have been simply more about space than psychology; eight people in two rooms would have been awfully crowded. Getting a place of his own probably gave him some room to breathe.

On January 18, 1918, Traynor applied for work as an unskilled laborer at the Boston Navy Yard, which boasted one of the top amateur baseball teams in the Greater Boston area. He began work a week later but the job didn't last long thanks to his puzzling inability to show up on time. He was drummed out after a week for missing six musters, although his bosses rated his conduct "good" and the quality of his work "very good."[2]

How Traynor occupied his time for the next several months is mostly a mystery. The only trace of him comes in a lone Ball Square A.C. box score that appeared in a Somerville newspaper in May.[3] By mid-summer, around the time his brother, Eddie, was wounded in France, Pie was gone. The War Department issued a "work or fight" order that was to take effect on July 1. Traynor opted for work, packed his things, and left his family for the first time in his life.[4] His destination was infernal Nitro, West Virginia.

America's entry into World War I created an urgent need for a huge gunpowder manufacturing operation. The War Department considered several locations, but after studying the climate, soil quality, availability of raw materials, and a number of other factors, decided to locate the plant on a large, almost completely empty swath of farmland about 15 miles south of Charleston, West Virginia. The new town needed a name. Since the specific kind of powder produced there was to be nitro-cellulose, the government landed on the name Nitro.

Ground was officially broken on January 2, 1918. With so many men off at war, finding manpower to build the plant and work there was a formidable challenge. The military contractor, Thompson-Starrett, set up recruiting offices in big cities throughout the country, including Boston, where Traynor signed up. Attracting men was hard; getting them to stay was even harder. During the 11 months between the start of construction and the end of the war, 110,000 people worked in Nitro. The average employee remained only 40 days.

In the decades following the armistice, Nitro evolved into a pleasant enough little town, but conditions in 1918 were abysmal. One man who arrived that summer, around the same time Traynor rolled into town, related, "Most of the streets were of mud, but wooden sidewalks were being built as fast as the help came from the farms and towns of the west, north, and south."[5] Environmental responsibility was not a high priority. "[T]he ether was so dad-burn thick in the air," carped gunpowder worker Averill Casto. "Especially on foggy nights and mornings, it was so bad that you couldn't see anything, just stagger like you were drunk."[6]

Meanwhile, lurking in the deep recesses of everyone's mind at Nitro was the very real possibility they might die there. It was not a safe place. By the end of the war, the plant was churning out 350 tons of gunpowder each day. As Traynor said, "How did I know but what there might be an explosion?"[7] Then beginning in September, the worldwide Spanish flu pandemic rampaged through and killed more than 200 people. At the local train station, the caskets of flu victims were lined up, awaiting shipment back home to grieving loved ones.

Each day saw the arrival of close to 100 railroad cars filled with raw materials to be converted into gunpowder. Traynor was a car-checker; his job was to ride around on horseback 12 hours each day, recording information about the arrival and departure of shipments. "It wasn't much fun," Traynor remembered.[8] It was a grueling job that required a man to be in shape, which Traynor certainly was, and to exhibit some degree of horsemanship, where his skills were passable, at best. One of Traynor's shifts came to an abrupt, bloody end after his horse threw him headlong to the ground. His enduring souvenir from Nitro was a small scar on his forehead that never completely disappeared.[9]

It is uncertain exactly how long Traynor stuck it out. A 1934 article suggests he probably remained at Nitro until the end of the war.[10] However, on September 11, 1918, he filled out a draft card, which is a clue that he might have left around this time and chosen to make himself eligible to fight.[11] Either way, November 11, 1918, must have been a happy day for him. It was his 20th birthday, but more importantly, it was when news of the armistice arrived in the United States. No more coal shortages, no more dreadful wartime jobs, no more risk of being shipped off to fight in Europe.

With the so-called "war to end all wars" over, Traynor returned to Somerville and re-focused on baseball. By June, he was playing for his town's premier sandlot team, the Somerville Base Ball Club. His teammates in 1919 included Ray Tift, who pitched briefly for the New York Highlanders in the American League in 1907. Traynor appeared in just six games with the Somerville B.B.C. in 1919 before moving on to bigger and better things. Years later, a Somerville reporter whipped up a fable that Traynor homered in all six of those games.[12] He did no such thing; in fact, there is no record that he homered at all. But he hit the ball well. Newspapers accounts exist for only four of the six games, but in those appearances Traynor came through with eight hits, including a double and two triples, in 17 at-bats.

But just as the Somerville B.B.C. season was beginning, Traynor found himself in the sights of a former major league pitcher who was trying to fill out the roster of the high profile independent team he coached in Cape Cod. Dave Morey was the scion of a prominent family from Malden, Massachusetts, not far from Somerville. His grandparents were pioneering abolitionists, and their Malden home was a busy way station on the Underground Railroad, which helped Southern slaves escape to freedom in Canada.[13]

Morey excelled in three sports in high school. On the diamond, he once struck out 25 batters in a game. He went off to Dartmouth College, majored in French, and developed into a feared runner out of Dartmouth's offensive backfield, making two Walter Camp All-American football teams.[14] After graduation, Morey quickly signed a major league contract with the Philadelphia Athletics. The Athletics were strapped for arms at the time, and team owner and manager Connie Mack threw Morey into the fire right away, with no minor league experience.[15] He allowed two earned runs in two innings out of the bullpen on his first day in uniform, sat for six weeks, and then worked two perfect innings of relief against the Chicago White Sox.

When Mack tried to send him to the minor leagues for some much-needed seasoning, Morey balked. He quickly concluded there was no reason a young

man with an Ivy League degree should waste his time toiling in a backwater nowhere while chasing a distant dream.[16] Instead, Morey hung up his baseball uniform and embarked on a long career as a college football coach and athletic department administrator.

His résumé included a short stint as the head coach at Auburn University (then known as Alabama Polytechnic Institute) from 1925 to 1927, followed by a two-year hitch as an assistant at Fordham, a national power in football in the 1920s and 1930s. Knute Rockne supposedly offered Morey a job on his coaching staff at Notre Dame, but Morey had to back out when he broke his leg just before the beginning of practice.[17] According to Milt Lindholm, who was a starting lineman for Morey at Bates College in Maine in the 1930s, "He was a warm-hearted person. He had the ability to get kids very dedicated and loyal to him. He was an intellectual ... very well read in many areas."[18]

In the summer of 1917, Morey, then in charge of athletics at Lowell Textile Institute (later known as the University of Massachusetts at Lowell) decided to assemble a team of premier Boston-area baseball players, all high school age or slightly older. Morey took his guys to Cape Cod, where the local semi-pro town teams played a highly competitive brand of baseball, taking on all comers.

On the Cape, the young men represented the town of Oak Bluffs, located on Martha's Vineyard. "(Morey's) teams were made up of ... players who had been hired as waiters by the hotels more for their athletic skills than their serving skills."[19] With the war on, it was mandatory that Morey's boys register for military service or war-related work. This was important because the locals, as a local newspaper put it, "wanted no 'slackers' to support."[20] In 1918, many of those non-slackers were in Europe, living in trenches, fighting for their country and their lives. Consequently, Morey found himself short of both good players and funding. So Oak Bluffs combined forces with a neighboring town team that was facing similar problems, the Falmouth Commodores.

Even so, in the spring of 1919 it still wasn't clear whether Morey would be able to get enough cash together to field another team. His club's financial solvency depended on contributions from fans, which came in the form of loose change collected when they passed the hat at games, and also from larger "subscriptions" solicited before the start of the season. With the bank account just about empty that spring, Morey and the Falmouth Board of Trade Base Ball Committee had to work hard at cajoling enough subscriptions out of the townsfolk before a self-imposed deadline of July 1. In the end, the fans came through and the combined Falmouth–Oak Bluffs squad survived to play another

Opposite: **Dave Morey (*far left in suit*), who discovered Traynor in 1918 and brought him to Cape Cod to play the following season. Morey is shown here in 1930, as coach of the Bates College baseball team in Maine (Edmund S. Muskie Archives and Special Collections Library, Bates College).**

season. With his finances finally in order by early summer, Morey was able to focus on more prosaic tasks, like finding a shortstop. The man he wanted and got was Pie Traynor.

Most likely, Traynor came to Morey's attention the previous year. In a game that took sort of a mythical hue, Traynor visited Falmouth in 1918, presumably with his Ball Square A.C. team, to battle Morey's Commodores. On the mound for Falmouth was Nathaniel Moor, a student at Kenyon College in Ohio. Moor spent the summer in Falmouth, where his family had a summer home, and earned a spot on Morey's roster.

As Moor told the story, Traynor led off the game against him by blasting a fastball out of the park. He later drove in two runs with a hit in the third inning, and then knocked Moor out of the box when his seventh-inning hit pushed across two more. Supposedly, Moor trudged to the bench and asked his teammates about that lanky kid with the hunched shoulders who had owned him all afternoon. All anyone knew is that it was someone named Traynor. Moor claimed that was the game that convinced him a professional baseball career probably wasn't in the cards and that it was time to get serious about going into the ministry.[21] (Coincidentally, Moor and Traynor became close friends after Moor accepted the post of Dean of the Trinity Cathedral Church in downtown Pittsburgh in 1931. He remained at Trinity for 32 years, increasing the size of the congregation at a time when most inner-city parishes around the country were losing members.[22] Following his retirement, he served as team chaplain for the Pittsburgh Steelers.)

Morey evidently remembered Traynor's performance and persuaded him to come and play for him on the Cape in 1919. As far as can be determined, Traynor played shortstop and batted clean-up for the Falmouth/Oak Bluffs team all season while waiting tables or washing dishes at a local hotel in the evening.

The Cape Cod League eventually grew into the leading amateur baseball league in America, a breeding ground for future big leaguers. The league often claims that Traynor was the first league alumnus to star in the majors, but technically that is not true. Although Falmouth later became a charter member of the Cape Cod League, there was no league, per se, when Traynor played for them. In 1919, and for decades before that, many Cape Cod villages fielded teams, but those nines were not connected to one another in any formal way. Ball clubs on the Cape took on semi-pro and amateur teams from all over southeastern Massachusetts, arranging games via personal contacts or through ads placed in the Boston Globe. There was a tournament each fall that was open to any town team that wanted to enter, but there was no central governing body to create a set schedule or to formally compile statistics or records. The Cape Cod League, as an entity, did not come into existence until 1923, by which time Traynor was playing in Pittsburgh. Even so, as of 2009, Traynor retained the distinction of being the only Hall of Famer known to have played a full season on the Cape.[23]

Traynor's team split its season between Oak Bluffs and Falmouth, taking a ferry back and forth across Vineyard Sound and alternating home parks and uniforms.[24] Falmouth Heights was considered the garden spot of Cape Cod ball fields. It was a beautiful setting, right along the ocean. The land sloped upward from home plate down the left field line, and fans in left could plop down on a hill and get a dramatic, amphitheater-like view of the action. If skies were clear, they could look across the sound and see all the way to Martha's Vineyard. "In those days, there weren't so many other things to do. People went to the ballgame, especially on the weekends," remembered Al Irish, who grew up on the Cape. "It was really crowded along the banks and the base lines. And you could look out over the water and enjoy the nice ocean breeze."[25] That was on a good day. At other times fog rolled in off the sound and enclosed the park in a damp, chilly, autumnal gloom.

Falmouth Heights was wedged into the surrounding neighborhood, which resulted in some quirky dimensions. It was an unremarkable 375 feet to left field and 400 feet to center, but the distance from home plate to the right field corner was 200 feet at most. Just beyond right field stood a corner store and a small house; a fly ball that landed on the porch was an automatic ground-rule double. The Commodores called the Heights home until 1964. Waban Park in Oak Bluffs also stood along the water and was subject to the same weather vagaries. Its distinguishing features were a large gazebo bandstand that loomed beyond first base and a collection of ornately styled summer cottages in back of home plate.

Falmouth/Oak Bluffs played all its games at home that season. It didn't play any other Cape teams; instead, it hosted some of the best clubs from the Boston area, including teams from the Boston Navy Yard and Western Electric and town teams from Attleboro, Middleboro, Brockton, and South Boston. Those teams usually would come down to the Cape and play a series of two, three, or four games.

There was no easy or convenient way to get around the Cape, so a road trip to Falmouth or Oak Bluffs could be a bone-clattering test of endurance. For some perspective, in Traynor's day, getting from Boston to Falmouth took almost five hours. By the twenty-first century, one could drive there in 90 minutes. While teams sometimes took trains or cars, another common form of transportation was horse-drawn buckboards that weaved their way through the tight, winding country roads.[26] Sometimes after games, the visiting team would sprawl out on the grass to enjoy a picnic lunch before embarking on the grueling ride out of town.[27]

Newspaper coverage of Traynor's season with Falmouth/Oak Bluffs is spotty. Full box scores exist for only 29 of the 46 games the team apparently played (along with line scores for a few other games), which makes piecing together a game-by-game account impossible. Although Morey's club opened the season on the Fourth of July, the first game for which results are available is a 2–0 win over the Knights of Columbus of New Bedford, Massachusetts, on July 8. The *New Bedford Times* noted that the only runs of the game came on "Trainor's [*sic*] hit to left field, [which] was carried over Jennings' head by a high wind which swept across the field."[28] It was the only home run Traynor is known to have hit that season. In the ten July games for which statistics are available, Traynor hit .289 and appeared to have played a solid shortstop.

The records, though incomplete, suggest Traynor went on to post some astounding numbers in August. He hit safely in 15 of the 18 games for which box scores exist, batting at a .385 pace across that sample with six doubles, a triple, 12 stolen bases, and 16 runs scored. His fielding percentage over those games was .965, which was exceptional. Not coincidentally, it was a good month for the club as a whole as it clicked off a nine-game winning streak from August 1 to 13 and won 15 of the 19 games reported in the papers.

Falmouth/Oak Bluffs was scheduled to wrap up its season at home against Fall River, Massachusetts, in a Labor Day doubleheader, with a band concert and eight field day events scheduled between games. Morning fog and rain wiped out the first game, but by afternoon the skies had cleared enough to play one game, plus the field day events, which Traynor dominated. He was fastest in circling the bases, getting around in 15 seconds; he won the 100-yard dash in a blazing 10.4 seconds; and he heaved the ball further than anyone else in the distance throwing competition.

Falmouth/Oak Bluffs prevailed, 8–2, over Fall River to conclude its season. The *Boston Globe* reported that the club finished with a record of 38–8, and that Traynor led the team with a batting average of .518.[29] It is highly unlikely, almost impossible, that those figures are accurate. In the games for which either final scores or boxes are available, Falmouth/Oak Bluffs went 24–8, while Traynor posted a batting average of .350. But regardless of the exact numbers, it is unmistakable that Traynor had taken a significant step in his career, more than holding his own against some of the stiffest competition in New England. Dave Morey had given him a break, he had made something of it, and the Boston Braves, in particular, had taken notice.

3

Portsmouth's $10,000 Beauty

Traynor was quite familiar with the Boston Braves. "I always wanted to play for the Braves, ever since I was a little boy."[1] Traynor not only rooted for them but also attended at least a couple of games at Braves Field as a young man. But it seems that watching the Braves was as much about cheering for his favorite team as it was about comparing his own skills against those of the men on the field. His uncle, Stephen Matthews, told a newspaper reporter that, for Pie, seeing a big league game up close was more stressful than anything. Matthews said Traynor once went to a game and left halfway through. "The play was much faster than he had imagined.... He was afraid if he remained longer he might become discouraged and never realize his lifelong ambition."[2]

At the invitation of a Boston scout, Traynor, now 21 years old but claiming to be 20, appeared at Braves Field for a workout on a crisp day in early May 1920. It was his chance to show his hometown team what he had and maybe entice them into offering him a contract, the opportunity he had been preparing for all his life.

Boston's manager was a hard-bitten martinet from Georgia named George Tweedy Stallings. Stallings, who, like Connie Mack of the Philadelphia Athletics, managed in street clothes, made his name as the leader of the 1914 "Miracle Braves," who rose from last place in July to win the National League pennant, and then swept Mack's Athletics four games to none in the World Series. (It is possible that Traynor was part of the throng that jammed into Somerville's Davis Square that October, watching the Series unfold on a large scoreboard that was updated continuously as the play-by-play came in over the telegraph.[3]) Stallings also was a forward-thinking baseball tactician, among the first managers to play the percentages by using a platoon system.

But a little bit of Stallings could go a long way. Away from the ballpark he was a somewhat reasonable guy. But in the clubhouse and on the bench he transformed into an ogre — monstrously vulgar and, at times, downright mean. "A game player fights when bawled out, and that's what I like," he once said.[4] According to Braves business manager Walter Hapgood, "There never was a ballplayer who did not want to get back at George Stallings. He was rough and sometimes abusive but ... he wanted to win."[5]

Traynor's tryout began well enough. "I got out on the infield and was having a great workout when a bell rang somewhere in the park. I heard it but I didn't pay any attention to it. I was having too good a time."[6] The bell meant batting practice was over — time for the Braves to take fielding practice and, therefore, time for Traynor to get out of the way.[7] But instead he tarried in the infield, not really sure what was happening or what he was supposed to do. Stallings, for some reason, judged this to be a grievous offense. "The next thing I know Stallings was bawling me out from the bench, 'Get the hell out of here and stay out!' So I got out — and stayed out."[8] Traynor claimed, maybe only half-jokingly, Stallings' explosion was so terrifying that he ran halfway back to Somerville.[9]

Some people would have been able to shrug off Stallings' tongue-lashing as nothing personal, just an irrational tirade from a crabby, foul-mouthed old man. But Traynor was not wired that way. "Pie was very sensitive to what he perceived as slights, which may or may not have been slights. He could hold a grudge," said Pittsburgh sportswriter Roy McHugh.[10]

In his more reflective moments, Traynor admitted maybe it was a misunderstanding; perhaps Stallings simply was unaware of who he was or why he was there.[11] But even so, Traynor saw no excuse for that kind of outburst, and he was inclined neither to forgive nor forget. "I vowed then that I would get even with Stallings; I never would play for the Braves, even if someday he begged me to."[12]

In the spring of the following season, by which time Traynor was highly valued Pirate property, Pittsburgh manager George Gibson gave the youngster his choice of minor league teams to be assigned to. Gibson informed Traynor one of the 11 clubs interested in him was Rochester, managed by none other than Stallings, who had resigned his post in Boston after a seventh-place finish. Traynor glared at Gibson and said curtly, "Tell Mr. Stallings for me he can go to hell."[13]

About a week later, Traynor enjoyed better luck at a workout for the Boston Red Sox in Fenway Park.[14] The Red Sox were a once-great franchise heading for deep trouble, just four months removed from owner Harry Frazee's infamous sale of Babe Ruth to the New York Yankees. From 1915 to 1918 Boston won three world championships with a glittering roster that featured the likes of Ruth, Hall of Fame outfielders Tris Speaker and Harry Hooper, and formidable moundsmen Dutch Leonard and Carl Mays. But by 1920, with the exception of Hooper, all of those men were gone and not very well replaced. In the nine seasons from 1922 to 1930, the BoSox would finish in last place eight times.

The fog of time and the malleability of memory make it tough to divine precisely how things unfolded during Traynor's Red Sox workout. Everyone who was there seemed to see things through his unique lens. By some accounts it was a one-day workout, but Traynor later remembered it stretching over two days. Depending on who was telling the story, Traynor's workout was arranged either by Boston sportswriter Ed Hurley or by his old Cape Cod coach, Dave Morey.[15]

Traynor said he began by throwing extra batting practice to the Red Sox's Wally Schang and Ossie Vitt before finally getting an opportunity to take some hacks himself. He swung the bat well. "I hit the fence some," he said cryptically. Traynor remembered that it was Vitt who tracked down Red Sox manager Ed Barrow and urged him to come take a closer look.[16]

Boston pitcher Joe Bush, later a teammate of Traynor's in Pittsburgh, recalled the young man from Somerville wowing everyone with his glove. "I grabbed a fungo stick ... and yelled to him, 'Hey, sonny, let's see you get the ones I'm going to hit you.' The kid was amazing."[17]

One man who professed skepticism was the Red Sox's Everett Scott. Of course, Scott had reason to be a wet blanket; he was Boston's starting shortstop and he was watching a talented prospect who basically was gunning for his job. Scott, a durable, good-field, no-hit player, supposedly watched the gawky Traynor take ground balls and scoffed, "He's too awkward. He's kicked so much of the surface around shortstop that it will take the [grounds crew] a week to get it in shape."[18]

Regardless of what his shortstop might have said, Barrow was impressed with Traynor. "He looked like a real ballplayer even though he appeared to be all arms and legs and [had] feet like violin cases."[19] But Barrow was not sufficiently intrigued to offer a contract. Instead, he suggested that Traynor go to the minor leagues, sharpen his skills, and come back to Boston for another workout at the end of the season.

Traynor had two slightly different recollections of that discussion with Barrow. In a 1929 interview, he said Barrow tried to convince him to go down to the Class B Virginia League and play for the Portsmouth Truckers, a team the Red Sox used as a *de facto* farm club. But Traynor, in this telling of the story, balked at Barrow's offer. "[Barrow] told me how much I would get there and it didn't seem enough, so I told him I wouldn't go."[20] But Traynor thought Barrow must have gone off and sung his praises to Portsmouth management because "a day or two later I got a wire from [Portsmouth] offering better terms than Barrow thought I could get, so I went down there."[21]

But in 1920, just a few months removed from the events, Traynor told a different story. "[Barrow] offered to get me a berth with ... Toronto ... of the International League. Then I received a telegram from [Truckers president Henry] Dawson with a new offer, which I showed to Barrow and he advised me to go to Portsmouth."[22] This seems like the more plausible scenario. All through his major league career, Traynor was a notoriously soft touch when it came to negotiating contracts. He never haggled; whatever management offered seemed to be fine with him. It is hard to imagine he drove a harder bargain as a callow, poverty-stricken kid than he did as a grown man and established star.

The Red Sox were not the only club to indicate interest. Connie Mack, whose Athletics were in town to play Boston at the time, made Traynor an offer similar to Barrow's—no contract, but a no-promises invitation to go to the

Michigan-Ontario League to show what he could do. Traynor said no.[23] He also allegedly turned down an offer from former Red Sox first baseman Dick Hoblitzel to play for Akron of the International League, where he would have been teammates with the great Olympian Jim Thorpe. Hoblitzel's refusal to pay Traynor's travel expenses supposedly was a deal-breaker.[24]

Portsmouth outfielder Lester Bangs, a Somerville native whom Traynor befriended following the 1919 Cape Cod season, apparently played a role in getting Traynor hooked up with the Truckers.[25] Bangs was a character. In 1916 he departed Massachusetts, played two seasons for the Class D Hagerstown (Maryland) Terriers, and then went off to serve in World War I. Bangs was working for a cement company after he returned from the war when, as the story goes, he sent a telegram to the owner of the Portsmouth team, Frank Lawrence, with the words "Terms accepted." He followed up with another wire that read, "Send transportation money immediately." The Truckers had never seen Bangs, probably never even heard of him, much less offered him a contract. But to Bangs' astonishment, they sent him the cash.[26]

Bangs jumped on the steamship *Virginia*, which caught fire and sank in the middle of Chesapeake Bay. He arrived in Portsmouth with nothing more than the clothes on his back, signed a contract, and immediately got tagged with the nickname "Shipwreck."[27] He became something of a local folk hero, a speedster who played mostly in the outfield and at third base and managed the team in 1925 and '26.

Sometime after the Fenway Park workout, Bangs spoke with Henry Dawson about Traynor, although who approached whom and when is unclear. Bangs vouched for his friend's talents, which was good enough for Dawson.[28] The Truckers promptly wired Traynor a contract offer of $200 a month. Before heading south, Traynor again spoke to Barrow, who assured him that his club had a working agreement with Portsmouth guaranteeing that if Traynor made good down there, the Red Sox would have first dibs on him. Barrow was sure to make the same point with Dawson. "I made it plain [Traynor] belonged in Boston, even though I hadn't signed him to a Red Sox contract."[29]

Barrow was making a huge assumption and, as it turned out, a huge mistake. Without a contract, the Red Sox had no rights to Traynor. In 1920 no major league team controlled a system of minor league affiliates; that was still some years away. Although a major league team might set up informal arrangements with a handful of minor league clubs (as the Red Sox did with Portsmouth), those outfits remained independent entities. Owners like Frank Lawrence were on their own, scratching and scrambling to make a buck any way they could. Getting a great, young prospect under contract and later auctioning him off to the highest major league bidder was one way to help keep the coffers flush.

Usually it was in the best interests of minor league teams to honor their handshake agreements. If a minor league owner broke his word too often, major league teams could stop funneling good players his way, which would make it more difficult for him to win games and sell tickets. Nevertheless, a big league team took a gamble anytime it encouraged a prospect to sign a minor league deal.

Of course, the Red Sox would have incurred a different kind of risk had they simply signed Traynor themselves. Not every great athlete develops into a good baseball player. Just because a kid has potential at age 20 does not guarantee he will be a good player at age 25. Traynor was not without talent, but at the same time he didn't have much pedigree beyond the suburban Beantown sandlots. If he had signed and fizzled, the Red Sox would have had nothing to show for their investment.

Lester Bangs, Portsmouth Truckers outfielder and Somerville native, whose endorsement helped Traynor land his first professional contract in 1920 (Joan Estienne).

Had Barrow been comfortable living with that uncertainty, his Red Sox would have controlled Traynor's rights. Essentially they could have snapped their fingers and brought him up to Boston whenever they thought he was ready. But as it was, Traynor became sole property of the Portsmouth Truckers. Frank Lawrence and Henry Dawson were free to do anything they wanted with him and legally there was nothing the Red Sox could do about it.

Traynor joined Portsmouth on Friday, May 14, 17 games into the 1920 season. The Truckers were off to a slow start with a record of 6–11, tied for fifth place in the eight-team Virginia League. In his first professional game Traynor batted clean-up and went 0-for-3 with a sacrifice bunt as the Truckers won on the road against Newport News, 4–1. He handled three chances cleanly at shortstop and participated in a double play. The next afternoon Traynor, batting fifth this time, tallied a single for his first professional hit.

Traynor did not play well in his first week or so. He had just four singles in his first 26 at-bats and was lifted for a pinch-hitter in an important late-inning situation. He hardly would have been human if his confidence were not wavering at least a little bit. Years later a newspaper columnist named Charles Reilly recounted a story of a prominent local resident happening upon a forlorn Traynor at the Portsmouth railroad depot as the young man prepared to take a train back home to Massachusetts and leave baseball behind. "I don't like Portsmouth.... I didn't have any business coming here in the first place.... I wasn't cut out to be a ballplayer."[30] In Reilly's telling, the man picked up Traynor's bag and dragged him back to Frank Lawrence's office, where 30 minutes later Traynor emerged smiling with his confidence restored.

Reilly's account may have been at least partially apocryphal. The specifics seem to smack a little too much of a trite Hollywood script to be wholly trustworthy, and many sportswriters in that era were loath to allow pesky facts to spoil a good story. Nevertheless, it would have been within character for Traynor to feel discouraged, and it is possible he might have considered packing it in. Even after he was well established in the big leagues, Traynor let slumps eat away at him. He could never accept that eventually things would work themselves out, even though they nearly always did. At Portsmouth he was especially frantic to succeed because his future was at stake; he assumed this would be his one and only chance. "If I didn't make good, I probably was through with baseball. The Red Sox didn't think enough of me to hold me on an option."[31] After struggling mightily over the first seven games of his professional career, all sorts of questions and doubts must have been dancing in his brain.

Traynor's fortunes turned soon enough. He enjoyed the first big day of his career on May 22, when he battered Newport News for three hits, including a double, and started a triple play. "We are very much pleased to see [Traynor] get into the limelight ... for he is a hard working lad and deserves credit for his work," wrote the *Portsmouth Star*.[32] Shortly thereafter, on May 26, the Truckers got a new manager when they hired former Pittsburgh Pirates second baseman Jim Viox to replace Jimmy Barton. Barton couldn't seem to settle on a lineup; he had Traynor bouncing everywhere from fourth to seventh in the order. But when Viox arrived, he planted Traynor in the number eight hole.

The move worked. From May 26 through July 7, when Viox moved him back up to fifth, Traynor's average rocketed from .242 to .339. In the middle of that stretch, he found his power stroke. On June 17, he connected for his first professional home run, off Norman Glaser of Rocky Mount. Later he rocketed a homer to straightaway center field in an 8–0 victory over Norfolk on June 20 — the longest ball hit at High Street Park to that point in the season, according to the *Portsmouth Star*.[33] The next afternoon, Traynor homered twice more and knocked in four runs. Then on June 28, he went 4-for-5 with two triples and another home run. Defensively, Traynor was a work-in-progress. Sometimes he looked brilliant, pulling off the occasional "hair-raising" play at shortstop.[34] But he was just as likely to botch an easy one; Traynor was charged with 15 errors in his first 26 games.

Thanks in large part to Traynor's emergence, the Truckers surged in June to a second-place finish in the season's first half, just behind Richmond.[35] (The Virginia League split its season into halves, with the winners of each half meeting in a playoff series at the end of the year to crown the league champion.) However, the city of Portsmouth was slow to warm to its team. After playing before a sparse weekend crowd in mid–June, one of the team's directors groused, "We are putting out a winning team these days and an attendance of a mere thousand at a Saturday game is not the most encouraging thing in the world."[36] Traynor had played before more people on Cape Cod and even with the Somerville B.B.C., which was known to draw crowds of 3,000 or more for important games.

As the second half began, Traynor was in the midst of what would be a 24-game hitting streak, and major league scouts were on his trail. On July 6, scouts from the New York Giants, Detroit Tigers, Chicago Cubs, and Boston Braves showed up in Portsmouth to get a firsthand look at this suddenly hot prospect. Sam Potts of the *Virginian-Pilot and Norfolk Landmark* newspaper reported on July 9 that Portsmouth had turned down an offer of $5,000 for Traynor.[37] Shortly thereafter came an offer of $7,500 from the New York Giants. Potts concluded, "If [major league teams] are willing to pay big money for some of the players reputed to have been sold recently in the Virginia League, can you blame Trucker moguls for ... demanding $10,000 [for Traynor]?"[38] The moguls themselves certainly didn't think so. They told the Giants no. New York manager John McGraw came to regret that he listened to his scout, Art Devlin, and refused to bid higher. He later moaned that after he missed out on Traynor, he spent $200,000 trying to find a third baseman.[39]

On July 16, Pittsburgh Pirate scout Tom McNamara caught Traynor on a very good day. He watched as the Portsmouth shortstop went 2-for-3 with a

double and successfully handled ten chances at short in a 3–2 loss to Petersburg. "Traynor's sensational fielding ... stood out as the feature of the
encounter," according to the *Virginian-Pilot and Norfolk Landmark*. "This
youngster's playing was almost phenomenal at times."[40] McNamara reported
to his boss, Pirate owner Barney Dreyfuss, that Traynor was worth Portsmouth's
eye-popping price tag. Four days later the deal was done. Dreyfuss purchased
Traynor's contract for $10,000, the highest figure ever attached to a player com-
ing out of the Virginia League. "Half a dozen scouts and minor league managers told me I was crazy," Dreyfuss crowed.[41] He would be proven anything
but.

The man responsible for bringing Traynor to the major leagues, 5' 4", 125-
pound, jug-eared Barney Dreyfuss, was the American Dream personified. Born
in 1865 in Freiberg, Germany, Dreyfuss crossed the Atlantic in 1883, in part to
avoid mandatory military service. He settled in Paducah, Kentucky, where he
was employed in the accounting office of Bernheim Brothers Distillery. Dreyfuss worked long hours crunching numbers during the day, and then went home
and spent his nights teaching himself English. Before long, he had worn himself into a state of exhaustion. A doctor recommended he get a life, go outside
once in a while, maybe learn to play a sport. Dreyfuss settled on baseball and
quickly took to the game, although perhaps not in the way the doctor had
hoped. He actually played very little baseball, maybe none at all, but he loved
the challenge of organizing local amateur teams. In 1890, he used money bor-
rowed from his bosses at the distillery to purchase a share of the National
League's Louisville Colonels. Within nine years, he was the club's sole owner.

The Louisville teams of the 1890s were, for the most part, a horror show.
Toward the end of the decade, just when the Colonels finally began to dig up
some promising young talent, the National League decided to eliminate four
teams, and Dreyfuss sensed his club was on the endangered list. Following the
1899 season he worked out a shrewd deal that allowed the league to dissolve
the Louisville franchise; in exchange, he received part ownership of the Pittsburgh Pirates, and the right to take 14 of his Colonels with him. Those players—including Tommy Leach, Deacon Phillippe, Fred Clarke, and the legendary
Honus Wagner—formed the nucleus of the Pirate ball clubs that captured three
straight National League pennants from 1901 to 1903 and a World Series crown
in 1909.

For a man who knew nothing of baseball until he was a young man, Dreyfuss proved a sharp evaluator of talent. He painstakingly kept tabs on minor
league players and, when he found one he liked, would dispatch his scouts to
take a closer look. His acumen paid off. In the 32 years Dreyfuss owned the
Pirates, his teams won six pennants and finished in the top half of the National
League standings 26 times. "I just couldn't—I wouldn't—stand for a second-
division team."[42]

A man with a resume like that has earned the right to be a bit full of himself, and Dreyfuss exercised the privilege. "Smartness pays off in baseball as well as in any other activity.... If I had put the same time, energy, brains, and money into another business, I would have succeeded just as well."[43] As that self-aggrandizing statement might suggest, Dreyfuss, while admirable, was hardly lovable. It is not even clear if he was likeable. Writer Fred Lieb, who generally was rather fond of the man, admitted he could be "severe, dominating, critical, and stubborn."[44] Dreyfuss studied everything that happened on the field with the eye of a scientist; his incessant questions, critiques, second guesses, and suggestions could drive a manager nuts. He would shell out big cash to sign worthy prospects like Traynor, but once he got those men in the fold, he proved an inflexible and intimidating negotiator, unafraid to sever ties with players who crossed him or tried to break the bank. Dreyfuss could be just as abrasive with his peers. He once publicly referred to a fellow owner, Charles Murphy of the Chicago Cubs, as a "rat" and a "sneak."[45] He was hard, but he was a winner.

Up in Boston, Ed Barrow was caught asleep at the switch. He thought his gentleman's agreement with the Truckers tied Traynor to the Red Sox, but in this instance at least, Henry Dawson and Frank Lawrence acted more like stone-cold capitalists than gentlemen. Attendance in Portsmouth had been disappointing that year; the $10,000 that Traynor brought was a welcome windfall. But that was irrelevant to Barrow, who went berserk when he heard the news. "I hit the ceiling. I grabbed the phone and called Dawson and called him everything I could think of," Barrow said.[46]

Tough luck, answered Dawson. "Boston turned down this man because he was too inexperienced.... I have a letter from Barrow in which it is admitted that Boston has no claim on Traynor."[47] Traynor backed up his boss. "I never signed any sort of agreement with [Barrow], nor am I obligated to him in any way except for the friendly assistance he gave me."[48] (Barrow, aggrieved as he was, didn't hold it against Dawson. In 1932, when he was general manager of the New York Yankees, he gave Dawson a job as one of his minor league executives.[49])

Barrow wasn't the only man who felt like he had been bamboozled. Washington Senators owner Clark Griffith had his own sob story. "I thought I had [Traynor] all sewed up. They owed me the pick of their club in exchange for three ballplayers I sent them the summer before. So I picked Traynor and thought he belonged to me. Then the owner weaseled out of it. He went against his word and told me I'd have to give him $5,000 extra."[50] Unlike Barrow, Griffith was still whining about it 20 years later. "If we had Traynor for third base and [Ossie] Bluege for shortstop, we'd have won four straight pennants instead of two."[51]

As part of the purchase agreement, Traynor remained in Portsmouth for the balance of the regular season. The performance of the "$10,000 beauty," as one reporter labeled Traynor, was erratic.[52] On July 23, he enjoyed another two-homer afternoon, but from there he immediately slipped into a 7-for-51 swoon that dropped his batting average from .316 to .281. His glove work remained unsteady, with sustained stretches of brilliance interrupted by periods of butchery. His complacent approach to a ground ball on August 23 cost pitcher Slim McLaughlin a no-hitter, and in 12 September games he totaled eight errors. For the season, in 104 games, Traynor batted .270 with 18 doubles, four triples, and eight home runs. He committed 31 errors for a fielding percentage of .947. Although his defense ran hot and cold, that fielding percentage was near the top among Virginia League shortstops, plus he seemed to cover a fair bit of ground.

Portsmouth won the second half with a record of 37–19, four games better than second-place Petersburg. The Truckers captured an exciting league championship series four games to three over first-half champion Richmond, but they did so without their star shortstop. At the conclusion of the regular season, Traynor headed north to begin living his big league dream as a member of the Pittsburgh Pirates.

The Pirate team that Traynor joined was well out of the pennant race, in fourth place. The Bucs organization went into a slow, steady decline after winning the World Series in 1909, bottoming out in 1917 when they went 51–103 and finished in last place for the first time in 26 years. Forty-year-old George Gibson, a longtime Pirate catcher, was trying to lead Pittsburgh back to prominence as a rookie manager in 1920.

The Pirates were the weakest hitting team in baseball that season, but their pitching was outstanding. Pittsburgh's 1909 World Series hero, Babe Adams, still could pick batters apart at age 38 with his impeccable control. He finished second in the league in 1920 with an earned run average of 2.19. Two slots behind Adams in the ERA race was left-hander Wilbur Cooper, as of 2009 still the Pirates' all-time leader in wins. Cooper, who once played for a minor league team owned by future United States President Warren Harding, won 24 games in 1920 and 202 over his long Pirate career. Cooper was an intense competitor — probably overly intense. His habit of throwing a tantrum whenever a teammate committed an error behind him was not one of his most endearing traits.[53]

Traynor often reminisced about a special pickoff play he and Cooper developed. "Cooper used to stand near the mound and when he stiffened his right hand, I walked near the bag and the ball would come over. I used to catch plenty of runners."[54] It is easy to be skeptical of that story. For a pitcher to pick a runner off third base is highly unusual, and Traynor was known to tell a whopper once in a while. But a review of the play-by-play accounts proves he wasn't kidding — they really did pull it off a few times.[55]

The Bucs' pre-eminent position player in the late 1910s and early 1920s was Hall of Famer Max Carey, who arrived in Pittsburgh as a 20-year-old in 1910. Carey's most notable attribute was his blazing speed. He led the league in stolen bases ten times and retired in fifth place on the all-time major league list with 738 steals. Carey also was a defensive whiz in both center field and left, covering acres of territory and cowing runners with his rifle arm.

Carey was a fascinating person. He had an active mind that led him toward a diversity of off-the-field interests. At various times throughout his life he speculated in real estate, wrote songs, shared a patent for a liniment called Minute-Rub, invested in a lime farm, and organized baseball leagues for Cuban refugees following Fidel Castro's ascent to power.[56] Carey also managed a team in the All-American Girls Professional Baseball League; a highly amusing but borderline creepy publicity photo shows a tanned, shirtless Carey, pushing age 60, sharing batting tips on a beach with a group of admiring young women in swimsuits.[57]

So here was Traynor, a shy youngster who had seen relatively little of the world outside of Boston, suddenly part of a fraternity of crude, skirt-chasing, hard-drinking, world-wise men. Longtime Pirate employee Art McKennan, interviewed in 1994, retained vivid memories of that atmosphere. "It was pretty rugged. I could swear as well as a sea captain when I was 13 just by being around that clubhouse."[58] At a glance, it didn't appear that Traynor belonged there. At six feet, he was taller than most of his new teammates but his body hadn't filled out yet, which made him look like an overgrown teenager. "He was the rawest-looking thing you ever saw in your life. Knock-kneed and big wide shoulders," observed McKennan.[59]

Ironically, Traynor made his major league debut on September 15 in Braves Field, where just four months earlier George Stallings had stripped off a chunk of his hide and sent him crawling home. Traynor entered in the sixth inning of the second game of a doubleheader, replacing Bill McKechnie at shortstop. In his first at-bat, against Boston's Dana Fillingim, Traynor popped out to his fellow Somervillian, shortstop Hod Ford. Two innings later against Fillingim, he tallied his first major league hit, an RBI double that scored Possum Whitted. That accounted for the only Pirate run in a 4–1 defeat.

The Pirates had been on a futile quest for a shortstop for three years, ever since Honus Wagner retired. That's why Gibson gave Traynor a good, long look over the season's final two-and-a-half weeks, in hopes he might prove worthy of the job. Traynor appeared in 17 games, including the first and third games of the major leagues' last regularly scheduled tripleheader, on October 2. He had his moments, including a three-hit game against Brooklyn, the eventual pennant-winners. But for the most part he looked anxious and overmatched at the plate, and his work at shortstop was wretched. A September 18 game against the New York Giants revealed his defensive problems in microcosm. He was charged with three costly errors—a low throw to first base, a high throw to second base on a force play, and a dropped relay on an attempted double play—in an 8–7 loss.

Gibson tried to be supportive and encouraging. After that second bad throw against the Giants, he was reported to have hollered, "Throw the next one into the balcony, kid. It's all right with me!"[60] Traynor showed the Pirates some good things; he certainly played hard and his speed and strong arm were unquestionable. But 12 errors, an .860 fielding percentage, and a .212 batting average said all that needed to be said. The kid just wasn't ready yet.

4

Killing Ushers in Birmingham

Though it wasn't easy to see in that first major league trial, Traynor's skill set was ideally suited for the Pirates' home ballpark, Forbes Field. Forbes was one of the jewels of baseball. Author Richard Peterson tells of "its towering white clay façade, its array of high-arched entrances topped by large awnings, and its green-painted steel girders holding the massive three-tiered concrete oval in place."[1]

For nearly 30 years the Pirates had played their home games at Exposition Park, a field derisively known as "Lake Dreyfuss" because it was prone to flooding from the Allegheny River, which flowed only 50 yards away. Exposition was crudely charming and contained a lot of history, but by 1909 it was no longer acceptable to play major league baseball in a ramshackle park located in a dilapidated neighborhood while outfielders splashed around in water that lapped against their ankles. As Dreyfuss put it, "The game was growing up, and patrons no longer were willing to put up with nineteenth century conditions."[2]

Dreyfuss erected Forbes Field in Pittsburgh's burgeoning Oakland neighborhood, which was becoming the educational and cultural hub of the city. It was about three miles from downtown and easily accessible by trolley. The Pirates played their first game there on June 30, 1909, a mere four months after the official groundbreaking. Thirty years later it took four months just to install light standards.[3]

The ballpark was gigantic. When Traynor arrived, it measured 462 feet to the deepest point of left-center field, 409 feet to straightaway center, and 416 feet to right-center.[4] The batting cage, which the Pirates stashed in the nether reaches of the outfield, right next to the flag pole, was in play. From 1909 to 1924, there was a set of low bleachers in right field. According to National League rules at the time, a ball that landed in fair territory and hopped over the short fence in front of the bleachers was a home run. (Traynor tallied three of these so-called "bounce home runs" at Forbes.)

The Pirates tailored their team to the dimensions of their park. Forbes Field could be cruel to power-hitting musclemen, so the Bucs leaned toward line drive hitters with good speed who could shoot lasers into the gaps and run forever. Most of the Pirates' great sluggers during the Forbes Field era — including Honus Wagner, Max Carey, Paul Waner, Kiki Cuyler, and Roberto Clemente — fit this mold. So did Traynor. He quickly learned to take advantage of Forbes' spaciousness by choking up slightly and spraying the ball to all fields while wielding one of the heaviest bats of anyone in the game at 42 ounces. That big club cut down on his power, but "[w]hat I'd do with a lighter bat is send nice, long outs."[5]

During Traynor's time, Forbes Field was one of the leading ballparks for triples, and inside-the-park home runs also were relatively common.[6] Traynor ranked in the top ten in the National League in three-baggers ten times. He hit 58 home runs in his career, 18 of which were of the inside-the-park variety. According to the Society for American Baseball Research, in Traynor's more than 14 seasons as a Pirate player, he hit only seven home runs over the fence on the fly in his home park.[7]

Playing the infield at Forbes Field was like playing on a cobblestone street. The park rested atop a layer of bedrock, which made the dirt portion of the field extremely hard; defenders had to be prepared for some crazy bounces.[8] "There were infielders who would not take infield practice because of the condition of that infield," recalled Steve Blass, who pitched for the Pirates in the 1960s and early 1970s.[9] It wasn't any better in the 1920s and 1930s. As a result, the so-called "hot corner" where Traynor plied his trade was much hotter at Forbes than at most other stadiums. It was no place for men with weak hearts or slow reflexes.

As he departed for spring training in Hot Springs, Arkansas, though, Traynor surely was aware he stood little chance of opening the 1921 season in Pittsburgh. Over the winter the Pirates had traded for 29-year-old shortstop Rabbit Maranville, who had spent the previous nine years with the Boston Braves. Maranville was one of baseball's biggest stars and the Pirates didn't get him to sit on the bench. Moreover, Traynor, with only one season of professional baseball under his belt, still needed to smooth the rough edges of his game.

The Pirates stayed in downtown Hot Springs at the elegant Eastman Hotel, a short trolley ride from the Pirates' training site at Fordyce Field. As Traynor recalled, the Pirates worked out from 10:00 A.M. until noon each morning, rode back to the hotel for a quick lunch, and then returned to the park for an afternoon session from 1:00 until 3:00 P.M. In the Eastman's basement was a huge room, big enough for 100 people, which contained mineral water baths. "There was no clubhouse, no locker room, [no] shower facilities at the training site, so after practice each day we had strict orders to take a bath back at the hotel in the basement," Traynor said.[10] To guarantee his team followed those orders, manager George Gibson issued each man a card that he was required to have punched each time he entered the bath.[11] Long after his career had ended, Traynor remembered that camp at Hot Springs as the best he ever attended. Surely, some of those feelings arose from the novelty and excitement of going through spring training with a major league team for the first time. But Traynor says he also loved the baths, which he felt gave him strength and cleansed his body of impurities.[12]

While Hot Springs left a lasting impression on Traynor, the young man made his own mark in the minds of the Pirates that spring. His improved physique and manic work ethic opened everyone's eyes. Heretofore, descriptions of Traynor made him sound gangly and awkward, like an adolescent who hadn't fully grown into his body. But he spent the winter of 1920-21 toiling as an ironworker and doing a lot of running and walking in his spare time.[13] It showed. He came to Arkansas that spring looking like a man. "He was in the condition of a well-trained fighter," observed one reporter.[14] His body was bulkier and sculpted, and he was ready to go at full throttle from day one.

While the rest of the team adjourned practice at midday and went back to the hotel to eat, Traynor frequently arranged for someone to bring him his lunch so he could remain at the field and continue working on his own. Usually he talked a more experienced teammate into hanging around and helping him. For example, after Gibson pointed out that Traynor had a bad habit of running the bases flat-footed, the youngster cornered speedy veteran outfielder Carson Bigbee and asked him to stay through lunch and give him some pointers. Bigbee obliged, teaching Traynor how to stay up on the balls of his feet and how to execute a proper slide. After that he got Bigbee to hit him some grounders before the afternoon session got underway.[15] "[Traynor] was the talk of all the vets," according to Chilly Doyle of the *Pittsburgh Gazette-Times*.[16]

On April 16, the Pirates officially farmed out Traynor to the Southern Association's Birmingham Barons.[17] As it happened, Birmingham, Alabama, was known informally as "the Pittsburgh of the South." It was the region's boiler room, a hub for iron and steel production. Unlike Pittsburgh, though, Birmingham was a relatively new city, founded in 1871. Its population boomed 245 percent from 1900 to 1910 and stood at around 180,000 by the time Traynor hit town in 1921.[18]

Baseball was woven into the fabric of Birmingham, where it proved a popular escape from the steamy monotony of life in the mills. Highly competitive (and racially segregated) industrial leagues flourished. Over the years, a good number of African Americans parlayed their success on the city's sandlots into careers in the Negro Leagues.[19] Professional baseball dated to 1885, the Barons' first season, while the Birmingham Black Barons, established in 1920, became one of the greatest clubs in Negro League history.

Traynor's manager in Birmingham was 45-year-old Carlton Molesworth. The rotund Molesworth had a very short, very unimpressive stint in the major leagues, working in four games for the National League's Washington Senators in 1895. In 1908 he took over as manager at Birmingham and found he had a gift for developing young prospects. By 1921 Barney Dreyfuss regarded him as one of the top minor league managers around. The Pirates trusted Traynor was in good hands.

Birmingham had an exciting team that season. The pitching staff was a little thin despite the presence of Earl Whitehill, who later enjoyed a long career in the American League. But the Barons could score some runs. Every starter on the infield batted over .300, and three of them had averages higher than .320. First baseman Dutch Bernsen led the Southern Association with 22 home runs. Molesworth had his team running wild on the bases, too, with four Barons among the league's top six in steals. They swiped 11 in one game against Chattanooga.

Twenty-three-year-old catcher Johnny Gooch, whose minor league career had been rather pedestrian to that point, put together a breakout season, catching almost all the Barons' games while hitting a solid .288. Gooch and Traynor roomed together on the road in 1921 and became close friends. They just didn't see eye-to-eye on the window blinds, according to Gooch's son, Beverley. "Pie liked it darker and Dad liked it lighter ... so the window shade kept going up and down and they never compromised. I don't know if that says anything about their ability to solve arguments or not!"[20]

Gooch went on to catch for the Pirates from 1922 until 1928. He was a popular figure among the Forbes Field faithful, partly because he had a fun name. When Gooch stepped to the plate, public address announcer Nat Moll bellowed, "Johnny Goooooooch," and Pirate fans replied in kind.[21] After Traynor took over as Pittsburgh's manager, he hired Gooch as a coach. They were on each other's Christmas card list for the rest of their lives.

Traynor joined the Barons three games into their season and wasted no time asserting himself. In his first game he went 4-for-5 with a double in a 7–3 victory at Nashville on Saturday, April 16. That same morning Birmingham found itself in the path of a devastating tornado, part of an outbreak of twisters that killed 90 people and injured nearly 700 across five southern states. One of the tornados touched down briefly in downtown Birmingham, and then leapfrogged over to the home of the Barons, Rickwood Field, where it shredded the bleachers and the outfield fence, causing $30,000 worth of damage.[22] Cleanup began that afternoon. On Sunday a crew of 125 volunteers worked from dawn until dusk to rebuild the fence and make sure the field was playable for the Barons' Monday home opener against Little Rock.

Traynor, who batted seventh, caught the home folks' attention immediately. He lashed three hits, including a triple to deep center field, and stole a base as the Barons thumped Little Rock, 15–3. The *Birmingham News* was suitably impressed. "Pie Traynor, who cost the Pirates $10,000, looked like he was worth a million.... Traynor is just as fast as any of the Baronial speed kings in getting down to first. When he stretches out on the base paths, he looks like a greyhound in motion."[23] All that speed came in a very unlikely looking package, around six feet tall and a solid 170 pounds. "My, but is he a big boy for a shortstop. He has a pair of [hands] as big as Tennessee hams and can almost touch third [while] ... standing ... on second."[24] After six sizzling games, Molesworth moved Traynor up to third in the order, where he cooled off a little. But after 15 games, he was tied for the league lead in hitting with a mark of .417.

Traynor poses in his Birmingham Barons uniform in 1921. Traynor batted .336 and stole 47 bases in Birmingham, which earned him another late-season promotion to Pittsburgh (Marilyn Lenick).

Molesworth dropped Traynor to the six hole for a while, and then moved him to the leadoff spot in mid–June. Traynor responded with his most torrid stretch of the season, stroking three hits apiece in six of the next eight games. At the same time, Traynor's defense at shortstop, shaky all season, collapsed. He could track down plenty of ground balls; that wasn't the problem. As *Birmingham News* sports editor Zipp Newman wrote, "Pie is not the most graceful fielder in the world but he sure covers the territory."[25] But when he uncorked a throw, he had no clue where it was going.

His issues seemed to be more mental than physical. On close plays, when he had to hurry, he often was fine, though he did have a bad habit of making crazy, off-balance throws in situations where he probably should have just hung on to the ball.[26] But where he got into an inordinate amount of trouble was on easy grounders that allowed him a moment to think about his throw; in those situations he never knew if the baseball was going to end up in the dirt, in the dugout, or somewhere among the fans sitting along first base. "I killed a few ushers," he once joked to his friend Tony Bartirome.[27]

Traynor committed errors in five consecutive games, from June 10 to 13. This was part of an alarming 13-game stretch in which he accumulated 15 miscues. With smaller gloves and infields that often were poorly manicured, errors were more prevalent in that era than they would be decades later. Even allowing for that, though, Traynor was a defensive liability in 1921.

But Birmingham fans and certainly the local newspaper seemed willing to overlook Traynor's defensive lapses. He was wildly popular thanks to his hitting, of course, but also due to the irrepressible zeal with which he played the game. The *Birmingham News* laid the hyperbole on thick. "Comparing Harold Traynor ... with other Southern League [shortstops] is like comparing the dim, phosphorescent glow of a lightning bug to the effulgent rays of the midday sun."[28] On July 1, at a point in the season when Traynor had more errors than double plays, the *News* shouted, "How this baby can field! If he isn't a better fielder than at least half of those in the big leagues, then we miss our guess."[29]

Traynor's 15-game hitting streak in early July helped the Barons surge into second place, although the first-place Memphis Chicks, who went on to take the league championship with 104 victories, were already far down the track. At the end of July Traynor was tied for second in the Southern Association with an average of .356, while his 42 stolen bases led the circuit. He also collected another 19 errors that month.

Although Traynor's bat cooled in August, his defense stabilized somewhat. Then on August 26, the Pittsburgh Pirates announced Traynor would be coming north for the final month of the season to help the first-place Bucs try to stave off a challenge from the New York Giants. His final home game at Rickwood Field came on August 27, designated Pie Traynor Day by the city of Birmingham. Traynor got a base hit along with a spirited ovation from the Barons' fans when the team honored him before the game. Traynor officially bade the team goodbye following a 3–0 win over Memphis on August 29.

It was an exceptional offensive season for Traynor, as he batted .336 (tenth in the Southern Association) with 47 stolen bases (tied for third in the league) and a slugging percentage of .455 in 131 games. He compiled 18 three-hit games and five four-hit games, along with hitting streaks of 15, 11, and 11 contests. He wasn't a perfect player — he walked just 18 times and his 64 errors and .918

fielding percentage were not good — but those who had watched him thought he looked like a young man who was bound for stardom. A seasoned Southern Association observer gushed, "He's the greatest ballplayer individually and for his team in the Southern League; there has never been another league short-stop who approached him in all around class."[30] Carlton Molesworth called him the greatest player he had seen in 20 years.[31] Team captain Dutch Bernsen, a minor league veteran, concurred. "I have never seen a finer big league prospect. He has every earmark of a real player ... and right determination to make good."[32] Barons owner Rick Woodward penned a glowing tribute to Traynor in the *Birmingham News* and years later still called him the finest player in the history of the franchise.[33]

The 1921 Pittsburgh Pirates were a good team for a greenhorn like Traynor to break in with. "[They] were most gracious to me," he said.[34] Lots of clubs hazed and ostracized young players as a rite of passage, but most of the veterans on the Pirates were too busy laughing and causing mayhem to deliberately make someone else's life miserable. Art McKennan, the team's batboy, likened the clubhouse atmosphere to that of a circus. "There was not much serious play with that crowd."[35] McKennan said things got quiet after losses, but after a victory he would find the players in the shower whacking each other with brooms.

Traynor fit in reasonably well with this wild bunch. Though he wasn't boisterous or rowdy, he was no stick-in-the-mud either. Traynor had an imp-ish, deadpan sense of humor that got him in trouble on occasion; it wasn't always clear whether he was being serious or just messing with someone. One time George Gibson got on him for striking out three times in an afternoon exhibition game. Traynor, with a straight face, quipped that he had trouble picking up the ball because the moon was right behind the pitcher.[36] One after-noon Chicago's burly Hack Wilson lashed a drive to right field that Paul Waner tracked down for the final out of the game. As Traynor headed across the field toward the clubhouse, he crossed paths with an enraged Wilson, who was spew-ing a geyser of vulgarities. Traynor shouted toward him, "When you get to be a good ballplayer, I'll listen to you." The joke was lost on Wilson, who was in no mood for levity. "He turned on me [but] I kept right on going," said Traynor. "I didn't wish to be twisted and torn into little pieces."[37]

But while Traynor's humor was understated, there was nothing at all sub-tle about the loony shenanigans that went on with the Pirates. The ringleader was pocket-sized shortstop Rabbit Maranville, the slightly wayward son of a Springfield, Massachusetts, cop. Had he been born two or three generations later, Maranville probably would have been medicated or placed into therapy at an early age. As it was he was free to careen through life, boozing, brawling, making merry, and gleefully trampling the rules of socially acceptable behav-ior.

Baseball executive Bill Veeck called Maranville "the first drunken player I was really aware of. Maranville was always loaded."[38] He once celebrated Ash Wednesday by parking himself in the lobby of a swanky hotel and flinging hand-fuls of ashes at unsuspecting guests as they walked through the door.[39] He enter-tained fans with in-game pantomime acts and caught pop flies by leaning back and letting the ball land on his chest, roll down his upper body, and into his glove.[40] He had a vaudeville act; one night while demonstrating his sliding tech-nique he skidded off the stage, sailed into the orchestra pit, and crashed into a bass drum.[41]

But Maranville only got away with his buffoonery because he was an out-standing player, a brilliant defensive shortstop who finished second in National League Most Valuable Player voting in 1914, as part of the world champion "Miracle Braves." He also was very solicitous toward Traynor, tutoring him on the finer points of defense, including such nuances as the most effective way to break in a new glove.[42]

Maranville's partner in crime was 22-year-old first baseman Charlie Grimm. Grimm wasn't as wacky as Maranville, but he was pretty far out there. "Charlie was tops as mime and pantomimist," Traynor remembered. "He had us laughing all the time."[43] Once when a slow-footed hitter bounced an easy grounder to him, Grimm surprised everyone by flipping the ball to second baseman Cotton Tierney and yelling, "Have we got him Mr. Tierney?" Tier-ney hollered back, "Absolutely, Mr. Grimm!" as he fired the ball over to first for the out.[44] Grimm enjoyed playing the banjo and formed a quartet with teammates Tierney, Johnny Morrison, and Possum Whitted. "[Traynor] wanted in, but he couldn't sing," chortled Grimm.[45]

The intensity of the pennant race that Traynor stepped into in September 1921 belied the frivolity; it was the first time in ten years the Pirates were play-ing meaningful games in the final month of the season. The Bucs were cling-ing to a 1½-game lead over the New York Giants, the National League's premier team during the first two decades of the twentieth century. The rivalry between the Pirates and Giants was intense and heated and sometimes crossed into some truly nasty territory.

The Giants' skipper was the larger-than-life John McGraw. In his youth, McGraw had been the starting third baseman and spiritual leader of the Balti-more Orioles, a combative and immensely talented gang of reprobates who bullied umpires and outsmarted opponents on their way to three consecutive National League titles in the mid–1890s. In 1902 "Little Napoleon," as he became known, took the reins as manager of the Giants and sculpted a team in his own image. By 1920, he had directed them to six pennants. Author Cait Murphy wrote, "The man and the city were a good match. McGraw was belligerent, gen-erous, contemptuous of authority, and a rotten loser — qualities not exactly unknown to Gotham."[46]

"Hate" is a potent word, not one to be casually tossed around. Barney Dreyfuss hated John McGraw. The malice between the two men and their teams dated to 1903 when, in the middle of a close race, New York catcher Frank Bowerman lured Pirates player-manager Fred Clarke into the Giants' clubhouse and beat the living daylights out of him.[47] Two years later came the peculiar "Hey, Barney" incident at the Giants home park, the Polo Grounds, in which McGraw spotted the Bucs' owner in the stands and repeatedly called his name while loudly accusing him of "owing money to bookies and welching on bets."[48] Dreyfuss tattled to the league office and got McGraw suspended for 15 days.

On August 24, a week before they recalled Traynor, the Pirates entered the Polo Grounds up 7½ games over the Giants with less than six weeks to go. It was the Pirates' last trip into New York, so before the opening game the city's many newspaper photographers beseeched them to pose for World Series pictures. The Bucs gleefully obliged, while McGraw and his Giants sat and burned. Grimm broke out his banjo in the dugout and strummed along as his teammates sang and taunted the Giants, which nearly sent the tightly wound McGraw over the edge. "Look at them! Look at the clowns!" he fumed.[49] McGraw had the last laugh; his Giants swept Pittsburgh five straight, and suddenly the Pirates found themselves in a race.

Traynor, down about 20 pounds after stewing in the oppressive heat of the Deep South all summer, was awaiting the Pirates when they arrived to begin a homestand on September 1. He met up with them in the Forbes Field clubhouse, an austere dungeon with bare, wooden floors and the pungent odor of liniment hanging in the air. Along the walls were wooden cubicles that served as lockers, with benches running in front of them. Teammates often gathered to play cards at a large table set up in the middle of the room.[50]

Gibson threw Traynor headlong into the fray. After a couple of pinch-hitting appearances in a September 1 doubleheader, Traynor took over as the starting third baseman for rookie Clyde Barnhart. Traynor had limited experience at third and as it turned out his leash was short — ridiculously short. On September 5, the Pirates and Cincinnati Reds were knotted, 1–1, as the Reds came up in the top of the 13th inning. With a runner at third and two out, Larry Kopf bounced an easy grounder to Traynor. He gobbled it up, took his time, reared back and fired the ball straight into the ground, off the glove of a lunging Grimm, as Sam Bohne crossed the plate with the deciding run. For Gibson, that was enough. Barnhart was back at third base in the nightcap and that's where he remained the rest of the season. In the Pirates remaining 23 games, Traynor saw action just twice, both times as a pinch-hitter.

The Bucs crumbled in September, going 11–16 as the Giants took the pennant by four games. ("You can't sing your way through this league," sniffed a self-satisfied McGraw.[51]) Barnhart, who hit .137 over the first two-and-a-half weeks after Traynor's benching, did not help. He turned out to be a very useful bench player for the Pirates over the next seven seasons, but he was miserable at the plate as a rookie. Nor was Barnhart a gifted defensive third baseman. He handled the easy plays well enough but his range was limited. It is not clear why Gibson would anoint Traynor his starter and then put him into cold storage after one error, even though that flub was a costly one. Max Carey, for one, didn't get it. "Traynor could play rings around Barnhart."[52]

Quite possibly, Gibson let negative emotions get the best of him. He remembered Traynor's struggles in Pittsburgh in 1920 and certainly knew about him piling up errors by the dozen in Birmingham. Every time a ball was hit toward Traynor, Gibson's heart rate probably doubled as he wondered if the young man was going to spike a throw into the dirt or launch one four rows into the stands. Although Barnhart was a lesser player, at least Gibson knew what to expect from him.

In many ways, things were looking up for Traynor by the end of the 1921 season. He finally had a little money in his pocket, and he used some of his earnings from his first two years of professional baseball to help his parents become homeowners. On September 21 they completed the purchase of a two-story flat at 48 Alpine Street, directly across the street from the first home they rented in Somerville.[53] James, Maud, and their youngest children would reside at that address until 1926, when they moved up again, this time to the more exclusive community of Arlington, where they remained until shortly after James' death in 1933.

On the other hand, in his two very brief shots at the big time, Traynor had not shown much. The Pirates still had questions about how good he was going be; most likely Traynor was asking himself some of those same questions. He was still young, of course, just 23 years old that November, and since Pittsburgh had paid a pretty penny for him, they were going to give him every opportunity to succeed. But the 1922 season would be a critical one. The Pirates' plan was to run him out there every day and see once and for all what they had.

5

I Wouldn't Trade Him for Half of the Brooklyn Ballclub

If Traynor was at all concerned about his immediate future during the winter of 1921-22, he need not have been. Although Gibson temporarily lost faith in Traynor during the 1921 pennant race, he still believed the young man's best days were ahead of him. "This boy has ability sticking out all over him," he told an audience in New York during the offseason. "By that I mean that I can put him anywhere on my team except in the box or behind the bat. He's one of those old-fashioned ballplayers who takes a real delight in playing ball."[1]

Traynor reported to camp at West Baden Springs, Indiana, on March 5. The players met each morning at 6:00 A.M. for a jog or hike, and then returned to the West Baden Hotel for a regimen of mineral baths and horrid-tasting mineral waters. The afternoons featured calisthenics, workouts with a medicine ball, and, during those rare days when weather permitted, some basic drills on the baseball field. After a miserable week of rain and cold, the team departed West Baden Springs on March 11 for a 27-hour train ride to Hot Springs, where more mineral baths and waters awaited.

When Rabbit Maranville was late to spring training because of the death of his sister, Traynor opened the spring as the team's starting shortstop. When the team split up into "Regulars" vs. "Yannigans" for intrasquad games, Gibson put Traynor with the "Regulars" for the first time. Maranville finally appeared and assumed the shortstop position, but Gibson kept Traynor with the "Regulars," shifting him to an unfamiliar position, second base.

Traynor hit well all spring against minor league teams and occasional big league pitching, but he made a hash of things at second. When the season began, the Opening Day lineup featured Traynor batting fifth and starting at third base. Gibson wasn't thrilled with that arrangement, but he felt it was the only way to get Traynor in the lineup. "[Gibson] told me, 'You've got to go to third.' He thought Maranville was a fellow who couldn't play anywhere but shortstop. And Maranville could play anywhere at all," Traynor recalled.[2] As would become his custom, Traynor got off to a slow start, getting just two hits in his first 19 at-bats as the Pirates split their first six games, all on the road, before heading home to Pittsburgh.

Pittsburgh was the city where Traynor would spend most of the rest of his

51

life. According to the 1920 census, it was the ninth largest city in the United States with a population just under 600,000, about a fifth of whom were foreign born.[3] The city boasted large communities of Irish, German, Polish, and Italian immigrants, and even today, Pittsburgh has a number of neighborhoods that still reflect the ethnicities of the people who settled in them a century ago or more — places like Bloomfield, known as Pittsburgh's Little Italy; Polish Hill; and East Allegheny, a North Side neighborhood often referred to as "Deutschtown."

Immigration helped fuel the steel industry, which made Pittsburgh one of the most important cities in America in the late nineteenth and early twentieth centuries. Andrew Carnegie, who arrived from Scotland, brought steel production to the region in 1875 when he opened the Edgar Thomson Steel Works in nearby North Braddock. Within two decades, Carnegie had purchased the rival Homestead Steel Works and other competitors and by 1892 had melded those companies together into an amalgamation known as Carnegie Steel, headquartered in downtown Pittsburgh. In 1901, Carnegie sold out to J.P. Morgan, who created U.S. Steel, the world's first billion-dollar corporation.

Though Pittsburgh is still known as "the Steel City," its biggest employers today include universities, hospitals, and financial services firms. But when Traynor came to town in the 1920s, heavy industry ruled the day, creating countless jobs and building staggering wealth for owners and managers. It also turned Pittsburgh into a place that resembled "hell with the lid off," as one observer put it.[4] In 1927, essayist and social critic H.L. Mencken wrote of his dismal experience in the city:

> Here was a scene so dreadfully hideous, so intolerably bleak and forlorn that it reduced the whole aspiration of man to a macabre and depressing joke. Here was wealth beyond computation — almost beyond imagination — and here were human habitations so abominable that they would have disgraced a race of alley cats.
>
> I am not speaking of the mere filth. One expects steel towns to be dirty. What I allude to is the unbroken and agonizing ugliness, the sheer revolting monstrousness, of every house in sight. From East Liberty to Greensburg, a distance of twenty-five miles, there was not one sight from the train that did not insult and lacerate the eye.[5]

The people of Pittsburgh lived, worked, and played in dirt. Every building wore a carapace of accumulated grime. Light-colored structures turned black. Office workers who ventured outside would find their white shirts speckled with dark soot by the time they returned. If the weather patterns were just so, a thick cloud of pollution would enshroud the city all morning long, blotting out the sun and keeping streetlamps and automobile headlights on until midday. Not surprisingly, the rate of respiratory illness was exceedingly high.

It was not until after the Great Depression, which devastated the local steel industry, that Pittsburgh's leaders finally got serious about making life in the city more tolerable. The smoke control ordinances of the 1940s and 1950s combined with a plan of urban renewal known as the "Renaissance" helped make Pittsburgh clean, modern, and highly livable, even a beautiful city if one looked in the right spots. But the Pittsburgh that Traynor first walked into was, in many ways, a dreadful place.

The Pirates beat the Cardinals in the home opener, 10–5, on a sunny, cold afternoon. But it was not a good day for the Pirates rookie third baseman. When Traynor botched a bunt by the Cards Del Gainer early in the game, it brought back memories of the struggles he experienced during his brief call-ups the previous two seasons. "Pie must become more confident in his ability or another shift may soon be made at the hot corner," said the *Pittsburgh Press*.[6] The *Pittsburgh Post* was just as harsh in its assessment. "Doubtful eyes were cast toward third base to watch the lumbering, anxious Traynor in action, and when he looked bad on the first ball, the shaking of heads became almost audible."[7]

The 1922 season was on-the-job training for Traynor defensively. He was not a natural third baseman and the position did not come to him easily; he had to strangle the position into submission. "Nobody taught me how to play third base and I'm glad they didn't," he once said. "It's easy to be confused by players offering well-meaning advice. The way I learned was simply to tackle each situation as it arose and master it before going on to something else."[8] He worked tirelessly. John McGraw told of spotting a young Traynor under the stands following a rain-out, long after other players had scattered, practicing fielding bunts.[9]

But even after he had completely conquered third base and become one of the best glove men in baseball, Traynor still felt like a shortstop at heart. "When you are playing third, that foul line looks like a stone wall," he noted in 1927. "When you are playing short, you've got the whole field to roam in.... You feel free and easy."[10]

For all the brilliance he eventually displayed at third, Traynor was no acrobat. He was a big man, pretty muscular for his day, with long arms and legs. One writer looking back at his career observed, "He leaped at a grounder with the actions of a tiger rather than a gazelle. There was a certain Lincolnesque ungainliness about him."[11] Traynor wouldn't give an inch to an oncoming baserunner, which resulted in more than his fair share of broken toes, scraped shins, and bloody knees. "Pie got hurt a lot of times when he shouldn't have," said Max Carey. "He should have been a little more shifty. He'd stand right in there in line with the runner coming in and got cut up easier than most fellows. I don't think he ever learned to give with the play."[12] Traynor was very much a self-taught genius, and in April 1922 he was still working hard to match his raw physical gifts to the demands of this new and unfamiliar position.

Traynor went on a modest seven-game hitting streak in late April, during which he hit his first major league home run, a three-run bounce home run on April 29 off Cincinnati's Eppa Rixey, a Pirate nemesis. Before that game, Reds manager Pat Moran told a reporter, "[Traynor] takes a proper position at the

Traynor flashing some leather, probably in spring training 1921. At this point in his career, Traynor was an erratic defensive shortstop. But he labored tirelessly to learn the intricacies of a new position and soon won acclaim as the best defensive third baseman of his era (Bain Collection, Prints & Photographs Division, Library of Congress, LC-DIG-ggbain-34019).

plate and handles his bat in a natural manner. He has a powerful punch."[13] Though Traynor's major league performance had been nothing special to this point, his immense potential was obvious.

Traynor soon began to get his feet under him, as did the Pirates, who had been a disappointment, hovering around .500 for the first weeks of the season. On Monday, May 15, Traynor's two-run homer in the tenth inning defeated Boston, 6–5. He went on to raise his average 50 points during that week as the Bucs drew closer to the first-place Giants. The *Pittsburgh Press* noted, "Traynor's play in all departments is improving."[14] His sacrifice fly put the Pirates ahead for good in a 7–3 win over St. Louis on May 25. Pittsburgh was just a half-game out.

But they couldn't keep it up for very long. The next two weeks were up and down. Traynor had four hits as the Pirates beat Philadelphia, 7–3, on June 8, which pulled them back to within 1½ games of the Giants. But a loss to Boston the following day triggered a freefall during which the Bucs lost 13 of 16 games. Traynor continued to hit well, ripping off a 15-game hitting streak and lifting his batting average over .300 for the first time. But in the middle of his club's tailspin, Gibson, trying to find some lineup combination that would work, shifted Maranville to second base and Traynor back to shortstop, where again he struggled. He committed three errors in a 15–14 loss to Brooklyn on June 21, and two more on June 24 as the Bucs fell to Cincinnati.

As Gibson's juggling suggests, many in the organization saw Traynor's long-term future at shortstop, not third base. The Pirates were bitterly disappointed that summer when they missed out on signing a major league–ready third base prospect named Willie Kamm. The Pirates supposedly had a handshake agreement with the Pacific Coast League's San Francisco Seals that would have given them first dibs on Kamm. But Pirate scout Chick Fraser claimed that when White Sox owner Charles Comiskey offered a record $100,000, the Seals immediately accepted. "Kamm would have been bought by us no matter what the cost," insisted Fraser. "Pie Traynor is a shortstop and he'd sooner play that position than be tied to third."[15]

The Pirates lost 17 of their 25 games in June, which concluded with an ugly 6–0 loss to St. Louis. The Forbes Field crowd booed Gibson with relish at every opportunity that afternoon. A tipping point had arrived. Gibson was upset with what he perceived to be a half-hearted effort by his players in the preceding weeks. Barney Dreyfuss had been on Gibson's case going back to the previous summer, when Dreyfuss believed Gibson let his guys get away with too much fun and carousing.[16] The Pirates' owner thought the lack of discipline had cost the team the pennant. Both men had pretty much had it.

After the loss to St. Louis, which dropped the team below .500, Gibson abruptly turned in his resignation, and Dreyfuss had no qualms about accepting it. "Not one of us had the slightest inkling that Gibby was going to resign. We were so completely knocked off our feet ... that nobody could say a word," stated an anonymous player to the *Pittsburgh Post*.[17] Nonetheless, Gibson was out, replaced by Bill McKechnie.

McKechnie was 35 years old, though his grim, American Gothic face made him look about ten years older. A native of Wilkinsburg, Pennsylvania, just a few miles outside of Pittsburgh, McKechnie had ended his 11-year playing career just two years earlier, when he appeared in 40 games as a utility infielder for the Pirates. His only previous managing experience came in the Federal League, where he served as a player-manager for the Newark Pepper in 1915.

He stood out in stark relief against the foul-mouthed, ill-bred sots who were still quite numerous in major league clubhouses at the time. McKechnie, nicknamed "Deacon" for his firm sense of propriety, never smoked or drank, rarely cursed, and was a member of his church choir at the Mifflin Avenue United Methodist Church in Wilkinsburg. Though a pious and honorable man, he was no milquetoast. He set rules and expected his players to abide by them. A sportswriter later wrote of him, "Players do not look at him as their boss; rather they regard him as their father."[18] In time, he would be considered one of baseball's greatest managers.

McKechnie was obsessed with defense, and he obviously saw something in Traynor that Gibson did not. Traynor started at shortstop in each of McKechnie's first two games as manager and committed three more errors. With that, McKechnie concluded it was time to shift Traynor back to third base and leave him alone. Traynor started at third against the Cubs on July 3 and remained there for most of the next 13 years.

Another important McKechnie move was reaching out to holdout catcher Walter Schmidt. Schmidt had been so insulted by Dreyfuss' contract offer that he chose to stay home in California and earn a living planting fruit trees. But McKechnie brought the two sides together, and Schmidt was in uniform by early August.

McKechnie also brought aboard 33-year-old Reb Russell, McKechnie's teammate with Minneapolis of the American Association the year before. Russell had been a reliable starting pitcher for the Chicago White Sox from 1913 to 1918 before injuring his arm, returning to the minors, and working his way back up as an outfielder. For the final two months of the season, Russell battered National League pitching, hitting .368 with 12 home runs in only 220 at-bats.

With McKechnie at the helm, Traynor ensconced at third base, and with the two new additions in the fold, the Pirates won 13 games in a row in August and drew to within 4½ games of first place. They tailed off toward the end of the month, as Traynor fell into a 6-for-46 slump at one point. But an early September charge got them back in the race, and they remained within striking distance of the Giants until almost the last week of the season. Pittsburgh ended the year in third place, with a mark of 88–66.

As is the case with many rookies, Traynor was inconsistent; there were times when pitchers couldn't get him out, other times when he looked liked he belonged back in Portsmouth. He wrapped up with a .282 average, about 20 points below the league average. His OPS (on-base percentage plus slugging percentage) of .694 also was below par. But his speed enabled him to crack the National League's top ten in triples and stolen bases. Just as importantly, after he settled in at third, his defense became less erratic and included the occasional spectacular play. His game was still raw, but he clearly was not far from becoming a very good player. He had begun to erase the question marks.

Over the winter, Traynor toiled at Boston's Commonwealth Pier, where he inspected incoming freight. The job was similar in some ways to the work he did in Nitro, West Virginia, during the war, only without the possibility of being thrown from a horse or blown to bits. He reported to spring training carrying a few extra pounds, but in pretty solid condition overall.

Although Dreyfuss hoped McKechnie would crack the whip harder than Gibson, the mood around Hot Springs remained loose and informal. Scrawny little Rosey Rowswell, one of the club's most enthusiastic fans and later its first regular play-by-play announcer on the radio, pulled on a uniform, took infield, and joined the players on their morning hikes. Traynor and pitcher Hal Carlson challenged each other to a senseless footrace, during which Carlson took a tumble and sprained his wrist. McKechnie had to reprimand Maranville for umpiring an intrasquad game while puffing on a cigarette. In the evenings, the players laughed along with the Tierney-Grimm-Morrison-Whitted quartet. Or they gathered around a radio while Carson Bigbee fiddled with the knobs and pulled in the crackling signal of one far-flung station after another.

There was some more serious work going on as well. McKechnie took Traynor aside in early April and recommended that he adopt a more compact swing, something along the lines of Bigbee's. Traynor was receptive. He spent most of the morning of April 5 working with Bigbee on his new approach.[19] The following day, Traynor busted out of a spring-long slump with two home runs in an exhibition game against Tulsa.

In later years, Traynor claimed that the most important advice he received early in his career came from his good friend Rogers Hornsby, who suggested that he switch to a heavier bat in order to more easily drive the ball to right field.[20] He gave no credit to McKechnie, whose relationship with Traynor was strained for many years. But whether it was Hornsby, McKechnie, or just the natural maturation of a young hitter, Traynor would take a dramatic and permanent step forward offensively in 1923.

The Pirates plodded along around the .500 mark for the first month of the season, despite sizzling starts by Traynor and Charlie Grimm. Grimm hit safely in the first 25 games of the season, while Traynor enjoyed multi-hit games in seven of Bucs' first 10 games and led the league in hitting for a short time in April. But beyond the two corner infielders, the Pirates had problems. The pitching was ghastly. Russell, anointed the starting right fielder, was hitting like the former pitcher he was, with an average of just .161 through 25 games. Maranville got himself arrested on suspicion of driving while intoxicated — at 9:00 in the morning, no less.[21]

In late May, the Pirates picked up steam, moving into second place on May 21 after winning the first game of what would be a three-game sweep of Philadelphia. Traynor went 9-for-13 in the series with two home runs, six runs scored, and a handful of dazzling plays in the field.

As that series concluded, the Bucs finally signed off on a trade that had been in the works for two weeks. They jettisoned Cotton Tierney and pitcher Whitey Glazner to cellar-dwelling Philadelphia, receiving in return disgruntled right-hander Lee Meadows and second baseman Johnny Rawlings, who had refused to report to the Phillies after they selected him off waivers. The 27-year-old Meadows, who would turn out to be the key man in the deal, had two claims to fame. He was the first twentieth century player to wear glasses on the field. Also, he was an outrageously fast worker. In 1919, he was the losing pitcher in the quickest nine-inning game in modern history, completed in an incomprehensible 51 minutes. Meadows would anchor the Pirate pitching staff for the next five years, winning a total of 87 games.

The Pirates ran their win streak to six the following day with an 11–4 victory over the Cardinals, as Traynor legged out his fifth homer of the year, the first of five inside-the-park home runs he would hit that season. Three days later, Meadows won his first game as a Pirate, giving Pittsburgh its eighth win in nine games as the team found itself 6½ games in back of the first-place Giants.

Traynor's dramatically improved play was attracting national attention. UPI reporter Henry Farrell called him "one of the best third basemen in the National League and he has not yet matured."[22] When a baseless rumor surfaced about the Pirates dealing Traynor to the Brooklyn Robins for pitcher Dutch Ruether, a fan from New York reportedly wrote to Dreyfuss and declared, "I would not trade him for half of the Brooklyn ballclub."[23]

Not only was Traynor hitting with authority, but he also had figured out how to play third base. As he stood at his position, Traynor still carried himself like an anxious rookie. The man simply could not remain still; every fiber of his body arced with nervous energy. But once a ball was hit in his direction, he had everything under control, turning in one diving, sprawling, or leaping play after another. He was blessed with huge hands ("If you gave him your hand, it disappeared," recalled a friend), which made it easy for him to charge in and scoop up bunts or weakly hit ground balls.[24] He is reputed even to have made barehanded stops on sharply hit balls over the bag, which sounds like a tall tale, but a number of people swore it was true.[25] Nothing got past him. "A hitter doubled down the line and Pie Traynor threw him out" was an oft-repeated joke that summed up his defensive preeminence. "Pie had the quickest hands, the quickest arm, of any third baseman," according to Charlie Grimm. "And from any angle he threw strikes."[26]

It was getting those strikes within the general vicinity of Grimm's mitt that had been a problem for Traynor. He was fortunate that his first baseman was so agile and sure-handed. "They always said Charlie Grimm saved Traynor's neck when he first came up," said Art McKennan.[27] But by 1923 he had discovered a solution that he stuck with for the rest of his career. "You'd hit a shot at [Traynor], a play that he could take his time on, and he'd catch it and throw it right quick, so that if his peg was wild the first baseman had time to get off the bag, take the throw, and get back on again," recalled the Chicago Cubs Billy Herman. "It was the only way Traynor could throw; if he took his time he was *really* wild."[28]

Shortstop Dick Bartell, who played alongside Traynor in the late 1920s, took issue with the way Traynor compensated for his natural wildness. Bartell didn't care for Traynor as a person — he thought he was selfish and a bit of a phony. Notwithstanding that, his point merits consideration. "The first baseman had to play close enough to the bag so he'd be there when the throw arrived; as soon as Pie got the ball he'd be throwing it. That forced the first baseman to play closer to first, cutting down his range. Things like that don't show up in the fielding stats."[29]

The Pirates remained lodged in second place from late May through early July, the deficit between them and the first-place New York Giants ranging between 3½ and 5½ games for most of that period. New York's pitching was nothing special, but their potent lineup — which included future Hall of Famers George Kelly, Frankie Frisch, Dave Bancroft, and Ross Youngs, with Casey Stengel adding some lefty thump off the bench — covered up the holes in the staff.

The Bucs pulled within three games of the Giants on July 7, pounding their old teammate Glazner and the Phillies, 18–5. Traynor led the barrage, hitting for the cycle for the only time in his career, scoring three times, and driving in six. Three days later, Pittsburgh visited the Polo Grounds for a critical five-game series. In the opener against New York, the Pirates took an 8–6 lead into the late innings. But Kelly hit a solo homer in the eighth, Frisch added another one in the ninth to tie it, then in the tenth, catcher Frank Snyder singled in the game-winner off Pittsburgh reliever Jim Bagby. That loss dropped the Pirates into third place for the first time in nearly two months. The Giants won again the next afternoon, 6–1, despite a 3-for-4 performance from Traynor. As was often the case in Pirate-Giant games, the mood was tense and tempers were short. Umpire Bill Klem ejected both McKechnie and Max Carey from the game; the two men had exploded after the always-charming Klem purportedly called Carey a louse.[30]

The Pirates salvaged two of the remaining three games in the series as Traynor contributed a remarkable leaping catch and a home run and stretched his hitting streak to 18 games. But the Pirates left the Polo Grounds in third place, 4½ games out, having squandered an opportunity to put some serious pressure on the Giants.

Traynor remained on fire at the plate as the Pirates pushed on to Brooklyn and Boston. He took an evening to visit his parents in Somerville on July 18, and then the next day extended his hitting streak to 24 games and started a triple play in an 8–6 win over the Braves. Boston righty Joe Genewich stopped the streak the following afternoon, but Traynor hit at nearly a .400 clip during those 24 games and in the process hiked his average to .367, among the top five in the National League.

But neither Traynor nor the Pirates were done. The next afternoon he tallied five hits with a home run in a doubleheader sweep of Boston. Back in Pittsburgh on July 25, Traynor terrorized the Braves again with six hits, including an inside-the-park home run to the deepest recesses of Forbes Field's vast centerfield, in another doubleheader sweep. The following day, Pittsburgh rallied from six runs down to send the game into extra innings. With the score tied in the bottom of the 12th, Traynor's scorching liner to center field skipped by a diving Gus Felix and rolled to the wall. While left fielder Ray Powell tracked it down, Traynor flew around the bases. Powell made a strong throw to the cut-off man as Traynor brazenly made the turn at third and headed home. He should have been out, but the relay sailed over the head of catcher Frank Gibson, allowing Traynor to make it safely with a game-winning inside-the-park homer while Forbes Field erupted. The Pirates took five straight from Boston to creep to within 2½ games of first place as they prepared for yet another five-game showdown with the Giants.

Though the Pirates were breathing down New York's neck, the Giants were confident they had the better team. One unnamed player told the *Pittsburgh Post*, "If we should run into a bunch of hard luck and happen to be nosed out, it will be the Reds and not the Pirates."[31] Pittsburghers, of course, disagreed. A record 34,600 of them wedged into Forbes Field for the series-opening doubleheader on Monday afternoon, July 30. "Fully grown men, warped into half their size, crouched in the iron girders of the grandstand ... fashionably dressed women, happy and contented, sitting on spread newspapers on the inner fringe of the vast crowd.... Children ... [were] perched in aisles and dangling from the upper tiers of the grandstand."[32] Many more fans wandered around outside, unable to get a ticket.

The Pirates gave the faithful a thrill in the first game, scoring five runs in the bottom of the ninth to pull out a 5–4 victory. But the Giants quickly stifled the Bucs' momentum, battering Johnny Morrison for seven hits and nine runs in 2⅔ innings in the nightcap as they won, 17–2. New York went on to win two of the next three to take the series. Traynor had three hits in the deciding fifth game, but he also made a costly error on a Heinie Groh grounder in the fifth inning. Groh came around to score what would prove to be the winning run.

The fight seemed to go out of the Pirates after that. The dismal Phillies, on their way to a 100-loss season, came into Forbes Field right after the Giants and took three of four while McKechnie seethed over his club's sloppy play.

Though Pittsburgh remained in second place, the Pirates were 7½ games out and their season was essentially over. The Giants led wire-to-wire, taking their third consecutive National League pennant. The Bucs, racked by injuries down the stretch, faded to third place, behind both New York and Cincinnati.

From a statistical standpoint, it might have been the finest season of Traynor's career. "That was my red letter year," he bragged.[33] He finished seventh in the batting race with a .338 average and drove in more than 100 runs for the first time. He tied Max Carey for the National League lead in triples with 19 and also established what would remain career highs in home runs (12), hits (a team record 208), and stolen bases (28), totals that ranked him in the top ten in the league in each of those categories. His performance earned him a sizeable raise; Barney Dreyfuss reportedly upped Traynor's salary to $8,000, a very nice pile of dough for a 25-year-old man with barely an eighth-grade education.[34]

With his youth, talent, and dashing style of play, Traynor quickly was becoming a fan favorite, though it took him a while to wholeheartedly return the fans' embrace. Traynor was still kind of green in the early 1920s. He was bright but not learned, hadn't traveled much outside of baseball road trips, and hadn't been exposed to a wide variety of people, which made him seem reserved and vaguely uncomfortable in certain social settings. But he always felt completely in his element around children. Traynor was accessible to young fans in a way that is inconceivable today, and was almost unheard of even then.

In September 1923, with the season winding down, Traynor accompanied Babe Adams and Max Carey to a sandlot game in Crafton, a suburb of Pittsburgh. Traynor hung around long after Adams and Carey headed home, signing autographs and talking baseball with a pack of children as he relaxed on the lawn of a nearby church and noshed on a sandwich. According to Ralph Davis of the *Pittsburgh Post*, a radiant Traynor lifted a toddler off the ground, cradled her in his arms, and "glorified in her innocent caress."[35] Years later a fan reminisced about standing outside of Forbes Field after games hoping to get some autographs. Usually the effort was in vain. "But when Pie'd come out all the kids would get around him and he'd stand at Boquet and Sennott and talk to us. And long after the other players and the ushers and the crowd had left, he'd still be talking to the kids and the old Italians from Boundary Street and the traffic cops and the guys who'd come out of 'Put' Tierney's saloon."[36]

And it wasn't just in Pittsburgh. Arthur Harrow was a Brooklyn kid who faithfully lingered outside the players' entrance at Ebbets Field every afternoon. One late afternoon, as Harrow was idly leafing through his autograph book, he felt a tap on his shoulder. When he spun around he found himself face to face with a smiling Traynor. "Would you like me to sign?" Traynor asked. "I was stunned," remembered Harrow.[37]

Richard Leeds, another young Dodger fan, was around the ballpark so much that he struck up a casual friendship with Traynor. "[Traynor] would recognize me. He'd walk with me all the way to the Franklin Avenue subway when the Pirates were in town."[38] In his later years, Traynor became a legendary raconteur, completely at ease with anyone regardless of age, gender, ethnicity, or station in life. But even as an elderly man, he retained an innocence and boyish enthusiasm that young people found especially captivating and relatable.

Traynor clowning around with a young friend on the golf course, probably in the mid-late 1920s. Though he never had children of his own, Traynor always had a way with kids (Paul Traynor).

Following the 1923 season Traynor turned down an offer to go on a barnstorming tour. "I am considerably underweight right now and I don't think that 20 games at the end of the season would do me any good physically."[39] They wouldn't have done him much good financially either. Traynor reportedly was offered $700, which was nothing compared with the $10,000 that Rogers Hornsby received for the same tour.

Instead, Traynor entered Bryant and Stratton Business College in Massachusetts, part of a national chain of institutions that taught bookkeeping and other rudiments of commerce. He said his goal was to earn enough credits to gain admission to Boston University, but soon his eyes began to bother him. A physician advised him to get glasses or quit school. Traynor, who was so fanatical about his eyes that he avoided movie theaters for a long time for fear that watching films in the darkness would affect his vision, dropped out and went to work as a salesman for a "nationally-known dental paste concern."[40]

McKechnie had found the weather at Hot Springs too unpredictable and the ground too hard for his players' legs. In 1924 he and Dreyfuss shifted the club's spring training headquarters to Paso Robles, California, about halfway between Los Angeles and San Francisco and 12 miles off the coast of the Pacific Ocean. It was the Pirates' spring home for the next 11 seasons.

Paso Robles was the hub of California's almond industry, but that's about all it had going for it. It boasted 2,900 residents, a movie house, a drug store, a couple of hotels, and an all-night Greek restaurant. "Paso Robles was just a bump on the map in those days," according to lifelong resident Karl Haueser. "It was a staid community. It wasn't growing very fast. It was just there."[41] Paradoxically, the town experienced a small boom after World War II, when the almond growers moved away. "People from Los Angeles would sell their $20,000 home down there for $200,000 and come up to Paso Robles and build a mansion because land that used to be the almond acreage was very cheap," said Haueser.[42]

When the Pittsburgh Pirates came to town, though, Paso Robles sprang to life, especially for youngsters like Haueser. He shagged baseballs outside the park for a dime a ball and, if he brought in three balls, a free pass to a Sunday game. Some of the townsfolk got up close and personal with the players. For example, Haueser's father, a Lutheran minister, had Traynor over for dinner one evening. "He was friendly but he wasn't overly friendly," said Haueser, recalling Traynor's demeanor that evening. "He was very serious, not a slap-you-on-the-back kind of guy. I think he felt a little bit out of place in a preacher's home. A lot of people do!"[43]

The Pirates pulled into the train station in Paso Robles on February 27 and were greeted by a brass band and almost the entire population of the town. The train was filled with new faces. Over the winter, the Pirates bolstered their pitching staff with the purchase of two submariners — 31-year-old Ray Kremer, who would win 143 games for Pittsburgh over the next decade, and the curiously named Emil Yde (pronounced E-dee), a lefty of Danish descent who had won 28 games for Class A Oklahoma City in 1923. Also joining the Bucs for the first time was rookie Glenn Wright, who would win the starting shortstop job, forcing Maranville over to second base.

Another promising rookie was Hazen "Kiki" Cuyler, who had enjoyed a couple of brief call-ups toward the end of the previous three seasons and was now deemed ready for full-time duty in right field by McKechnie. Cuyler was born in Harrisville, Michigan, and worked in an automotive plant while playing in a highly competitive industrial league in Detroit. It didn't take long for scouts to find him. Like Traynor, Cuyler had blazing speed, a rocket arm, and drove the ball from one foul line to the other. The Pirates purchased Cuyler's contract from Bay City in the Michigan-Ontario League in September 1921. He appeared in one game with the Pirates later that month, going 0-for-3, and eventually earned a permanent spot in Pittsburgh after batting .340 for Nashville of the Southern Association in 1923.

There are a couple of different accounts for how Cuyler picked up his alliterative nickname (pronounced Ky-Ky, not Kee-Kee). Cuyler stuttered. According to one story, when he tried to pronounce his last name it sometimes came out as "Cuy-Cuy-Cuyler." Another legend has it that in the minor leagues, the shortstop and second baseman each would call out "Cuy!" when a fly ball was hit over their heads and toward Cuyler in center field. Sportswriters are supposed to have picked up on this and slapped him with the nickname.[44]

Though he was married to his high school sweetheart, Cuyler became something of a heartthrob. He had curly dark hair and hypnotic hazel eyes that appeared almost translucent. Woody English, a teammate later in his career with the Cubs, thought Cuyler a peculiar man. "He was a loner. He kept to himself. He ... never palled around with a single player on the club. They didn't really dislike him, but he wasn't one of the boys."[45] Cuyler was a devout Catholic; he was one of the first major leaguers to make the sign of the cross before stepping into the batter's box.[46] He was a teetotaler and didn't smoke. Singing and dancing seemed to be his only two indulgences. Cuyler retired in 1939 after a stellar 15-year career, most of it spent with the Pirates and Cubs. The Veterans' Committee selected him posthumously for the Baseball Hall of Fame in 1968.

With an improved lineup, Pittsburgh expected to be serious pennant contenders in 1924, but the first half of the season was miserable for both the Pirates and Traynor, and it might have nearly cost McKechnie his job. Through the first 14 games of the campaign, Traynor was hitting just .204. On April 30 McKechnie juggled the lineup, moving Traynor from fourth to third in the order. He responded by going 0-for-6 and hitting into four double plays in a 14-inning game against the Cubs. On May 22, after a 4–2 loss to Brooklyn dropped his club three games under .500, Barney Dreyfuss felt compelled to issue McKechnie a public vote of confidence. "There isn't going to be any change in the management of the Pirates."[47]

But for the next month, the Pirates continued to go nowhere. Fans were really letting McKechnie have it, and he understood where they were coming from. "The (fans) no doubt are as thoroughly disgusted as I am, and that is saying a lot. But what can I do?"[48] Regis Welsh of the *Pittsburgh Post* wondered, "What's the matter with the Pirates? The fire is not there. There is no pep or fight.... Somewhere the aggressiveness and quick thinking ... [are] sadly lacking."[49]

Babe Adams was out of action with a sore arm; Maranville, Bigbee, and Cuyler were having their problems at the plate; the new shortstop, Wright, was struggling with his defense. But the biggest disappointment was Traynor. McKechnie bounced him all over the lineup, even inserting him in the leadoff spot for a brief time. But no matter where he appeared in the order, he was just this side of useless. On June 18, lost in a 14-for-85 funk, Traynor found himself benched. He was hitting just .239 — this in a season where the National League average was .292. Among players with at least 160 at-bats, Traynor had the second lowest batting average in the major leagues.

A writer covering the Pirates for the *Sporting News* noted, without offering any detail, that Traynor was playing while less than 100 percent healthy.[50] Following the season, after a tonsillectomy, Traynor complained about "the effect a pair of diseased tonsils can have upon the physical as well as mental side of an athlete."[51] Regardless of what was causing the slump, Traynor, a compulsive worrier even in the best of times, was going bonkers—"nervous and overwrought" in the words of the *Sporting News*.[52] William Peet of the *Pittsburgh Post* figured that sitting out for a while would give Traynor some much-needed time to get his head straight. "There is nothing over which to be too alarmed about Traynor. The boy will soon come out of his batting slump. He has been too anxious, too eager to listen to advice handed him by every member of the club."[53]

What happened over the next two weeks must have been even more unsettling for Traynor. Pitchers found his replacement, 5'7" rookie Eddie Moore, almost impossible to get out. In the 13 games he started at third base, Moore batted .423 from the leadoff spot, and the somnambulant Pirate offense snapped awake. On June 23 McKechnie declared Moore to be his man, at least for the foreseeable future. "I intend [on] using Moore as long as he performs as capably as he has.... It would be folly for me to bench him and send Pie back, for I need all the hitting strength it is possible to muster."[54] With Moore in the lineup, the Bucs won 10 of 13, including a stretch of seven in a row. But on July 1, Moore suffered a dislocated left shoulder when he was hit by a pitch from the Cardinals' Johnny Stuart. Just like that, Traynor had his second chance.

McKechnie would have faced a dilemma had Moore stayed healthy and continued to hit. The Pirates had a lot invested in Traynor and they certainly believed in him. At the same time, the team was supposed to be challenging for a pennant and Traynor was a big reason why that was not happening. Moore was no .400 hitter, but he was a solid player who started at second base and performed well for the Pirates' World Series club in 1925. There is no reason to think he couldn't have hit enough to justify a spot in the lineup through the end of the 1924 season, but his injury made a potentially tough decision easy.

During that era, Pittsburgh fans were among the toughest in baseball. They demanded a winner and showed little tolerance for players who were not living up to expectations or managers who couldn't get the most out of their teams. After Traynor had become an established star, someone suggested to him that Pirate fans might burn Forbes Field to the ground if he were traded. Traynor operated under no such delusions. "Wait until I start booting a few.... They won't burn down the park, they'll burn down my house."[55] But in 1924 the fans stuck with Traynor, giving him a rousing ovation when the club returned from a road trip for a July 4 doubleheader. He responded with two hits in each game and went on to hit safely in his next nine outings.

Over the next six weeks the Pirates played good baseball, bolstered by Traynor's return to form and by the purchase of a rowdy, hard-drinking catcher named Earl Smith, whose act had worn thin with the Boston Braves. (Smith's former manager, John McGraw, described him as "a goddamned anarchist. He has no respect for law and order."[56]) Splitting time with Johnny Gooch over the final two-and-a-half months of the season, Smith batted .369 with an equally impressive on-base percentage of .435.

Pittsburgh couldn't gain much traction in their pursuit of the league-leading Giants; they remained between 7½ and 11 games out most of June and all of July. But at least they were able to hurdle a couple of the teams in front of them. The Pirates moved into third place on July 17, when Traynor's inside-the-park homer and Smith's three hits led them past New York, 4–3, and then into second place with a 5–3 victory over Brooklyn on August 4.

The nature of the race changed dramatically in mid–August, when the Giants entered Forbes Field for a four-game series. The Bucs had taken three of four from the Giants in Gotham a couple of weeks earlier, a series marked by a clash between Cuyler and New York second baseman Frankie Frisch. As he applied a tag to Cuyler at second base, Frisch smashed the baseball into Cuyler's head, knocking him out of the lineup for several days. McKechnie was incensed; he claimed he had overheard the Giants vowing before the game that they were going to "get" Cuyler.[57]

Pirate fans serenaded Frisch with boos during the series opener on August 13. Cuyler got some measure of revenge, going 3-for-4 as the Pirates won their sixth straight, 4–2. Traynor's sensational leaping grab of George Kelly's liner in the ninth inning robbed the Giant first baseman of extra bases and helped preserve the win. The next day Wilbur Cooper won his 16th game, 3–1. The lead was down to five games, and the Giants were showing signs of frustration. McGraw went ballistic on a fan who loudly referred to him as "Muggsy," the nickname he so detested. Normally mild-mannered third baseman Heinie Groh slammed his unique bottle-shaped bat to the ground after hitting a weak grounder back to Cooper.

It would get worse for New York. In the third game, Cuyler's homer highlighted a five-run third-inning outburst as the Bucs won, 6–4. Then Pittsburgh concluded the four-game sweep, rallying from three runs down to win, 5–4, on Glenn Wright's RBI single in the twelfth inning. The Pirates had drawn within three games of the Giants, the closest they had been to first place since the first week of the season. Though their heretofore easy march to the pennant had been rudely interrupted, New York coach Hughie Jennings was unimpressed, firing a shot across the Pirates' bow in the *Pittsburgh Post*. "They won't win it. It takes guts to win a pennant. They thought they had [it] sewed up three years ago but they blew up at a critical stage, and they will blow up again this season."[58]

Pittsburgh initially made Jennings look prophetic by immediately losing four straight. But then they reeled off winning streaks of five and six games, edging to within a game of the Giants following the sweep of a Labor Day doubleheader against Chicago. But meanwhile, the Brooklyn Robins, 13 games out and left for dead a month earlier, were charging hard, led by a trio of geezers playing some of the best baseball of their careers— 34-year-old first baseman Jack Fournier, 36-year-old left fielder Zack Wheat, and 33-year-old right-hander Dazzy Vance. A 15-game winning streak pushed the Robins past Pittsburgh and into second place.

Entering a three-game weekend series at Brooklyn's Ebbets Field on Friday, September 19, the Pirates were in third place, 2½ games out of first, exactly where they had been for the last week. The Giants still led; Brooklyn was a half-game back. Pittsburgh needed a sweep to have a legitimate shot at going to the World Series. Yde, on his way to a 16–3 rookie season, won the first game of the series, 4–2, despite nine Brooklyn hits and three errors by Maranville at second base. The Giants also won, and the Pirates remained 2½ back.

Pittsburgh had its work cut out for it on Saturday because Dazzy Vance was on the mound for the Robins. Vance had been a Pirate very briefly; he started one game for them in 1915 before going back down to the minor leagues, where he injured his elbow. A doctor told Vance he would need to give his arm a rest. Vance asked how long. "About five years," came the reply.[59]

Vance kicked around the minors for a few seasons, pitching a limited number of innings, keeping his career alive while hoping his arm would magically come back to life. And after about four years it did. He returned to the majors as a 31-year-old rookie in 1922 and won 18 games. In 1924, Vance was far and away the best pitcher in baseball, leading the National League in wins, complete games, strikeouts, and earned run average. Heading into this pivotal game with the Pirates, he had won 15 straight decisions, had a record of 27–4, and had beaten Pittsburgh ten times in a row. Opposing Vance was Wilbur Cooper, the Bucs' ace, who was seeking to become a 20-game winner for the fourth time in his career.

The game went into extra innings tied at 4–4. With two outs in the 11th, Traynor singled. Then with Traynor running on the pitch, Maranville blooped a single to center. Brooklyn center fielder Eddie Brown was a notoriously poor thrower (he wasn't nicknamed "Glass Arm" for nothing). With his speed, Brown's lousy arm, and the element of surprise on his side, Traynor gambled. Brown rainbowed the ball toward second base, where shortstop Johnny Mitchell nonchalantly took the throw. As Mitchell turned, he was stunned to spot Traynor flying around third, barreling through McKechnie's stop sign, and heading home. After a brief hesitation, Mitchell snapped off a throw to the plate. Catcher Hank DeBerry swept his glove down, but Traynor slid under it for the go-ahead run.

In the bottom of the inning, Cooper wiggled out of a two-on, none-out jam to preserve the 5–4 victory. Vance's streaks were history and the Bucs were tied with the Robins, 1½ games behind the Giants, thanks in large measure to Traynor's mad dash. "I wasn't so much a veteran then, accustomed to thrills," he said years later. "Believe me, that ... gave me the biggest thrill I ever got in a ball game."[60]

The Pirates missed an opportunity to pull to within a half-game of New York in the series finale. Pittsburgh, held in check by Burleigh Grimes all afternoon, finally broke through in the ninth when Traynor singled and Maranville doubled him home to tie the score. But Brown's RBI single off former Brooklyn star Jeff Pfeffer gave the Robins a 2–1 victory, dropping the Pirates back to third place.

Next for Pittsburgh was a decisive series against the Giants in New York. The Giants, who had three key players fighting through minor injuries, used the clouds that hung over New York in the morning as a lame excuse to call off the opener. By the scheduled game time, the sun was shining brightly with no hint of rain. Dirty pool, cried Dreyfuss, but National League president John Heydler said there was nothing he could do about it. The Giants dealt the Pirate hopes a crippling blow the next afternoon, winning, 5–1, behind Hugh McQuillan, who had to be held back from attacking Traynor after the Pirate third baseman trampled him while ostensibly trying to beat out a bunt up the first base line in the ninth inning. Traynor seldom tried to bunt for a hit, and that was not really what he was doing in this case either. McQuillan had worked around the heads of a few Pirate hitters that afternoon, and Traynor simply was meting out some frontier justice to settle the score, as often happened in baseball in those days.[61] New York went on to sweep the series, winning the next two games by 5–4 counts and dashing the Bucs' hopes. The Giants captured the pennant by 1½ games over Brooklyn and three games over Pittsburgh, and then lost to Washington in a thrilling seven-game World Series.

Regis Welsh of the *Pittsburgh Post* put a bleak spin on the season, claiming, "This was the year. The best [fans] can look forward to is another year of experiments which in the hands of the same bad mechanics may turn out to be another bloomer."[62] In the *Sporting News,* under the headline, "Spineless Bucs Dig Their Own Graves," writer Ralph Davis blamed the Pirates' defeat on a persistent lackadaisical attitude that, in his opinion, lingered from one year to the next.[63]

But looking back, it is a little hard to understand all the hand-wringing. The Pirate roster was brimming with talented young players who were just about to enter their primes. The 25-year-old Cuyler wobbled down the stretch as he tried gamely to play through a shoulder injury, but he still finished fourth in the league in hitting with a .354 mark. Wright, another rookie, had a solid year, and he was only 23. Yde, unhittable at times, was just 24 years old. Traynor's second-half rally brought his average back up to .294; not a great year, but not bad considering where he had been in June. Plus, his defense continued to improve; for the first time Traynor was significantly above the league average for third basemen in both fielding percentage and range factor (the number of chances accepted per game). And he wouldn't turn 26 until November. Moreover, old hands like Carey, Meadows, and Cooper showed no signs of slowing down.

The Pirates hadn't won a pennant since 1909, and the recent near-misses were maddening, so perhaps that's where all the doom and gloom talk was rooted. Or maybe it was the apparent invincibility of McGraw's Giants, who had won four pennants in a row. But there appear to have been many reasons for optimism as the Bucs got ready to make another run at New York in 1925.

6

World Champions

Traynor found himself a bit player in a tangle of controversies that ensnared the New York Giants just prior to the 1924 World Series. Baseball was only five years removed from the infamous Black Sox gambling scandal that marred the 1919 World Series, and people around the game were on edge at even the slightest hint of impropriety. Commissioner Kenesaw Mountain Landis, a former judge, dealt with any transgressions swiftly and decisively, often leaving due process by the curb.

Prior to a September 27 game against the Phillies, New York's Jimmy O'Connell sidled up to Philadelphia shortstop Heinie Sand and offered him $500 "if you don't bear down too hard."[1] Sand told O'Connell to shove it and reported the attempted bribe to his manager, Art Fletcher. Fletcher alerted National League president John Heydler, who relayed the news to Judge Landis. O'Connell, a trusting and naive sort, claimed he was simply following orders from Giants coach Cozy Dolan. Landis dismissed O'Connell's claim that Frank Frisch, Ross Youngs, and George Kelly all knew what was going on, and banned O'Connell and Dolan for life.

And thus the stench of scandal again wafted over the World Series. Barney Dreyfuss and another John McGraw adversary, American League president Ban Johnson, led calls for the Series to be postponed, in response to which Landis blustered, "This is a good time for gentlemen in baseball who have no responsibility in the matter to keep their shirts on."[2] Then Dreyfuss dropped another small bomb, claiming that Dolan, acting, he suspected, under orders from McGraw, had tampered with Traynor the season before. He told Landis that Dolan "advised Traynor to hold me up for $15,000 in 1924."[3]

Dolan admitted he advised Traynor to ask for more money, but that there was nothing malicious or illegal about it. The bribery scandal sealed his fate anyway, so it doesn't appear that Landis looked too closely into the Traynor incident. Plus, the commissioner didn't need baseball getting any more bad press. When Dreyfuss tried to arrange a meeting with him to discuss the tampering, Landis brushed him off, and the incident quietly went away.[4] But McGraw was peeved nonetheless, and suggested Dreyfuss was just "sore because he built a lot of new stands in 1921 and seldom had a chance to use them."[5]

Traynor was lying low while all this was brewing. His physician suggested he head to a warm, dry climate for the winter after he had his tonsils removed.

After a short time back home in Somerville, Traynor met up with Carson Big-bee, Emil Yde, and Max Carey in St. Louis in early November for a long car ride to the West Coast. On the way, they stopped off in Winfield, Kansas, for a few days of duck hunting on the Little Pirate Ranch, owned by former Pitts-burgh outfielder and longtime manager Fred Clarke. Eleven days after conven-ing in St. Louis, the men reached California, where another ex–Pirate, George Cutshaw, had arranged for them to camp, hunt, and fish at Big Bear Lake near Los Angeles. The men spent virtually all winter in California and met their teammates in Paso Robles for the start of spring training in late February.

The makeup of the team had changed dramatically during the offseason. In late October the Pirates made a blockbuster deal, sending three of their most popular players—Cooper, Maranville, and Grimm —to the Chicago Cubs for stocky right-hander Vic Aldridge, who had won 47 games for the Cubs the pre-vious three seasons; George Grantham, a butcher at second base, but a dan-gerous hitter; and first base prospect Al Niehaus. Dreyfuss, never a fan of all the practical jokes, music-making, and other tomfoolery that went on in his clubhouse, was exultant. "I got rid of all my banjo players," he boasted.[6]

Reaction in the newspapers and among fans was mixed at best, but in the end Dreyfuss probably got the better of the trade. Cooper, just off a 20-win season, lasted only two more years in the majors. Supposedly he was so devas-tated by the trade that he lost his heart for pitching. More likely, at age 33 and with eight straight years of 260+ innings behind him, his arm wore out. Maranville hung around for another decade but he was past his prime, too. Grimm was young and he remained as slick a defender as anyone, but he never consistently produced the offensive numbers typically expected from a first baseman.

On the other side, Niehaus gave the Pirates nothing, but Grantham, who the Pirates shifted to first base, and Aldridge proved to be major contributors. And Maranville's departure cleared the way for Eddie Moore to start at second. Moore wasn't the defensive savant that Maranville was, but at that moment, before injuries and dissipation sapped his skill, he was a markedly better hit-ter.

With the "banjo players" out of his hair, McKechnie was determined to have discipline. He wanted his club to take spring training much more seri-ously. To that end, he banned the consumption of liquor. "If I have to break up my entire club, I am going to see that such a rule is strictly adhered to. I am through covering up the faults of others."[7] Technically, of course, the "rule" was called the Eighteenth Amendment, but Prohibition was kind of a joke. Those who wanted booze could find it — and the Pirates usually wanted a lot of booze. "Some of those guys knew the spots [to buy alcohol]," said longtime Pirate employee Art McKennan. "One was a drugstore where my father [a physician] wrote his prescriptions. It was back counter stuff. Some of those guys overdid it."[8]

While McKechnie was enforcing the Volstead Act, Traynor was lifting the hood and tinkering some more with his approach at the plate in the wake of his struggles during the 1924 season. "I'm not trying to murder the ball like in years past," he later pointed out. "I am driving the ball through the infield and laying it in short outfield sections more than ever before.... [In the spring of 1925], I decided on a plan to chop my hits rather than take free swings as I had since I began playing ball."[9]

Traynor enjoyed good results in March and April and McKechnie elevated him to the clean-up spot in the order. But when the games started to count, Traynor tumbled into his familiar early-season void, hitting a meager .220 through the first ten games. His teammates weren't doing much either. The pitching, in particular, was execrable. In early May, Yde, Kremer, and Babe Adams all owned bloated earned run averages around 7.00. On May 7, the Cardinals rallied for six runs off Yde and Adams in the eighth inning for a dramatic 10–9 victory, dropping the Pirates into last place (although Glenn Wright provided a memorable moment in the ninth inning when he turned an unassisted triple play, only the fifth in major league history).

It seemed like something bad was happening almost every day. The afternoon following the loss to the Cardinals, the Phillies bounced Lee Meadows

The starting infield for the 1925 Pittsburgh Pirates. *Left to right:* Traynor, shortstop Glenn Wright, second baseman Eddie Moore, and first baseman George Grantham (Boston Public Library, Print Department).

from the box in the first inning on their way to a 15–7 win. Moore, sixth in the National League in hitting at .391, re-injured his shoulder in that game. His replacement, Johnny Rawlings, filled in for a few games, but then his father died unexpectedly, forcing Moore back into the lineup at less than 100 percent.

The next day in Boston, Earl Smith was headed toward the stands in pursuit of a foul pop when he found himself nose-to-nose with a vicious heckler who had been riding him all afternoon. The combustible Smith reacted the best way he knew how — he leaped the wall and started to pound the man senseless. Umpire Cy Rigler, a former football player, wrestled Smith away and was leading him toward the clubhouse when another fan, who had remarkable aim, busted Smith's head open with a flying metal chair. Smith snapped again and another near riot ensued. Though the first fan charged Smith with assault and battery, the National League suspended him only three games. Rigler's sympathetic report to the league office noted that Smith took a ton of abuse before he lost his mind. The criminal charges became an ongoing saga. The complainant, who apparently was about as crazy as Smith was, no-showed for two scheduled hearings in Boston before the district attorney said to heck with it and dropped the charges.

The night of Smith's brawl, Traynor went home to Somerville, where that night he became a member of the Masons at the John Abbott Masonic Lodge.[10] Traynor was becoming something of a joiner, getting his name on the rolls of several different fraternal organizations in Somerville — the Elks and the Loyal Order of Moose, as well — even though he was seldom in town and apparently not an active member of any of them. It is unclear what his motivation was other than the fact that, in that era, joining these kinds of brotherhoods was a cool thing to do.

The Pirates completed a two-week road trip with a 10–1 loss to the Giants on May 23. That put them at 14–16, nine games behind the Giants, in fifth place. After a rainout, the team's return to Pittsburgh was delayed for hours by a freight train accident in Harrisburg. That forced the bleary-eyed Pirates to roll back into town and head directly to the ballpark, where they beat the Cubs, 5–3, in a dismal game, with temperatures in the lower 50s and just 2,000 fans shivering in the seats. That was the first unlikely step on the Pirates' long road back into contention. They won their next six games. Smith was a driving force, hitting in 19 straight games and pushing his average to .409, second in the league. Traynor was hitting the ball well, too; he had his average up to .328 by mid–June.

One of the key series of the year was a four-game sweep of the Giants at Forbes Field. New York arrived in Pittsburgh on June 12 6½ games in front in the National League. But the Giants were in the middle of a ridiculous 20-game road trip, and playing without two injured starters in the infield, Frank Frisch and Freddie Lindstrom. Traynor played a huge role with a pair of hits in each of the final three games. In the finale, Pittsburgh choked on a 9–3 lead and was forced to go to extra innings. New York tallied two runs in the top of the tenth to take the lead, but in the home half of the inning Cuyler walked, Clyde Barnhart tripled him home, Traynor doubled to left to bring in Barnhart and tie the score, and then Glenn Wright homered off Art Nehf to give the Pirates a dramatic 13–11 victory. Just like that, the Pirates were in second place, only 2½ out. Harry Cross of the *New York Times* thought the Giants looked like a team in deep trouble. "Their temperature is far above normal, respiration is alarming, blood pressure is kiting, and they are suffering from housemaid's knee and their appetites have gone blooey."[11]

The patient's health would continue to decline. In addition to the injuries to Lindstrom and Frisch, several of McGraw's hitters were enduring terrible years. Ross Youngs, in the early stages of the kidney disease that would kill him two years later, saw his average drop nearly 100 points from the year before. Aging catcher Frank Snyder, young shortstop Travis Jackson, and center fielder Hack Wilson also were puttering along well below expectations. The Giants fell from first in the National League in hitting in 1924 to fifth in 1925.

Throughout Traynor's career, June often was the month when he really got hot, and that was the case in 1925. On the heels of his standout play in the New York series, he lashed out three multi-hit games against Brooklyn to raise his average to .350, followed by a grand slam in a wild 24–6 win at St. Louis. Joining him in carrying the load was Clyde Barnhart, who had a 25-game hitting streak earlier in the season and whose .400 average was second only to Rogers Hornsby in late June. By the end of the month, the Pirates were tied for first place. After sweeping a July 4 doubleheader, the Bucs found themselves alone in the lead.

Pittsburgh struggled on a 14-game road trip that stretched into late July. They won only six of those games and fell back into second place by a half-game. It was on this trip that Fred Clarke, hired by Dreyfuss a month earlier and given the title of "assistant to the president," began to alienate nearly everyone in the Pirate clubhouse. Clarke was one of the owner's favorites. He managed Dreyfuss' Louisville Colonels from 1897 to 1899, and then remained in charge when Dreyfuss merged his Louisville team with the Pirates in 1900. Clarke was a highly successful manager, guiding the Pirates to four National League pennants and a World Series title in 1909. All the while he was starting in left field and putting up numbers that consistently ranked him among the top hitters in baseball.

Clarke was loaded, easily a millionaire, thanks in no small part to some oil he discovered underneath his ranch in Kansas.[12] But by 1925, restless with counting his money and hunting, Clarke needed a new challenge. Dreyfuss not only invited Clarke to return to the Pirates, but also, inexplicably, to sit in the dugout in uniform alongside McKechnie, who technically ranked below Clarke on the organization chart.

Clarke proved to be a nuisance, a know-it-all who had little regard for

McKechnie's authority. His presence became an uncomfortable and awkward situation for all involved. After each of two losses to Boston on the long July road trip, Clarke took center stage and gave the team a postgame tongue-lashing. Before long he was tinkering with the players' batting stances and openly second-guessing McKechnie's decisions. The power struggle between the two men would simmer at a low boil all season; it would explode and destroy everything around it in 1926.

The Pirates put some space between themselves and the Giants a couple of weeks later, taking a pair of games from Brooklyn on August 8. Traynor's bloop single in the seventh inning of the second game drove in Cuyler with what proved to be the winning run, as the Pirates turned a 4–0 deficit into a 5–4 win. It was Pittsburgh's sixth win in their last seven. New York, meanwhile, fell for the sixth straight time, dropping an 8–2 decision to Cincinnati and fading to five games out. Next, New York and Pittsburgh split a tense four-game series at Forbes Field. Traynor went hitless in the first two games and committed a critical error. Then in the third game, in a rare flash of temper, he shoved George Kelly and went chest-to-chest with him after Kelly bowled him over on a rundown play.

The Pirates departed for a 16-game road swing on August 15. They would have to get through it without Max Carey, who stayed home to nurse an injured ankle (at age 35, Carey hit .343 and stole 46 bases that season). They showed up in New York for a five-game series versus the Giants with their lead pared to three. "Practically every town of any size at all in Western Pennsylvania" was represented at the Polo Grounds.[13] After the first game was rained out on August 21, Pirate fans feted the club at luncheons during the day and at theater parties that night.

A standing-room-only throng of 51,000 crammed in to watch a series-opening Saturday twinbill. Two radio stations broadcast the games live back to Pittsburgh, a rare happening in those days. Kiki Cuyler set the tone immediately with a first-inning home run off Virgil Barnes. The Giants tied it on a Frank Frisch solo shot in the third. But the next half-inning the Pirates put two on the board thanks to consecutive singles from Barnhart, Traynor, and Glenn Wright, followed one out later by an RBI single from Johnny Gooch. Lee Meadows surrendered just six hits, and five more Pirate runs in the ninth sealed the 8–1 victory.

In the nightcap, with his club down, 1–0, in the fourth, Traynor's quick thinking snuffed out a Giant rally and changed the course of the game. With runners at second and third, Freddie Lindstrom grounded to Wright at short. His throw home trapped Bill Terry in a rundown. Traynor tagged Terry, then alertly whipped the ball to first base to nail Lindstrom, who had wandered too far off the bag. Traynor led off the seventh inning with a single, and was on base when Wright blasted a game-winning two-run homer to left field. The Pirates won, 2–1, as Vic Aldridge outdueled Jack Scott.

It was another doubleheader on Sunday, again with a full house and 1,000 more disappointed people outside who couldn't get in. New York took the first game, 7–4. Game two went to Pittsburgh, 3–2, as Traynor elicited a grudging ovation from the New York crowd with an amazing stop of an Irish Meusel smash in the fifth inning. Giant fans were beginning to lose faith. Only about 15,000 of them showed up on Monday to watch their team lose again, 9–2, as the Giants self-destructed, committing three errors in six-run Pirate fifth. For once it was the Giants who had blinked. The Bucs took four out of five and built a six-game lead with 38 games to play. The National League flag was theirs to lose.

The Pirates continued on to Boston where, on August 25, the people of Traynor's hometown of Somerville organized a "Pie Traynor Day" at Braves Field. Somerville held three different Traynor Days in Boston over the years — the first one in 1922, the last one in 1927 — but the one in 1925 probably was the biggest. Traynor's buddies at the Elks Lodge planned the event. Among the organizers was Perry Nangle, younger brother of the man who slapped Traynor's nickname on him so many years before.

This was big doings for Somerville. The organizing committee raised almost $300 from individual donations. Still more money came from the sale of 6" × 3" paper tags, featuring Traynor's photograph, that were available at stores all over town. Fans paid $1.60 for the tag. Fifty cents went toward Traynor Day expenses, and then fans could redeem their tags at Braves Field for a grandstand ticket.[14]

Around 1,000 Somerville fans, including a band, came out on August 25. The crowd included Traynor's father, sister LuLu, brother Charley, and uncle Stephen Matthews, who came in from Nova Scotia. Players from both teams gathered around home plate before the game as Somerville dignitaries presented Traynor with a bevy of gifts, including a traveling bag, a pair of diamond-studded cufflinks and a diamond-encrusted stickpin. The festivities got a little weird near the end. A man draped an Elks Lodge blanket over a goat and persuaded Traynor to pose alongside it for a photograph. As Traynor handed off the goat to Kiki Cuyler, his friends presented him with a massive 15-pound apple pie — "about the size of an automobile wheel without its tire," according to one account — which Traynor quickly sliced up and passed out to the other players.[15]

Traynor tripled in the second inning and scored the Pirates' only run as they lost, 2–1. Traynor, who was notoriously absent-minded, left his cufflinks and stick pin in the dugout, where a young boy snatched them and took them home to his mother. She was not amused. Traynor got his jewelry back the next day.

Pittsburgh took two of three in Boston, then wiped out the Phillies five straight, piling up 54 runs and 78 hits in a bloodbath of a series at Baker Bowl. The grueling East Coast swing turned out to be no problem at all. The Pirates

"Pie Traynor Day" at Braves Field in Boston, August 25, 1925. A beaming Pie is flanked by (*left to right*) his father James, sister Lulu, brother Charles, and uncle Stephen Matthews (Hal Traynor).

went 13–3 on the trip, and then stretched their winning streak to nine in a row with home victories over the Reds and Cardinals.

The final month was a breeze. In Pittsburgh on September 23, the Pirates clinched their first pennant in 16 years as Emil Yde won his 17th game, 2–1, over Philadelphia. "We had been chasing the flag for so long and it had eluded us with such regularity that often my players felt as though it was a hopeless job," McKechnie confessed.[16] In a fitting twist of fate, the hated Giants, who had shattered those pennant dreams so many times, arrived in town the next day. Before the opening game Earl Smith and coach Jack Onslow nailed black crepe and a bouquet of flowers onto the roof of the New York dugout.

Thanks to a scheduling quirk the Pirates played a game on September 27, and then had a week off before finishing the regular season with a meaningless doubleheader against the Reds. During that week, the Bucs were the toast of the town. On Monday they attended a reception at the Nixon Hotel. On Tuesday they visited McKechnie's hometown of Wilkinsburg, where 300 people paid tribute to them at the local Elks Lodge. On Wednesday dinner was followed by a raccoon hunt at a country club in nearby Tarentum. Then on Thursday the

Pittsburgh Chamber of Commerce honored them at a luncheon. The city was thrilled to have a winner again.

Dreyfuss erected a special set of bleachers in right field, boosting Forbes Field's capacity for the World Series to 42,000. Box seats cost $6.00, reserve seats were $5.50 — an outrage. As one Pirate fan put it in the *Pittsburgh Post*, "Nothing could be more disgusting to the average fan than the absolute commercial spirit that has taken hold of the great game of baseball."[17]

The Pirates' opponent was the Washington Senators, led by intense 28-year-old player-manager Bucky Harris, the so-called "Boy Wonder" who guided Washington to its first World Series the previous October when they beat the Giants in seven games. The Senators were the joke of baseball for the first decade of their existence; they finished sixth or worse in the American League every year from 1901 to 1911. But Washington's fortunes improved when it hired Clark Griffith to manage the club. Griffith overhauled the roster and built a smart, young team. From 1913 to 1920, Washington was respectable, finishing in the first division five times. But the real breakthrough came after Griffith purchased 40 percent of the team and bumped himself upstairs in 1921.

The Senators' biggest star was 36-year-old right-hander Walter Johnson. Johnson was a Kansas farm boy playing for an industrial team in Idaho when the Senators unearthed him. They gave him a crack at the major leagues at age 19 in 1907. Johnson went just 5–9 as a rookie, but right from the start he combined splendid control with an overpowering fastball that was basically his only pitch during the early part of his career. Johnson had an effortless sidearm delivery; it didn't look like he was throwing hard, but in fact he might have been throwing harder than anyone ever had. There were no radar guns in those days, but Johnson's fastball possibly approached or topped 100 miles per hour. "You can't hit what you can't see," cracked an awestruck opposing hitter.[18]

Johnson's 1912 and 1913 seasons, when he went 33–12 and 36–7, respectively, are among the greatest in baseball history. His 417 career victories put him second only to Cy Young on baseball's all-time list, and his 3,509 strikeouts stood as a record until 1983. By 1925, Johnson wasn't Johnson anymore, but judged against mere mortals he was still awfully good, ranking fifth in the American League in earned run average and second in strikeouts. "I would have hated to face him ten years earlier ... but he still had some speed," said Eddie Moore.[19]

Johnson anchored a superb pitching staff that included Hall of Fame right-hander Stan Coveleski, whom Griffith acquired in a trade with Cleveland the previous offseason. The veteran spitballer, who slaved in the anthracite coal mines of northeast Pennsylvania as a teenager, led the American League in ERA. Tom Zachary and Dutch Ruether rounded out an excellent group of starters, but Harris decided before the World Series to hold those two out because of the Pirates impressive record against lefties. If a starting pitcher ran out of gas, Harris could call on dominant right-hander Fred Marberry, one of baseball's first relief specialists. Like many of the great closers who would come along decades later, Marberry had an intimidating demeanor on the mound, complete with a big fastball and a savage delivery that often sent his cap flying off his head.[20] He declared himself ready after missing the final five weeks of the season with elbow trouble.

Veteran shortstop Roger Peckinpaugh, the American League Most Valuable Player, anchored the infield along with Harris, who doubled as the second baseman. Defensively challenged left fielder Goose Goslin approached fly balls as if they were on fire, but he was a fearsome young slugger in the middle of the order who finished third in the American League in extra-base hits in 1925. In center field was lithe, slap-hitting leadoff man Sam Rice, a former pitcher who overcame unspeakable personal tragedy (his parents, wife, two sisters, and both of his children were killed when a tornado ripped through the family farm while Rice was off playing minor league ball) and ended his career just 13 hits shy of 3,000.

The combination of great stars at or near their prime, compelling storylines, controversial plays, and a madcap seventh game combined to give baseball perhaps its most riveting World Series ever. Game One on October 7 was played on a crisp, sunny afternoon in Pittsburgh. Hotels were sold out all the way to Greensburg, 30 miles away. Loudspeakers in public places around the city blared out the broadcast from radio station WCAE, while storefronts and buildings featured manually operated scoreboards to help passersby and assembled multitudes keep an eye on how the game was unfolding. After Pennsylvania governor Gifford Pinchot tossed out the ceremonial first pitch, the Pirates took the field behind Lee Meadows. On the hill for Washington, of course, was Walter Johnson.

The Senators reached Meadows for the first run of the Series, thanks to Joe Harris' solo homer in the second inning. They added two more on Rice's two-out, bases-loaded single in the fifth. That would be plenty on a day when the old master Johnson had the Pirates twisted up into knots. Through four innings Johnson held Pittsburgh to just two hits—singles by Traynor and Cuyler. In the fifth, Traynor drove a solo home run into the temporary bleachers in right field, but that was about all the Pirates could muster.

The Forbes Field crowd was aware it was witnessing a bravura performance; when Johnson came to the plate in the eighth inning, Pirate fans gave him a standing ovation. He checked the Pirates on five hits and struck out ten. The final score was 4–1. "I believe I had more 'stuff' [that afternoon] than I ever had before, even back in 1912 and 1913 when I was supposed to be at my best," said Johnson.[21] Max Carey was flabbergasted. "We just couldn't see Walter's fastball ... [and] I don't ever recall seeing a pitcher with such a sharp-breaking curve," he raved.[22] To add to the Pirates' troubles, Meadows was in agony after the game with a sore arm. He was done for the Series. The only Pirate who had a really good day was Traynor, who, in addition to his two hits, made a diving, backhanded catch of a Muddy Ruel liner in the third inning.

For Game Two, both teams wore wide black armbands in memory of New York Giants great Christy Mathewson, who had died of tuberculosis the previous evening. Aldridge and Coveleski were locked in a 1–1 duel until the bottom of the eighth. After Eddie Moore reached on a Peckinpaugh error to lead off the inning, Kiki Cuyler blasted a two-run homer to right field to give the Pirates the lead. Aldridge, who had escaped a bases-loaded, none-out jam in the fifth inning, got himself in trouble again in the ninth. A Buddy Myer single sandwiched between a pair of walks loaded the bases. Pinch-hitter Bobby Veach's sacrifice fly pulled the Senators within a run. But Aldridge struck out pinch-hitter Dutch Reuther and induced Rice to hit one on the ground to second base. Moore booted it but recovered in time to get the speedy Rice, preserve the 3–2 victory, and tie the Series, 1–1.

Following a rain-out, the stage shifted to Griffith Stadium in Washington for Game Three on Saturday, October 10. The Pirates met President Calvin Coolidge on the White House lawn before the game, and then Coolidge followed them over to the park to throw out the first pitch. Ray Kremer was on the mound for Pittsburgh, while the Senators bypassed Zachary and Reuther, who had won 30 games between them, and went with nondescript righty Alex Ferguson, a late-season acquisition with a bloated 6.18 earned run average. The Pirates jumped ahead early when Traynor's second-inning drive skipped past right fielder Joe Harris for a triple and Glenn Wright followed with a sacrifice fly. But Ferguson kept the Pirate bats under control for the most part. Washington rallied for two runs in the bottom of the seventh on a Joe Judge sacrifice fly and an RBI single from Joe Harris. That put Washington up, 4–3, as Marberry came in to close it down.

After Wright and Grantham struck out to open the eighth, Earl Smith caught hold of a 2–2 pitch from Marberry and hammered it deep into right field. Rice, who shifted from center to right for defensive purposes at the start of the inning, gave chase, racing back toward the low right field wall. "I jumped as high as I could and backhanded [the ball] ... but my feet hit the barrier about a foot from the top."[23] Rice tumbled backside over teacups into the first row of the bleachers. "I hit my Adam's apple on something which sort of knocked me out for a few seconds but (center fielder Earl) McNeely arrived about that time and grabbed me by the shirt and pulled me out."[24]

Was it a catch or a home run? Second base umpire Cy Rigler couldn't see whether or not Rice had held onto the ball; no one really could except for Rice and the handful of people he nearly squashed as he flew into the seats. But Rice managed to clamber out of the stands with the ball in his glove, and that's all Rigler needed to see. He punched his right fist into the air — Smith was out.

The Pirates went crazy. McKechnie was screaming at Rigler, "You didn't see him catch the ball!"[25] Rigler stood fast. McKechnie hustled over to Commissioner Landis' box seat to complain, but he didn't get any satisfaction there either. Landis said it was Rigler's call. It remained a one-run game.

The Pirates had another chance in the bottom of the ninth, as they loaded the bases with one out. Barnhart popped out to Ruel for the second out, which brought Traynor to the plate with a chance to be the hero. He got ahead in the count three balls and no strikes, as the Washington crowd grew uneasy. Marberry's next two pitches were called strikes. It was a full count, the runners would be off with the pitch, and even the shallowest single to the outfield would be enough to score Carey from second and win the game. But all Traynor could do was lift a lazy fly ball to center field, which McNeely hauled in, as the Senators took a two games-to-one lead.

The furor surrounding Rice's catch would not die. Two Pirate fans who were seated in right field came to the clubhouse and offered to swear out affidavits asserting that Rice lost control of the ball. "Rice did not catch the

Traynor sprints past Senators catcher Muddy Ruel to score the first run of Game Three of the 1925 World Series at Griffith Stadium. Traynor, who tripled to lead off the second inning, came home on Glenn Wright's sacrifice fly. Ruel is moving into foul territory to take the throw from left fielder Goose Goslin while umpire Barry McCormick, pitcher Alex Ferguson (emerging from shadows) and first baseman Joe Judge look on. Washington rallied to win the game, 4–3 (National Photo Company Collection, Prints & Photographs Division, Library of Congress, LC-DIG-npcc-14761).

ball at all. Instead, a boy picked it up and gave it to him," stated one of the men.[26] McKechnie was still steaming and wanted to protest the game, but Dreyfuss nixed the idea. "We will take our medicine like men," he insisted.[27] Years later Traynor claimed that both Peckinpaugh and Zachary admitted that Rice didn't make a clean catch, but that's not what Rice was saying. Commissioner Landis demanded to speak to him after the game to find out whether it was, in fact, a clean catch. Rice stepped neatly around the question. "Judge, the umpire called Smitty out," he said. Not much of an answer, but good enough for Landis.[28] "That's exactly what I wanted you to say and that's the way I want you to answer anybody else asking you that question," the commissioner ordered.[29]

People asked Rice about that catch for the next 50 years. The controversy amused him and he milked it for all it was worth, playing coy with the public just as he had with Landis. A waiter approached Rice at a dinner party the weekend he was inducted into the Baseball Hall of Fame in 1963 and asked whether he had caught the ball. "The umpire said I did," he replied.[30] Asked the same question in a television interview a few years later, he said, "I'll have to take the Fifth Amendment."[31] In the 1960s, Rice authored a letter to Hall of Fame president Paul Kerr, with orders that it not be opened until after his death. When Rice died in 1974, Kerr unsealed the letter and revealed its contents. Rice had finally let everyone in on his secret: "At no time did I lose possession of the ball."[32]

Game Four featured more Johnson domination. He scattered six hits—two of them by Traynor—as he again went the distance in a 4–0 whitewashing, becoming the oldest man in World Series history to throw a shutout. Not only were the Pirates down three games to one, but they looked totally inept at the plate. They had scored just seven runs through the first four games and now they had to beat Coveleski in Game Five in order to send the Series back to Pittsburgh.

McKechnie benched first baseman George Grantham, 2-for-14 through the first four games, and replaced him with veteran Stuffy McInnis, a mid-season pickup who had started at first base for the world champion Philadelphia Athletics more than a decade earlier. Goslin, whose large and protruding nose impelled Earl Smith to taunt him with loud quacking noises from behind the plate all Series long, belted an RBI double off Aldridge in the first inning and gave Washington a 1–0 lead.[33] But Coveleski, pitching with a sore back, couldn't hold it. The Pirates went ahead, 2–1, in the third on an RBI single by Clyde Barnhart and a sacrifice fly by Traynor. After Joe Harris' homer tied the score, the Pirates broke through for good in the seventh inning on back-to-back RBI singles by Cuyler and Barnhart. Aldridge went the distance in the 6–3 victory. Equally important, Marberry, summoned to mop up in the ninth inning, faced two batters and then walked off the mound with his balky elbow throbbing. He was done for the Series.

Again it was Kremer and Ferguson on the mound, this time on two days' rest, for Game Six back in Pittsburgh. Attendance was just under 44,000, including 20 fans perched atop the large *Pittsburgh Post* clock beyond right field. They booed Rice mercilessly, prompting columnist Ring Lardner to muse, "The way not to get booed in Pittsburgh ... is to ignore fly balls or muff them."[34] Washington scored a run in each of the first two innings, but the Pirates came back in the third to knot it up, Traynor's two-out single bringing home Carey with the tying run. In the fifth inning Moore, despite aggravating a thumb injury in batting practice before the game, powered a Ferguson pitch over the left field fence for what proved to be the deciding run. The Senators had the tying run at second base in the eighth and ninth innings, but Kremer squirmed out of the jam each time. Ossie Bluege's grounder to Traynor ended it, and the Pirates had won, 3–2, to force a seventh game.

McKechnie probably endured a long, restless night as he pondered his choice of a starting pitcher for Game Seven. Meadows was hurt. Neither Aldridge nor Kremer were options since they had just started Games Five and Six. Yde, who pitched poorly in Game Four, had struggled with his endurance all season, so bringing him back on two days' rest probably wasn't the best idea. McKechnie told the press he was considering going with journeyman Red Oldham. But instead, he decided on "Jughandle" Johnny Morrison, who had pitched 4⅔ innings of shutout ball in relief of Yde in Game Four. Morrison was a 17-game winner in 1925, and had won 25 games two seasons earlier thanks largely to a wicked, knee-buckling curveball. He would have to be at his best, though, because the Senators were countering with Walter Johnson, who had been unhittable to that point in the Series.

The Pirates got what appeared to be a lucky break when Game Seven was rained out. That gave them a chance to come back with Aldridge on two days' rest, after he had thrown 145 pitches in Game Five.[35] The next day, October 14, brought more lousy weather to Pittsburgh. The rain poured down all morning and tapered to a steady drizzle by early afternoon. Commissioner Landis, seeing that the forecast for the next few days looked no better, ordered that the game be played, regardless of the rain. When Aldridge threw the first pitch of the game at 2:30 P.M., puddles had formed in the infield and the outfield resembled a Slip 'n' Slide. A good portion of the crowd arrived in the second inning or later because most people assumed the game would be postponed.

James Harrison of the *New York Times* called Game Seven "the wettest, weirdest, and wildest game that 50 years of baseball has ever seen ... the best and worst game of baseball ever played."[36] The first inning was a disaster for the Pirates. Aldridge was horrible, slipping all over the muddy mound and struggling to grip the wet baseball. He walked three and threw two wild pitches. After third baseman Ossie Bluege singled in a run to make it 2–0, McKechnie, perhaps thinking his lucky underwear had lost its magic (he hadn't changed since before Game Five), summoned Morrison from the bullpen. But the Senators tacked on two more runs against him — one on a bases-loaded catcher's interference call against Earl Smith, another on an Eddie Moore error. Morrison retired Johnson and Rice with the bases loaded to prevent a knockout blow, but Pittsburgh was definitely on the ropes, trailing, 4–0. "The way Walter Johnson was pitching, it was hard to imagine him blowing such a big lead," Traynor admitted.[37]

But Johnson wasn't at his best either. He had injured his leg while running the bases in Game Four, and he worked Game Seven with his hamstring heavily wrapped. Bucky Harris dismissed the importance of that injury prior to the game, asking rhetorically, "He doesn't pitch with his leg, does he?"[38] But the discomfort clearly affected Johnson, and the mound conditions were driving him crazy, too. Between innings, the grounds crew dumped wheelbarrows full of sawdust on the infield and the mound to absorb the water. But the dirt remained too slick for the Big Train, who periodically scooped up even more sawdust in his cap and scattered it on the mound. One writer observed that all the leftover sawdust that settled onto Johnson's head and uniform made him look like he was covered in oatmeal.[39]

The Pirates scored three runs off Johnson in the third. Morrison started the inning with a bloop single. Moore doubled him home, then Carey singled in Moore. Two batters later, Barnhart knocked in Carey to trim the lead to a single run. The Senators added on in the fourth inning, though, as Joe Harris' two-run double made it 6–3. The Pirates posted a run in fifth, then drew even in the seventh. Moore reached on an error by Roger Peckinpaugh, his seventh of the Series. Carey, who had four hits on the afternoon, followed with a run-scoring double. Two batters later, it was Traynor's turn. He had been enjoying a brilliant Series, with three multi-hit games, and he had been the only player to enjoy any success against Johnson in Games One and Four.

Traynor rifled a Johnson pitch deep into right field, scoring Carey with the tying run to make it 6–6. As Carey crossed the plate and Joe Harris tracked down the ball, Traynor raced toward third. He had an easy triple, but with the score tied and the chance that the game could be called at any moment, Traynor tried to stretch it into a home run, which would have put the Pirates on top. But the relay throw was on target, and catcher Muddy Ruel applied the tag in plenty of time. Traynor made a squishy, inelegant slide into the bog that had formed around home plate. The *New York Times* complimented Traynor on his display of "daring and good baseball."[40]

Ray Kremer came in on one day's rest to pitch the eighth. After one out, Peckinpaugh temporarily shed the goat horns, driving a home run to left field to put the Senators back on top, 7–6. Traynor's diving stop of Ruel's sharply hit ground ball helped prevent further damage. Johnson went back out to pitch the bottom of the eighth although he clearly was laboring. This would have been a perfect spot for Marberry had his arm not fallen off in Game Five. Even so, Harris still had Reuther and Zachary waiting in reserve, fresh as could be. But this was Johnson's game.

After retiring the first two hitters in the eighth, Johnson called out the grounds crew; he needed more sawdust to help dry the mound. The field conditions had deteriorated to the point of absurdity. "It was pouring like mad from the third inning on," said Goose Goslin, "and by the seventh inning the fog was so thick I could just about make out what was going on in the infield from there in the outfield."[41] In the stands, rain was pouring off the brims of fans' hats in rivers.

Ready to work again, now with a newly landscaped mound, Johnson melted down. He allowed back-to-back doubles by Smith and pinch-hitter Carson Bigbee as Pittsburgh tied the score, 7–7. After a walk to Moore, Carey hit a routine ground ball to poor Roger Peckinpaugh for what should have been the third out. But Peckinpaugh's high throw to second base pulled Bucky Harris off the bag and Moore was safe. The bases were loaded for Kiki Cuyler.

Cuyler worked the count to 2–2 before fouling off several pitches. Johnson came back with a fastball that looked good. Johnson and Ruel both started toward the dugout but home plate umpire Barry McCormick called the pitch a ball. Johnson thought he should have been out of the inning twice. Cuyler capitalized on the break, slashing the next pitch just fair down the right field line and into the Pirate bullpen. Bigbee and Moore scored. Joe Harris' throw got away, which allowed Carey and Cuyler to come around, but after a conference the umpires ruled the ball had been temporarily wedged under the tarpaulin in foul territory, meaning it was a ground-rule double and Carey and Cuyler had to return to their bases. But the two unearned runs gave Pittsburgh a 9–7 lead going to the ninth inning.

McKechnie, having lifted Kremer for a pinch-hitter in the eighth, was just about out of available pitchers. The man he settled on was Red Oldham. If someone had asked baseball fans in 1925 who they would have wanted on the mound in the ninth inning, trying to nail down Game Seven of the World Series for their team, Red Oldham's name would have been pretty far down the list. The Pirates purchased the 32-year-old from Des Moines on August 10. He had appeared in just 11 games for Pittsburgh over the final two months, usually in mop-up roles or as a starter in relatively meaningless games. Prior to August, he hadn't pitched in the majors in three years. His best season had come in 1921, when he went 11–14 for the Detroit Tigers. Traynor recalled Earl Smith walking out to the mound at the start of the inning and trying to get the nervous left-hander to relax a little bit. "You'll be alright," Smith told Oldham. "Your feet are so big you can't slip in the mud. Just throw the ball where I hold my glove."[42]

And that's what he did. In his only career World Series appearance, Oldham, working against the top of the Washington batting order, struck out Rice looking, got Bucky Harris to line out softly to Moore, and then wrapped it up with a called third strike on Goslin. The Pirates were world champions.

Forbes Field burst into hysteria. "The fans swarmed out and ripped up the

The 1925 World Champion Pittsburgh Pirates. *Left to right, front row:* George Haas, Eddie Moore, Bernard Culloton, Tom Sheehan, Jewel Ens with mascot Billy McKechnie, Jr., Glenn Wright, Kiki Cuyler, Ray Kremer, Johnny Gooch. *Middle row:* Red Oldham, Earl Smith, Pie Traynor, Stuffy McInnis, Max Carey, Bill McKechnie (manager), Fred Clarke (vice president), Carson Bigbee, Fresco Thompson, Roy Spencer, George Grantham, George Austen (trainer). *Back row:* Chick Fraser (scout), Bill Hinchman (scout), Jack Onslow (coach), Clyde Barnhart, Vic Aldridge, Sam Watters (secretary), Barney Dreyfuss (owner), Sam Dreyfuss (treasurer), Johnny Rawlings, Emil Yde, Babe Adams, Johnny Morrison, Lee Meadows (Paul Traynor).

plate and the bases. They stole caps off the players' heads and took everything they could find," Traynor said. "We were lucky to get into the clubhouse alive."[43] The fence in front of the right field bleachers collapsed under the weight of thousands of fans streaming onto the field, while a band clad in red jackets blared out a raucous musical accompaniment. Pittsburghers following the game elsewhere clogged downtown streets as soon as the final out was recorded, blowing horns, banging pans together, and pushing one another around in wheelbarrows as confetti fluttered down on their heads from office buildings. The revelry continued until the wee hours of the morning. Meanwhile, the scene in the Pirate clubhouse was just as emotional. "[H]ardened ball players ... some crying from pure joy, others in fond embrace with a brother ball player."[44] Traynor called it "one of the happiest moments of my life."[45]

There were endless recriminations on the Senators' side. Roger Peckinpaugh, in tears in the clubhouse afterward, would be forever branded as the klutz who blew the World Series. But Bucky Harris was in line for criticism as well. He went just 2-for-23 in the Series, but what people really questioned was his decision to go the distance with Johnson in the deciding game. Traynor thought Harris made a wise decision, even though the Big Train allowed 15 hits. "He might have survived even that if his defense hadn't cracked."[46] But American League president Ban Johnson was not so forgiving. He addressed a note to Harris, reading, "You put up a game fight. This I admire. Lost the game for sentimental reasons. This should never have happened in a World Series."[47] Johnson later told reporters, "Walter Johnson never should have been permitted to continue in the box after the third inning."[48] Harris struck back. "Ban Johnson's statement is impudent and uncalled for. He knows very little about baseball and certainly nothing about the management of the Washington team."[49] He went on to add, in reference to Walter Johnson, "I went down with my best."[50]

These seven games established Traynor as one of baseball's true superstars. Giants coach and former Detroit manager Hughie Jennings called Traynor "the real hero of the World Series. He not only covered his own territory but he was down in front of Wright half the time scooping up slow rollers and always getting his man."[51] Even before the Series, some of his contemporaries were beginning to speak of him in reverential tones. The usually grumpy John McGraw allowed in September, "He will go down in history as one of the really great third basemen."[52] Traynor's .346 Series average and flawless play at third base helped the entire world see exactly what McGraw was talking about. The *New York Times* called Traynor "the greatest third baseman since Jimmy Collins."[53] Veteran New York sportswriter Joe Vila agreed, writing, "I do not recall a greater third baseman than Pie Traynor."[54]

Traynor batted .320 in 1925 and appeared in the National League top ten in runs, hits, extra-base hits, and RBIs. Defensively, he participated in 41 double plays, a league record for third basemen that stood for 25 years. Traynor finished eighth in league most valuable player balloting and made the first of his seven appearances on the *Sporting News'* all-star team.

In the afterglow of the World Series celebration, some latent bad feelings rose to the surface. The team elected Traynor, Carey, Smith, and Babe Adams to make recommendations for how to divide the club's World Series money (a full share was worth $5,300 per man). The committee recommended Fred Clarke be awarded a half-share. But when it came to a vote, the team decided Clarke should get nothing at all. Carey tried to work out a compromise solution and eventually persuaded his teammates to give Clarke $1,000. When Clarke found out, he hit the roof and went howling to Dreyfuss.

Barney Dreyfuss was upset with McKechnie for letting the team get away with shortchanging Clarke. McKechnie, in turn, felt like Clarke had stabbed him in the back by running to the owner. Clarke eventually tried to return the check, but Dreyfuss talked him out of it.[55] The upshot was a whole lot of resentment and hurt feelings as the team prepared to defend its title.

7

A Great Club Melting Away

For the next few months Traynor enjoyed the freedom that came with life as a comfortably well-off bachelor. He had nowhere he had to be that winter, nothing pressing to do, so he went wherever the wind took him. Originally he planned to visit Clarke in Kansas, then head to the West Coast for some hunting. But instead Traynor bagged those plans and returned to Massachusetts, where he spent three weeks on Stuffy McInnis' 100-acre farm in the town of Athol, chopping wood and shooting raccoons. Although he had done a little hunting in California the previous offseason, it still was a relatively new experience for a city boy, and he liked it. Hunting became one of Traynor's offseason pastimes.

From there he went home to the Boston area to be with his family and take in a few college football games. Then he returned to Pittsburgh on New Year's Eve to undergo a minor surgical procedure to resolve some persistent sinus problems. While in town Traynor ran into Max Carey, who persuaded him on the spot to head to Miami. Carey was going down south to meet with Emil Yde and Lee Meadows to try to make quick money buying and selling land during Florida's real estate bubble. Traynor probably wasn't into that, but doctors thought warm weather would help with his breathing.

After a few weeks in the sun Traynor went back north to New York for the National League Golden Jubilee and then took off for California and reported to spring training early, opening camp with the pitchers and catchers in Paso Robles in late February.

On March 4, Pie was joined in camp by his 23-year-old brother, Arthur, a third baseman who was there to make a quixotic bid at a roster spot. One can assume Pie pulled some strings to wrangle an invitation for his brother; nothing in Art's spotty baseball record would suggest he was there on merit. Art Traynor (or "Att Tray-nuh," as Pie would have pronounced it in his Boston brogue) came out of school and enlisted in the navy in May 1920. He spent almost 18 months in the military, departing at the rank of seaman second class in December 1921. The next year Art signed contracts with both Birmingham and Atlanta in the Southern Association, but there is no evidence of him appearing in a game for either team. In 1923 he played in 42 games as a third baseman with Crisfield of the Class D Eastern Shore League, where he hit .245 with three home runs.[1] After two years in obscurity, presumably playing semipro ball somewhere, Art popped up in Paso Robles.

Traynor family legend has it that Art was a better athlete than Pie. That is hard to believe, but he did look the part. A friend described Pie as having the build of a football defensive back.[2] Art, on the other hand, looked more like a tight end. He was a couple inches taller than his brother, with a thicker, more powerful-looking build.

Physical traits aside, Pie had something intangible, unseen inside him that his brother lacked. Pie was almost fanatical about improving, doing better. That meant grueling sessions of extra batting or fielding practice when he was in a slump; it meant going to business school in the offseason in an effort to qualify for admission to college; it meant reading great books, something that apparently engaged him for a while. When George Stallings humiliated him at that workout at Braves Field, he became all the more driven to succeed, in part so he could rub Stallings' face in it. Beneath Pie's affable persona and self-deprecating sense of humor burned intense ambition. And, as with many people who rise from nothing to make it, Traynor's drive seemed to be fueled by a deep-seated fear of failure. Every slump was torture. When he became a manager, every loss was a small catastrophe.

Art's perspective hardly could have been more different. He didn't take baseball too seriously. He didn't take much of anything too seriously. He just wanted to live for the moment and have a little fun. Pie, realizing this, took on the challenging task of saving Art from himself in the spring of 1926. Ed Ballinger of the *Pittsburgh Post* noted that Traynor "acts just like a daddy in looking after the welfare of his kid brother."[3] Pie roomed with his brother and tried to manage every aspect of his life, going so far as to dictate his bedtime. Teammates found the dynamic between the two men hilarious. "Isn't it time for you to put your kid brother to bed?" they razzed Pie one evening.[4]

Try as he might, Pie could not transform his brother into something he wasn't. Injuries and immaturity dogged Art all spring. First he suffered a sprained ankle that put him on the sidelines. Then just when his ankle was better, he missed a March 22 game when he showed up to the park stiff and sore following a senseless, bone-jarring horseback ride through the woods.[5] Later than evening he got into a playful wrestling match with a teammate, smacked his face off a bedpost, and emerged with a black eye.[6]

But as it turns out Art's biggest problem, beyond his self-discipline and injury issues, was a simple, profound lack of talent. He didn't hit during the few opportunities he received that spring, and his play at third base was brutal. Arthur got a ticket to the minors, where he surfaced later that year with Lawrence of the Class B New England League. He was out of his depth even there, hitting .215 with just two extra-base hits and eight errors in 21 games. After appearing in 26 games with the Class D Waynesboro Red Birds in 1928 (and batting a hollow .271), Art drifted out of baseball.[7]

Without baseball or the military to impose discipline on him, Art's life spun out of control. He lived in the New York City area, drank more than he should have, got into trouble with the law, and even lived as a drifter in China for a period of time. Eventually he returned to Massachusetts where he moved back in with his mother. He had pretty much bottomed out.

Then in 1942, at age 39, Art finally began to get his act together. He enlisted in the United States Maritime Service and rose from the rank of able seaman to that of second mate by the time he received his honorable discharge on August 14, 1945, the day Japan announced its surrender, marking the end of World War II.[8] After leaving the service, Art settled in Baltimore, where he worked as a pipe fitter and supposedly became a successful real estate investor.[9]

He remained a fun, life-of-the-party kind of guy. Photos of him in his later years show a portly, jolly-looking man with a welcoming smile spread across his moon face.[10] Art, the only one of his siblings who never married, invited his mother to join him in Baltimore during her last years and they lived together until her death in 1970. Arthur died on November 4, 1984, the last remaining Traynor sibling.

Coincidentally, on the same day Art injured his ankle in spring training, Pie also tweaked his when he stumbled rounding second base. Pie's injury was the more serious of the two. He missed two weeks of action, walking with a cane for a portion of that time. He made a pinch-hitting appearance in a March 25 exhibition game, but it was all he could do to hobble down to first base. On April 4, he collided with another player while shagging fly balls, was knocked unconscious, and aggravated the ankle. But within a few days he was well enough to challenge Vic Aldridge to a footrace and the Pirates breathed a sigh of relief when they learned he would be able to answer the bell on Opening Day.

The Pirates improved their outfield corps with the addition of rookie right fielder Paul Waner, who had starred with the San Francisco Seals and played against the Pirates in exhibition games in previous springs. Waner was a brittle-looking left-handed hitter, just 5'8" and around 135 pounds as a rookie. He grew up in Harrah, Oklahoma, near Oklahoma City, excelled in track and base-ball in high school and then spent three years at a teachers college. "My father was a farmer and he wanted his sons to get a good education."[11] But a contract offer from the Seals was enough to convince his father to let Paul drop out of school and go west. Waner batted .369, .356, and .401 for San Francisco from 1923 to 1925. The Pirates bought him for $100,000.

The *Pittsburgh Post* called Waner "a boy of excellent habits ... brought up with the proper ideas of clean living."[12] Perhaps the writer had him confused with someone else. Waner was an alcoholic, and even in that hard-boozing era, his consumption was legendary. He drank before games, after games, even during games. Traynor once joked that he didn't realize Waner drank until he came to the ballpark sober one day.[13] "He had to be a very graceful player," Casey Stengel observed, "because he could slide without breaking the bottle on his hip."[14] In those days alcoholism generally was looked upon as a personal failing or a source of amusement rather than a serious disease. Waner never got in any trouble and performed at a consistently high level, so no one in base-ball seemed to care much about what he was doing to himself. Whether his drinking adversely affected his hitting is hard to say. If it did to any apprecia-ble extent, then without alcohol Waner might have been one of the four or five greatest hitters who ever lived. He was plenty good as it was, finishing his 19-year career with 3,152 hits and earning election into the Baseball Hall of Fame in 1952.

The Pirates were widely expected to repeat in 1926. Irving Vaughan, a well-respected writer with the *Chicago Tribune*, predicted they would win the National League by 15 games.[15] Other than the addition of Waner, it was essen-tially the same team that had won the World Series the season before. But Pitts-burgh's offense got off to an inexplicably slow start. The team batting average stood at .190 while Pittsburgh won just three of its first 12 games and fell briefly into the National League basement. After a May 6 loss to Boston, McKechnie, faced with a 9–12 record, benched Carey, who was hitting just .161, and replaced him with Carson Bigbee. Waner was batting .150 in limited action. Barnhart was at a dismal .127. Traynor's first week was a disaster, as he hit .207 and man-gled his toe while making a tag on a rundown play. But he warmed up earlier than usual, putting together a stellar May and raising his average to .370 by late in the month, second best in the league.

Traynor's bat helped bring the Pirates out of their doldrums. The Bucs won 15 of 20 games from late May through early June to pull into first place by per-centage points over Cincinnati. But they spent most of June back in second place, as Traynor maintained his spot among the top five in the National League in batting average.

July was a fantastic month for Pittsburgh, which went 21–10 and moved back into first. But this push coincided with a complete disintegration of team discipline. On July 12, McKechnie fined Yde and Moore for "indifferent play" following a doubleheader loss to the Giants. Moore committed an error in the first game of that doubleheader, which drew boos from the fans at Forbes. Moore had a habit of smiling when he became frustrated. When Fred Clarke saw Moore grinning after his miscue, he mistook it as a sign of apathy. After the inning, the two men got into a loud confrontation, during which Moore, who had a short temper and a big mouth, screamed at Clarke to "get off the bench!"[16] Moore never played another game for Pittsburgh; the Pirates sold him to the Braves a week later.

On July 21, Aldridge's sore arm forced him from a game against Brooklyn after facing only three batters. He immediately left the clubhouse, a violation of team rules, which drew a $50 fine. The team suspended Johnny Morrison without pay when, without warning, he picked up and went home to Kentucky for a few days.

Additionally, Kiki Cuyler had become *persona non grata* in the clubhouse. Though he was one of the best hitters in the league, Cuyler had been in the doghouse because McKechnie thought he made too many mental errors and didn't always do what he was told.[17] However, the *Pittsburgh Press* noted that something had happened to alienate him from his teammates as well.[18] The *Press* did not get into details, but it did reveal that the Pirates had become riven along religious lines.[19] Cuyler was unabashedly Catholic in a time when anti–Catholic bias was still alive and well in America. It seems reasonable to speculate that those ugly societal prejudices might have followed Cuyler through the clubhouse door.

Under different circumstances, perhaps McKechnie could have kept the team together. His kind but firm personality was well suited for it. But Dreyfuss had inadvertently cut the legs out from under his manager by allowing Clarke to sit on the bench and openly question McKechnie's authority. McKechnie was losing the team.

The big pot of venom and chaos that had been brewing around the Pirates all season finally bubbled over on August 7 during a doubleheader loss to the Boston Braves. The Pirates looked terrible that day, losing both games by shutout. Carey, who was suffering through an awful season after missing much of the spring with pneumonia, looked especially bad. After one of Carey's at-bats, Clarke looked over to McKechnie in disgust and muttered, "Put in the batboy. He couldn't be much worse."[20] Carson Bigbee overheard the remark and told Carey, who became irate. Carey once had been a Clarke ally, but even he had grown tired of the older man's meddling. "No team can thrive under two managers," Carey declared.[21] It was time to bring the issue to a head and address it man-to-man with McKechnie.

Before speaking out, Carey and Bigbee approached Babe Adams, the wise old man of the clubhouse, for a reality check, just to see where he stood. Adams concurred wholeheartedly. "I think the manager should manage and no one else should interfere," he told them.[22] With Barney Dreyfuss on an overseas vacation, even McKechnie seemed unclear about who was supposed to be running things. "[Clarke] is supreme. He is the president of the club right now. Mr. Dreyfuss gave him full authority when he left for Europe."[23] Asked whether that authority extended over him, the Pirate manager replied, "I would say that it does." Detroit newspaper writer Harry Salsinger claimed the two men bickered over strategy going back at least to the 1925 World Series.[24]

Following the doubleheader, Carey, Bigbee, and Adams pulled McKechnie aside on the porch of the Brunswick Hotel while they waited to depart for their train. McKechnie heard them out, realized he had a problem on his hands, and scheduled a team meeting for the next morning to clear the air. But then McKechnie made two misjudgments. First, just 30 minutes before the team meeting was to begin, he cancelled it because he believed that he and Pirates vice president Sam Watters had found a "diplomatic way" to remove Clarke from the bench.[25] Second, McKechnie told Clarke about his meeting with the three players at the Brunswick. Clarke responded as one should have expected, with verbosity and indignation, demanding that the so-called mutineers be punished.

When he saw Clarke ranting and raving, McKechnie realized he should have kept his mouth shut. Carey, Bigbee, and Adams were the three most senior Pirates in terms of length of service. All had stellar reputations; they were hardly troublemakers and McKechnie knew it. But now the storm was beyond his control. Clarke called his own clubhouse meeting on Monday, August 9, prior to the first game of a series against Brooklyn and ripped the team up one side and down the other, reminding them who was in charge and bitterly vowing to leave the bench if he was not wanted. On Tuesday, the team relented and voted 18–6 to allow Clarke to remain in the dugout.

Clarke, however, wanted his pound of flesh. When the team returned to Pittsburgh on Friday, Barney Dreyfuss' Princeton-educated, 29-year-old son Sam, who was running things while his father was away, called a clubhouse meeting, during which he informed the club that Adams and Bigbee had been given their unconditional releases, while Carey had been suspended without pay and placed on waivers. Brooklyn quickly claimed Carey, and his long Pirate career was officially over. Neither Bigbee nor Adams ever appeared in another major league game.

Public opinion fell strongly on the side of the three players. One fan, T.J. Crowe, wrote a letter to the *Pittsburgh Press* stating that the players' termination was "one of the most coldblooded and ridiculous performances that ever came under my notice."[26] Another fan declared, "I'd like to take Fred Clarke by the shoulders and give him a good shake."[27] *Pittsburgh Press* beat writer Ralph Davis bemoaned Clarke's "vindictiveness."[28]

Circumstantial evidence strongly suggests Traynor probably felt much more loyal toward Clarke than McKechnie. Traynor and Clarke were friends and remained so for years. When Traynor was concerned about losing his managerial job in 1937, it was Clarke who gave him a crying shoulder and tried to boost his spirits. Clarke also attended Traynor's Baseball Hall of Fame induction in 1948.

On the other hand, Traynor and McKechnie did not get along at all, for reasons that both men apparently took to the grave. The *Pittsburgh Press*, without elaboration, noted that "beginning in 1925, their personal relations were strained."[29] In the 1930s, when McKechnie was managing the Braves, he rejected a couple of trades with the Pirates that Traynor assumed were done deals. After a trade for Wally Berger fell through in 1937, Traynor publicly criticized his former manager. "Bill McKechnie just doesn't like to deal with the Pirates. I don't know what the trouble is."[30] After that, the two men refused to speak to each other for some time. Traynor was extremely well liked, as was McKechnie. But for some reason their personalities just never meshed.

With Carey gone, Traynor assumed the role of team captain, a title he would hold for the next eight years. In the immediate aftermath of the controversy, the Pirates did not skip a beat on the field. They won 10 of their next 14 games, but remained locked in an extremely tight race with St. Louis and Cincinnati. For about two weeks in late August the three clubs were never separated by more than two games. Then in late August into early September, Pittsburgh lost eight out of nine, including four straight to the Cardinals. With little margin for error in such a close race, that stumble buried them in third place, 3½ games out, and they never recovered.

The Pirates' struggles over that two-week period coincided with a total implosion by Traynor, who went 11-for-69 at the plate (a .159 clip) from August 29 to September 12. He ended the season with a somewhat disappointing average of .317, and statistics suggest his defensive work was off slightly from where it had been in 1925. It was a rough year. "We lost our spirit," Traynor asserted. "We had no zip. We slopped around and finished third when we had the best team in the league. The players started to slump off. You never saw a great club start to melt away so fast."[31]

The bloodshed continued following the season. Clarke resigned. Stuffy McInnis, a Clarke supporter who reportedly leaked details of the story to reporters, was cut loose. And in what was a surprise to some, Barney Dreyfuss fired McKechnie. Dreyfuss insisted that the Carey incident had nothing to do with it, but did admit that the fans' displeasure with the manager played a role. Of course, the fans' scorn was a direct consequence of the "mutiny." Once the messy details became public, Pittsburgh fans rode McKechnie relentlessly every time he popped his head out of the dugout, hollering things like, "Did Clarke tell you to come out?" or "Better make sure of your orders, Bill!"[32] In McKechnie's mind Dreyfuss was a Judas. Their relationship was irretrievably broken, and McKechnie held a quiet grudge against the Pirate organization for many years.[33]

Traynor spent three weeks immediately following the season at a hunting camp near Yellow Lake in northwest Wisconsin, where Brooklyn pitcher Burleigh Grimes owned property.[34] Upon leaving Wisconsin and returning to the Boston area, Traynor was besieged by requests for public appearances. "He was bothered half to death by giving talks, answering foolish questions, writing his autograph, and performing other such stunts," according to the *Pittsburgh Post*.[35] The 1926 season was miserable and stressful; the Pirate clubhouse had not been a fun place to go to work. Traynor no doubt wanted to put all that behind him and find some peace, but instead he kept letting people drag him into speaking engagements. "For one solid week I never went to bed before two in the morning, and never in my life did I see so much cold roast beef and potato salad."[36] Traynor couldn't help himself, though. Incapable of saying no to people, he did the next best thing — he got out of town. He caught a train back to Yellow Lake, where he spent the rest of the offseason.

In the summer, the area of Wisconsin where the camp was located was a popular vacation getaway. In the winter, the place was a snowy, arctic ghost town. "Thirty below was nothing out of the ordinary," according to Traynor.[37] But after Grimes purchased land there in 1925, it became a regular offseason retreat for a handful of ballplayers, including Traynor, who spent most of the next four winters there. Grimes, Dave Bancroft, and Fred Lindstrom (who also purchased property on the lake) were Traynor's most frequent companions, though other players visited at various times. Traynor loved the outdoors, and the lifestyle suited him perfectly. "There's nothing like the tug of a big northern pike," he crowed.[38]

Yellow Lake was tucked away in a secluded corner of one of the remotest parts of the country. Burnett County, Wisconsin, had a population of only 10,735 according to the 1920 U.S. Census. More than 60 percent of the land was forested, with 508 lakes, 10 rivers, and hundreds of miles of shoreline.[39] Grimes captured what life was like for the guys who wintered there. "I troop miles every day in the snow with my gun. I breathe crisp, frosty air many hours out of the 24. I eat a lot of wholesome, well-cooked food. I go to bed early and sleep like a badger in a burrow."[40] Grimes was the top marksman in camp. Traynor claimed he once saw him shoot a buck in the head with a high-powered rifle from nearly a mile away. "It was the best shot I ever saw."[41]

The cabins were located next door to Ike Walton's Resort. The players took their meals at the resort lodge, which featured a big dining room and kitchen, and a back porch where, in the fall, the players would gather for a beer after dinner. Opal Larson, who worked at the resort as a young girl, recalled that the cabins where guests like Traynor lived were spartan, but clean and livable. "I think they had two beds in each cabin and then a little kitchenette on the end," Larson said.[42] On the days when the winter weather was just too harsh for hunting, hiking, or ice fishing, Traynor sometimes holed up in his cabin with his stash of books and magazines. Other times he joined his buddies for a game of bridge, possibly an illegal beverage or two, and, no doubt, hours of animated, testosterone-fueled discussion about baseball, women, and life.

The 1927 edition of the Pirates looked remarkably similar to that of the previous season with one exception: Paul Waner's younger brother, Lloyd, took over in left field. New manager Donie Bush had penciled in Clyde Barnhart for left — that is, until Bush saw Barnhart waddle into spring training. "He was just a butterball," recalled Paul Waner. "They gave him steam baths, and exercised him, and ran him, and ran him, and ran him. Well, they got the weight off all right, but as a result the poor fellow was so weak he could hardly lift a bat."[43]

Lloyd Waner, a quieter, more sober and slightly smaller version of his brother, hit .355 as a rookie and finished sixth in the National League Most Valuable Player voting. Despite that brilliant first act, Lloyd was never quite the player that Paul was and some historians have criticized his 1967 election to the Baseball Hall of Fame.[44] He lacked power and missed a lot of games due to injuries and illness during the prime years of his career. But he had great speed, was a superb defensive player, and was a fixture in Pittsburgh alongside his brother until 1941. In his later years, whenever he was sitting back sharing old war stories, Traynor would go on and on about the way Lloyd Waner patrolled Forbes Field's vast outfield. "No better center fielder ever lived and that includes Tris Speaker."[45]

Most experts again thought the Pirates were the best team in the National League in the spring of 1927. Through the first two months of the season, there appeared little doubt they were right, and Traynor was one of the primary reasons why. From May 18 to 22, he homered three times in a four-game sweep of the New York Giants, which propelled Pittsburgh into a first-place tie. One

Traynor takes a swing at Baker Bowl in Philadelphia in the mid–1920s. Choking up on a huge 42-ounce bat, Traynor hit .342 and knocked in 106 runs in 1927 to lead the Pirates to the World Series for the second time in three seasons (National Photo Company Collection, Prints & Photographs Division, Library of Congress, LC-DIG-npcc-14198).

of his shots was a 12th-inning grand slam; the next afternoon he broke up a tie game by driving a Hugh McQuillan pitch off the right field scoreboard at the Polo Grounds.

From there Traynor went to Cincinnati, where he put up back-to-back four-hit games, upping his average to a season-best .397, second in the National League. Although Traynor cooled off some over the next couple of weeks, his team continued to plow forward. Traynor's two-run single lifted the Pirates to a 9–6 win over New York on June 7, as Pittsburgh climbed five games ahead of the second-place (and defending World Series champion) St. Louis Cardinals.

By that summer Traynor had grown more popular than ever in Pittsburgh. Whenever he was in town, he was almost guaranteed to be making a public appearance in the morning before a game or in the evening after one. A meet-and-greet with kids at a marbles tournament, dinner with a youth league team, speeches to clubs and organizations—if anyone wanted Traynor, all he had to do was ask. The man's private life was almost non-existent. "He has been over-booked in the entertainment game and he is still booked up far in advance," reported the *Pittsburgh Post*'s Ed Ballinger. "He wishes he could get out of it, but wants to be accommodating."[46]

Traynor had emerged as the Pirates' unofficial community ambassador. He sometimes griped about it and resisted it, but he also was very good at it. He had developed a preternatural social intelligence that revealed itself most unmistakably in intimate, up-close interactions with fans. Though Traynor was the star around whom people gathered, he had a gift for making those people feel important and valued in their own right.

For example, he had an uncanny memory for names, faces, and the minutiae of people's lives. "If I would tell him I was playing in some sport or going off to some summer camp, then the next time I would see him he would ask about it," said Jack Berger, who was a young man when he knew Traynor.[47] Al Crouch, Traynor's colleague at KQV Radio in the 1960s, agreed that Traynor was an exceptional listener. "He had twinkly eyes, and when you talked to him, he would look you straight in the eye. You would have his absolute attention. It was like you were the biggest thing on his mind at the time."[48]

There were no strangers in Traynor's world. "He would always make you think that he knew you even if he didn't, which is a public relations gift," asserted Pittsburgh sports historian Jim O'Brien.[49] This came through in a 1967 television documentary, in which a cameraman followed Traynor and his wife, Eve, to Forbes Field, where the Pirates were playing their home opener. It took them forever to get there because every few steps someone stopped Traynor for an autograph, a handshake, or just to say hello. As they finally entered the stands, an elderly gentleman hobbled up to Traynor and burst out, "Hi! How have you been? I haven't seen you for 35 years!" Traynor had no idea who the guy was. But he grabbed the man's outstretched hand, leaned in toward him, and exclaimed with a warm smile, "Thirty-five years!? Glad to see you! How have you been?"[50] Traynor was one of the most popular athletes in Pittsburgh history, and that had almost as much to do with how he carried himself off the field as what he achieved on it.

Though the Pirates were impressive early in 1927, winning a pennant is seldom a snap. Sure enough, a few potholes appeared on the Bucs' road to the World Series. On June 18, in the seventh inning of a game against Boston, the Braves' Lance Richbourg singled home player-manager Dave Bancroft. Bancroft had a running dispute with Pirate catcher Earl Smith, dating to when Smith played for the Braves in 1923 and 1924. As Bancroft crossed the plate, Smith, out of nowhere, delivered a left hook that knocked Bancroft out. Bancroft lay prone in the dirt, his face busted open and his jaw shattered. As players from both teams milled around the Braves' fallen leader, Traynor said something that deeply offended Boston pitcher Joe Genewich, who had to be restrained from whaling on Traynor with a bat. National League president John Heydler called Smith's sucker punch a "violation of decency" and suspended him for 30 days.[51]

Ten days later, the Pirates suffered another key loss when a fastball from the Cardinals' Vic Keen struck Glenn Wright in the temple. Doctors said Wright probably would have been killed had the pitch been a few centimeters higher. As Wright recuperated, Traynor filled in at shortstop for nine games, with newly acquired veteran Heinie Groh taking Traynor's spot at third. Traynor held his own at his old position; he only committed one error, but that miscue led to the only run in a 1–0 loss to the Cubs on July 8. It was Chicago's ninth straight victory, and it catapulted them into first place, the first time the Pirates had been out of the lead in six weeks.

With the Pirates back atop the standings on July 28, Traynor chalked up a career first by finally getting thrown out of a game. In a game against Brooklyn, umpire Pete McLaughlin ruled the Robins' Max Carey safe at third on a double steal. This was the second time in a week Traynor found himself on the wrong end of a questionable call by McLaughlin. He spun around, fired his glove to the ground and, according to third base coach Otto Miller, screamed at McLaughlin, "I'm sick and tired of your decisions!"[52] McLaughlin immediately tossed him. The *Pittsburgh Post* called McLaughlin "typically hasty and consistently wrong" in ejecting Traynor.[53] But McLaughlin felt like Traynor left him no choice. "Since he said he wasn't feeling well, I thought he ought to go to the clubhouse," the umpire noted sarcastically. "And he threw the ball on the ground, which he ain't supposed to do."[54] Traynor would be ejected only once more during his playing career.

By August 16, the Cubs had surged 6½ games in front of the Pirates. While Chicago was winning 13 of 14, the Pirates were working through another clubhouse soap opera, this time involving Donie Bush and Kiki Cuyler. Cuyler had been whining all year about Bush's decision to bat him second in the lineup instead of down a little further, in the heart of the order. Bush found Cuyler's moaning and uninspired play to be constant sources of irritation. During a game against the Braves, Cuyler went in standing at second base instead of sliding to break up a double play. The pivot man dropped the ball, but Cuyler overran the bag and was tagged out. It looked bad, though Cuyler insisted it was a smart play; he argued he went in standing in order to block the relay throw to first. But all Bush saw was a disenchanted player dogging it. He fined Cuyler $50 and benched him for the rest of the season.

Barney Dreyfuss, no fan of Cuyler's, had his manager's back. "It isn't the player who talks loudest about himself who is the most indispensable," adding later, "I'm not satisfied with [Cuyler] or his playing and I don't think anybody else is for that matter."[55] Traynor thought both Bush and Cuyler were acting like children, stating years later that their quarrel "made it bad for the whole club. It was very silly."[56] Lloyd Waner moved over to take Cuyler's spot in center field, while Clyde Barnhart entered the lineup in left.

It looked like a promising season was again about to dissolve in internecine bickering. But from mid–August through mid–September, in the wake of Cuyler's benching, the Pirates won 24 of 31 games, including 11 straight at one point. During that same stretch, the Cubs won just 11 of 33 and fell off the pace. The Pirates held a narrow lead over the hard-charging Giants and Cardinals during the last two weeks. They finally clinched the pennant on the next-to-last day of the season when Traynor's two-run single off Cincinnati's Jakie May broke open a close game and propelled the Bucs to a 9–6 victory. "He gave me one in my groove inside," said Traynor, who had three hits that afternoon.[57] For the second time in three seasons, Pittsburgh was headed for the Fall Classic.

Awaiting the Pirates was perhaps the greatest team in baseball history — the mythical 1927 New York Yankees, record 110–44, making their fifth World Series appearance in seven years, with their "Murderer's Row" lineup featuring Babe Ruth, Lou Gehrig, Tony Lazzeri, Earle Combs, and Bob Meusel. Ruth's 60 home runs that season stood as a major league record for 34 years. Gehrig was right behind him with 47 blasts. By contrast, the Pirates hit just 54 home runs *as a team*.

New York also had assembled the best pitching staff in the American League, anchored by Hall of Famers Waite Hoyt and Herb Pennock and a veteran spitballer by the Dickensian name of Urban Shocker. Hoyt was complex — a heavy drinker who ran around with Ruth and stayed out until the wee hours, but also sort of a renaissance man who expressed himself through writing and painting. Pennock, a wiry junkballer, was a Main Line Philadelphia blue blood, polished and well-bred. He raised thoroughbreds and hosted fox hunts on his estate in tony Kennett Square, Pennsylvania. Shocker was a taciturn grouch who spent much of his day poring over newspapers and working crossword puzzles. He had a heart ailment that would kill him within a year.

These guys were excellent pitchers, but it certainly helped to be supported by one of the most fearsome lineups in history. New York averaged 6.29 runs per game. Right-hander George Pipgras, a rookie in 1927, recalled, "When we got to the ballpark, we knew we were going to win. That's all there was to it. We weren't cocky. I wouldn't call it confidence, either. We just *knew*. Like when you go to sleep you know the sun is going to come up in the morning."[58] The Yanks were self-assured almost to the point of narcolepsy. "This is the most blasé team we have ever seen go into a world's series [*sic*]," wrote the *New York Times*' James Harrison on the eve of the Series.[59]

The Yankees were larger than life on the field and off. Although a few of them, most notably the painfully shy Gehrig, shunned the nightlife, many of the Yankees lived like Roman emperors, none more so than Ruth. In his biography of Gehrig, Jonathan Eig writes, "Babe Ruth liked to rent a hotel suite, put on a red robe and a pair of Moroccan slippers, and hold court for anyone interested in a good time. He had plenty of company. There were always women in the Ruth suite and they were not the sort who required seduction."[60] Before the Series, Traynor boasted that he could "eat Babe under the table."[61] When Ruth heard that, he just smiled; it is hard to imagine Traynor or any other human out-excessing Ruth in any way.

The Yankees put on a mighty display in batting practice the day before the Series opener on October 5. Legend has it that the Pirates, watching slack-jawed as Ruth, Gehrig and the rest drove ball after ball over the Forbes Field walls, were so intimidated that the Series was over before it even began.

On the surface, the story has a whiff of incredulity about it. For one, Pittsburgh knew full well what the Yankees were all about; they had seen it with their own eyes earlier in the summer when they hosted New York in an exhibition game, during which all of the Yankees big guns had played. Three Pirates—Joe Harris, Heinie Groh, and Earl Smith—had competed against New York before coming over to Pittsburgh. Moreover, the Pirates were a battle-tested group. They had won a World Series two years earlier and had been in the middle of intense pennant races four years in a row. In fact, they had just edged out the Cardinals for the pennant, the same Cardinals who beat the same Yankees in the World Series 12 months earlier. As Paul Waner put it, "We didn't scare as a club. Why should we have been scared?"[62]

This tale and its implication that the Pirates were a bunch of star-struck, weak-kneed wimps bugged Traynor to no end. "It's high time that story was debunked. It's just not true," he said prior to the 1960 World Series, when the Pirates and Yankees battled again.[63] As he remembered it, the Pirates took batting practice first, and then immediately retreated to the clubhouse for a team meeting. They weren't even watching the Yankees. Lloyd Waner's recollection was slightly different in some details, but the gist of it matches what Traynor said. "I never even saw the Yankees work out that day," Waner insisted. "We had our workout first and I ... was leaving the field just as they were coming onto the field. I know some of our players stayed but I never heard anybody talk about what they saw."[64]

Perhaps the biggest indictment against the veracity of the story comes from one of the sportswriters who first promulgated it, Ford Frick. Frick was covering the Series for the *New York Journal*; he later became commissioner of baseball. Asked in 1960 whether he still believed the Yankees' show of pregame muscle had wrecked the Pirates, Frick wavered. "As a sportswriter in 1927, I thought it meant something. In 1960, as the commissioner, I cannot subscribe to such a theory."[65]

That said, whether the Pirates were intimidated or not, it wasn't much of a Series. Game One in Pittsburgh matched Hoyt against Ray Kremer. More than 41,000 watched from the stands while millions more listened to Graham McNamee's loud, over-wrought, and frequently inaccurate description over NBC radio.[66]

Before the first pitch, a group of fans in the bleachers unfurled a banner reading "We Want Cuyler." Cuyler did not appear in the Series despite occasional pleas from the crowd. Not only did Barnhart start in left field, but when it came time for a pinch-hitter, Bush went with the likes of the decrepit Groh, who had appeared in only 14 games all season, third-string catcher Roy Spencer, and 20-year-old spare outfielder Fred Brickell, while Cuyler moldered on the bench. "The whole thing is a mystery to me," said Cuyler.[67] Barnhart was no slouch — he hit .313 during the World Series — but he was no Cuyler, either. Most managers seem to believe that the best way to win a World Series is to put the best players on the field. Bush might have felt that way, too, but he had a point to prove.

In the opener, errors by second baseman George Grantham and catcher Earl Smith led to three unearned runs as the Yankees broke out to a 4–1 lead in the third inning. The Pirates clawed back to within a run in the eighth when first baseman Joe Harris — picked up on waivers from the Senators in February — singled in Glenn Wright. But with runners at the corners, relief ace Wilcy Moore got Smith to ground out, and then set down the Pirates in order in the ninth inning to preserve a 5–4 victory. It was a maddening day for Traynor, who failed to come through three separate times with a man on third base and two out.

Pipgras overcame first-inning jitters to shut down the Pirates on seven hits in Game Two, 6–2. "I was fast that day," he said. "Didn't throw but three curves. They kept coming up there looking for the curve but never got it."[68] Yankee pitching again dominated in Game Three in New York. Pennock almost wrote history, taking a perfect game into the eighth inning, but Traynor spoiled it with a one-out single to left field. The next batter, Barnhart, doubled him home but the Yankees still won comfortably, 8–1. "Pennock smoothed us out with very little trouble," mourned Lloyd Waner. "He wasn't the type who threw the ball past you — he just made you hit it right at somebody."[69] As Pennock explained, "When I have got control I can pretty near [make] the ball do anything I want."[70]

The Yankees finished off the Pirates the next afternoon. With the game tied, 3–3, New York loaded the bases with no one out in the bottom of the ninth inning. Pirate reliever Johnny Miljus struck out Gehrig and Bob Meusel and was on the brink of escaping the jam. But while working to Tony Lazzeri, Miljus unleashed a big, sidearm curveball that sailed past catcher Johnny Gooch and allowed Earle Combs to scramble home from third with the winning run. "What a funny way the crowd took it," thought Traynor. "It seemed as if most of the fans didn't know what was going on."[71] Lloyd Waner reacted just like the fans. "For a couple seconds I didn't budge, just stood out there in center field. Couldn't believe it, I guess. It's no way to end a ball game, much less a World Series, on a doggone wild pitch."[72]

Traynor later argued that the grueling pennant race had left the Pirates "worn to a bone," while the Yankees, who cruised to the pennant by 19 games were well-rested and in peak form.[73] "We'd have given those Yankees plenty of hell if we hadn't been all in. I guess they were a better ballclub, but we'd have given them plenty of hell."[74]

Traynor was a quiet 3-for-15 in the Series, causing one writer to declare, "The utter inability of Wright and Traynor to help in the pinches was one of the greatest weaknesses of the Pittsburgh team."[75] It was an anticlimactic coda to a solid year in which Traynor batted .342 and drove in 106, the first of five consecutive seasons of more than 100 RBIs.

Traynor collected his $4,000 loser's share of the World Series money and instead of going back home, headed directly to Wisconsin. He went to Massachusetts to see his parents and siblings for a few days over the holidays but then immediately beat it back to Yellow Lake. One gets the impression that Traynor was beginning to drift apart from family for some reason, but it is impossible to know what the problem was, or even if there was a problem.

A researcher seeking to decipher the dynamics of Pie's relationship with his family is like an archaeologist trying to understand a lost civilization. It comes down to analyzing the few fragmentary clues available and trying to make some educated guesses. In the end it feels like the more one knows, the less one knows. The people who had the most direct knowledge have been dead for years. No diaries or other such memoirs seem to exist. What's more, Traynor simply did not discuss family with outsiders. Bill Cardille, one of Traynor's pallbearers and a close friend, wasn't even aware that Traynor had siblings.[76] According to Don Riggs, who worked alongside Traynor at a Pittsburgh television station in the 1960s, "He came off as a hale-fellow-well-met guy, but when it came to talking about life, he'd clam up."[77] There were certain topics that were off limits and Traynor's family apparently was one.

However, there are tiny shreds of information that, when stitched together, seem to suggest that perhaps the Traynors weren't the closest family in America. This isn't to say they didn't love one another, but they didn't express their love in all the traditional ways. Pie's niece, Marilyn Lenick, recalled that the

Traynors were not a family that went out of its way to spend time together, not even at holidays or funerals.[78] Pie, once he found his refuge at Yellow Lake, spent only a few days at home each winter. After he married, he almost never went back. It doesn't appear that any members of Pie's family attended his wedding. No blood relatives showed up for his Baseball Hall of Fame induction ceremony. Most curious of all, Pie's father was buried in an unmarked grave. Certainly Pie, pulling in a major league salary, could have provided his father a headstone but, for whatever reason, he didn't. From all that is known, the Traynors were a stable, tightly knit household when Pie was growing up, despite their financial insecurities. But over time Pie's bonds with them seemed to weaken.

Over the winter the Pirates committed an act of baseball managerial malpractice, shipping Cuyler to the Cubs for a fringe major league outfielder, Pete Scott, and an aging, fungible second baseman named Sparky Adams. Barney Dreyfuss was a shrewd operator who made many more good decisions than bad ones. This one, however, was a clunker. Cuyler surely was glad to be out of purgatory and away from a manager who treated him like an infectious disease. But he admitted later, "I was hurt and puzzled and filled with a desire for revenge."[79] In Chicago he recaptured much of the magic that had made him such a bright prospect a mere two years earlier.

Another offseason deal turned out much better for Pittsburgh. They sent Aldridge, one of Cuyler's few friends on the club, to the Giants for Traynor's pal, 34-year-old Burleigh Grimes. Grimes had begun his career in Pittsburgh in 1916, but after a pier-six brawl on a train with manager Hugo Bezdek, during which he nearly gnawed Bezdek's finger off, Dreyfuss figured everyone would be better off if Grimes were employed elsewhere. He was a four-time 20-game winner for Brooklyn, then spent 1927 with the Giants before returning to Pittsburgh.

Traynor and the Pirates were terrible for the first three months of the 1928 season as the age of the veteran pitching staff began to peek through. Other than Grimes, who was brilliant in winning 25 games, all the regular starting pitchers battled injuries and periods of ineffectiveness. Traynor was hitting .338 in early May, only to see that average plummet to .264 over the next three weeks.

Bush had fallen out of favor inside the clubhouse and out. The fans refused to forgive his shoddy treatment of Cuyler, while his players questioned his strategy and resented his ham-fisted attempts at discipline. (For a time Bush forbade his players from attending any form of public entertainment — no movies, no shows, no concerts.) The team played like it had a hangover. "I can't get a man to say a word," lamented Captain Traynor late in the season. "It's the quietest team I ever saw. They are playing ball ... like a lot of ghosts playing in a cemetery."[80] A July 4 holiday doubleheader sweep at the hands of the Cardinals dropped them to 13 games out of first place.

Three days later, July 7, was "Pie Traynor Day" in Pittsburgh. Before a doubleheader against the Giants, the Traynor Juniors, a youth league team from nearby Dormont, presented Traynor with a 51-volume set of the *Harvard Classics*. The Traynor Day committee had planned to purchase him a hunting rifle. But when they checked with him, Traynor, who enjoyed reading on trains and in hotel rooms, told them he preferred the books. After the Bucs swept the twinbill, Traynor hustled over to the Schenley Hotel, where more than 500 people paid $10 apiece to attend a banquet on his behalf. The evening dragged on for four hours with one interminable speech after another, but in the end a bleary-eyed Traynor walked away with a chest filled with $2,000 in gold coins.[81]

From late July through the end of August Traynor went on the longest tear of his career and almost single-handedly pulled the Pirates back into the pennant race. By the time August ended he had hit safely in 36 of the previous 38 games and in the process had boosted his average from .297 to .352. He had 12 hits and 13 RBIs as Pittsburgh took four straight from Philadelphia. Later he went 7-for-8 with eight RBIs, three triples, and three runs scored in a doubleheader sweep of those same pathetic Phillies. Over the course of a three-game series against the Braves, Traynor piled up ten more hits and moved into the top five in the league in hitting. The Pirates went 23–9 in August, set a team record with 247 runs scored that month, and drew to within 6½ games of first. However, they ran out of steam in September and crossed the line in fourth place, 8½ out.

Traynor finished with a mark of .337, sixth in the National League and second on his own team behind Paul Waner's .370. He was second to the Cardinals' Jim Bottomley with a career-best 124 RBIs (despite just three home runs), and made his best showing in the Most Valuable Player voting, coming in sixth. For what it was worth, he also established a major league record with 31 sacrifice flies, although he benefited from a new scoring rule that, for a time, credited a batter with a sac fly even when runners advanced without scoring.

The Pirates were transitioning into a new era. Old pitching stalwarts Meadows, Yde and Morrison were gone or on their way out, while the trusty Kremer was showing signs of decline. Dreyfuss had given away Cuyler for a couple of buttons, a paper clip, and a pile of string. Glenn Wright reportedly partied too much, never quite met the Pirates' lofty expectations, and got himself traded in December. Management broke up the venerable catching tandem of Smith and Gooch. Smith was released, fittingly, after a clash with Bush, while Gooch was traded to Brooklyn. Traynor was about to turn 30. Injuries and illness would chisel away at him for the rest of his career.

The future looked so promising for the Pirates at the end of the 1924 season. They were young, immensely talented, and had the look of a team that could have built a National League dynasty throughout the mid-to-late 1920s. They did win two pennants and a World Series, so it would be inaccurate to call them a bust, but there was nothing dynastic about them, either. And now the window had slipped shut.

8

Not a Kid Anymore

Traynor, who never bothered to get a driver's license, caught a ride out to Wisconsin with the Pirates colorful clubhouse man, Caleb "Socko" McCarey. They stopped at Burleigh Grimes' home in Ohio, stocked up on hunting supplies, and headed north. McCarey's heap broke down twice — first in Indianapolis, then again as they crossed the Wisconsin border — before it finally wheezed and belched its way into the camp in mid-late October.

Traynor and McCarey had a Felix Unger/Oscar Madison kind of relationship. "Socko was very cantankerous and they were always arguing. If you said the sky was blue, Socko would say it was white. He would argue about anything," recalled Bob Gustine. "Pie would jab at him good-naturedly. He would argue religion and politics with Socko all the time, just for the sake of arguing."[1] But beneath their little pseudo-quarrels thrived a long and rich friendship. That scene with McCarey at the wheel, Traynor riding on the passenger's side, the two men sniping at one another relentlessly, would be re-enacted countless times over the next 40-plus years.

Traynor again found the relative solitude of Yellow Lake to be exactly what he needed. His attitude at the outset of spring training 1929 surprised the *Pittsburgh Press'* Ralph Davis. According to Davis, Traynor had always brimmed with enthusiasm for the start of baseball season, but not this year. He longed for a little more time hiking through the snow and playing bridge with the guys.[2]

With Glenn Wright now in Brooklyn, Donie Bush revived the idea of moving Traynor back to shortstop full-time. Bush thought he had a suitable replacement at third base in rookie Jim Stroner, who hit .367 and belted 42 home runs for Wichita in 1928. Bush was making a gutsy call. Third base is a more physically demanding position than shortstop; therefore, it is fairly common for a player in his late 20s or early 30s, whose range is diminishing, to switch from short to third. But moving successfully from third to short in mid-career, as Bush was demanding of Traynor, is rare indeed. Furthermore, this wasn't just any third baseman. Traynor was almost universally regarded as the best in the game, one of the top defensive players who had ever played the position. Barney Dreyfuss thought Bush was out of his mind.[3] But if Traynor was nursing any similar thoughts, he didn't let on. By all indications he not only was eager for the challenge, he also took Stroner under his wing, as he often did with young infielders, helping him learn the ropes at third base.

The experiment was short-lived because Stroner simply was not ready to compete. He had undergone an appendectomy in the offseason and was still far from full strength. In addition, both Stroner's mother and young wife had died within the past year. The man was a physical and emotional wreck. He appeared in only six games with the Pirates, was sent down to the minors, and never made it back. Stroner's minor league statistics look like those of someone who probably could have played in the majors, someone who might have played well, in fact.[4] But he never got a second chance.

Traynor, meantime, had his own troubles. Early in camp, he felt some soreness in his hip and lower back, a problem that had first surfaced over the winter. He indulged in mud baths, which helped for a while, but then the pain returned on March 18 while the Pirates were in San Francisco for a pair of exhibition games. An X-ray revealed what a physician ominously described as "a slight twisting of the lumbar spine sacrum and some calcification along the tuberocity of the ischium." ("It must be terrible to have anything like that," mused Bush.[5]) Traynor tried to play in a couple more exhibition games, but it was torture. By March 31, he could hardly walk.

He left the team in Houston the next day and traveled to Fort Worth, Texas, to meet with Dr. G.F. Nemitz, a chiropractor who had practiced in Hot Springs, Arkansas, when the Pirates trained there. Nemitz solved the puzzle, at least partially, and after a week of treatment, Traynor was healthy enough to work out again. Over the coming months Traynor underwent heat treatments several times a day. The discomfort, which most often bothered him at night after games, would flare up in varying degrees of intensity all season. He was never 100 percent, but he declared himself ready to go for the April 16 season opener. Traynor started at third base and batted cleanup, going 3-for-5 with two runs scored to lead the Bucs over Chicago, 4–3.

Traynor's back problems and Stroner's myriad difficulties forced Bush to abandon his dreams of Traynor, the shortstop. Instead, the skipper filled the hole at short with 20-year-old Dick Bartell. Bartell was an intense, hard-nosed player. He also was cocky, prickly, and loud, the kind of guy who rubbed a lot of people the wrong way. He and Traynor would spend the next two years getting on each other's nerves.

Bartell caustically referred to his time playing alongside Traynor as "a real learning experience."[6] Though he acknowledged Traynor was "a great ball player," he also called him "the toughest third baseman to play alongside that I'd ever played with."[7]

Like many others who played his position, Traynor believed that a third baseman's duty was "to range as far as possible on grounders to your left."[8] But to Bartell's way of thinking, that was selfish. "A ball would be hit toward me at short. As I came in to field it, Pie would cut across in front of me trying to get it. Usually he would miss it, but as he crossed in front of me I'd lose sight of it. I was charged with plenty of errors that way."[9]

In his autobiography, Bartell tells of approaching Traynor and asking him to stay a little closer to the bag at third. The request, which Bartell probably did not phrase in the most diplomatic of terms, was not well received. "Don't you call me off," Traynor snapped. "I'll tell you what to do. I'm going to take everything I can."[10] There wasn't much Bartell could say to that. "[Traynor] wasn't my idea of a great team player. But I never called him off again."[11]

Traynor never struck out much, but in the early weeks of 1929, he wasn't striking out at all. His first whiff did not come until May 30, when the Cubs' Charlie Root got him. For the season, he fanned a mere seven times in 540 at-bats, one of the 20 best ratios in modern baseball history. Over his entire major league career, which spanned 14-plus seasons, Traynor struck out just 278 times. As a point of comparison, Mark Reynolds of the Arizona Diamondbacks struck out 204 times in 2008 alone. To be clear, though, one could hardly describe Traynor as a selective hitter. He swung early, often, and at anything, and was nearly as difficult to walk as he was to strikeout. But his superior hand-eye coordination and bat control let him venture out of the strike zone and not only hit bad balls, but hit them with authority.

Though Traynor was making lots of contact in April and May, he was not hitting particularly well. But come June, as was typical, he sizzled. From May 28 through June 11, he hit safely in 12 straight games, with an average of .438. The day after his streak ended he went 3-for-5 with three RBIs, singled in the tying run, and scored the winning run in a 7–6 ninth-inning comeback over the Giants, a victory that moved Pittsburgh into first place. The next day he stroked two triples and scored three more times as the Pirates downed New York again. For June, Traynor batted .395 and drove in 29 runs, despite playing part of the month with a broken nose, suffered when he was hit in the face by a fastball from the Cubs' Pat Malone. The Pirates entered July in second place, trailing Chicago by just a half-game.

Traynor's hits were coming off a hefty old 42-ounce bat he shared with Paul Waner. The two men had salvaged the bat a couple of years earlier, from either Giants catcher Shanty Hogan or a minor league outfielder from the San Francisco Seals, depending on which version of the story is believed.[12] "We had taped it and nailed it together as long as we could," Traynor reflected. "I guess Paul and I must have made more than 600 hits with it."[13] Traynor scavenged bats wherever he could find them; he told a writer in 1931 that he hadn't used a brand new bat since his rookie season. "I liked to get old ones, with the lumber well-seasoned ... they had more oomph and drive in them."[14] Teams in those days didn't have bat racks; they just lined up their bats in the dirt in front of their dugout. Traynor often would amble over to the opposing dugout, look over the lumber and, if he found a heavy one that looked good, he'd swipe it. "I'd find one that suited me in the Giants' [bats], for instance, and I'd tell Bill Terry I was taking it. What could he say but, 'Sure, go ahead, Pie.'?"[15]

On the other hand, Traynor was as meticulous as could be about his gloves.

Some players develop close, quirky, almost familial relationships with their gloves. Not Traynor. He would use a new glove for a month, maybe two, and then swap it out for a new one. He went through three gloves a season, minimum.

Traynor preferred his gloves with a felt lining, unlike most of his peers, who chose all-leather models. "The felt glove gives with the impact and makes a pocket to hold the ball or at least drops it at your feet, where you can pick it up and throw out the runner."[16] For a better grip, Traynor would rip open a new glove and remove the padding from the thumb. It was as if he wanted his glove to mold itself to the contours of his hand like an extra layer of skin. In 1939, when he was managing the Bucs, Traynor tried to foist one of his minimalist gloves on his protégé, rookie third baseman Frank Gustine. "I couldn't break it in. It was like a pancake, but Pie swore by it," Gustine marveled.[17] In a 1959 interview, Traynor questioned whether he could have played with the larger gloves that had come into vogue by that time. "The glove, not the hands, does the work now. I wonder how players can ever handle the weight [of the glove] and be dexterous at the same time."[18]

Traynor shows New York Giants manager John McGraw how it's done before a game at Forbes Field in 1925. Traynor preferred small gloves with minimal padding, trusting his massive hands to do most of the work (National Photo Company Collection, Prints & Photographs Division, Library of Congress, LC-DIG-npcc-14724).

Propelled by Traynor's hot hitting, the Pirates slipped into first place again early in July before injuries quickly dashed their pennant hopes. On July 11, Traynor homered and drove in three runs as the Pirates beat Philadelphia, 6–2, and extended their lead to two games. But he also hurt his groin while stretching for a ground ball. That injury, combined with his recurring back pain, put him out of action for three weeks. On July 20, Burleigh Grimes, who had a record of 16–2, was struck in the hand by a line drive. He didn't pitch again for a month, and when he returned he was ineffective. Less than a week later, sweet-swinging second baseman George Grantham suffered shoulder and ankle injuries when he collided with Paul Waner in shallow right field. Grantham missed two weeks. By the time Traynor got back in the lineup August 2, the Bucs were five games out and falling fast.

Pittsburgh played barely better than .500 ball the rest of the way. The Pirates simply didn't have the horses to keep pace with the Cubs and their army of bashers that included Kiki Cuyler, Rogers Hornsby, Hack Wilson, and Riggs Stephenson. In late August, after a disastrous 5–12 road trip, Donie Bush surprised everyone by handing in his resignation. Bush was miserable in Pittsburgh. He had wearied of the constant sniping from Pirate fans, didn't have a great relationship with his players, and found Barney Dreyfuss to be dictatorial and hyper-critical. Bush returned to his beloved hometown of Indianapolis, declaring, "I am back in a good town now and I believe my lifespan will be longer."[19]

Dreyfuss elevated Traynor's good friend, coach Jewel Ens, to the managerial post on an interim basis. Ens was a former Pirate infielder and longtime member of the coaching staff, an easygoing man who was popular with players and fans. Pittsburgh played decent ball under Ens, but Pirate fans didn't seem to care; they already had checked out. Two games against Brooklyn in mid–September were intimate little gatherings, with only 400–500 people in the stands. Pittsburgh finished 10½ games out, a distant second to the Cubs.

Traynor, whose average had been up to .372 in early September, labored through his injuries for the remainder of the month and slumped to .356, still good for seventh in the National League. For the fourth time, the Baseball Writers Association of America named him their all-star third baseman. There were rumors that Traynor would be offered the Pirates' managerial position, but Dreyfuss was satisfied with the way the Bucs played under Ens and asked him to return in 1930.

Some medical specialists, along with Dreyfuss, urged Traynor to remain in Pittsburgh following the season to receive ongoing treatment for his back. Specifically, they wanted to encase him in a body cast to strengthen his spine.[20] Traynor, however, was a man who couldn't sit still for 30 seconds at a time. Years later, dying of emphysema, he was still running around giving speeches and doing TV commercials. Dreyfuss might as well have asked him to spend the winter in a coffin. Instead, Traynor devised his own rehabilitation plan:

more hunting and fishing in Wisconsin. "I'm the kind of fellow who can't stay indoors," he once said.[21] That winter the back pain vanished just as quickly and mysteriously as it had appeared a year earlier. As Traynor came into spring training, his offseason companion, Burleigh Grimes, assured everyone, "Traynor is in the greatest condition of his life."[22]

Instead of going home at Christmas, Traynor enjoyed a rollicking holiday season with Pirate pitcher Heine Meine, who owned a speakeasy in the St. Louis area. Legendary *New York Times* columnist Red Smith, then a young writer with the *St. Louis Journal*, spent a few hours with Traynor and Meine and later recalled, "Heinie's store was genteel in a knock-down-drag-out way, and the specialty of the house in those prohibition days was a brand of moose milk that would peel the paint off a battleship."[23]

One day Traynor and Meine passed up the lure of the bar and headed into the woods for some duck hunting. After a fruitless start, Traynor finally gunned down a couple of birds, only to watch them tumble out of the sky and splash down into a swamp. "I told Pie he had better forget about the ducks because the only possible way to get across there was to swim," Meine recalled.[24] He was talking sense. It was the dead of winter. Taking an outdoor dip in cold, fetid, watery goo was not going to be fun.

On the other hand, Traynor really wanted those ducks.

So he stripped buck naked, swam 50 feet across the swamp, tied the ducks around his neck, and swam back to land. Meine stood there dumbstruck, his jaw nearly on the ground right next to Traynor's drawers. "When Pie decides to do anything, he believes in going through with it."[25]

The big storylines in spring training 1930 involved Grimes and Traynor. Grimes was a holdout, demanding a two-year contract, which would have been unprecedented for the Pirates. Dreyfuss always firmly insisted on one-year deals for all players, coaches, and managers. A pair of other issues further complicated the negotiations. One, Ens did not really want Grimes around after the two men had an angry confrontation the previous September. Second, Grimes was in the middle of an ugly, embarrassing divorce, the lurid details of which were splattered all over the papers. Burleigh's wife of 17 years claimed her husband was an adulterer and offered as evidence syrupy love letters that two of Grimes' female admirers had sent him. Grimes countered that his wife was a spendthrift who bounced checks, ran up debts, and frittered away $50 on a punch bowl that she used as a laundry basket.[26]

Dreyfuss met with Grimes on April 7 and concluded that although he had won 42 games for the Pirates over the last two seasons, he wasn't worth the trouble. "No man can expect to have a good season on the diamond whose interests are divided," the Pirates owner declared. "I discovered that his marital difficulties were much more in his mind than baseball."[27] On April 9, Dreyfuss pawned Grimes off on the Boston Braves for pedestrian left-hander Percy Jones, who would appear in just nine games for the Pirates before disappearing from the majors forever. Grimes only had two more good years left in him, but, all in all, it was a rotten trade for Pittsburgh. Traynor was disappointed to see his buddy sent away, but he knew the drill. "It's all in the game. You're here today and somewhere else tomorrow.... Every player understands that."[28]

Traynor's problems, though much less titillating than Grimes', were potentially more serious. He had experienced strange sensations in his left eye while he was in Wisconsin over the winter — some involuntary twitching and mild pain — but he didn't think anything of it until he arrived in California. "After a time in Paso Robles, I took the salt water baths and I don't think they did it any good.... After I had taken a couple of those baths my eye became inflamed."[29] A major infection had taken hold.

Physicians initially leaped to the conclusion that bacteria had spread from two of Traynor's teeth into his eye, and their first line of treatment was to extract those diseased teeth.[30] This was typical of the half-baked thinking that often passed for modern medicine at the time. Many physicians' first inclination when presented with any number of symptoms was to reflexively yank teeth or cut out tonsils. Only when that failed would they start thinking critically about what was causing the patient's problem.

As Traynor accompanied the Pirates on exhibition games up and down the coast, he bounced from doctor to doctor, none of whom did anything that helped. Finally on March 30, as the club made tracks for Texas, the Pirates sent Traynor back to Pittsburgh to see Dr. Stanley Smith. An April 2 photograph shows Traynor arriving in the city, walking through the train station bareheaded despite the cold weather (unlike most men, Traynor seldom wore hats; he feared they would make him go bald) and wearing sunglasses to shield his eye.[31] He was optimistic. "The doctor in 'Frisco told me that it would be 3 to 6 weeks before my eye would be OK. I am hoping, however, that I will be ready for Opening Day."[32]

Though he could hardly see out of his eye at the time, Traynor maintained a gallows humor about his plight, joking that if his vision didn't improve he might try umpiring.[33] Nonetheless, it would have been out of character for a worrywart like Traynor if he were not freaking out a little bit, especially given that early in his career he had been somewhat obsessive about his eyesight.[34]

Dr. Smith's treatment helped for a while. Traynor could have played in the opener at Cincinnati but it was raining, and the doctor recommended that the Pirates hold him out; no need to take a chance. But within days the infection came raging back. Traynor missed Pittsburgh's first 16 games before finally breaking into the lineup on May 6. "My vision isn't perfect, but I believe it will do no harm to play."[35] He had trouble focusing when he turned his head quickly, but he successfully handled two chances and banged out a pair of hits in his season debut, an 11–9 loss to the Giants. That evening a crowd of more than 500 gave him a rousing ovation when he rose to speak at a testimonial dinner for Ens at the Schenley Hotel.[36]

Traynor's vision rapidly deteriorated again, and now he really was concerned. He described it as like a film that had spread across his eye.[37] On May 10 he found himself at the renowned Wilmer Eye Institute at Johns Hopkins Hospital in Baltimore, where he remained for a week while doctors ran a battery of tests. Traynor was back on the field May 21, although his eye remained sensitive to glare for at least another month.[38]

The 1930 edition of the Pirates was Dreyfuss' least competitive outfit since 1923. In addition to Traynor's eye problems, Lloyd Waner sat out almost the entire first half after undergoing an appendectomy in January. It was rough sledding for the pitching staff early on, too. Other than Ray Kremer, Erv Brame, and 22-year-old Larry French, Ens couldn't find anyone who could stay healthy and get people out. The Pirates couldn't catch a break. On August 18, Havey Boyle of the *Pittsburgh Post-Gazette* wrote, "Ens right now would not be greatly surprised if a girder from the grandstand tore itself loose, walked over and bumped Jewel on the bean, and then moved back into its place."[39] Though they were in first place for most of the season's first three weeks, Pittsburgh faded rapidly and never seriously threatened, ending in fifth place, 12 games out. Their record of 80–74 was their worst in a decade.

In the midst of this Traynor quietly enjoyed a sensational season at the plate. His best day came, as was often the case, in Baker Bowl against the Phillies in a July 23 doubleheader. His homer in the ninth inning of the first game won the game, 2–1. Later that afternoon he drilled a three-run homer in the 13th inning to break a 13–13 tie and give Pittsburgh a 16–15 victory in one of the wackiest games in history. It ran three hours, 41 minutes, nine minutes shy of a major league record. The Bucs and Phillies set records for at-bats and total bases in a single game. Traynor was 5-for-7 and accounted for nearly half the Pirate runs, with four scored and four more driven in.

Traynor hit .366 in 1930 with nine home runs and 119 RBIs in just 130 games. His on-base percentage of .423 was the best of his career, the only season in which he registered an OBP higher than .400. He did not play well defensively. His fielding percentage of .941 was the lowest of his career to that point. Traynor still covered a lot of territory around third and, in fact, for most of the season he performed at his typically high level. But in early August, out of nowhere, his old problem with wild throws returned as suddenly as if someone had flipped a switch.

Though no one said so at the time, it is quite possible Traynor was experiencing the first trace of the shoulder problems that would dog him throughout the latter part of his career. There is no other obvious explanation for such an overnight loss of accuracy. Though most fans and writers continued to praise Traynor as baseball's premier defensive third baseman for a few more years, his reputation outlasted reality. After August 1930, he was never the same.

Also in August the Pirates were playing an exhibition game in Terre Haute when Traynor showed up at the park with a surprise for his teammates—a dia-

mond engagement ring. Traynor had proposed to his girlfriend, 26-year-old
Eva Helmer, a telephone operator at the Havlin Hotel in Cincinnati, where the
Bucs stayed when they were in town. Eve (as she preferred to call herself) apparently had met Pie sometime in 1929, and they carried on a long-distance
courtship, mostly on the telephone.[40]

Eve was born in Aberdeen, Ohio, about 60 miles southeast of Cincinnati,
on November 21, 1904, the oldest child of Jacob and Adelia Helmer. She had a
younger sister, Jean, and a baby brother, Dale. When Eve was an infant, the
family relocated to another exurb of Cincinnati, Brookville, Indiana, a town
at the crossroads of the Midwest and the South. Eve never lost the faint echo
of a Southern twang that crept in around the edges of her voice.

The Helmers were a solid, respectable, middle class, small town family.
Jacob, the son of German immigrants, was a tradesman who made his living
hanging wallpaper and painting houses, while Adelia tended to the kids at
home.[41] But their divorce in 1923, and Jacob's subsequent marriage to a woman
almost half his age, barely older than his oldest daughter, surely set some
tongues wagging around Brookville.[42]

Eve's parents were very different people. Actually, Jacob was a little like
Pie, outgoing and popular with a good word for everyone. "[Jacob] was a real
people person, real engaging," recalled Eve's nephew, Mike Helmer. "Right
before he died, he and my step-grandmother took a trip to California. That was
something he really wanted to do. When they came back from that trip he
brought back some oranges, and he walked around the small community of
Brookville and found various people that he knew and gave each of them an
orange."[43]

Eve took after her mother in many ways. "[Adelia] was much more of a
sophisticated kind of person [than her husband]; someone I would have seen
a small-town life being pretty dull for," Mike Helmer believed. "She was very
polished in her appearance. I saw characteristics of my Aunt Eve in my grandmother in terms of that."[44]

After their split, Jacob remained in Brookville, while Adelia, who never
re-married, moved to Cincinnati and forged her own way. She owned some
rental properties and apparently did quite well for herself.[45] Eve and her sister,
Jean, joined their mother in Cincinnati. Jean actually moved in with her mom
but Eve, perhaps the more independent of the two sisters, lived at the YWCA,
about a 10-minute walk from her job at the Havlin.

Though he was well-to-do, famous, and handsome, Traynor had always
been uneasy around women. It is impossible to trace Traynor's romantic history pre–Eve, but certainly he had opportunities aplenty. Even in the 1920s,
baseball players were popular targets for attractive gold diggers with a taste for
cash, and randy, young ingénues looking for a romp.[46] If Eve was Traynor's first
woman, either his self-discipline or his awkwardness must have been unfath-
omable. But a Lothario he was not. One reporter called him "girl shy."[47] Traynor

confessed that before meeting Eve he had become resigned to lifelong bachelorhood.[48]

Eve was an unlikely mark for a man with such insecurities. She was dauntingly hot, a leggy brunette with dramatic features and a slightly reticent manner — a nice person, just not one who warmed to strangers easily. But Pie melted her reserve, hanging out in the Havlin's lobby when he was in town, making idle conversation. When she was too busy to talk, Pie would linger around her workstation, looking nonchalant, awaiting an opening.[49]

He was smitten. "Aunt Eve was a presence — very, very striking and attractive in her appearance and her manner," according to Mike Helmer. "She was someone who would enter a room and people would just gravitate toward her. It seemed like that's how the relationship was between Eve and my uncle. He was a pretty well-established bachelor, but I think he was charmed by her."[50] Eve was a baseball fan, too, so presumably that helped mitigate any bashfulness Pie might have felt; at least they had some common ground upon which to launch a conversation and build a relationship.[51]

Traynor and his fiancé intended to marry in the offseason, but first there was more baseball to be played. He attended the first two games of the Athletics-

Unwinding with a cold brew in Cuba in October 1930. Traynor was part of a contingent of major leaguers selected to play in a series of exhibition games in Havana that fall. *Left to right*: Traynor, Brooklyn third baseman Wally Gilbert, Washington outfielder Heinie Manush, and Cincinnati catcher Clyde Sukeforth (Helen Zimmerman).

Cardinals World Series in Philadelphia and then headed outside the United States for the first time in his life, sailing to Havana, Cuba, as part of a contingent of 27 major leaguers invited to the island by wealthy brewery owner Don Julio Blanco Herrera. Herrera was eager to shine a spotlight on his country and generate more national interest in baseball. To that end he came up with the idea of a seven-game series, beginning on October 10, featuring some of the top baseball talent from the States. Nine future Hall of Famers participated. The players split into two teams, one led by Jewel Ens, the other by Braves manager Dave Bancroft. Ens' unit, which included Traynor, won five of the seven games.

The Cuban fans were enthralled. "They had tremendous crowds," related Brooklyn catcher Al Lopez. "They didn't have enough capacity in the grandstands so they roped the field off on ... the left field side and the right field side."[52] The grandson of Red Sox outfielder Russ Scarritt was under the impression that each player was paid $1,000 per game, but historians Bill Nowlin and Kit Krieger speculated in 2005 that it was more likely that Traynor and each of his teammates received $1,000 for the entire series rather than per game.[53]

For the first time since 1925, Traynor did not winter in Wisconsin. Instead, he spent a month at home with his parents in Arlington, Massachusetts, before departing for Cincinnati right after Christmas to meet up with Eve for their wedding. The ceremony on January 3, 1931, was a tiny affair in the parlor of the First Presbyterian Church of Walnut Hills in Cincinnati.

The Traynors' honeymoon took them first to Missouri, where they spent three weeks as guests of Heinie Meine and his wife.[54] Then they drove out to Southern California, which would become their favorite winter vacation spot. (Eve fantasized about someday settling down with Pie in a cozy home in a small town along the Pacific coast.[55]) In San Diego they met up with a friend from Pittsburgh, Art Rooney, and his wife, Kathleen, who also were enjoying their honeymoon. Rooney was a noted amateur athlete and horse player in the Pittsburgh area; within two years he would help create the National Football League and become the longtime owner of the Pittsburgh Steelers.

San Diego was kind of a sleepy city, not much happening. But Tijuana, just over the Mexican border, was nuts. Alcohol flowed freely and legally (unlike in the United States) and people could lay their money down at the track (unlike in California, which had banned gambling on horse racing). It was a good spot for young couples who wanted to have some fun. The Traynors and Rooneys had hotel rooms in San Diego, but in the evening they often slipped into Tijuana where they dined at elegant restaurants, probably enjoyed some drinks, and wagered at a popular horse racing park known as Agua Caliente, where "the racing was lawless and wild and the Americans loved it."[56]

One night the Rooneys and the Traynors got carried away and stayed too late. When they arrived back at the border crossing, customs officials told them it was closed for the night. "Oh, they were upset," said Art Rooney, Jr., as he

Harold and Eve Traynor, at their wedding ceremony on January 3, 1931, in Cincinnati (Bettmann/Corbis).

related the story that has become legend in the Rooney family.[57] The newlyweds were forced to get creative. "They had to go up to one of the gates in their dresses and everything and crawl under the fence, just like the illegal immigrants did."[58]

Having survived Meine's speakeasy and the adventures in Tijuana, Eve accompanied her husband to spring training. This was somewhat unusual for the time, but Eve made it a habit, appearing at spring training every year for the rest of Pie's career.

Traynor's erratic throwing continued to haunt him that spring and into the season. Several years later, the *Pittsburgh Post-Gazette* confirmed that Traynor played the 1931 season with a torn ligament in his shoulder.[59] He compensated by altering his throwing motion and dropping down sidearm. That was easier on his shoulder, but both his arm strength and accuracy fell off dramatically. Decades later, with advances in sports medicine, a surgeon probably could have gone in and cleaned up the problem area, and after some rehab Traynor likely would have been almost as good as new. But in 1931 there were not many solutions. He just had to suffer through it and manage as best he could.

He was troubled by what was happening to him. Any prolonged slump, either in the field or at the plate, always drove him to the brink. As one scribe put it, "Few players chafe under adversity as does Traynor."[60] Prior to the Pirates' game on May 7, after committing his third error in the first 20 contests, Traynor spent an hour taking extra infield, working on his throwing. It didn't help. Actually, as the season went on, he got much worse, chalking up a career-high 37 errors and a grisly .925 fielding percentage, second from the bottom in all of baseball among regular third basemen.

Traynor's defensive decline was an apt metaphor for what was happening to the Pirates. They bore not even the faintest resemblance to a pennant-contending team, spending only one day in the first division all year; after May 25, they never climbed higher than fifth place. Barney Dreyfuss, dwelling on his club's problems and mourning the loss of his son, Sam, who died of pneumonia in February, confessed in August, "This season has been a nightmare for me."[61] The Pirates' record of 75–79 was their first losing mark since 1917. Dreyfuss dismissed Ens following the season and brought back George Gibson to manage the team.

Traynor did not let his defensive problems compromise his hitting. He played in every game, batted .298 (in a season where offense was down markedly league-wide thanks to a deadened baseball) and knocked in 103 runs, the seventh and final time he exceeded 100 RBIs. He ended in the top 15 in league MVP voting and was named to the *Sporting News* all-star team for the fifth time.

On September 23, Traynor appeared at the grand opening of the Wagner Traynor Company, a sporting goods store he founded in partnership with Pirate legend Honus Wagner at 709 Liberty Avenue in downtown Pittsburgh. A newspaper ad featured a banner reading "The Old and the New" with pictures of the two Pirate greats side-by-side.[62]

Looking back, it is glaringly apparent their venture was doomed from the start; the United States was, after all, in the early days of the Great Depression. But in fairness, at the end of 1930, the Pittsburgh Chamber of Commerce was confident the city had escaped the worst of the economic downturn. Unemployment was at 12 percent — significant, but not as bad as the 15–25 percent figures in nearby cities like Cleveland, Buffalo, Cincinnati, Philadelphia, and Baltimore. In 1931, however, the bottom dropped out. Pittsburgh's production of pig iron and soft coal were down over 40 percent. The steel industry was operating at 40 percent capacity.[63] Joblessness spiked. Hoovervilles popped up. During those years it was not uncommon to see people rooting through garbage cans scavenging for a half-eaten sandwich. There wasn't much disposable income left over for baseball mitts and golf clubs.

The Wagner Traynor Company went bust in little more than a year, although the friendship between the two men remained strong. Traynor dined frequently at Wagner's home and was on a committee that raised $50,000 to finance a statue of Wagner, which was unveiled outside Forbes Field in 1955, months before the old shortstop's death.[64] But the disastrous sporting goods venture combined with steep losses in the stock market devastated Traynor's net worth. Though he never hit skid row, he never felt financially comfortable again, and he long rued his decision to go into business. "A man can't pay attention to two things at once," Traynor declared in 1950. "His nerves can't stand it — especially if he is worn down physically."[65]

Traynor's life was transforming steadily and profoundly. Only a few years earlier he was a footloose kid — perfect health, no responsibilities, money hanging out his ears. His ballclub was a winner and he played the game with an exciting combination of childlike exuberance and brash, swaggering confidence. But it was all changing now. His money was vanishing down a rat hole, his arm was falling off, and his team had descended into mediocrity. Furthermore, the rumors of his becoming a manager, which first surfaced in 1929, were soon to become reality, for better and for worse.

9

Endings and Beginnings

Traynor spent six weeks in Wisconsin with Eve, then rode to California where they spent the remainder of the winter of 1931-32. It was a busman's holiday for Traynor, who spent much of his time at Los Angeles' Wrigley Field working with Frankie Jacobs, the Los Angeles Angels trainer, to get his arm back into shape.

On February 5, just before the start of spring training, Barney Dreyfuss died at the age of 66 following a two-month battle with pneumonia. His passing sent the day-to-day operations tumbling into the hands of Dreyfuss' owlish, mild-mannered son-in-law, 39-year-old Bill Benswanger. Just a year before, Dreyfuss had persuaded a reluctant Benswanger to walk away from a thriving insurance business to help him run the Pirates in the wake of Sam Dreyfuss' death. "I was just there because I was the only man in the family," Benswanger once said.[1]

The new Pirate president had been a baseball fan since he was kid. He attended Pittsburgh games at old Exposition Park, and was in the right field bleachers for the opening of Forbes Field in 1909.[2] Over the years he developed a nuanced appreciation for the game and its history. His first love, though, was music. He was a classically trained pianist and served on the board of the Pittsburgh Symphony.

As a club president, Benswanger wasn't meddlesome, but he was involved. He attended home games, pencil in hand, keeping score and jotting down his observations while chewing on his ever-present pipe. Benswanger also had a flair for creativity and innovation. He spiced up the Pirates bland uniforms by adding a bright red "P" on the chest of the home jerseys and the word "Pirates," also in red, on the road jerseys (black and gold didn't replace red and blue as the team colors until 1948). He instituted promotions like Kids Days and Ladies Days and gave the go-ahead for the installation of lights at Forbes Field in 1940.[3]

All in all, though, life as a baseball executive provided Benswanger little joy. It was one thing to be a fan, but to be in charge of a major league team was a heavy burden that left him bent and bowed. A writer once labeled Benswanger "a baseball fatalist."[4] He was anxious, jittery, and sometimes relentlessly pessimistic. Later in life, ruminating about his 15 years running the Pirates, he sounded like a man who wished Dreyfuss had left him alone to sell insurance. "We had nothing but trouble. I took over in the depths of the Depression. After that it was World War II. Then came the effort to unionize players [in 1946]. It was one headache after another."[5]

It appeared Benswanger had inherited a bad ballclub. Manager George Gibson admitted he expected 1932 to be a rebuilding year. Other than Traynor, the infield, in particular, was very green. At first base was 26-year-old Gus Suhr, entering his third year with the Pirates. Suhr looked like a superstar in the making when the Bucs purchased him after he posted outlandish numbers for the San Francisco Seals in 1929, including a .381 average with 51 home runs.

Suhr never quite lived up to his advance billing and a lot of fans resented him for it; he heard more boos and catcalls over the years than he probably deserved. The Pirates, however, could have done much worse than Gus Suhr as their starting first baseman. He was a remarkably durable player, appearing in 822 games in a row at one point; only his mother's funeral forced him out of the lineup. He did not hit for average but compensated by drawing a lot of walks, popping 10–15 home runs a year, and playing solid defense.

In the middle infield, Gibson put his chips on a pair of rookies. At second base was Tony Piet, a former gymnast who grew up in the anthracite coal region of northeast Pennsylvania. Light-hitting veteran Tommy Thevenow began the year at shortstop, but after he hit just .196 through the first two weeks of the season, Gibson benched him in favor of a 20-year-old from Arkansas named Joseph "Arky" Vaughan, who had just one year of minor league experience. Vaughan had trouble in the field early in his career, but Honus Wagner, who joined the coaching staff in 1933, tutored him (and roomed with him) and helped transform him into a solid defender. At the plate, Vaughan didn't need any help. He finished in the top 10 in the National League in batting average and OPS (on-base percentage plus slugging percentage) seven times and led the majors in both categories in 1935.

Vaughan never seemed to get the respect he deserved, either. There are several possible explanations for this. First, he did not play on great teams. His World Series record consisted of two at-bats at the tail end of his career. Second, he split his career between Pittsburgh and Brooklyn, and players who are not strongly identified with a single team sometimes, for some reason, get lost in history.[6] Third, he had the personality of a hubcap; a thoroughly decent and honorable fellow, but very quiet and very serious, not the kind of person who was destined to be a darling of writers or fans. Historian Bill James surprised even himself when he landed on Vaughan as the second greatest shortstop ever, behind only Wagner.[7]

Twenty-four-year-old Larry French was back to anchor the pitching staff after winning 32 games in 1930 and 1931. Joining him was rookie Bill Swift and 28-year-old Steve Swetonic, a local boy who once killed a batter with a pitch while on the mound for the University of Pittsburgh.[8] Swetonic had amazing stuff but a long history of arm problems. Gibson had his fingers crossed that Swetonic could get through the season without shredding his elbow.

The Pirates, along with Traynor, did a pratfall coming out of the gate. The Pittsburgh third baseman hit just .206 in the spring, and then committed errors in each of the Pirates' first two regular season games; the second error cost his team the game. The Pirates lost 12 of 15 from late April into early May and dropped into last place, 10 games out. The season had hardly begun, but already it appeared to be over.

Despite all the trouble his aching shoulder had caused him, Traynor, to his credit, had never begged out of the lineup. But on May 27 his streak of 316 consecutive games came to an end after he slammed that shoulder into the shinguard of St. Louis catcher Jimmie Wilson in a close play at the plate. He missed a week of action. This was the first in a long series of tête-à-têtes between Wilson and Traynor, who spent much of the next decade exchanging physical and verbal haymakers. The following season, Traynor came in spikes-high on Wilson, which nearly triggered a brawl between Traynor and his friend, Burleigh Grimes, Wilson's teammate. In 1934, Wilson fell on Traynor's arm in another close play at the plate and further wrecked his shoulder. When both men were managers, Wilson publicly accused Traynor of double-crossing him and cheating him out of a gifted right-hander named Russ Bauers. In 1940, Traynor cited the 40-year-old Wilson's presence at catcher for the world champion Reds as evidence that the quality of the game had gone to seed.[9]

The Pirates worked their way up toward .500 near the end of May and into June. Then in late June Traynor finally broke free of his early-season malaise and helped the Pirates make a big push. On June 25 he hit a pair of home runs in a doubleheader sweep of Cincinnati, which moved Pittsburgh into second place. The next afternoon, the Pirates swept the Reds again 5–0 and 9–5, for their fifth and sixth consecutive victories, and moved into first place by percentage points over the Chicago Cubs. Traynor's three-run inside-the-park home run in the first game broke a scoreless tie, and his leaping stab of a Wally Gilbert liner helped preserve Larry French's first shutout of the season. On June 30, with the Pirates wearing numbers on their home jerseys for the first time, Traynor (sporting uniform number 20) went 4-for-5 and stole a base in a 9–6 win over St. Louis that kept the Pirates in first place by a half-game.

But for all the damage he was doing at the plate, Traynor was killing his club at third base. His error on the Fourth of July was his 18th, which dropped his fielding percentage to an unacceptable .911. His injured arm had been his biggest problem, but now at age 33 it looked like his legs and reflexes were starting to go, too. A writer observed, "Pie is not the agile fellow he once was and there has been a perceptible slowing up in his movements around third."[10] However, he pumped his batting average up to .342 shortly after Independence Day and the Pirates, with a 3½-game lead, were the surprise of baseball.

Traynor attributed his outstanding offensive first half to a change in eating habits. "I have taken to eating meat again," he told the *Pittsburgh Post-Gazette*. "I was a vegetarian for quite a while, but I am now convinced that meat is essential for anyone in active life.... I've got more heft to my swing."[11]

Unlike many of his contemporaries who saturated themselves with alcohol or gorged on unhealthy foods, Traynor was keenly mindful of what he was putting into his body. Much of his adult life he liked to experiment with his diet, although some of his ideas about nutrition were unorthodox, to say the least. For example, shortly after returning meat to his plate he became fixated on eating spinach. "There's no arguing with Pie once he makes up his mind," said his wife. "Spinach is good for him, he's certain. He should have it every day. So he does."[12] Traynor also recommended a dish of applesauce every morning to help stay fit.[13] When he managed the Pirates, he forbade his players from consuming bottled drinks and shrimp for a time out of a fear they would lead to stomach problems.[14] His friend, Jack Henry, wrote, "Pie's health views would rock the medical fraternity yet I can vouch for several people who have profited by his unusual tips on diet."[15]

Traynor obviously was doing something right. He was never out of shape and always reported to spring training in peak condition. Even into his 70s, he looked strong and lean, hardly a hint of a belly on him.

On July 7, in the middle of a 14-game hitting streak, Traynor suffered a stomach-churning injury. A throw from pitcher Heine Meine glanced off Traynor's poorly padded glove and bent back the tip of his left index finger at a macabre angle. For the next two weeks, Traynor was limited to pinch-hitting duty, but he was still able to make an impact, funky finger and all. The day after the injury he delivered a pinch-hit single and came around to score the winning run in an 8–7 victory over the Giants. A week later his pinch-hit single and stolen base were key to a two-run ninth-inning rally as the Pirates completed a doubleheader sweep of Boston.

The Pirates were playing marvelous baseball. From May 18 until July 29, they won 50 games and lost just 21. Swetonic's record was 11–2, Swift was 10–3, and Paul Waner was challenging for a batting title. Pittsburgh's lead over the Cubs was six games and Pirate fans had reason to be excited again. A July 28 *Pittsburgh Post-Gazette* headline trumpeted that the Bucs were "Marching Along to the World Series."[16]

But without warning their march came to a halt. After taking six of seven from the staggering New York Giants, the Pirates went to Philadelphia, where they lost four straight to a better-than-usual Phillies team (this would be the only season from 1918 to 1948 in which Philadelphia would finish above .500). That triggered a catastrophic stretch in which the Pirates lost 14 of 15 and watched their six-game lead morph into a one-game deficit in just two weeks. George Gibson initially pooh-poohed the suggestion that his young club was shrinking under the pressure of a pennant race. "It's nonsense to say a thing like that. We just haven't been getting the breaks."[17]

By August 25, Swetonic's elbow had given out and he was done for the season. Traynor was hitting just .265 for the month (an especially unproductive pace given that he seldom drew walks), which prompted Gibson to drop him from the clean-up spot to sixth in the batting order. Pittsburgh had fallen to third place, seven games back, just four games over .500. "I'd say the team has been pressing too hard," Gibson conceded. "That's the only answer I can give."[18]

The Pirates won 10 straight from late August through early September but it didn't do them much good because the league-leading Cubs won 14 in a row during that same stretch. Chicago, which went 37–18 after replacing cantankerous manager Rogers Hornsby with Traynor's old teammate, Charlie Grimm, won the pennant by four games over Pittsburgh (and went on to vote Hornsby a zero share of their World Series bonus money).

Traynor returned to form both offensively and defensively during the season's final weeks. He racked up two milestones: his 2,000th career hit on August 30 and his 1,000th run scored four days later. (In May he had appeared in his 1,500th major league game.) Overall, despite his injuries, Traynor put together a fine season at the plate. He finished with a batting average of .329 and an OPS of .806, which was 64 points above the National League average. He ran third in the *Sporting News* National League MVP voting behind Philadelphia's Chuck Klein and Brooklyn's Lefty O'Doul. The Baseball Writers Association of America named him the game's top third baseman, even though his glove work was inconsistent and, as a whole, unexceptional.

Traynor left the Pirates at the end of the season knowing his father was gravely ill. James Traynor had been stricken by colon cancer that spring. A few weeks after the baseball season ended, James checked into Pondville Hospital in Norfolk, Massachusetts. Pondville was about 40 miles away from the Traynor home in Arlington, but it boasted one of the first cancer treatment centers in the United States.

He never made it out. James died at 4:30 in the morning on January 5, 1933 (former President Calvin Coolidge died about eight hours later, less than 100 miles away).[19] He was 56 years old. Word of James' death spread quickly to Pie's teammates scattered across the country, many of whom sent flowers to the funeral ceremony. With her husband gone, Pie's mother went to work cleaning office buildings to support her three children remaining at home.

The Depression that was laying waste to the country did not make an exception for baseball. The game was suffering through hard times and clubs were hemorrhaging money. Traynor questioned baseball's reaction to the crisis. For one, he criticized teams for scheduling what he felt was an over-abundance of doubleheaders. The intent was to draw larger crowds by giving fans a bargain, two games for the price of one, but Traynor believed it was a short-sighted tactic. "I suppose you might draw a parallel with a fellow who likes ice cream. He may eat a pint a day, but suppose he was given a quart. It probably would spoil his appetite sooner or later.... I think baseball will come back without such [an] artificial stimulant.... All we need [in Pittsburgh] is a year of steady work. Then the folks will begin to get their debts paid off and will be back with us."[20] He also thought the doubleheaders exacted an unacceptable physical toll on players. Ten years earlier, he might not have minded, but in his mid–30s one game a day was plenty.

Clubs cut corners everywhere to make ends meet. They eliminated coaching positions, slashed salaries, and benefited from a new rule that reduced the major league roster size from 25 to 23 players. But some owners didn't think it was enough. "The overhead must come down," pleaded Cardinals owner Sam Breadon. "Club owners, in view of the times, realize that something must be done to give us all a chance to break even. This means still greater reductions in the pay of players than was the case [for] 1932."[21]

Traynor thought the owners' public bellyaching, legitimate though it might have been, was counter-productive. "It's bad for the customers and very bad for the athletes," he declared. "Constant crying about the necessity of reducing overhead and news that this player has been traded because of his high salary and that fellow [is] dissatisfied because of a sliced salary will make the public wonder if the baseball is going to be inferior."[22]

There was no crying from Traynor. Benswanger held his 1933 salary at $13,000, down from where it had been from 1929 to 1931. He had absorbed a $1,000 pay cut in 1932 and was proud that he "took [it] without moaning."[23] Of course, Traynor was well aware of the suffering the country was going through; he was going through a little bit of it himself now that his sporting goods store had gone toes up. He was grateful for every paycheck. "We're so lucky to be making a living this way," he said.[24]

But over the years, he might have been thankful to a fault. Uncomfortable with face-to-face disagreement and direct confrontation, he never once held out for more money during his career. In fact, it seems he never really negotiated a contract. Negotiations, such as they were, consisted of Traynor acquiescing to the Pirates' first offer and signing as quickly as possible, often before leaving Pittsburgh for the winter. He certainly made much more money than the average major leaguer, but among the game's elite players, his salary was at the low end of the spectrum.[25]

It is hard to say whether a more secure person with a stronger stomach might have wrung a few more dollars out of ownership. Dreyfuss and Benswanger were notoriously tight with a buck, and under the reserve clause, without the possibility of free agency, players had little leverage. But either way, if Traynor had never bargained with the Pirates, he certainly wasn't going to start in the early 1930s, with millions of Americans hungry and the economy in tatters. "I was making a lot more than a lot of my friends back home who were on WPA."[26]

One man back home with one of those Works Progress Administration jobs was Pie's brother, Robert Creswell Traynor. Bob was the third-oldest child, born just 10 months after Pie, on September 24, 1900. He was a man of diverse interests—he loved opera, played a mean piano without being able to read a note, and enjoyed cooking. But like his father and most of his siblings, Bob was a blue collar guy all the way. During the Depression he worked in a mill until his younger brother, John, arranged for him a construction job helping to build the Quonset Naval Air Station in Rhode Island.

While working at Quonset, Bob was the victim of a near-fatal industrial accident. In some ways he recovered, in other ways he didn't. Physically he was fine. But his daughter, Marilyn Lenick, felt like she grew up with two different fathers—one before the accident and one after.[27] Bob always had been happy-go-lucky, quick with a smile. He still flashed that side from time to time, but he also became prone to moodiness and unpredictability, though he wasn't violent in any way. His wife, Laura, was the steady hand who kept the family of six on an even keel. Bob later worked at the University of Rhode Island for 15 years and then became the caretaker of the Bonnet Shores Beach Club in Narragansett, Rhode Island. He was 83 years old when he died on December 27, 1983.[28]

The Pirates' surprising second-place finish created some high expectations coming into the 1933 season. "We have an experienced pitching staff.... That counts for a lot," said Traynor.[29] They also had acquired former New York Giant Fred Lindstrom, who was expected to add some punch to the lineup as the everyday left fielder, while Lloyd Waner shifted to center field. In addition, Arky Vaughan, who batted .318 as a rookie, was only going to get better.

The first month of the season went mostly as planned. Traynor, enjoying an unusually productive April and May, went 2-for-4 on May 19 to help the Pirates to a 6–2 win over the Phillies. The victory rounded out a series sweep and put the 19–8 Pirates 1½ games in front of the New York Giants atop the National League. Traynor was leading the team with a .376 average, and just as importantly, he was playing third base like the Traynor of old. He again had received treatment on his arm throughout spring training and he was hopeful that his problems had been cured. His throws were strong and sure.

But by early June, cracks were beginning to show and Pittsburgh slipped out of first place. Vaughan had committed 18 errors in 38 games at shortstop. Heine Meine, one of the Pirates most reliable hurlers the previous two seasons, was pitching reasonably well with a record of 5–3, but Gibson was frustrated with his inability to finish games. "Meine has bogged down on us the last few tries.... That isn't helping us get back into first place."[30] He went from May 15 to June 18 without completing a game. Lindstrom, who as a Pirate appeared to play baseball as if it were "nothing more than a prosaic job, a thing of routine and hours," temporarily lost his starting job on June 3 after a .269 start.[31]

On top of all that, Traynor suddenly could not get the ball across the infield. The *Pittsburgh Press'* Volney Walsh marveled at how Traynor's arm "acts very naturally on some days and resembles a rubber hose on others."[32] That pretty much summarizes how it went from late 1930 onward. Traynor would go weeks without an error, looking great, and then just like that he would hit a streak where even the most routine play could turn into a debacle.

A bad throw on a sacrifice bunt attempt on May 30 led to four unearned runs in a 6–2 loss to Chicago. The next afternoon another throwing error on a simple force play resulted in three more unearned runs, all the Cubs would need in a 3–1 victory. On June 8, he made three wild throws, two on consecutive plays, in an 8–2 loss to the Reds. He accumulated nine errors in June, hit a weak .250 for the month, and, with his frustration boiling over, was thrown out of a game for just the second time in his career. The Pirates June record was 12–18, which dumped them into third place, six games out of first. "The last month has been a nightmare," said Gibson.[33]

Nearing the season's halfway point, excitement was building for the first major league All-Star Game, scheduled for July 6 at Comiskey Park, home of the Chicago White Sox. The game was the baby of Arch Ward, sports editor of the *Chicago Tribune*. By the 1990s, the All-Star Game had lost much of its competitive spirit, but at the outset and for many years thereafter, it was a heated battle for supremacy between the American and National leagues. Woody English, who represented the Cubs in the inaugural game, captured the intensity of the rivalry in an interview more than 60 years later, when he was 87 years old. "To this day I still root for the National League. I'm a National Leaguer. That's your family."[34]

Fans voted on which stars they thought deserved to be at Comiskey. Traynor was the sixth-highest vote-getter in all of baseball, receiving 304,101 votes. He was far and away the leader among National League third basemen, receiving more than three times the number of votes as Pepper Martin of the St. Louis Cardinals.[35]

In Traynor's mind, the honor of playing in the All-Star Game represented a capstone for his career. Traynor was not a notably sentimental man. He did not hold on to much memorabilia from his career (unlike his wife, who apparently was determined to clip and save every newspaper article that so much as mentioned her husband's name). But it seems telling that one of the few keepsakes he retained was his uniform from the 1933 All-Star Game.[36]

Given the personal significance he attached to the game, it is understandable why Traynor was fuming when he arrived in Chicago and discovered Martin was starting at third base. In later years, fan voting would determine the starting lineup. But in 1933, fans simply voted for the players they wanted on the team. The managers could start whomever they pleased. Traynor was well aware that being the top vote-getter at third base did not guarantee a spot in the lineup; nonetheless, he was stunned to find himself on the bench. "And so was Pepper Martin," said Traynor.[37]

Pirate fans and Pittsburgh writers pointed accusatory fingers at National League manager John McGraw. "We feel a great injustice has been done Traynor as well as the fans who voted for him," stated B.N. Leonard, in a letter to the

1933 NATIONAL LEAGUE ALL~STAR TEAM

HARTNETT, WILSON, FRISCH, HUBBELL, WALKER, WANER, ENGLISH, SCHUMACHER, TRAYNOR, LOTSHAW,
HALLAHAN, BARTELL, TERRY, McKECHNIE, McGRAW, CAREY, HAFEY, KLEIN, O'DOUL, BERGER.
HASBROOK, MARTIN, WARNEKE, CUCCINELLO.

Pittsburgh Press.[38] Many fans believed McGraw put Traynor on the bench because he hated the Pirates, but that probably was not the case. True, the rivalry between Pittsburgh and McGraw's Giants had been bitter, but McGraw had tremendous respect for Traynor and heaped acclaim on him every chance he got.

In fact, it was Traynor's understanding that McGraw, in very poor health and out of baseball for a year, had deferred the lineup selection to Brooklyn manager Max Carey, a member of the National League coaching staff.[39] Traynor believed it was his old friend and teammate who had knifed him in the back. "Carey was funny like that. Martin was the hero of the 1931 World Series and Carey thought the crowd wanted Martin. Carey did funny things."[40]

The wound never healed, according to sportswriter Roy McHugh. "I don't think Pie ever got over what Carey did. He thought about that for the rest of his life."[41] Martin arguably was enjoying a slightly better season than Traynor to that point, but McHugh believed Traynor's overall body of work, which spanned more than a decade, should have carried the day. "If anyone deserved to [start] the first All-Star Game, it was Pie, even though he was nearing the end of his career."[42] The kicker was that Martin had never played a full season at third base. He was mostly an outfielder prior to 1933.

McGraw summoned Traynor to pinch-hit for Dick Bartell in the seventh inning. After fouling off a handful of two-strike pitches from the great Lefty Grove of the Philadelphia Athletics, a resolute Traynor ripped a double. "I wasn't going to let him strike me out," he said.[43] Grove escaped the inning unscathed, however, and went on to preserve a 4–2 victory for the American League.

The Pirates continued to look like a very ordinary team in the second half. Late in August, with Pittsburgh still in fourth place, a reporter asked Benswanger if Gibson would return in 1934. "I haven't made up my mind yet," Benswanger answered.[44]

Following that less-than-robust endorsement of their skipper, the Pirates ripped off eight straight wins to move into second place, though they remained seven games behind New York. Traynor hit .447 with nine RBIs during that span, including a pair of ninth-inning game-winning hits. In order to remain in contention the Pirates needed to win at least four games of a five-game set against the Giants, which began on September 5. Pittsburgh won three, enough

Opposite: The National League squad for the inaugural All-Star Game, July 6, 1933, at Comiskey Park in Chicago. *Left to right, front row:* Gilly Hasbrook (batboy), Pepper Martin, Lon Warneke, and Tony Cuccinello. *Middle row:* Bill Hallahan, Dick Bartell, Bill Terry, Bill McKechnie (coach), John McGraw (manager), Max Carey (coach), Chick Hafey, Chuck Klein, Lefty O'Doul, and Wally Berger. *Back row:* Gabby Hartnett, Jimmie Wilson, Frankie Frisch, Carl Hubbell, Bill Walker (batting practice pitcher), Paul Waner, Woody English, Hal Schumacher, Traynor, and Andy Lotshaw (trainer) (Sporting News/ZUMA Press).

to take the series, but not sufficient to change the tenor of the race. Traynor made a critical error in the third inning of the final game of the series, when his wild throw allowed Jo-Jo Moore to reach base. Moore eventually came around with New York's first run, and the Giants went on to win, 2–1. The next afternoon, when he threw one away on an easy play against Brooklyn, Traynor received a rare chorus of boos from Pirate fans.

The Pirates ended the season in second place, never a serious threat to the Giants. Traynor put up solid numbers at the plate, including a .304 average with 82 RBIs and a .342 on-base percentage, 15 points above league average. He came in eighth in the National League Most Valuable Player voting, although he finished ahead of some players who had much better seasons statistically, including Arky Vaughan. He was the third baseman on the *Sporting News* all-star team for the seventh and final time.

Traynor again spent the bulk of the winter in California undergoing treatment on his shoulder, but by the time spring training rolled around, his wing was worse than ever. At the time, it was common for regulars to play full games during the exhibition season, but Traynor couldn't do it in 1934. He would play five, six, or seven innings before heading to the bench; the pain was more than he could bear. On April 15, two days before Opening Day, the *Pittsburgh Press* wrote, "Pie is just getting to the point where he can begin to whip the ball across the diamond without fear of seeing his arm wing its way toward first base, too."[45]

It was all he could do to throw the baseball back to the pitcher after an out. A reporter described his way of lobbing the ball back to the mound as "about as unorthodox as any similar toss in the league. There is almost a feminine air about it."[46] The man many thought was the greatest third baseman ever to walk the face of the earth had been reduced to throwing like a girl.

After committing three errors, all on throws in the dirt, in the season's first four games, Traynor requested that George Gibson remove him from the lineup. He needed time to get well. "I've been doing the club more harm than good.... When I throw the ball it feels as though it weighs a ton. I simply can't get the ball across the diamond."[47] The pain in his shoulder was so bad, so relentless, that he had trouble sleeping through the night.

Although the original plan was for Traynor to sit out three or four days, it was a full two weeks before he felt well enough even to throw a baseball on the side. But then after a few practice tosses on May 6, he walked away with his shoulder throbbing again. Traynor made the occasional pinch-hitting appearance, but for the most part he sat and stewed for more than a month, discouraged at how his body had let him down. He acknowledged he had become "pretty sick and tired of sitting on the bench. I go out and make the speeches while the rest of them play ball.... I've been chairman of the Pirates' lecture bureau."[48]

Traynor's injury was "the only semblance of a cloud in an otherwise high sky" for the Pirates.[49] Thanks in large part to Vaughan, who was leading the National League in hitting, Pittsburgh was just a half-game out of first place by the time Traynor got back into the lineup on May 23. He hit well upon his return. By June 6, his batting average was .405 and Gibson had elevated him to third in the order.

By mid–June, however, that high sky had started to look gray. The Pirates lost three of four at home to Brooklyn, and then proceeded to drop three straight to the Giants. The final game of the series, played at Forbes Field before a sizeable Sunday crowd on June 17, was a fiasco. Pittsburgh looked terrible, losing, 9–3, as the fans booed Gibson lustily every chance they got. The Bucs had fallen to fourth place, 7½ games back. For the third straight year a promising start to the season had come a cropper.

Two days later, on the morning of June 19, Traynor was at his apartment when the phone rang. It was Bill Benswanger, who asked Traynor to report pronto to the Pirate offices in the Flannery Building. Benswanger and Gibson had just concluded a morning meeting, during which the Pirate president apparently asked Gibson to consider stepping aside. "If you think I'd better quit, release me today," Gibson replied. "Otherwise, let me finish out the season."[50] Benswanger took the first option. Gibson was out.

When Traynor arrived, Benswanger offered him the job of player-manager and Traynor immediately accepted. "We have been in a bad slump, much worse than we think a team of our caliber should be in, and the change is an effort to secure better results," Benswanger said. He added later, "I didn't fire Gibson. The fans of Pittsburgh did that. I just carried out their orders. Sentiment crystallized very suddenly against him."[51]

Traynor flips through a stack of congratulatory telegrams in the clubhouse at Forbes Field shortly after being named the Pirates' manager on June 19, 1934 (copyright © 2009 *Pittsburgh Post-Gazette*; all rights reserved; reprinted with permission.).

Gibson, Traynor, and Benswanger broke the news to the team just before they were scheduled to leave the clubhouse for pre-game warmups. It was an awkward meeting, with Gibson shaking Traynor's hand and exhorting the club to give their new manager their best effort.[52] Gus Suhr took over Traynor's role as captain.

Traynor spent much of his time before the game posing for photographers in the Pirate dugout. With Eve decked out in a dark patterned dress and wide-brimmed hat, watching from her usual spot in the first row of the second level at Forbes Field, the Pirates lost Traynor's managerial debut, 5–3. Traynor started at third and collected two hits while letting coaches Doc Crandall and Honus Wagner handle the work along the coaching lines.

Traynor described himself as "excited" about his new job.[53] Havey Boyle of the *Pittsburgh Post-Gazette* visited Traynor at home that evening and came away with a slightly different impression. "[Traynor] was fired with nervous ambition and anxious thoughts.... He knew it was no easy affair."[54] Eve was concerned about what her husband had gotten himself into. "I'll worry more than ever now because Pie is a worrier. He worried so much as a player, think what he'll do as a manager."[55] She knew her man. Traynor would run the Pirates for 5½ seasons and not without some success. But that success carried an emotional price tag. It soon would become apparent that in many ways Traynor — sensitive, neurotic, and averse to confrontation — was psychologically unsuited for the role of major league manager.

The Pirates won for the first time under their new manager on June 20, when they beat the Braves, 6–5. Traynor largely had himself to thank. He went 4-for-5 with three doubles and three runs scored, including the game-winning run in the bottom of the ninth inning. Traynor had his Pirates playing better for a while, as they won 10 of their first 16 games for their new skipper. Granted, half of those games were against Philadelphia and Cincinnati, the dregs of the league, but the new manager appeared to be making an impact. When he was hired he insisted, "We have a fast team and we must take advantage of our speed if we are to get anywhere."[56] For a few weeks it looked like that message had gotten through. "Traynor has done something to them. They're hustling," wrote Volney Walsh in the *Pittsburgh Press*.[57]

Moreover, one of Traynor's first personnel decisions proved to be an astute one. He made a starter of 34-year-old right-hander Waite Hoyt, the former Yankee who defeated the Pirates in the 1927 World Series. After New York traded him in 1930, Hoyt bounced from the Tigers to the Athletics to the Dodgers and then to the Giants, with limited success at each stop, before he signed with the Pirates in 1933.

Hoyt made his first 22 appearances out of the bullpen in 1934 before Traynor converted him back into a starter, where he was brilliant, finishing with a 15–6 record and a dazzling 2.93 ERA. It might have helped that Hoyt, an alcoholic, hadn't had a drink in more than a year.[58] The veteran right-hander's approach to his craft endeared him to Bill Benswanger. "It always made me think of an architect and his design. Every pitch had a meaning and a purpose, whether or not it succeeded."[59]

Traynor again received more all-star votes than any other National League third baseman and this time he started the game, which was played July 10 at the Polo Grounds. In the seventh inning he became the first player — and, as of 2009, the only one — to steal home in an All-Star Game, scoring on the front end of a double steal with Mel Ott of the Giants. He also drove in a run on a fifth-inning single and scored on a Joe Medwick home run, but the American League was able to survive and pound out its second straight victory, 9–7.

The apparent jolt the Pirates received from the managerial switch was fleeting. On July 17, with Pittsburgh back near .500, 11 games out of the race and in fourth place, Traynor gave a characteristically blunt assessment of the Pirates' pennant prospects—he didn't think they had a chance. "Perhaps the manager of a fourth place club should make a lot of claims and threats, but I'm being honest instead of optimistic."[60] It might not have been the tactful thing to say, but astute observers, including Havey Boyle, seemed to agree. "It is not ... indifference.... There is no serious dissension.... It is only because the boys can't put good pitching and good hitting together. And this can only mean one thing: It is a bad ball club."[61]

Traynor knew he couldn't perform miracles with the limited talent on hand, but that didn't ease his mind or reduce the intense strain he felt. By early August, just six weeks into the job, he already was losing ground. "I just can't help it. I go to bed at night and can't get to sleep. Often I awaken more tired than when I crawled between the sheets. I'm of a nervous temperament at all times, and piloting a team which isn't going anywhere has taken its toll."[62] He apparently wasn't eating properly; in his first two months as manager, his weight dropped ten pounds and his batting average tumbled right along with it. "I was discouraged and downcast and often wished I was just a player with no other worries."[63]

Traynor beat himself up like this throughout his entire tenure as manager. He worried incessantly, lost alarming amounts of weight during the season, and smoked like a fiend; at particularly stressful times, he was known to inhale an entire pack between games of a doubleheader. The moments of satisfaction were fleeting. The apprehension and torment were endless. It was not a healthy situation, either physically or emotionally.

All of this begs the question of why Traynor would put himself through this torture for as long as he did. In a perverse way, leading the Pirates probably gave him a feeling of comfort and safety. Given his age and chronic shoulder trouble, he certainly realized the end of his playing days was drawing near — a disconcerting thought for a lot of professional athletes. For nearly two decades baseball had been Traynor's life. Without the game, he would have been forced not only to find a new job but also, just as importantly, create a new identity for himself. It seems Traynor figured that managing, despite all of the angst it brought him, was more meaningful and lucrative than any other career options that were out there. He probably was right.

The 1934 Pirates finished 74–76, well out of contention. Paul Waner and Arky Vaughan had tremendous seasons and Gus Suhr was decent, but no one else in the lineup did much of anything. The Pirate pitching staff, with the exception of Hoyt, was similarly undistinguished. Traynor missed small chunks of the second half with a series of minor injuries, including another smashed nose suffered when he failed to handle a tricky hop on a low throw. His hitting declined after he became manager and his OPS was below league average for the first time since his rookie year. Traynor's appearance on the Associated Press all-star team, where he barely beat out Pinky Higgins, who had a career year with the Athletics, said more about his reputation than his performance.

Traynor's recent offseasons had been easy and laid back, as he camped in Wisconsin or cavorted with Eve in the Southern California sun. But major league managers didn't have the luxury of five months of downtime. They spent their winters sitting in meetings, negotiating trades, and occasionally soothing the hurt feelings of a player bent out of shape over his latest contract offer. As Traynor was quickly learning, his new job provided precious little time for escape and a mountain of unfamiliar challenges.

10

Squeezing Orange Juice from a Potato

The way the final weeks of the 1934 season went down had Traynor steamed, and he poured those feelings out at a banquet held for Pittsburgh sportswriters that fall. "I did not go through the latter part of the season with my eyes closed," he said. "I did not fail to notice that several of the so-called sick boys got their health back when the season closed. It was no secret to me that one or two ballroom favorites didn't show much on the field, but probably would win prizes as dancers."[1]

Unvarnished comments like that endeared Traynor to the press, if not always to his players. He was good copy and always gave it to the reporters straight. "[Traynor] pulls no punches ... [and] is at all times entertaining," wrote one columnist. "He discusses the strengths and weaknesses of his club as casually as a mailman talking about his daily route."[2] For instance, in the middle of praising his team for a splendid month of play in 1936, he took time out to make one pointed exception. "I don't think [Al] Todd has been a great catcher for us the last few weeks."[3] In 1938, the Pirates needed a spare infielder and re-signed 34-year-old Tommy Thevenow. Asked what he expected out of Thevenow, Traynor replied flatly, "Not much."[4]

Traynor's candor did not stop with assessments of his own team. According to Bill Nash of the *New York World-Telegram*, "As a player, Pie never opened his kisser, but since being manager he has popped off about all the trades made by other pilots."[5] He ventured that Giants manager Bill Terry had ruined New York's pennant chances by acquiring Burgess Whitehead to play second base in 1936. He also infuriated his old *bête noire*, Dick Bartell, in 1938 by suggesting that the Cubs made a mistake trading for Bartell because he was too old to hold down the starting shortstop job.

Traynor enjoyed the daily give-and-take with writers. He was brutally honest but also easy to talk to—patient, courteous, completely without pretense. In 1934, his first season as manager, Traynor sat down in the Wrigley Field dugout with a very young reporter named Steve Snider. Snider, nervous and struggling to keep his thoughts straight, sensed the interview was going nowhere ... until Traynor rescued him. "We're rookies together, so I'll just start talking and we'll see what happens," Traynor said.[6] He went on for the next hour. At the opposite end of his tenure, after he had resigned under pressure, Traynor alerted Les Biedermann of the *Pittsburgh Press* that Bill Benswanger was planning to replace him with Frankie Frisch. "How many times does a departing manager tip you off on his successor?" Biedermann asked rhetorically.[7] "I never forgot the favor."[8]

In return, writers seemed to give him the benefit of the doubt when his teams failed to meet expectations. Under Traynor, the Pirates usually were a reasonably competitive first-division club, but many around baseball felt they should have been better. Traynor's teams had a reputation for lethargic play on the field and wild, out-of-control behavior off it. "His players didn't respect him," accused Bartell. "When one got into a brawl and wound up in the police station, Pie would bail him out and keep it quiet. No fines. No suspensions. No leadership."[9] But for the most part, the press defended Traynor, castigating the players rather than criticizing the manager for his failure to effectively crack the whip.

Traynor spent the winter of 1934-1935 zipping back and forth between Pittsburgh and Brookville, Indiana, Eve's hometown and the place where the Traynors made their offseason home. They lived well in Brookville. For a time they shared a roof with Eve's father and stepmother, then rented a beautiful 14-room mansion called the Hermitage, which once had been an artists' colony and home of noted Indiana painters J. Ottis Adams and T.C. Steele.[10] Pie and Eve wanted to buy the place, but one of Adams' heirs refused to part with it. "They wanted that Hermitage so bad," said Eve's half-sister, Mary Jessop.[11] Traynor spent his winters in Brookville hanging out at the Valley House Tavern, hunting, and visiting friends. Jessop also recalled him playing baseball with some of the local children and doling out a dime to every kid who got a hit.[12]

Pie returned to Pittsburgh in late October for talks with Benswanger and Pirates vice president Sam Watters, thinking he would be in and out in 24 hours. He didn't even bring an overnight bag. To his surprise, the meetings took four days as the men plotted offseason strategy and got Traynor officially signed for the coming year at a salary $16,500, a $2,500 raise.[13]

Benswanger gave his manager considerable leeway in negotiating trades and signing free agents, and Traynor set about using that autonomy to dramatically re-shape his pitching staff. One of his first decisions, though, was a staggering blunder. In New York, the Giants grouchy manager, Bill Terry, was at odds with his brilliant southpaw, Carl Hubbell. Hubbell's signature moment had come just a few months earlier, when he struck out future Hall of Famers Babe Ruth, Lou Gehrig, Jimmie Foxx, Al Simmons, and Joe Cronin in order at the All-Star Game. But Hubbell, who set career highs in innings pitched and appearances in 1934, complained to reporters that his manager was overworking him.[14] Terry, in a snit, put Hubbell on the trading block and offered him to the Pirates. His demands were modest; all he wanted in return were Larry

The Hermitage in Brookville, Indiana. It was a one-time artists' colony where the Traynors made their offseason home in the mid–1930s (Martha Shea).

French and Fred Lindstrom.[15] Traynor, given a chance to acquire the best pitcher in baseball, said no.

It is not clear what exactly Traynor was thinking. Perhaps he believed Hubbell, who was 31 years old and threw his screwball with such violence that he permanently disfigured his arm, was a likely candidate for elbow problems. Instead of bringing Hubbell on board, which might have instantly made the Pirates the favorites to win the National League, Traynor dealt French and Lindstrom to the Cubs for pitchers Guy Bush and Jim Weaver and colorful outfielder Babe Herman.

Terry, who, like Traynor, told it like it was, predicted the Bucco skipper would regret his decision. "Weaver and Bush are not going to win as many games as some of their boosters are predicting. Bush is a good pitcher, but he's not what he once was."[16] Terry was prophetic. Weaver actually wasn't bad; he gave the Pirates a couple of solid seasons. But Bush was a major disappointment and Herman was worthless. Hubbell's elbow did indeed blow up, but not until he won 23, 26, and 22 games for the Giants from 1935 to 1937.

The Pirates shifted their training camp site south in 1935, moving from Paso Robles to San Bernardino, about 60 miles from Los Angeles. They relocated, in part, so it would be easier to play exhibition games against the

Chicago White Sox, who trained in Pasadena. The San Bernardino Chamber of Commerce had financed a new 3,500-seat park for the Pirates, called Perris Hill Park. It was a beautiful location, with the snow-capped San Bernardino Mountains looming behind home plate and hills beyond the outfield fence where fans could gather to watch the action.

Pie arrived in California a few weeks early for some much-needed down time with his wife. They went horseback riding at a Sonoma County ranch once owned by author Jack London and had dinner with a Hollywood buddy named Dick Powell, a Pittsburgh native and box office star of the era.[17] Traynor hit it off well with show biz types. As early as 1927 he went on a fishing excursion with a small group that included Harpo Marx.[18] Other acquaintances included Ray Bolger (who played the Scarecrow in *The Wizard of Oz*), the Three Stooges, and Joe E. Brown, a well-known vaudeville comedian whose teenage son, Joe L. Brown, worked out with the Pirates during spring training in Paso Robles and many years later became the club's general manager.[19] (In 1951, Traynor did a bit of a star turn himself when he made a cameo appearance in the movie, *Angels in the Outfield.* Eve was an extra.)

Herman's presence provided much of the buzz that spring. The longtime Brooklyn Dodger had a reputation as a clownish oaf who made silly baserunning mistakes and let fly balls clank against his glove or thud off his head. But, as he put it, "I was always a pretty fair country hitter."[20] The Babe finished in the top 10 in the National League in home runs eight times and in batting average four times. In 1930, his best season, he hit .393 with 35 homers. Traynor was willing to overlook Herman's deficiencies because he thought he was just what the Bucs needed: a big middle-of-the-order run producer. "Every season he drives in 85–95 runs. We didn't have a real slugger on the club, but now we have Babe."[21] Benswanger, though less effusive, also predicted Herman would be an important addition. "[He] isn't such a bad ballplayer. I wouldn't call him an outstanding star, but I believe he is way above the average."[22]

Herman, who raised birds at his home in California, showed up in San Bernardino with a parakeet for his new manager. The bird proved to be of more value to Traynor than Herman did. Pie and Eve had "Pete" flying around their apartment for the next couple of years. Herman played only 26 games, batting .235 with no home runs, before the Pirates gave up the ghost and sold him to Cincinnati in June.

Traynor made two nice moves in the offseason, acquiring a pair of young pitchers: Mace Brown, whom the Pirates purchased from Kansas City of the American Association, and Darrell "Cy" Blanton, who had struck out 18 and 20 batters in consecutive games for Albany of the International League in 1934. Blanton, who hunted and fished with Carl Hubbell every offseason in Oklahoma, became the talk of baseball early in 1935. On April 19, he allowed just one hit in a complete-game smothering of St. Louis (a magnificent diving catch by Traynor in the ninth inning preserved the one-hitter and ended the game).

The core of the Pirate braintrust at spring training in San Bernardino, California, on February 27, 1935. *Left to right*: **Coach Jewel Ens, Manager Traynor, and team president Bill Benswanger (National Baseball Hall of Fame Library, Cooperstown, New York).**

In his next start, Blanton fanned 11 Cincinnati Reds in a 5–2 victory. A few days later he outdueled the great Dizzy Dean and beat the Cardinals again, 3–2. Then came a three-hit shutout of Brooklyn.

Blanton kept batters guessing with a diverse repertoire that included a screwball, a blazing fastball, and a "downer," probably something like a forkball, which Hubbell called "the strangest ball I've ever seen. It breaks downward as if he were standing on top of the batter."[23] Two-and-a-half weeks into his career, Blanton was 4–0 with an ERA of 0.75.

Traynor, on the other hand, was a train wreck. He was hitting below .200 through early May and, with his bad shoulder, was flinging the ball all over the place. He contributed to Blanton's first defeat in the rookie's next start, committing three errors that led to two unearned runs in a 3–1 loss to Hubbell and the Giants. On May 13, Blanton won his fifth game, a 10–1 win over the Phillies, as Traynor went 3-for-5 with three RBIs. But the Pirate third baseman also committed two more errors, giving him seven in his last eight games and drawing boos from Pittsburgh fans.

Four days later Traynor threw away another grounder for his tenth error of the season. That was the last straw. The next afternoon, he benched himself indefinitely. It was the first time since 1924 he had sat out for any reason other than an injury. A week later, sitting on the bench observing batting practice, he said wistfully to a reporter, "Gee, I wish I was as young as some of those kids out there."[24] Except for a handful of emergency appearances, Traynor remained out of the lineup until late August.

Since he wasn't playing, Traynor was free to take his place along the coaching lines for the first time. Just watching him in the first base coach's box would have been enough to make one squirmy. He didn't say much, but he was in constant restless motion, like a man on the edge of a seizure. He paced and fidgeted and twitched and developed a nervous habit of juggling pebbles in his hand.

Perhaps the restlessness was a physical manifestation of what was happening in his mind. Between his chronic sinus trouble, the pain in his shoulder, and the excruciating strain of managing, Traynor was unable to sleep. It's not that the Pirates were playing poorly in the season's early weeks; they were slightly over .500, in the middle of the pack in the National League, about where most experts predicted they would be. But that was cold comfort for Traynor, who simply could not get out of the way of his own thoughts. "I always worried a lot as a player, but now I'm worse than ever. I can't shake myself of that habit of worrying, worrying, worrying."[25]

Perhaps the most memorable series of Traynor's managerial tenure came May 23–25, when the great Babe Ruth rolled into Pittsburgh with the Boston Braves. The Bambino had joined the Braves that winter with the understanding that owner Emil Fuchs eventually was going to give him a chance to manage. But Ruth quickly figured out that was not going to happen. By the time he arrived in Pittsburgh, he was a dispirited man, lugging around too many extra pounds and a batting average below .200.

Looking back, it is clear that Ruth was used up — 40 years old, rotund, tired, and slow, squeezed into a uniform that looked so wrong on him after all those years in Yankee pinstripes. Nevertheless, opposing pitchers and managers still handled Ruth as if he were plutonium. He drew more than 100 walks in 1934 and was on pace to approach that total again in 1935. If Ruth could do nothing else, he still could hit with power, and a lot of people didn't want to mess with him. "He was fat and old but he still had that great swing," remembered Guy Bush. "Even when he missed, you could hear the bat go swish."[26]

Prior to the series opener, Traynor sat down with his pitchers to figure out a game plan. The Pirate skipper encouraged his staff to approach Ruth very carefully. According to Waite Hoyt, Traynor stated that Ruth had "no weaknesses."[27] However, a few Bucco pitchers, most notably Bush, piped up in dissent, arguing that the Bucs had nothing to fear, that they should challenge Ruth. Bush's argument appears to have won the day. The Pirates went right at him.

Ruth muscled a couple of deep fly balls off Bill Swift in the series opener, but ended up 0-for-4 as the Bucs whipped the struggling Braves, 7–1. Swift was not one of Traynor's favorites, but performances like this one were helping him emerge from his manager's doghouse. "Bill always had plenty of stuff, but he was careless. [Now] he's getting left-handed hitting out. That means he is using his head."[28]

Following the game, Traynor and Ruth both spoke at a testimonial dinner for Rabbit Maranville at the Schenley Hotel; the former Pirate and now Brave who was about to retire. Ruth, unusually maudlin and probably pondering the end of his own career, broke down in tears during his speech. Against Jim Weaver the next afternoon, Ruth went 1-for-4 as the Braves fell, 7–6, but he did give the crowd a thrill when he pushed Paul Waner back to the right field wall in the eighth inning.

In the series finale on May 25, a bright, sunny afternoon in Pittsburgh, Ruth ventured back in time. In the first inning, he went deep off Red Lucas, the 712th home run of his career. In the third, facing Bush, who was on in relief, Ruth hit a towering shot into the second deck of the right field stands. Bush managed to keep Ruth in the park in the fifth inning, surrendering a single.

Paul Warhola (the brother of artist Andy Warhol) was 12 years old and sitting behind home plate that afternoon. As Ruth stepped in to face Bush in the seventh inning, the crowd cheered in appreciation and respect. As Warhola told it in a story that might be too good to be true, "[Ruth] pointed to a group of old guys clapping for him and said he'd put it over the roof."[29] A called shot. It was the same thing he had done (allegedly) in the 1932 World Series, when he was near the height of his powers.

Bush snapped off a curveball, which Ruth absolutely destroyed. "I never saw a ball hit so hard before or since," said Bush.[30] Not many people have. The ball soared over the 86-foot-high right field roof, caromed off the top of a house, bounced into Boquet Street, and rolled into a far-flung backyard. No one knows how far Ruth hit it. One estimate put the distance at more than 600 feet. It was the first time any batter had cleared the right field roof at Forbes Field.

The Pirates won, 11–7, but after the game all anyone could talk about was Ruth. Even a hard-bitten veteran like Traynor, who had seen Ruth in his heyday, was in awe. "Forbes Field is a triple ballpark and it didn't seem possible for anyone to hit three home runs there. But who could tell Ruth that?"[31] The Pirate manager added that the Babe's display "gave me a thrill and a chill at the same time."[32] But the homers didn't do much for Ruth's mood. According to Sam Sciullo, who was waiting in vain for an autograph, Ruth left the park radiating gloom. "Kids started running up [but] he [didn't] say a word. He was not rude, he didn't push anybody. He just put his head down and walked.... He was the original sad sack."[33]

Not long after, Traynor was a guest at a Friar's Club dinner in New York, where he was seated with a pair of legendary comedians, Milton Berle and Ed Wynn. Naturally, the subject of Ruth's three-homer day came up.

"We shouldn't have awakened him," Traynor said ruefully.

"You say he hit three home runs?" asked Wynn.

"Three big fat home runs," replied Traynor, taking the bait.

"Then he was still asleep," Wynn zinged.[34]

Ruth later told Waite Hoyt, "That was the day I should have quit. That was the end."[35] Ruth hung around for a few more grim days before announcing his retirement on May 30. His 714 career home runs stood as a major league record until 1974.

Beginning with those games against the Braves, the Pirates won 15 of 18 to improve to 31–20 and skyrocket to within three games of the first-place Giants on June 12. Better-than-expected pitching, especially from Blanton and Swift, carried the Bucs, as did the slugging of Arky Vaughan, who was hitting near .400. But a long road trip from mid–June through July 4 did them in. The Pirates won just 10 of 22 during that period, as an injured leg sidelined Vaughan for eight games and appendicitis knocked out both Blanton and Weaver.

Traynor remained hopeful his team could mount a charge. "The Giants are not going to get good pitching all the way. They cracked last year and they can crack again."[36] But the return home didn't help as the Bucs dropped nine of their next 11 to fall 14 games out on July 18. That afternoon Casey Stengel, manager of the Brooklyn Dodgers, who had just swept four in a row from Pittsburgh, said of the Pirates, "I've never seen a team with so many fine players having such a listless spirit."[37] Cubs manager Charlie Grimm came away with a similar perception when his team faced Pittsburgh. "I never saw a deader ballclub in my life."[38]

On August 20, Traynor re-inserted himself in the starting lineup, replacing Tommy Thevenow, who for a time had played surprisingly well while filling in at third base, but who by this point had come crashing back to earth. Traynor went 0-for-4 that afternoon as his average fell to .226. But over the next few days, he got on one of his absurd hot streaks where no pitcher seemed to stand a chance. On August 24, he bounced a single past shortstop Billy Urbanski in the eighth inning, knocking in the go-ahead run in a 3–2 win over Boston. Twenty-four hours later he went 4-for-6 with three RBIs in a doubleheader sweep of the Braves.

From there, the Pirates journeyed to the Polo Grounds, where Traynor enjoyed a landmark day: 5-for-5, six RBIs, and the final home run of his career (a first-inning grand slam off the Giants' Al Smith) as the Pirates battered New York, 10–2, to keep the Giants a half-game behind the Cardinals in the race for the pennant. After a rainout, the Pirates swept a doubleheader from New York, with Traynor driving in a pair of runs in each game. The Bucs ended August on a 10-game winning streak. With Traynor alive again and Arky Vaughan now over .400, the Pirates quietly had inched to within six games of first place.

But any faint pennant hopes the Bucs had faded quickly in September. The

Cubs topped the Pirates on September 1 behind Roy Henshaw, a little left-hander who beat Pittsburgh eight times in 1935. After a doubleheader loss to the Cardinals the following day pushed the Pirates eight games out, Traynor conceded, "The outlook is virtually hopeless."[39]

It was on this day that the 36-year-old Traynor made his final start of the season. It took just one terrible throw that afternoon to remind him of how badly his shoulder had deteriorated. "The ball did not carry [more than] 30 feet. I went through the motion of throwing, but the arm would not function."[40] Though Traynor would appear in a handful of games in 1937, his playing career was, for all intents and purposes, over. Had the National League had a designated hitter, he might have been able to play a while longer. After all, he still could hit a little bit. But it had come to the point where he simply could not play defense. His arm was ruined. "I hate to admit these ailments, but I can't kid myself longer. I'm getting old.... It's high time the Pittsburgh club had a brand new third baseman."[41]

Pittsburgh finished a distant fourth (behind Chicago, which reeled off 21 straight wins late in the season to capture the pennant) with a record of 86–67. Vaughan, who flirted with .400 well into September, ended up at .385 with a club-record 19 home runs. Blanton's rookie season was highly impressive — a mark of 18–13 with a 2.58 ERA, the best in baseball.

Before the season was out, Traynor had re-upped for another year at the same $16,500 salary. "His work has been highly satisfactory," declared Benswanger. "We've never had a more conscientious or loyal manager."[42] Conscientious was a good descriptor. He reportedly spent every morning before home games in conference with Benswanger, discussing the state of the team. After tough losses, it was common for Traynor to linger in his stuffy, smoky, windowless office deep within the bowels of Forbes Field. He and coach/confidant Jewel Ens would sit beneath the single bare light bulb that dangled from the ceiling, rehashing over and over what went wrong and what they should have done differently.

Traynor headed into the offseason hoping to improve his club in a handful of key spots. "I'd like to have an experienced catcher, another outfielder, and a sure-fire pitcher. But where can I get them?"[43] He also wanted to inject some youth into his team; he believed his veterans had a penchant for coasting much of the season before turning it on at the end when it was too late.[44]

Traynor had particular reservations about the leadership and pitch-calling abilities of his catcher, Earl Grace. He initially targeted a pair of future Hall of Famers to replace Grace, Cincinnati's Ernie Lombardi and Al Lopez of the Boston Braves. Reportedly, Braves manager Casey Stengel came to the minor league meetings in Dayton, Ohio, ready to swap Lopez for Paul Waner and was irate when the Bucs backed out of the trade, although the Pirates insisted Stengel had jumped the gun in assuming the deal was done.[45] Instead, the Pirates completed a deal with Phillies president Gerry Nugent that sent Grace and pitching prospect Claude Passeau east in exchange for catcher Al Todd.

For the second year in a row, Traynor had shot himself in the foot. Traynor praised Todd's "rifle-like" arm, but others were skeptical of the trade.[46] Regis Walsh of the *Pittsburgh Press* wrote, "In obtaining Todd, the Bucs didn't get the smartest catcher in the league."[47] The Pirates didn't even know how old Todd was. They thought he was 27.[48] He turned out to be 33, a huge difference, especially for a catcher, who absorbs a lot of wear and tear.

But it wasn't Todd's acquisition *per se* that made the deal such a stinker. Passeau, an afterthought in the trade, had come up to the Pirates at the end of 1935 and gotten shelled in his one appearance. It had been a long season for the 26-year-old, who had piled up 20 wins and 244 innings for Des Moines of the Western League. "My arm was shot," he recalled. "The Pirates gave me that one chance and said, 'He isn't going to make it.'"[49] The Pirates were wrong. Over the next 12 years, Passeau won 162 games for the Phillies and Cubs. Traynor would spend his whole tenure searching desperately for a staff ace. He had something resembling that in Passeau, didn't recognize it, and gave him away.

Traynor might have been better off had he been working under Barney Dreyfuss, more of a hands-on baseball man. Dreyfuss drove his managers crazy with his tendency toward micromanagement, but he knew talent when he saw it and did what needed to be done to make his club better. Understandably, Benswanger delegated more of the team-building responsibilities to his field managers, but unfortunately that was not Traynor's forte. More often than not, he came out on the short end of trades.

Perhaps part of his trouble was that he seemed to evaluate his men more on their weaknesses than their strengths. He did not offer praise easily.[50] Like many stars-turned-managers, he tended to be "supercritical and to judge a player's performance by his own standards."[51] In a stunningly honest self-critique, Traynor, in 1938, conceded, "When I was a player, I was a much better judge of prospective players than I am now."[52]

Although Traynor understood intellectually that he no longer could play third base, he had a much harder time accepting that reality emotionally. In the wake of the 1935 season, his arm had not improved. "Seldom have I experienced a night in which I did not awaken with a groan every time I happened to roll over upon that damaged shoulder."[53] He admitted at the minor league meetings in Dayton that it hurt him just to shake hands.[54] But he was desperate to play again and he was going to lift every rock and peek into every corner hoping to find the magic elixir that would turn him back into what he used to be.

Over the winter he initially sought help from a physician in Cincinnati.[55] Then when he went to Chicago for the major league winter meetings, he visited another doctor who discovered what Traynor called "a crystallization in my throwing muscles."[56] The man applied a substance that caused Traynor's arm to swell, and then manipulated the shoulder while it was swollen to break up the "crystallization." This bit of quackery was enough for Traynor to declare himself "absolutely sure" that his throwing problems were history.[57]

In late January, Traynor spent two weeks in California working with Detroit Tigers trainer Denny Carroll, who assured reporters, "As far as we can determine now, Traynor's arm is as sound as it was many years ago."[58] But once Traynor started throwing, the pain recurred and Traynor surrendered third base to perennial prospect Bill Brubaker and young Cookie Lavagetto.

Even after that setback, Traynor just could not come to grips with the inevitable, and his denial was beginning to cloud his judgment. At the Pirates new spring training site in San Antonio, he expressed his determination to play in 2,000 career games (he was at 1,936), and said he might platoon himself with Gus Suhr at first base.[59] In preparation for this scheme, Traynor, who didn't even own a first baseman's mitt, went out and picked one up at a Memphis sporting goods store about a week before Opening Day. As it turned out, Traynor didn't play in 1936, but he kept himself on the active roster, in essence forcing the Pirates to play a man short all season.

It was one headache after another for Traynor that spring. Two of his star players were unhappy with their contract offers. Traynor traveled to Arky Vaughan's home in Fullerton, California, in mid–February for a round of golf and, presumably, to figure out what his shortstop's beef was. Vaughan signed less than a week later. Paul Waner, whose average plunged 41 points in 1935, held out briefly before swallowing a pay cut. Waner was vocal about his displeasure. "I was stunned. I thought for a moment that somebody in the office had made a mistake and mailed me the wrong contract," he said.[60] "I was in there hustling and giving the best I had all the time, even though at times my arm and side were so sore I could hardly raise my bat."[61]

Paul's brother, Lloyd, had been hospitalized with pneumonia in January and missed the first two weeks of the season. The pitching staff was in disarray. Waite Hoyt apparently was back on the sauce ("He's got to take care of himself," declared Traynor, otherwise "he's off the ball club"), while the over-the-hill Bush and the out-of-shape Blanton pitched poorly all spring.[62] "After what has happened to Blanton and the others, our pitching staff is open to anyone who can show me he can win. We haven't any first-string pitchers anymore," Traynor asserted.[63] Moreover, the new catcher, Todd, didn't exactly knock anyone's socks off. "Al was far from being a hard worker," said Jewel Ens.[64]

On top of all of this, there was, for a time, some doubt about whether the Pirates would be able to play their home opener as scheduled. After a particularly harsh winter, Pittsburgh was deluged by a massive St. Patrick's Day flood. Melting snow and heavy rain combined to send water pouring into the city. Pittsburgh's famous Point, where the city's three rivers come together, was 21 feet above flood stage as rescuers navigated downtown streets in canoes, picking up people who were stranded in the second and third floors of buildings.[65] More than 60 people died in the Pittsburgh area, and damage estimates ran as high as $250 million.[66]

Despite all the ominous signs, the season began well. Traynor, a boxing aficionado, received a good-luck telegram from former heavyweight champion Jack Dempsey before the opener in Cincinnati on April 14. The Bucs then went out and clipped the Reds, 8–6, as rookie Bud Hafey, filling in for Lloyd Waner in center field, had three hits, including a home run. "We've got a dangerous club and the opening game proves it," Traynor proclaimed.[67]

The Pirates were just a game out of first place on May 9 with a record of 12–8. But their dearth of reliable pitching soon caught up with them. Blanton's performance, in particular, was appalling. Through early June, he was 2–4 with a 7.36 ERA. His low point might have come on May 23 at Cincinnati's Crosley Field. The Pirates led the Reds, 3–0, in the ninth inning when Cincinnati loaded the bases against Bill Swift. Traynor brought Blanton out of the bullpen to face pinch-hitter Sammy Byrd. Byrd, batting .083, promptly took Blanton's first pitch over the wall for a game-winning grand slam. Within a few days, with the Pirates under .500 and seven games out, the *Pittsburgh Press* was reporting talk that Traynor's job was in jeopardy.[68]

But by mid–June, Blanton had worked himself back into shape and started looking dominant again. Pirate fans' favorite whipping boy Gus Suhr was batting over .350 and providing some power. Weaver, a 14-game winner in 1935, had piled up a team-high eight wins. A 7–6 victory over the Phillies on June 21 pulled Pittsburgh back to within 1½ games of the lead. A couple of weeks later the Pirates entered the all-star break in third place, five games behind league-leading St. Louis and one back of the second-place Cubs. Traynor thought his club was poised for a big second half drive. "We are getting better pitching than ever, our hitters are making plenty of trouble, and our defense has tightened up. We ought to be able to get somewhere."[69]

Traynor returned to his hometown park, Braves Field, as a coach for the National League All-Star team, which finally won one from the American League, 4–3, on July 7. But after he arrived back in Pittsburgh, it wasn't long before he saw his pre-break optimism proven baseless. The Pirates opened the second half by crushing Philadelphia, 16–5, in 103-degree heat. But their fall began the next day when, with temperatures in the triple digits again, Chuck Klein tied a major league record with four home runs as the Phillies dumped the Pirates, 9–6, in 10 innings. Pittsburgh dropped eight of its next eleven to fall to fourth place, 10½ games back. For the rest of the season, they were just playing out the string.

During periods like this, when his team was losing, Traynor tended to grow visibly "sullen and morose," but he usually swallowed any anger he might have felt.[70] He was not the type of person who was comfortable throwing chairs, overturning tables, or cursing people out, although some believed that's exactly what the Pirates needed. Traynor thought that was bunk and bristled at the suggestion that he was too soft on his men. "I'm going to win or lose along my lines," he snarled on July 15. "I left a player [Cookie Lavagetto] in the clubhouse the other night with tears in his eyes. Do you want me to give that player hell?"[71]

At times, of course, a player did set Traynor's blood boiling. Physical errors or an honest lack of production he could sort of understand, but what really got to him were players who didn't take their careers as seriously as he took his—lazy players, underachievers, drinkers, womanizers. But even when faced with problem children like these, Traynor, it appears, often adopted a passive-aggressive stance rather than addressing the issues directly. "When as a player you do something Traynor doesn't like he just starts acting as if you were on the arctic patrol and beyond the confines of civilization," wrote Havey Boyle in the *Pittsburgh Post-Gazette*.[72] "Certain [players] on the club would feel better if they got a good rousing bawling out and [had] it over with."[73] The silent treatment is never a good way to resolve conflict and Traynor swore he never consciously behaved that way. But he developed a reputation as a pushover, too much of a nice guy who either couldn't or wouldn't lay the hammer down on players who drifted out of line.

Benswanger felt compelled to issue his manager a public vote of confidence in late July. "While the record of the Pirates has been disappointing to the public and the club, we want to express our complete confidence in Manager Traynor."[74] He probably should have left it at that, but instead went on to add, "Perhaps he isn't the greatest manager in the game today, but on the other hand he wasn't the best third baseman when he broke in with us. The point is that Traynor is improving as a leader, just as he did as a player."[75]

The Pirates finished in fourth place. In the opinion of Chet Smith of the *Pittsburgh Press*, Traynor took the 1936 version of the Bucs as far as anyone could have. "In some ways the Pirates have been a disappointment, but by and large they have delivered what was in them. You can't squeeze orange juice out of a potato."[76]

A veteran who could anchor the pitching staff again topped Traynor's winter wish list. To that end he spent much of the offseason haggling with St. Louis over Dizzy Dean. Cardinals president Branch Rickey had grown tired of Dean's obnoxious behavior; more importantly, he might have had some private concerns about the health of Dean's arm. The day before Thanksgiving, Traynor took a train to St. Louis to meet with Rickey at his home to see if they could work out a deal. Rickey demanded the world—seven players, including Arky Vaughan, plus $175,000. Traynor was okay with those terms with one exception: "I'll trade anyone on the ballclub—except Arky Vaughan."[77]

Rumors swirled for another few weeks, but neither side would budge on Vaughan. When Phillies manager Jimmie Wilson inquired at the winter meetings about the state of the negotiations, Traynor dismissed the question with a joke. "I'm leaving for Pittsburgh tonight to wrap up Forbes Field and deliver it to Rickey. We'll have Dean but no place for him to play and nobody for him to play with."[78] Dean remained a Cardinal for one more year.

Out of the running for Dean, Traynor attempted to shore up his staff by picking up veteran Ed Brandt from Brooklyn. Brandt had won 105 games in nine years of hard labor with some truly rotten teams. "We've got a sure winner in Brandt," Traynor chirped. "Ed ought to be good for 18 or 20 [wins] next year. The Pirates haven't had an outstanding left-hander since Wilbur Cooper ... but we have one now."[79]

Traynor developed a blind spot when it came to Brandt. He was a dependable pitcher for the Pirates, but he also drank and ran around a lot and Traynor couldn't get past that. Traynor simply didn't like the guy, probably didn't use him as much as he should have, and ran him out of town after a spring training incident two years later. Meanwhile, one of the players he dealt for Brandt, Cookie Lavagetto, immediately took over at third base for Brooklyn and became a four-time all-star.

At Traynor's request, the Pirates moved their spring headquarters back to San Bernardino. The city of San Antonio had invited the American League's St. Louis Browns to train there, assuming the two teams would want to work out together, but Traynor wanted no part of that arrangement. He headed off for California a week later than planned. In late January the Ohio River overflowed its banks, inundating Brookville, Indiana. Traynor stayed behind to assist with rescue work and help his neighbors whose homes had been destroyed.[80]

The spring headlines focused on a rancorous contract dispute between the Pirates and Paul Waner, who enjoyed a tremendous comeback in 1936 as he captured his third batting crown. "Last year I signed a contract with a $1,000 cut on the understanding I'd get the money back if I had a good year. Well, I had one of my best years ... and I didn't get the bonus."[81] When Waner approached Traynor to request his bonus during the final series of the 1936 season, the Pirate manager reportedly brushed him off with a terse, "We don't give such things."[82]

The disagreement got ugly, personal, and nasty fast. "I'll fish and play golf before I'll sign for what they're trying to pay me now. The management called by telephone from Pittsburgh nearly a week ago and agreed to pay me so much.... Then they sent me a contract but they cut $500 off it. I sent it right back."[83] A furious Benswanger dug in his heels; he felt like Waner was impugning his integrity. "Waner can stay in Florida and fish all summer."[84] When Waner boasted, in the parlance of the day, of being "a sit-down striker," Benswanger snapped, "Let him sit!"[85]

Chet Smith of the *Pittsburgh Press* said managers often interceded with ownership on behalf of holdout players, but Traynor never lifted a finger to help Waner.[86] "Paul promised to sign and then reneged," Traynor said. "I'll get along without him if I have to."[87] Finally, less than two weeks before Opening

Day, Waner signed. After Waner committed three errors in his first exhibition game back, Traynor wryly observed, "Paul Waner came back to the club saying he had worked out all winter, but ... he looked as if he might have been working out on a Ping-Pong table."[88] He swore it was just a joke.

Job security weighed heavily on Traynor's mind all spring. "I'm on the spot this season. If we don't win, I'll be the one that gets the blame."[89] Despite the addition of Brandt, he worried that pitching would be his club's downfall. He hoped he could find enough reliable arms to contend, but columnist John Kieran of the *New York Times* suggested Traynor had "a better chance of finding 12 oil wells in his cellar."[90]

The Pirates again came flying out of the chute. Nearly a month into the 1937 season Brandt had won his first three decisions; Joe Bowman, picked up in a trade with the Philadelphia Phillies right before the season opener, was 5–0; Paul Waner was hitting .370; Al Todd was up near .400. A 5–2 victory over Boston on May 22 staked the Bucs to a 4½-game lead. But a 7–11 road trip left Traynor in a "dark mood" and knocked the Pirates down to fourth place, 3½ games behind. "Our hitters weren't hitting when it counted and our pitchers were being hit when it counted."[91]

Accusations that the Bucs were loafing had surfaced again. Havey Boyle reported in the *Pittsburgh Post-Gazette*, "One manager confided ... that he does not like to play the Pirates because his team starts acting as they do."[92] Traynor found it hard to argue with that perception. He knew his team often was guilty of playing sloppy baseball and that, at times, it almost looked like they didn't care.[93]

Injuries to shortstop Arky Vaughan and versatile infielder Lee Handley forced Traynor, who again had wasted a roster spot on himself all season, back to third base on July 20 in Brooklyn. It was his first start since September 2, 1935. During infield practice before the game, Traynor glanced toward a friend and said, "I'm nervous as a bride. I really am."[94] He had reason to be; he hadn't taken infield or batting practice for weeks.[95]

Traynor, hitting eighth, went 0-for-4. He handled four chances flawlessly, but "you could have driven a load of hay" underneath his weak, looping throws to first base.[96] He started the next two days as well, went 2-for-12 in the series, and contributed one vintage Traynor play, a diving stop that robbed the Dodgers' Lindsay Brown of a hit. They were the last starts of his career.

Traynor's playing days melted away without fanfare. On August 14 he entered as a pinch-runner against St. Louis and scored the winning run on a Paul Waner single. And that was it. When the Pirates acquired backup catcher Ray Berres on September 2, Traynor quietly removed himself from the active roster.

His brilliance endures. At the conclusion of the 2008 season, more than 70 years after his final game, Traynor still ranked fifth on Pittsburgh's all-time career list in hits (2,416) and total bases (3,289), and fourth in triples (164) and

RBIs (1,273). His name also appeared among the Pirates top ten in batting average, runs, doubles, and games played.

Pittsburgh won 21 of its last 29, including its final ten games in a row; the big September push was purely cosmetic, though. The Pirates finished 86–68 in third place, their highest finish in the standings under Traynor, but at no point down the stretch were they ever in contention. Nonetheless, there were signals that 1938 could prove more promising. Paul Waner showed his comeback season in 1936 was no fluke, as he topped 200 hits for the eighth time. Twenty-three-year-old rookie Russ Bauers, a big right-hander described as "a comic-reading lumberjack from the Wisconsin woods," came out of nowhere to go 13–6 with a 2.88 ERA.[97] Vaughan remained far and away the best shortstop in baseball. Most importantly, perhaps, there would be no dominant teams in the National League in 1938. The New York Giants won the pennant in 1936 and 1937, but their pitching would betray them in 1938. The Pirates were well positioned to make a legitimate run at the flag provided they could stay healthy and Traynor could keep them focused.

11

The Homer in the Gloamin'

Traynor attended a couple of games of the 1937 World Series in New York and shortly thereafter put his signature on another $16,500 contract for the 1938 season. Benswanger was getting a deal. By comparison, Giants manager Bill Terry earned $40,000, Joe McCarthy of the Yankees $35,000, the Tigers' Mickey Cochrane $30,000, and the Cubs' Charlie Grimm and the Reds' Bill McKechnie $25,000.[1]

Traynor and Benswanger were determined to re-shape their team during the offseason. Asked whom on the roster he would be willing to trade, Traynor replied, "Everybody."[2] He made two good moves in mid–October, selecting 29-year-old right-hander Bob Klinger from St. Louis in the Rule V draft, and exchanging backup catcher Tom Padden for Johnny Rizzo, a hard-hitting Texan who was buried in the Cardinals minor league system. But those were the only significant transactions. As usual there were plenty of rumors and talking without much getting done.

Traynor almost pulled off a blockbuster deal at the minor league meetings in Milwaukee in early December. He arrived with his eye on pitcher Van Lingle Mungo, who was feuding with manager Burleigh Grimes in Brooklyn, but within a day his attention shifted to the Cubs. On December 2, Traynor and Bill Benswanger huddled with Charlie Grimm in a smoky room at the Schroeder Hotel, with Arky Vaughan the focus of their discussions. According to the *Pittsburgh Press*, Grimm rejected Traynor's offer of Vaughan, Red Lucas, and Woody Jensen for veteran shortstop Billy Jurges and center fielder Frank Demaree.[3] In retrospect, it sounds insane that Traynor would make this offer and even nuttier that Grimm would shoot him down. Vaughan was the Pirates best player, in the middle of a Hall of Fame career. But at the time, it looked as if Demaree might have been on that same path. He was only 27 and coming off two tremendous seasons. No one could have anticipated the drop off that was coming; Demaree had a poor year in 1938, got himself traded to the Giants, and was basically finished by age 30. Traynor had lucked out.

Traynor and Benswanger never bothered to follow up on one historic offer that was laid upon their doorstep that winter. Chester Washington of the black newspaper the *Pittsburgh Courier* sent Traynor a telegram with a tantalizing proposition:

KNOW YOUR CLUB NEEDS PLAYERS STOP HAVE ANSWER TO YOUR
PRAYERS RIGHT HERE IN PITTSBURGH STOP JOSH GIBSON CATCHER
FIRST BASE B. LEONARD AND RAY BROWN PITCHER OF HOMESTEAD
GRAYS S. PAIGE PITCHER AND COOL PAPA BELL OF PITTSBURGH
CRAWFORDS ALL AVAILABLE AT REASONABLE FIGURES STOP WOULD
MAKE PIRATES FORMIDABLE PENNANT CONTENDERS STOP WHAT IS
YOUR ATTITUDE? STOP WIRE ANSWER[4]

For those who appreciate baseball history, it is fun to consider how the course of the game and the fortunes of the Pirates would have changed had Traynor's answer been "Yes." Josh Gibson was just 26 years old, Paige and Brown were 30, Leonard was 31. All were at or near the peak of great careers. Bell was 35, a little long in the tooth, but still with some years left in him. Put these players in Pirate uniforms and Traynor would have been presiding over a dynasty. More importantly, the color line would have been broken nine years earlier than it was, and a tremendous wrong would have been made right.

Regrettably, Traynor did not reply. Historians such as Ken Burns and John Holway have rebuked Traynor, framing his non-response as a metaphor for organized baseball's indifference to the plight of African American players.[5] That is not entirely fair. Traynor simply did not have the clout to autonomously decide it was time to break baseball's color barrier. He would have needed support from higher up, from Benswanger. Did he ever ask his boss for that support? No one knows, but it is not inconceivable. Traynor appreciated the talent that Negro Leaguers possessed. "I have seen countless numbers of Negro ballplayers who could have made the grade," he said.[6] In May 1939 Traynor told Wendell Smith of the *Courier* that he would have no qualms about using African American players if only he could, adding, "Personally, I don't see why the ban against Negro players exists at all."[7] Some years later, when Traynor was working as a radio commentator, he was vocal in urging the Pirates to integrate.[8] In short, Traynor evidenced more racial tolerance than a lot of his contemporaries did.

But regardless of what Traynor did with that telegram, Benswanger, though ostensibly a supporter of integration, clearly didn't have the stomach to lead the battle. "If [the race question] came to an issue I'd vote for Negro players," Benswanger insisted. "I know there are many problems connected with the question, but after all, somebody has to make the first move."[9] But it wasn't in his personality to be that man. Benswanger was no revolutionary. He was quiet, retiring, and somewhat nervous; he lacked the boldness and audacity required to fight baseball's establishment.

In the late 1930s, when Washington sent his telegram, there was a sense in the African American community that the Pirates were the team most likely to integrate the game. But Benswanger, though tempted, would not nor could not make it happen. In 1942, the Communist Party newspaper the *Daily Worker* reported Benswanger had agreed to offer tryouts to three African American players: Roy Campanella, Sammy Hughes, and Dave Barnhill. But according to the *Courier*, he reneged once the story started attracting national attention, claiming that the *Daily Worker* "put words in my mouth."[10] He later contended, "I tried more than once to buy Josh Gibson," but that Homestead Grays owner Cum Posey had talked him out of it.[11]

Wendell Smith grew disillusioned with Benswanger's back-and-forth, calling him "baseball's number one phony."[12] But another of the era's prominent African American reporters, Dan Burley, thought Negro League owners were part of the problem. They had a good thing going financially and didn't necessarily want to see their biggest stars leave to play in the major leagues.[13] In short, this situation was a lot bigger than Pie Traynor. Washington's telegram surely deserved an answer, but under the circumstances it is hard to see how anything Traynor could have done or said in response would have made a whit of difference.

In early January, Traynor was home in Brookville when he caught wind of two unhappy Pirates who took their gripes public. One was Paul Waner, who was fuming over money yet again. Earlier in the offseason, Benswanger had declared that he wanted "new faces" on the Pirates in 1938. On January 8, upon receiving what he felt was a low-ball contract offer, Waner told a reporter, "Benswanger probably wants cheaper faces.... He just wants a bunch of bums at two for a nickel."[14]

Two days later, outfielder Woody Jensen fired an unexpected salvo in Benswanger's direction. "For years he's tried to run a [team] without knowledge of the game or understanding of player psychology. He ought to let someone who knows the business run it for him."[15] Strong stuff, but Jensen was just getting rolling. He called the Pirates "nickel nursers," and scoffed at their attempts to acquire the high-priced Mungo from Brooklyn.[16] "Bill Benswanger wouldn't give $10,000 for two Babe Ruths in their prime."[17] Then for good measure he ripped Traynor's policy of requiring players to eat with the team at the hotel on the road and his ban on golf on days off. "You'd think that we were running an orphan's home."[18]

Traynor did not have much to say to the press about Waner's remarks. He was accustomed to his right fielder's grousing by this point and, not insignificantly, Waner was still an outstanding player. Jensen was a different story. He was an all right guy, not really a troublemaker, but he had a reputation for being a little bit lazy and not getting the most out of his ability — exactly the kind of player who drove Traynor nuts. Perhaps that is why, when asked to respond to Jensen's rant, Traynor went for the jugular. "A mediocre ball player has got to say something pretty sensational to break into print. I could understand it if a star player popped off but a mediocre player like Jensen seldom rates the headlines this way."[19] A week later, in case anyone misunderstood the first time, he followed up with, "A .276 [*sic*] hitter like Jensen getting the headlines is something that amazes me."[20] Jensen soon fell back on a tried and true alibi, claiming to have been misquoted. Benswanger maintained all was forgiven, but Jensen's days as a Pirate were numbered.

In the end, Waner resolved his contract dispute without too much hassle, signing on February 18, well before the start of spring training. For the second straight year, Traynor's departure for San Bernardino was delayed by flooding. This time, he and Eve were marooned at the Biltmore Hotel in Los Angeles, watching from their window on February 27 as flood waters rose below them. The flooding killed more than 100 people in Los Angeles and damaged thousands of homes. San Bernardino also was hit by floods, but Perris Hill Park was unaffected. Traynor met his pitchers and catchers there on March 6.

Despite the offseason fireworks, it turned out to be an uneventful camp. Rizzo quickly established himself as a genuine prospect and easily took the starting left field job away from Jensen. Rizzo boasted that he planned to be the National League version of Joe DiMaggio. Traynor didn't go that far, though he did believe the youngster would become "Pittsburgh's best left fielder since Fred Clarke."[21] The most competitive position battle took place at third base, where Bill Brubaker and Pep Young looked equally inept. After failing in a springtime bid to land Pinky Whitney from the Phillies, Traynor, in desperation, persuaded Brubaker to change his batting stance. The adjustment made a difference; Brubaker got hot and won the job coming out of spring training.

The Pirates' slate of exhibition games was bizarre. They left San Bernardino and barnstormed their way back east, playing against ragtag teams in small towns that had never seen major league baseball, places like Taft, California; Winslow, Arizona; and Clovis, New Mexico. In terms of getting the team ready to start the season, the trip was all but useless. Games were wiped out by a Biblical plague of bad weather — rain, fog, dust storms, and blizzards. In the games the Pirates did play, the competition was wretched. Chet Smith wrote in the *Pittsburgh Press* that the Pirate pitchers "have been throwing to an assorted collection of barnyard hitters who can be counted on to miss any garden variety ... curve by at least two feet."[22] The Pirate hitters, meanwhile, were "standing up to the plate while some crossroads hooligan pumps in his Sunday pitch, which is more often than not a straight ball, waist high."[23]

On April 4, the Pirates were in Barstow, California, for an exhibition game, a bush league affair in every conceivable way. The Pirates took a school bus to the ball field, which also doubled as the town airport. When they arrived, they met their opponents, a group of men wearing giant sideburns and huge beards. A carnival was coming up in a month, and the men with the bushiest goatee and longest sideburns were to win prizes. Nearly every man in the ballpark was appropriately hirsute. The Barstow club wore mismatched uniforms. One guy batted in street clothes. The town's sheriff played shortstop with his badge pinned to his chest.

Afterward, the residents of Barstow supplied their guests with plenty of alcoholic refreshments, which set the stage for a near-calamity on the train to

Clovis, New Mexico, that night. That evening on one of the Pullman cars, Russ Bauers, the Waner brothers, Cy Blanton, and a couple of other well-lubricated teammates got into a friendly wrestling match. According to one report, five players grabbed the hulking Bauers and tried to wrestle him to the ground.[24] In the process, Bauers injured his knee. The first doctor to examine him predicted he would be out of action for two months.

Traynor was stunned, angry, and probably feeling betrayed. Although most experts were picking the Pirates third or fourth, Traynor thought this was the Pirates' year. "If we don't land higher than all you fellows say I'm going to be disappointed."[25] Moreover, he knew his window of opportunity was closing; the team was getting old and there were not many top prospects coming up. This was serious stuff for Traynor. In his mind it wasn't just his job that was on the line, it was his legacy. "If you don't win a pennant after you've been a player and a manager you are remembered not as a pretty good player, but as the manager who failed. That is why a pennant is so important."[26] And now his chances for that pennant appeared to be slipping away because the ace of his staff—a man Giants manager Bill Terry described as one of the four or five best young pitchers in the league and who Traynor thought had raw talent comparable to that of Dizzy Dean—couldn't stop himself from behaving like a capering loon.

While Bauers flew back to St. Louis with Benswanger for treatment, Traynor gathered his team together in a room at the Hotel Clovis and blistered them with a withering, profane tirade. He levied fines against all six players involved in the incident but, after learning that Bauers' injury was not as severe as initially feared, apparently rescinded all of the fines. But he remained upset. "Acting like a lot of wild schoolboys is no way to get ready for a major league season."[27] Weeks later, he still couldn't believe what had happened. He claimed Bauers was the only pitcher in ideal physical condition when they broke camp. "He was in such magnificent shape that I would not have hesitated to let him work a 15-inning game."[28]

While Traynor simmered, the Cubs made a deal that rocked baseball and appeared to set them up with the best group of starting pitchers in the league. They sent three players and $185,000 to the Cardinals for Dizzy Dean. Some felt the Cubs had made themselves the odds on favorites to win the pennant. Pepper Martin of St. Louis remarked, "There goes our World Series money."[29] But Traynor was unconvinced. "I have a grave doubt about the condition of his arm."[30] Traynor would be proven largely correct; Dean went on the shelf just two weeks into the season with a sore arm and only won 17 more games the rest of his career. But one of those wins would come at a most inopportune time for the 1938 Pirates.

The Pirates left behind the chaos of their spring trip and started fast, as they usually did under Traynor. Vaughan's two-run homer in the top of the ninth beat St. Louis, 4–3, in the season opener, and from there the Bucs went on to win their next six games. Bauers made his debut in the final game of that streak, struggling through seven innings and earning a no-decision in an 8–6 win over the Cubs. The loud-mouthed Dean was unimpressed. "The Pirates can win 15 games in a row at the start of the season and fold up as usual in the middle of the summer."[31]

The Bucs didn't wait that long, losing six of their next seven. Brubaker justified Traynor's decision to award him the third base job, batting .317 with an on-base percentage of .500 through the first 11 games. But then he made a mess of that 11th game in the field, committing four errors, which prompted Traynor to yank him from the lineup for good the following day. Lee Handley (who wore his manager's familiar uniform number 20, while Traynor switched to number 35) moved from second base to third, while Pep Young took Handley's spot at second. The shaky situation at third encouraged Traynor to continue to pester the Phillies about Whitney. Manager Jimmie Wilson reportedly liked Traynor's offer of Jim Tobin and $10,000, but Phils owner Gerry Nugent was reluctant to trade a fan favorite like Whitney.

Pirates manager Traynor in 1938 (National Baseball Hall of Fame Library, Cooperstown, New York).

By the middle of May, the Pirates were struggling to stay above .500, largely because Paul Waner was playing dreadful baseball. Legend has it that Waner, a notoriously heavy drinker, had acceded to Traynor's preseason request to lay off the booze. After watching him sink neck-deep into a 2-for-41 morass that dropped his average to .175 through 20 games, Traynor reportedly took Waner to a bar and personally ushered him off the wagon.[32] After sitting on the bench for a few games, Waner snapped out of it, but his drought was the first warning that age was catching up to the Pirates 35-year-old star. It would be the worst season of his career to that point.

But Waner was far from the only culprit. No one was hitting, and Traynor rapidly was becoming unglued. A 10-game road trip in May was the low point. On May 17, Bauers combined with 31-year-old rookie Rip Sewell for a one-hitter, but lost the game to Boston, 1–0. That defeat dropped Pittsburgh six games behind first-place New York. In game two, Bob Klinger made his first start of the year and allowed only five hits through 12⅓ innings but the Pirates lost in the 14th inning on a Pep Young error. Traynor was ejected earlier in that game for arguing with first base umpire Lee Ballanfant.

The following day, the score was tied, 3–3, in the bottom of the eleventh, the Pirates' sixth extra-inning game in the last seven. Al Lopez dropped a double into short left field, in front of Rizzo, who had been playing deep. With an open base, Traynor elected to allow Sewell to pitch to Rabbit Warstler, who had gone hitless in the series. But Warstler's single brought home Lopez, won the game for Boston, and dropped the Pirates to .500 and into fourth place. Pittsburgh won in Brooklyn the next day, but Traynor was ejected for arguing balls and strikes with Larry Goetz. After not being ejected in almost four sea-

Traynor watches the New York Giants throttle his Pirates 18–2 on May 22, 1938, at the Polo Grounds. This loss forced Traynor and Bill Benswanger to re-evaluate the direction of the ballclub (AP/Wide World Photos).

sons as manager, Traynor had been thrown out twice in four days. The next afternoon the Giants hammered Ed Brandt and beat the Pirates, 18–2. An Associated Press photographer snapped an image of Traynor gazing out at the field, his chin cradled in his right hand, a weary, disgusted scowl spread across his face.

Pittsburgh was in fifth place now. Benswanger and a demoralized Traynor had seen enough. They met after the game to chart their course for the rest of the season. They resolved, in Benswanger's words, "to start immediately to build a new team — and build it around younger men."[33] The Bucs ended the road trip 4–6. Rizzo hit .152 on the trip and came home with a sore wrist that would keep him out of the lineup for two weeks. Todd hit .135 over those ten games. Young had only three hits and hit into seven double plays.

At the end of May Pittsburgh stood one game under .500 and 7½ games out of first place. The plans to revamp the roster weren't off to a good start. In early June, Traynor was ready to pull the trigger on a trade with the New York Giants. Bill Terry wanted Young, and offered the Pirates Traynor's old crush, Wally Berger, utility man Lou Chiozza, and $25,000. Traynor wanted more cash so he could go out and buy a second baseman to replace Young. He got Terry to bump up the cash portion of the offer to $35,000 in exchange for a promise to throw in young outfielder Johnny Dickshot. But after consulting Benswanger, Traynor changed his mind.[34] Or perhaps Benswanger simply refused to sign off on the trade, although Traynor denied that.

Terry was upset. "It's the first time I knew that Pie Traynor didn't have a free hand in making deals."[35] If Benswanger did overrule Traynor, it probably was a good decision. Berger was in his 30s, Chiozza was 28 and had played regularly for four seasons without showing very much. Their acquisition hardly would have been in line with Benswanger's professed desire to build with youth.

One youngster Traynor came across who really had him salivating was a kid from nearby Donora, Pennsylvania, who stopped by Forbes Field for a workout early in the season. Over the winter, 17-year-old Stan Musial had signed with the St. Louis Cardinals for $65 a month. In the spring of 1938, Commissioner Kenesaw Mountain Landis ordered the Cardinals to release 91 players they had buried in their expansive minor league system. Musial hadn't heard from the Cardinals since signing the contract and thought he might have been one of the players who had been released. "If the Cardinals were as bad as Judge Landis said they were, I didn't want to be a part of them," Musial told author Peter Golenbock. Irv Weiss, who knew both the Musial family and Traynor, arranged for the young man come to Pittsburgh and show the Pirates what he had. He had a lot. "Pie Traynor liked me," Musial said. "I was pitching batting practice to the Pirates when I got a notice to report to [St. Louis'] farm club at Williamson, West Virginia." Musial didn't know what to do, so he approached Traynor.

"Did your Dad sign the contract?" Traynor asked.

"Yeah," Musial responded.

"That sort of makes it official," sighed Traynor. "But if you're ever out of a job, come see us."[36]

Musial wouldn't be out of a job for a long, long time. "Traynor could have told me to report [to Williamson] and look bad deliberately so that I would be released and he could sign me. I liked him so much I think I would have done it."[37]

The disappointment over Musial, which surely was minor at the time, was just one of a number of bad breaks Pittsburgh endured early in 1938. But then suddenly, before Benswanger and Traynor could make good on their pledge to rebuild, the Pirates started to win. They escaped fifth place on June 11 as pitcher Bill Swift helped himself with a three-run homer in a 4–3 win over Philadelphia. The next day Rizzo, healthy once more, snapped an 0-for-30 slump with a home run as the Bucs beat the Phillies again, 11–5. Paul Waner was in the midst of a 15-game hitting streak, while Gus Suhr, who also had a miserable first two months of the season, was putting together a 16-game streak.

On June 25, Pittsburgh finished off a 7–3 road trip with an 8–7 win over Boston. It was the tenth victory, all in relief, for Mace Brown, who hit a two-run homer to break a 6–6 tie. The Pirates were still in fourth place, but only 2½ games out of first. Then after a loss to Cincinnati to start a homestand, the Pirates ripped off 13 consecutive wins. They moved into second place on June 30 as Cy Blanton, making just his second start in six weeks, beat Cincinnati with a three-hitter, 3–1. On July 12 they leapfrogged the league-leading Giants by percentage points, whipping the Cubs, 14–6, as Al Todd homered and knocked in five. The Bucs had won 29 of 37. Brown and Klinger were each 6–0 during this stretch. Rizzo and Suhr were red-hot at the plate. Over the next few days, the Pirates and Giants traded first place back and forth.

The city of Pittsburgh was sucked in. "Anywhere you find a radio, you will find a group surrounding it, hanging on every word by the announcer," wrote Al Abrams in the *Pittsburgh Post-Gazette*.[38] A crowd of 43,241 jammed Forbes Field on July 17 for a doubleheader against New York. It was a charged atmosphere. Al Todd and the Giants Alex Kampouris got into a shouting match, and fans whipped bottles at Goetz after he ejected Rizzo for complaining about ball-strike calls. (Traynor had to walk out and stand beside Goetz to make the fans stop.)

The Giants won the first game, 2–1, but Suhr prevented a defeat in the nightcap, singling in the tying run in the bottom of the ninth, just before Pittsburgh's 7:00 P.M. curfew. Pittsburgh took over the league lead from New York for good when they beat the Giants, 7–4, the following day, and they kept pouring it on over the next two weeks. Cy Blanton's 9–2 win over Brooklyn on July 30 was his seventh straight win, the Pirates' 33rd in their last 42. It gave them a five-game lead in the National League and the best record in the major leagues at 57–31. It had been an astonishing turnaround.

Traynor was cleverly milking every last drop out of a nondescript pitching staff. In the middle of the pennant race, New York catcher Gus Mancuso scoffed, "The Pirates can't beat us with the pitching staff they have. Only Cy Blanton can throw hard and he can do it only so long. Tobin? Klinger? Soft stuff. Home run pitching."[39] Mancuso's evaluation was a bit harsh, but Traynor admitted that his staff was less than overwhelming. "No Fellers, no Groves, no Deans, but a lot of good boys."[40]

There was not a weak link in the group, but there were no true aces either, no stars. Traynor knew he could only ride his starting pitchers so far and that he had to be careful not to over-expose anyone. As a result, he handled his bullpen in a way that would not become common until a few decades later, piecing together innings from two, three, four different pitchers, whatever it took to get through a game and get a victory. Only the last-place Phillies and Athletics had fewer complete games as a team. Traynor didn't like to manage this way. He still possessed the old-school mentality that pitchers should finish what they start, telling the Detroit Tigers' Bobo Newsome after the season, "I wish I had a complete-game pitcher like you last September. We wouldn't have lost that National League pennant."[41] But Traynor was perceptive enough to recognize the limits of the talent on hand and deserves credit for altering his managerial style accordingly.

The Bucs increased their lead to 6½ games on August 7 with a doubleheader sweep of the crumbling Giants. After an off day, Bauers blanked the Cardinals, 1–0, to maintain that lead. But it was around this time that the Pirate leadership — Benswanger and Traynor — started acting weird. "I was that nervous watching Bauers try to protect that one-run lead that my hand was actually shaking when I was writing down things," said Benswanger. "These games are getting a little too tough for me."[42]

It was odd talk for a man whose team possessed a solid lead, though perhaps there was some reason for him to start to worry. His club, which put up a 40–14 record in June and July, was inevitably going to slow down sometime, and that time had arrived. They went 11–13 the rest of the month as the offense went into a tailspin. Traynor briefly benched Suhr after his average plummeted from .335 to .293 over a stretch of several weeks. The streaky Rizzo suffered through an 0-for-17 slump. During a 10-game span in mid-late August, the Pirates failed to homer and left a total of 106 men on base. They ended that stretch by losing three of four to the dismal Phillies.

The drought didn't hurt very much because the Pirates nearest challengers were struggling, too. Klinger's 6–0 shutout of the Giants on September 1 (his fourth win over New York that season) gave the Pirates a season-high seven-game edge over the Reds and Cubs, and dropped New York to seven-and-a-half back. The Pirates' lead appeared to be nearly insurmountable, but that did nothing to soothe the minds of the two men in charge, both of whom by now were beginning to really crack up. Benswanger admitted to the *New York Times* that he had begun taking two different anti-anxiety medications.[43] Traynor couldn't stop obsessing about the race, joking in the September 7 *Pittsburgh Post-Gazette*, "I only let baseball take up 24 hours a day of my time. The rest of the day I go in for the European situation."[44] He couldn't sleep, had lost 20 pounds, was smoking constantly, and generally looked awful.

It was almost as if Traynor and Benswanger couldn't understand how this unremarkable group of players, whom they had all but given up on two-and-a-half months earlier, was on the brink of going to the World Series. Nor did they seem to have any confidence their club had enough talent to finish the job. Sportswriter Havey Boyle remembered no such insecurity around the Pirates last pennant winner, 11 years earlier. In the August 29 *Pittsburgh Post-Gazette*, he wrote, "In contrast to the pained looks one receives around nervous Pirate headquarters if the World Series is mentioned ... there was no jittery feeling prevailing then, although the desperate boys of '27 were staggering and tottering right down to the stretch."[45]

The Pirates shored up their pinch-hitting corps for the last month of the season, acquiring former Tigers and Senators star Heinie Manush from Toronto of the International League, where he had been hitting .303. "We lost at least five games the past month which we would have saved with a hit or even a long fly ball," said Traynor in the September 1 *Pittsburgh Press*.[46] "Woody Jensen isn't hitting the ball for us and Red Lucas [a slugging pitcher who often drew pinch-hitting duties] ... hasn't even driven a ball out of the infield in a pinch this year."[47] Traynor was right; the Pirate bench was atrocious. Their pinch-hitters were hitting only .123 (8-for-65) on the season. Manush was a nice little pick-up; he hit well in September and gave the bench a boost.

Following Klinger's September 1 shutout of the Giants, the Pirates lost five of their next seven. The mini-slump coincided with injuries to Arky Vaughan, who was out of the lineup during this period first because of a spike wound on his hand, and then because of a stiff neck. Cincinnati trimmed the Pirates' lead to four games, defeating Pittsburgh, 5–3, under the lights at Crosley Field on September 8. This was a particularly galling defeat. Three of Cincinnati's five runs were unearned thanks to three errors by Rizzo in left field. Four of the eight hits off Blanton never left the infield. "I lost that game," remarked a downcast Rizzo afterward.[48] Traynor struggled to put a positive spin on things. "We've been beating ourselves. We'll likely break out in a five or six game winning stretch and put the pennant out of reach."[49] Meanwhile, he was fuming at Bill Terry, who had suggested to reporters that the Pirates should quit baseball if they lost the pennant.[50]

The reeling Bucs began an eastern trip on September 14 with a four-game lead over the Chicago Cubs. The Cubs had replaced manager Charlie Grimm with Gabby Hartnett on July 20. At first, the move made no difference at all; in their first 33 games under Hartnett Chicago went 16–17, prompting their new manager to describe his team as "highly overrated."[51] But as the Pirates were beginning their September East Coast swing, the Cubs had won 14 of their last 21.

The next week or so would be grueling for both teams; Pittsburgh was to play four doubleheaders over an eight-day stretch, while the Cubs had four doubleheaders in six days. It did not begin well for the Pirates. While the Cubs were defeating Boston, the Giants swept a twinbill from the Pirates, 3–0 and 10–3, which cut the lead to 2½. Traynor's troubles began before the first pitch was even thrown. His scheduled starter in the first game, Bob Klinger, developed a sore arm while warming up in the bullpen. Cy Blanton had to jump in and make an emergency start. He pitched decently, but the Pirate hitters could not touch Hal Schumacher. In the second game, New York put it away early, pounding Ed Brandt and Bill Swift for seven runs in the second inning. After the game, reporters found a "tragic looking" Traynor slumped atop a trunk near the Pirate clubhouse "looking for all the world like a fellow upon whom the whole world had tumbled."[52] Beside him sat Benswanger, trying to lift his manager's spirits. "Quit worrying," Benswanger insisted. "We're still in front."[53] Benswanger assured Traynor that whether the Pirates won or lost the pennant, he would return as manager in 1939. But Traynor found this to be small consolation. He moped back to his hotel room, unable to eat or sleep that evening.

The Pirates rebounded the next day, defeating the Giants, 7–2, thanks to five home runs, two of them by Paul Waner. Shortstop Dick Bartell broke his finger in this game, which dashed any of New York's remaining pennant hopes. On September 16, while the Cubs were rained out, the Pirates split a doubleheader in Boston. In the 11th inning of the opener, a searing Rizzo blasted his 20th home run of the year, which not only won the game but also broke Vaughan's single-season team record. In the nightcap, Traynor was forced give relief ace Mace Brown only his second start of the season. The pile of doubleheaders was stretching Traynor's pitching staff to the limit, and to make things worse they were down a man because Red Lucas had just left the team to spend ten days with his wife, who was suffering from pneumonia. Brown gave the Pirates seven quality innings, but Swift, making his third appearance in four days, allowed three runs in the bottom of the ninth as the Braves pulled out a 5–4 win.

Klinger's six-hitter beat Boston, 2–1, in the series finale on September 17. The Pirates trailed, 1–0, heading into the ninth, but Suhr led off the ninth with a fly ball that became a double when center fielder Vince DiMaggio and right fielder Johnny Cooney collided. Lee Handley's single scored Suhr and tied the game; three batters later Lloyd Waner knocked in Handley with what proved to be the winning run.

The Pirate clubhouse was ecstatic afterward. Todd said of Klinger, "That guy had as much stuff and as much heart as I've seen in a long, long time."[54] Klinger had been an ongoing source of frustration for Traynor. He had been in and out of action all season with arm problems, but privately Traynor suspected that Klinger's troubles were more in his head than his arm.[55] He commented after the game, perhaps with a tinge of sarcasm, "You saw Klinger pitch today ... with a sore arm. Wonder what he'd be like with a good arm?"[56] The Cubs, however, shaved another half-game off the lead as they took a doubleheader from the Giants. Chicago was back to within 2½ games.

Bauers followed with a superb performance the next afternoon as he tossed a four-hit shutout at the Phillies, allowing just one man to reach third base. The second game of the doubleheader against Philadelphia was rained out. Thanks to Brooklyn's defeat of the Cubs, the Pirates ended the day with their lead back up to 3½ games.

Traynor and his team then traveled to Brooklyn, where they spent the next three days holed up in their hotel watching it rain. The Great Hurricane of 1938, the first hurricane to strike New England in almost 70 years, was rampaging up the East Coast. The Cubs had their games rained out, too. Reporters at the time depicted this storm as a bit of good fortune for the Pirates; it was too late in the season to make up these lost games, which meant the Pirates were able to maintain their lead while knocking a few games off the schedule.

Shirley Povich wrote in the September 21 *Washington Post* that the pennant race was over "unless the Pirates suffer a complete collapse."[57] The *New York Times'* Roscoe McGowan agreed, concluding that the Pirates "would have to make the greatest flop in history" for the Cubs to sneak into the World Series.[58] Even the *Chicago Tribune* conceded in a headline, "Cubs Must Work Miracle."[59] The Pirates began selling World Series tickets on September 19 and ordered the construction of a new press box to accommodate the expected World Series media crush.

Benswanger later rationalized that the hurricane cost his team the pennant. "As we sat around hotel lobbies during the storm a hot team cooled off and never regained its winning momentum."[60] The rain did cost the Pirates four games against bottom-feeder teams Brooklyn and Philadelphia. But it also deprived the Cubs of two games against the lowly Phillies. And the idea that it stripped the Pirates of momentum is simply nonsense. The Pirates had won four of their last five before the storm hit, and after the skies cleared they won four of their next five.

The Pirates had seven games remaining on their schedule as they entered Wrigley Field on Tuesday afternoon, September 27 for a three-game series with Chicago. Though Pittsburgh had been playing well, the Cubs still managed to gain ground. Chicago was on a seven-game winning streak, had won 10 of its last 11, and trailed by just 1½ games. "Traynor Feels Confident, Or So He Claims," read the headline in the *Chicago Tribune*. "We have the edge and will continue to have it as long as we're in first place," Traynor insisted, possibly trying to convince himself.[61] "We took over first place July 12. We've been under pressure for more than two months. The worst kind of pressure.... Now we'll see what the Cubs do when the heat is on. I don't think they'll stand up."[62]

With his pitching in shambles after that string of doubleheaders, Hartnett handed the ball to a lame-armed Dizzy Dean, who hadn't started a game in more than a month. Dean had been battling arm problems all season and he knew his brilliant fastball was gone for good. "I throw hard enough but I don't throw fast enough no more."[63] But Hartnett was desperate and, in this era before the advent of set starting rotations, called on Dean out of nowhere. "I stuck my neck out but I had a feeling he'd come through for us," Hartnett later recalled.[64]

Initially it appeared the Pirates would make Harnett look like a fool. Though they didn't score in the first inning, the Pirates got two solid hits while Paul Waner and Suhr both hit lasers that the Cub defense turned into outs. Apparently they had Ol' Diz measured. But from that point on, Dean was remarkable. Relying on slow curves, changeups, good control, and guts, Dean left the Pirates baffled. He carried his club into the ninth inning with a 2–0 lead. He hit Vaughan with a pitch to lead off the ninth. Suhr followed with a pop-up, and pinch-hitter Jensen forced Vaughan at second. Handley then rapped a double to left center, advancing Jensen to third base. With that, Hartnett removed Dean and brought in his ace, Bill Lee. Dean strode off to a standing ovation.

Lee's first pitch eluded catcher-manager Hartnett for a wild pitch, allowing Jensen to score and Handley to move to third with the potential tying run. But Lee, the best pitcher in the National League in 1938, regrouped and struck out Todd swinging to end the game and pull the Cubs to within a half-game of the Pirates. Chicago's veteran utility man Tony Lazzeri called Dean's effort "the greatest exhibition of sheer nerve I've ever seen on a diamond."[65] Dean admitted he was in agony but added, "I wasn't going to have that stop me from winnin' the greatest game of my life."[66]

The next afternoon, Wrigley Field was packed again for what would be one of the most memorable games in baseball history. Chicago's young 19-game winner Clay Bryant went to the mound, while Traynor countered with Bob Klinger. The Pirates handed Chicago a 1–0 lead in the second inning. Todd's passed ball on a third strike to Billy Jurges put runners at first and second and led to the first run of the game when third baseman Lee Handley threw Bryant's ground ball into the Pirate dugout.

The score remained that way until the sixth inning, when the Pirates put three runs on the board after two men were out. Rizzo hit his 21st home run of the year to tie it; later in the inning Handley singled in two more runs to put Pittsburgh on top. But Chicago bounced back to re-tie the game in the bottom of the sixth.

The first of two controversial umpiring decisions came in the top of the seventh. With runners at the corners, Rizzo was at the plate awaiting a two-ball, one-strike delivery from Cubs reliever Vance Page. As Page went into his motion, Ens, from the third base coach's box, screamed that Page had balked. Traynor, coaching at first base, claimed he saw umpire Dolly Stark flinch, as if he were ready to call a balk. But there was no call. Page delivered the pitch, which Rizzo bounced to third baseman Stan Hack. Hack leaped high in the air, snared the ball, and started an inning-ending double play. Traynor, Ens, and several players surrounded home plate umpire George Barr and pleaded with him for five minutes but neither Barr nor Stark would budge. "The president of the league sends us quantity in umpires, but no quality," Ens snarled after the game.[67] "[Stark] saw it.... Why the hell didn't he call it?"[68]

In the top of the eighth, with the score still knotted, 3–3, and Pirate runners at first and third and no one out, Hartnett summoned former Pirate Larry French from the bullpen. Traynor countered with Manush, who batted for Pep Young. Manush won the battle, singling home Vaughan to break the tie. Out went French, in came Lee. Handley greeted him by smacking a run-scoring single to make the score 5–3, while Manush lumbered around to third base — and still no one was out.

Todd came to the plate, facing a drawn-in infield, with a chance to put the game out of reach. But he tapped weakly to Jurges, who gunned down Manush at the plate. Next, in a questionable move, Traynor let the weak-hitting Klinger bat for himself. Not only did Traynor not pinch-hit, he also let Klinger swing away rather than bunt. Lee got Klinger to ground into a double play to end the inning, pitcher to shortstop to first base. The Bucs had taken a two-run lead but had blown a prime opportunity to add on.

Ripper Collins led off the Chicago eighth with a single to center. Traynor immediately called Swift out of the bullpen, which made his decision not to pinch-hit for Klinger in the previous half-inning all the more puzzling. Swift promptly walked Jurges. Another Todd passed ball allowed Collins to sneak into third. Then Lazzeri, batting for Lee, laced a double to right field, scoring Collins and advancing Jurges to third. After an intentional walk to Hack, which loaded the bases with no one out, second baseman Billy Herman singled to right, scoring Jurges with the tying run. Pinch-runner Joe Marty tried to score on the play, but a perfect throw from Paul Waner nailed him at the plate. On came Mace Brown, who ended the rally by enticing Frank Demaree to ground into a double play.

The Pirates went quietly against ancient Charlie Root in the top in the ninth inning. By this time, it was dusk; from the stands it was difficult to see the baseball. The umpiring crew met to discuss calling the game. Had they ended play with the score tied, the clubs would have replayed the contest in its entirety as part of a doubleheader the following day. Given that Chicago had churned through six pitchers that afternoon, the Pirates would have entered the doubleheader with a distinct advantage. However, the umpires elected to play on. "Just 60 seconds and it might have been different," Traynor mused. "Dolly Stark told me he was going to call it."[69] But the two teams would finish out the ninth.

The bottom of the inning started innocuously enough with Phil Cavarretta flying out to Lloyd Waner and Carl Reynolds grounding out to Tommy Thevenow at second. Hartnett was next. Brown jumped out in front in the count no balls and two strikes on a couple of curveballs. Ray Berres, who was watching from the bench, remembered years later, "He made Hartnett look bad on a couple of curves that went down. Then he came back with one more. He was really going to snap one off. And like so often happens when you try too hard, he hung it."[70]

Hartnett guessed right. "I figured Brown for a curve on that pitch and I got set.... I gambled on a home run or nothing."[71] He hammered it to left field. "I felt it was gone the second I hit it," said Hartnett.[72] So did Brown, who at the crack of the bat raised his hands to his face in angst. In the semi-darkness, fans couldn't see the ball very well, but a roar built as they watched Rizzo creep closer and closer to the wall before he looked up helplessly as the ball sailed over his head and into the left field bleachers for a game-winning home run. The shot became known as "The Homer in the Gloamin'."

Wrigley Field went mad. Fans poured out of the stands and surrounded Hartnett as he circled the bases. Photographs show a beaming, barrel-chested Hartnett crossing the plate with legions of fans right on his heels. Teammates carried Hartnett off the field on their shoulders. "That was the greatest thrill of my life," Hartnett said.[73]

The Pirates were experiencing significantly different emotions. "It was a nightmare," said Brown.[74] Paul Waner told author Lawrence Ritter, "I just stood there in right field and watched Hartnett circle the bases, and take the lousy pennant with him."[75] The Pirate clubhouse was a dark place. "It was heart-breaking," recalled Bauers. "You figure on something and all of a sudden the skids were pulled out from under you."[76] Brown sat in front of locker sobbing. "I stayed with him all night, I was so afraid he was going to commit suicide," said Paul Waner.[77]

Traynor looked like he had witnessed a murder, sitting silently at his locker, staring into space. Eventually he got up, dressed, and trudged back to the Belmont Hotel alongside his faithful confidant, Ens. The length of that walk seemed to grow and grow each time Traynor re-told the story over the years. In reality it was only about a mile, although it must have seemed endless. "I was so wrought up inside I was ready to explode. Ens must have known how I felt. He never said a word," said Traynor.[78] "If Jewel had so much as opened his mouth, I believe I would have slugged him."[79]

Pittsburgh remained only a half-game out of first place, but emotionally they were done. And the Cubs felt indestructible. "We could've beaten nine Babe Ruths," boasted Billy Herman.[80] The Pirates went out the next day against Lee, who was making his fourth consecutive appearance and second start in four days, and did nothing. They lost, 10–1. It was Lee's sixth win of the month, his 22nd of the season. After the game, Traynor was spotted wearing a sweatshirt and uniform pants, drawing on a cigarette, and saying to Ens, "You can never give up."[81] But some months later he admitted, "I felt as bad as I'll ever feel, I think, that night we left Chicago."[82] The Cubs were home free; they clinched two days later.

It was an expensive defeat for the Pirates. They had to refund $1.25 million in World Series ticket money. Postage for those refunds and the cost of building the press box addition totaled $50,000. Traynor's colleagues were sympathetic. The normally crusty Terry sent a touching telegram, reading, "I have been through what you are going through now. I think you did a great job." ("That's one of the nicest things that's ever happened to me," Traynor said of Terry's note.[83]) Casey Stengel offered, "If Traynor had pitching he would have breezed in."[84] The media spin was that Traynor had done yeoman work keeping an inferior team in the pennant race for so long.

Traynor gamely appeared at Games Three and Four of the World Series between Chicago and the New York Yankees at Wrigley Field, where he was forced to watch the Cubs break with tradition and unfurl the National League pennant, a ceremony which usually waited until the following year. Traynor took it in good humor. "Gabby still thinks he's dreaming. He wants to get that pennant hung out for fear he wakes up."[85] After watching the Yankees dispose of the Cubs four games to none, Traynor went back to Brookville and then took refuge in the woods of Wisconsin for the first time in seven years, hanging out with Burleigh Grimes, Frank Crosetti of the Yankees, and Morrie Arnovich of the Phillies, undoubtedly reliving the September disaster and trying to forget it at the same time.

Brown, the victim of Hartnett's home run, recovered and had a few more productive seasons. At an old-timers day many years later, he claimed to have no regrets. "I threw three curve balls to Hartnett then and I would do the same today."[86] But Paul Waner didn't think his friend ever totally got over what had happened. "He can laugh about it now, practically 30 years later. Well, he can almost laugh about it anyway. When he stops laughing, he kind of shudders a bit, you know, like it's a bad dream that he can't quite get out of his mind."[87]

Traynor couldn't escape it either. Through the years, he joked about it and rationalized it and sort of made it sound like no big deal. But, quietly, it ate at him. "The Yanks knocked off the Cubs in a hurry, four straight. Imagine what they would have done to us. But I would have liked to have tried it anyway," he said.[88] A friend from many years later, Chuck Reichblum, noted, "He always claimed they never should have played that last inning because it was too dark. He thought they should have called the game. I think he was still very bitter about that. That was probably the biggest disappointment in his life. I'm sure it was. That was the only time I ever heard him be in any way bitter or regretful."[89]

It is a natural human tendency to search for causes and explanations. People are uncomfortable with ambiguity and uncertainty. In sports, someone can be hailed cavalierly as a hero and another branded as a goat, but seldom is the truth really that simple. Some baseball historians place blame for the Pirates second-place finish squarely on Traynor's shoulders.[90] Supposedly his reluctance to use his reserves left his regulars with nothing left in the tank down the stretch. It is an easy explanation, an obvious explanation, but probably not an altogether accurate explanation. A close look at the numbers suggests that Traynor has gotten a bum rap.

Roster management was never one of Traynor's strengths, and there is no question he worked his starting players like dogs in 1938. The only regulars to appear in fewer than 140 games were Handley, who was injured for an extended period, and Todd, who nonetheless played in more games than any other catcher in the major leagues. Among the bench players, no one received more than 125 at-bats—Tommy Thevenow was on the roster all season and played in only 15 games. Clearly Traynor believed that the way to win games was to run his best eight position players out there day after day after day.

Less clear is whether this philosophy actually hurt the team in 1938. None of his hitters suffered a dramatic dropoff the last month of the season. Vaughan lost eight points off his average in September and early October. Suhr lost seven points, Handley five. On the other hand, Rizzo (.313 with nine home runs and 29 RBIs) had an incredible final 29 games, and Lloyd Waner also played well down the stretch, batting .365. The Pirates did see their runs scored per game tail off significantly, falling from 5.48 runs in June and July to 4.44 runs in August, September, and October. But, then again, they averaged only 4.00 runs per game in April and May and they certainly weren't tired then. Among the pitchers, Blanton and Jim Tobin had a rough final month, but the staff work-horse, Bauers, was solid and Klinger was stellar. In sum, there is little evidence of a team-wide malaise.

No one could reasonably expect the Pirates to have maintained the blazing pace they set in June and July, when they won nearly 75 percent of their games. They tailed off in August, finishing the month with a 16–16 record, but they were still playing good baseball for most of the month. Despite the .500 mark, they outscored their opponents by an average of nearly one run per game that month, which suggests they might have simply run into a little bit of bad luck. Heading into the fateful Chicago series, Pittsburgh was 12–10 in September and had scored 107 runs to their opponents' 89. Not exactly a torrid pace and not what one might want from a team that was trying to nail down a pennant, but better than most would expect from a group that was purportedly so exhausted that it couldn't function.

There was no huge collapse here. This wasn't like the 1964 Phillies, who lost 10 straight in late September, the 1969 Cubs, who dropped eight in a row in the final month, or the 2007 Mets, who lost 12 of their last 17. The Pirates were doing well until one bad series. The story wasn't so much about the Pirates falling to pieces; rather, it was much more about the Cubs, who went 21–5 in September, playing out of their minds.

It is not obvious what Traynor should have done differently given the talent at his disposal. It is hard to pinpoint any glaring strategic errors that he might have made. Regarding the Cubs series, rookie right-hander Rip Sewell later claimed, "I pleaded with Pie to use me in that series, but I could understand when he told me he simply had to go with his regular starters."[91] This wasn't mere sentiment on Traynor's part; it was a very pragmatic decision. The starters weren't pitching badly and Sewell, an unproven commodity at that point in his career, hadn't pitched all that well in 1938.

Red Lucas later griped that he should have received more work, declaring, "If Pie Traynor had given me, and one other pitcher I know of [presumably Ed Brandt], regular turns, we'd have won that pennant."[92] If by "regular turns" Lucas meant starts, then his claim is absurd. During the season reporters and others around the league talked about Traynor as if he were some kind of brilliant mad scientist, mixing and matching his starters to perfection. There is nothing in the record of Lucas or Brandt to suggest they had more to offer than the guys who were making regular starts. But if Lucas meant that he should have pitched in relief more often, he might have an argument. Brown was shaky during the second half of the season. Perhaps he was worn out, but considering that his workload was not much heavier than it had been in 1936 or 1937, it is more likely that he was just due to regress to normal following an incredible first half. Perhaps Traynor could have salvaged a game or two by using someone other than Brown, but who knows? Lucas was hurting much of the season, Sewell was green, and though Traynor undervalued Brandt, it is impossible to say definitively whether the lefty could have made a difference.

In terms of the everyday players, Traynor second-guessed himself for not replacing Paul Waner with Manush in the starting lineup in September, but that probably would have been a mistake.[93] Waner hardly had a bad month, while Manush had just 12 more major league at-bats left in him following the season; he did a good job in limited action the final few weeks, but the tank was close to empty. Some players apparently were urging Traynor to activate coach Johnny Gooch and insert him at catcher in place of Todd, but it is not clear how a 40-year-old man who hadn't played a major league game in five years was going to help matters.[94]

This is not to say Traynor is blameless. His ongoing September psychodrama was not what one would expect from a strong leader and certainly could not have inspired confidence. Research supports the notion that emotions are contagious.[95] Those who spend time around neurotic, pessimistic people become more likely to be neurotic and pessimistic themselves. Moreover, expectations can impact performance in any aspect of life. "Confidence breeds success" is not just some piece of motivational claptrap that self-help writers feed to their readers; the statement carries a lot of psychological truth. Conversely, if people expect others around them to fail, that can be sensed and it can become a self-fulfilling prophecy.

If members of the press corps could read Traynor's woe-are-we attitude, then certainly his players could, too. It was almost like he expected to lose. So when it came to the Cubs series, perhaps his players unconsciously also expected the worst. Chicago, on the other hand, was brimming with confidence and probably felt almost destined to win. And they performed accordingly.

There was no single reason for what happened, no elegant explanation. The Pirates played a little over their heads in June and July to put themselves in position to win it all. They might have had a little bad luck in August, and then got beaten out in the end by a Chicago team that not only got very hot at the right time, but also probably was, on balance, a slightly better ballclub. Traynor deserves some blame, but there is plenty of blame (and credit) to go around. As Traynor said later, "Nobody knows what starts a thing like that, and after it starts there's not a thing in the world you can do about it except just sit and suffer."[96]

12

Keen Regret

True to his word, Benwanger did not hesitate in offering Traynor a new contract for 1939. "We are more than satisfied with Pie's direction of the team and do not blame him in the slightest for the loss of the pennant."[1] Traynor promised changes. "I know the fans here won't support the same team that faded in 1938 and I'm going to do everything possible to remedy the situation."[2] He even rented an apartment in Cincinnati over the winter in order to be closer to railroad transportation in the event he had to travel on short notice to discuss a trade.

Traynor identified the catching spot as a particular area in need of an upgrade. "[Al] Todd was a poor thrower. [Ray] Berres was just an ordinary catcher," he offered years later.[3] Todd also apparently had a formidable ego and the Pirate pitching staff found him difficult to work with. His sluggish performance in the Chicago series at the end of the 1938 season was enough for Traynor; he made no secret of his desire to get Todd out of town. At the end of the winter meetings in December, he dealt Todd and outfielder Johnny Dickshot to Boston in exchange for catcher Ray Mueller, who had been Al Lopez's backup with the Braves.

Following the deal, Todd ripped Traynor. "Traynor had to put the rap on somebody and he made me the goat. It's a funny thing why he let me catch [more games] than any other catcher in the league the last two seasons if I was so lousy behind the plate."[4] Todd speculated that things would have worked out differently had he delivered in the first game of the Cubs series, with two men on in the ninth inning. "If I had [gotten a hit] Pittsburgh would have won that game and possibly the pennant and I would have been a great guy. But I struck out and now they say I am not a championship catcher."[5] Traynor called the 27-year-old Mueller "the coming catcher in the league."[6] But unfortunately, like many of Traynor's trades, this one didn't turn out well. Mueller would enjoy three very good seasons with Cincinnati later in his career, but his time in Pittsburgh was a disaster. This trade weakened the Pirates in an already-weak area.

Despite Traynor's promises, that would be the only significant transaction of the offseason, though it wasn't for lack of effort. At the winter meetings, the Pirates fell agonizingly short in their bid for 20-year-old Fred Hutchinson, a right-handed pitcher who had won 25 games for Seattle in the Pacific Coast

League in 1938. The Pirates were prepared to send Seattle Dickshot, Joe Bowman, Woody Jensen, and Rip Sewell, plus $25,000 for Hutchinson. Everyone thought the deal was done; rival executives were congratulating Traynor and Benswanger. But the Detroit Tigers sneaked in under the wire and offered a better deal (fewer players, but much more cash) and stole Hutchinson away. Benswanger claimed he had been "double crossed" by Seattle owner Emil Sick. Traynor described himself as flabbergasted. "I thought we had him. Why does the American League have to get all the promising young players?" he moaned.[7]

At one point the Pirates were in the running for hulking slugger Zeke Bonura of Washington, but the Giants won that bidding war. Traynor also hopped a train to St. Louis, where he met with the Cardinals' Branch Rickey. Rickey wasted no time getting to the point. "Everybody that wants to trade with me asks for Medwick or Mize. I'll start the same way with you. Give me Vaughan or Rizzo."[8]

"He had me kind of stumped there," recalled Traynor.[9] The talks with Rickey went nowhere.

Thus, Pittsburgh entered 1939 with almost exactly the same group of players with whom they ended 1938. Brooklyn's new player-manager Leo Durocher looked over the Pirate roster and shook his head. "The Pirates should have changed 90 percent of the faces on that team after what happened last year."[10]

Traynor reported to San Bernardino with Eve and her sister, Jean. Eve had injured her back in a fall over the winter and was experiencing some discomfort, but she postponed surgery to join her husband on the coast. Pie came to California free of the "haunted look" that he wore at the end of the previous season.[11] But while the look may have been gone, the ghouls were still floating around. "What the Pirates will need is a good course in psychology," Traynor admitted, later adding, "Even if we're out in front by ten games next September 1, we'll keep looking back over our shoulders."[12] The rest of the team evidently felt the same way as their manager, which is why cleaning the house of aging veterans and starting over from scratch might not have been a bad idea. First baseman Elbie Fletcher, who joined the team in a trade midway through the 1939 season, told author Donald Honig, "That's all they talked about on the Pirate club that year: Hartnett's home run. I knew they weren't going to win it. That home run was still on everybody's mind, haunting them like a ghost."[13]

In what had become an annual rite of spring, Paul Waner was unhappy again. The 1938 season was by far the worst of his long career; his .280 batting average was a 74-point drop-off from the year before. Age, the enemy of every athlete, had hit him hard and fast. Waner's new contract for 1939 called for a 45 percent pay cut, which he described as "nothing short of an insult."[14] Traynor did not seem to be concerned. He thought (inaccurately, as it turned out) that Heinie Manush still had some life left in him, and was excited about rookie Fern Bell. "Even if Paul does come into camp he's going to find a couple of fellows standing ahead of him."[15] Furthermore, Traynor was drooling over 23-year-old rookie Bob Elliott, a Pirate farmhand who worked out with the team at spring training in San Bernardino. "This fellow right now is one of our best outfielders."[16]

Traynor and Waner had been the two faces of the Pirate franchise for 13 years, pretty good friends at one time, but by this point they had had about enough of each other. In mid–March, Traynor omitted Waner's name when replying to a reporter's question about the status of his outfield. When the reporter asked specifically about the old Pirate mainstay, Traynor put on an acerbic smile, "Darned if I didn't forget about Paul Waner. I hadn't even thought of him."[17]

Years later, it did sometimes seem like Traynor had purged all memories of Waner from his mind. "He liked Lloyd Waner and talked about him a lot. He always said Lloyd Waner was a better defensive center fielder than Willie Mays. But I never heard him talk about Paul Waner," said sportswriter Roy McHugh. "I don't know if he didn't care for Paul or not. But it was striking that he talked so much and so favorably about Lloyd Waner but never said much about Paul."[18]

In 1967, television station WIIC in Pittsburgh filmed Traynor taking a tour of the Baseball Hall of Fame with the Hall's director, Ken Smith. The two men stopped in front of Paul Waner's plaque, as Smith noted that Lloyd would soon be joining his brother in the Cooperstown shrine. Traynor replied with a long, spirited tribute to Lloyd. About Paul, he said not a word.[19]

As always, Traynor was preoccupied with his pitching staff that spring. "I need pitchers. Two pitchers anyhow."[20] The Pirates had released Lucas. Klinger had spent the winter receiving treatments on his arm, but Traynor had no idea what to expect from him. He wanted to trade Blanton, whom he thought was talented but lazy; and the enigmatic Bauers showed up fat, with a shoulder that was sore from an offseason car accident. Traynor also recognized he was going to have to carry promising but untested rookies Ken Heintzelman and Bill Clemensen on the staff or else risk losing their rights to another team. "The pitching staff is a pain in the neck," he stated bluntly.[21]

The pain grew sharper. The Pirates were playing poorly in their early exhibition games and Traynor was even edgier than usual. On March 22, the Pirates returned to their hotel in San Bernardino after playing a game in Los Angeles. Most of the players dropped their luggage in the hotel lobby, went immediately to the dining room, and then picked up their luggage after dinner and proceeded to their rooms. But as Traynor was on his way back to his room, he spotted the luggage of Bauers and Ed Brandt sitting alone in the lobby unclaimed, its owners nowhere to be found. Traynor decided to camp out in the lobby and wait for his pitchers, two notorious carousers. He was there until 3:00 in the morning before he gave up and went to bed. Bauers and Brandt staggered in sometime closer to dawn. When they arrived at the ballpark the next morning,

Traynor was waiting. He released Brandt on the spot. After dinner that evening he met with Bauers, read him the riot act, and threatened him with a fine. "I'm sick and tired of these playboys and I'm going to have discipline if I have to run one or two more players off the squad," he vowed.[22]

At the time, Traynor probably assumed that the loss of Brandt would be offset by the signing of 31-year-old Tiny Chaplin, a former Boston Bee who had won 43 games over the previous two seasons with San Diego in the Pacific Coast League. Traynor and Chaplin went way back; they were together for that postseason exhibition series in Cuba in 1930, and Chaplin's excellent mound work in that series surely stuck in Traynor's mind. At the time of Brandt's release, it seemed the acquisition of Chaplin was all but a done deal. But two days later, Chaplin was killed in an automobile accident.

The staff suffered another blow on Easter Sunday, April 9, when the Pirates were in New Orleans for an exhibition game with the Cleveland Indians. It had been an eventful day. Paul Waner had finally ended his holdout, signing for $12,000, $3,000 less than he had been demanding. Early in the game, immediately following a home run, Cleveland's Johnny Allen fired a fastball into Lee Handley's skull. Handley suffered a concussion and was admitted to a hospital, where three days later he had a blood clot removed from his left ear without anesthetic. Handley was lost to the team for the first two weeks of the regular season.

But the biggest story of the day involved Blanton. "I had intended to allow Blanton to go about six or seven innings," Traynor related years later. "I never saw Cy look as good as he did that spring. He was in great shape and his arm was loose and strong that year."[23] Blanton had a perfect game through five innings. He walked Earl Averill in the sixth, but escaped the inning with the no-hitter intact. Traynor decided to leave him in. "When Blanton went out for the seventh, I could see him bearing down all the harder. He actually forced himself in those late innings and that isn't any good from a pitcher in the spring."[24] Blanton put down the Indians in order the next inning. He had given his manager the seven innings he had been hoping for, but against his better judgment, Traynor sent Blanton back out there. "I remember talking to a friend of mine and telling him I hoped the Indians would get a hit and break the spell. I didn't want Cy to go the full nine innings, yet I couldn't take him out with a no-hitter coming up," said Traynor.[25] Blanton got his no-hitter; he lost his career in the process. Three weeks later, an x-ray revealed torn ligaments in his right elbow.

Traynor's decision to let a worn-out Blanton go the distance in a meaningless exhibition game is beyond comprehension; that he knew his staff was thin made the move that much more inexcusable. Indirectly, the decision played no small part in Traynor losing his job.

The Cy Blanton story does not end well. He pitched ineffectively in a handful of games at the end of the 1939 season and was released in 1940. He spent a few lackluster seasons with the Phillies, got released in 1942, and three years later died in a mental institution at the age of 37.[26]

The Pirates got off to a dreadful start in the regular season, losing eight of the nine games they played in April. Ray Mueller was hitting .161 and had lost his starting catcher's job, Lloyd Waner was relegated to hitting eighth for a time, Manush was useless off the bench, and Blanton was on the shelf. But the Pirates' luck turned a bit in May. Handley returned to the lineup and Rip Sewell was doing a decent job carrying some of the burden left by the injuries to Blanton and Bauers. Klinger threw a three-hitter and then a six-hitter during an early May road trip. During one stretch the Bucs won 16 of 24 games.

One particularly sweet win came on May 26 against the Cubs. Leading, 8–5, in the sixth inning at Wrigley Field, Traynor brought Mace Brown out of the bullpen in a one-on, one-out situation. The first batter he faced was, of all people, Gabby Hartnett, the man who homered off Brown to wreck the Pirates' 1938 season. This time Brown struck out Hartnett looking, and ended up fanning six of the 12 batters he faced to earn a save. It was a great symbolic triumph for Brown after the disaster of the previous September. "Striking out Hartnett was worth a month of salary to me."[27]

Sewell picked up his sixth victory on June 1, 5–2 over the Phillies, a win that moved the Pirates into third place, 5½ games behind league-leading Cincinnati. But beneath the surface, there were signs of trouble. The Pirates' lack of pitching depth was catching up to them. Traynor really had only six pitchers upon whom he could rely. Blanton was out, Bauers was hurting again, and Traynor had no faith in the two youngsters, Heintzelman and Clemensen, and hardly ever used them. In the second game of a doubleheader against Brooklyn on June 4, Traynor let Heintzelman take a brutal beating — ten hits and nine runs over three innings. He felt bad about it but, "I [was] in a jam for pitchers. I had no one I could throw in to relieve [him]."[28]

On June 7, the Pirates finally released Manush, who was 0-for-12 and had played in only one game the previous month. They replaced him with another aging future Hall of Famer, Chuck Klein, a former Triple Crown winner whose career had fallen off a cliff in Philadelphia. With Paul Waner recovering from appendicitis and a struggling Johnny Rizzo nursing a sore leg, Klein would receive plenty of opportunities to play, but he was of little immediate help. The Pirates lost eight of nine on an early June East Coast swing to fall to sixth place with a record of 23–26.

Baseball took a few days off in mid–June to celebrate the game's 100th anniversary. Traynor was among the guests on hand in Cooperstown, New York, for the dedication of the Baseball Hall of Fame. When someone suggested to Traynor that it was inevitable that he would be honored with a Hall of Fame plaque someday, he joked, "If they want to sculpt, they better get me now while I look like something. Another three months and ol' Traynor'll never look the same."[29]

Sure enough, by this time Traynor's physical appearance was changing. From the time he broke into the league until the mid–1930s, he hardly seemed to age at all. When one studies photographs of Traynor from his playing days, it is very difficult to tell by looking at his face or body exactly when the picture was taken. He looked pretty much the same at 25 as he did at 35. But managing aged him in dog years. By 1939, wrinkles had developed around his eyes, his hair had grown thinner and grayer, and he appeared perpetually exhausted. Photos from the late 1930s and early 1940s reveal the first hints of what Traynor would look like as an old man.

The Pirates made an excellent deal as they returned from the break, trading a minor league infielder to the Boston Bees for first baseman Elbie Fletcher. Fletcher, who broke into the majors at age 18, had a skill set remarkably similar to Gus Suhr's. Both were solid defenders who had some power and compensated for mediocre batting averages by drawing a lot of walks. However, Fletcher was ten years younger than Suhr, who was struggling at the plate and whose defense, in Traynor's mind, had slipped. Fletcher almost immediately took over the first base job from Suhr and kept it until 1946.

Nonetheless, the Pirates continued to play uninspired baseball and their fans were becoming frustrated. They booed the team resoundingly in an 11–2 loss to Philadelphia on June 17. Rip Sewell gave up seven runs in just two innings, and the Pirates committed three errors. With the Pirates mucking around near the bottom of the standings, the name of former Cardinals and Giants star Frankie Frisch began surfacing as a possible replacement for Traynor. Frisch was spending the year out of uniform after the St. Louis Cardinals fired him as their manager in 1938. He signed a $20,000 contract to broadcast Braves and Red Sox home games over the Colonial Network, which stretched across New England.

At the end of June, with the Pirates ten games out and going nowhere, Traynor benched Paul Waner, going with an outfield of Klein, Lloyd Waner, and Rizzo. Traynor suspected that the over-the-hill Klein, who the Pirates picked up for a $300 waiver claim plus $13 in train fare, still had something to offer, and he was right. For about a month, Klein morphed back into the beast he had been with the Phillies earlier in the decade when he was one of the most feared sluggers in the game. He ripped off a 21-game hitting streak, blasted five home runs on one road trip and took over the club lead in runs batted in. "It's because I'm playing regularly. When I was in the game [in Philadelphia] I pressed too much. Pie Traynor kept me in the lineup and I got loose."[30] Klein became so popular so quickly that the *Pittsburgh Sun-Telegraph* hastily threw together a "Chuck Klein Day" at Forbes Field. Among the loot he hauled away that afternoon were two radios, 200 cigars, two pigeons and a flashlight.

On July 26, the Pirates swept a doubleheader from Klein's former club, which moved them into sole possession of second place, although they remained nine games behind Bill McKechnie's Reds. In late July, Traynor speculated, "If

Bauers could have given us about six wins at this stage and Blanton about eight or nine, we'd be in first place."[31]

The pitching situation had gotten out of hand. While the Pirates were winning a lot of games, Traynor was killing his staff. Klinger injured his ankle just before the all-star break, and that had him hobbling for about a week. In the first game following the break, Jim Tobin injured his shoulder while sliding. Bauers still wasn't right. His shoulder was so painful that he could hardly throw a breaking ball; when he tried, the pitch had no bite. After his appearance against Brooklyn on July 14, Leo Durocher commented, "Bauers threw me a curve and I almost laughed at it."[32]

From early July until early August, Traynor had, for all intents and purposes, a five-man pitching staff. The workload was incredible. At one point Bill Swift started four games and relieved in three others in a span of 13 days. Bob Klinger, who had complained of arm problems throughout the previous season, made three starts and two relief appearances over a 10-day stretch. The Pirates finally got some help at the end of July when they plucked Max Butcher and his 2–13 record off the waiver wire from Philadelphia. At the time, the word on Butcher was that he was carrying a few too many pounds, but Mace Brown wasn't concerned. "If he sticks around us for awhile it won't take him long to get in shape."[33]

In the short term, Traynor's tactics worked. As in 1938, he was adept at selecting the right matchups for his pitchers and having a sense for just the right time to get them out of a game. The staff held up well through July and even August. But another problem cropped up in August — suddenly, just about every hitter went cold. The Pirates averaged a meager 3.3 runs per game that month and fell out of the race, winning just eight games while losing 22.

It was ugly. Among the regulars, Rizzo hit .225 in August, Klein and Young .211, Handley .187, Bell .132. They were shut out five times. Mixed in there was a 12-game losing streak, the Pirates' longest in 25 years. Pittsburgh blew leads in seven of the first eight games of the skid. Most painful was a loss to Cincinnati on August 14. Pittsburgh led the Reds, 7–0, in the fifth inning, and held an 8–5 lead after one out in the ninth, only to have Sewell and Brown blow it. After the game, Traynor and Ens re-enacted their long, silent Chicago walk from the previous September, dragging themselves two miles from Crosley Field to the Sinton Hotel to be alone with their phantasmagoric thoughts. "I'd wake in the middle of the night and jump, turn on the light, smoke a cigarette, then try to go back to sleep," Traynor said.[34]

Though the Pirates did not really collapse in 1938, this was a full-scale implosion. Traynor felt like his team had quit on him, and he was "angered to the point of bitterness" according to one writer.[35] "Some fellows can say, 'Oh, what the heck.' But for me something died down here," confessed Traynor, pointing to his heart. "I'm like a kid. It really hurt."[36] In late August, Benswanger admitted to the press that Traynor was on shaky ground, though he tried to take the edge off his comments. "I've given some thought to changing managers ... but if a few of our high-priced men had delivered for us, we wouldn't be worrying about those things."[37] An unnamed coach stated bluntly, "This team just doesn't have it."[38]

In September, the Pirates decided to make a full commitment to youth. They brought in center fielder Bob Elliott, who had made such an impression on Traynor in the spring. "I was a scared kid," Elliott recalled of his call-up two decades later. "Pie Traynor and his wife took me out to dinner. I'll never forget it. He made me feel at home."[39] Along with Elliott came teenage third baseman Frank Gustine, left fielder Maurice van Robays, and pitchers Oad Swigart and Johnny Gee.

Gustine was Traynor's pet project. "Everything I have I owe directly or indirectly to Pie Traynor," he said many years later.[40] A native of the Chicago area, Gustine first met Traynor at age 15. His next-door neighbor happened to be an old friend of Traynor's, Sam Roberts. Roberts brokered a meeting between the two at the Parkway Hotel. They talked in the lobby for two hours. "It was the thrill of my life," Gustine said. "Remember, Pie always was my hero."[41] The meeting ended with Traynor advising the skinny youngster to drink some milk shakes with eggs in them to put on some weight, and inviting him to work out with the team at Wrigley Field the next day. A couple of years later, Gustine turned down a four-year scholarship to the University of Chicago and signed with the Pirates. "Whenever the Pirates came to Chicago Traynor would call my mother and invite her to the ballpark. He'd always talk to her before the game and give her a progress report on me."[42] When Gustine received his call-up, Traynor was particularly generous, letting the young man crash at his apartment and providing him with a new glove.

The two men remained close over the years. Right up until his death, Traynor frequently visited the Gustine home on weekends for dinner, after which he would play catch in the yard with Gustine's sons while attired in a suit and tie.[43]

The Pirates had a losing record in September, largely because their overworked veteran pitchers finally gave out. But the rookies showed promise. The 6'9" Gee struck out 11 in his first major league start. Swigart threw a shutout against Boston. Elliott, who went on to play 15 seasons in the major leagues, hit .333 with three home runs. So there were some signs of hope, but with their team in the process of finishing lower than fifth place for the first time since 1917, not many Pittsburgh fans cared. The Pirates drew fewer than 1,000 fans for two of their September games, and overall attendance was down more than 40 percent from 1938.

By September 24, the Frankie Frisch rumors had resurfaced. The Colonial Network announced that Frisch would not return to its broadcast team in 1940 "because, to the best of our knowledge, he has been engaged to manage one of the big league clubs."[44] Asked if the Pirates were that club, Benswanger bluffed,

"I know nothing about it."[45] On September 27, the Pirates lost a doubleheader to Chicago, falling to 67–83. The next afternoon, a year to the day after the "Homer in the Gloamin'," a worn-out Traynor shuffled into Benswanger's office and submitted his resignation. According to the *Pittsburgh Press*, "It was apparent that the resignation was not voluntary."[46] In fact, J.G. Taylor Spink of the *Sporting News* reported that Traynor and his coaching staff knew by the middle of September that they were finished.[47]

Benswanger expressed "keen regret" and noted that Traynor's "loyalty, his devotion to duty, and his conscientiousness have won him an envied place in baseball."[48] As Benswanger made his announcement to three newspaper men assembled in his office, Traynor sat solemnly off to the side in front of a window, occasionally nodding his head. Given a chance to speak his peace, Traynor threw up his hands and conceded, "Well, it had to be done.... The fans want a winner. They don't want a sixth place club. And when they show it by staying away from the ball park you have to do something.... Maybe it isn't my fault, maybe it isn't anybody's fault, but you have to give the fans what they want.... So we talked it over, Bill and I, and we decided that the fans wanted a new manager, and so I resigned. That's all there is to it."[49]

Barney Dreyfuss once promised Traynor that he could have a job with the Pirates as long as he wanted it, and Benswanger wanted to make good on his father-in-law's pledge. Traynor accepted Benswanger's offer to remain with the organization as a scout, assisting farm director Joe Schultz. Sportswriter Havey Boyle thought Traynor seemed relieved, but syndicated columnist Bob Considine excoriated Benswanger for forcing Traynor's exit. "He fired the manager in the simple-witted belief that he was taking the customers' minds ... off the fact that [he] had failed to provide Pie with a ballclub. It is the cheaper way out, financially and morally."[50]

Two days later, Frisch officially agreed to manage the Pirates. In a move that probably galled Traynor, Benswanger gave Frisch a two-year contract (Traynor and other Pirate managers historically signed one-year deals). The Pirates split a doubleheader with Cincinnati on the season's final day to finish with a 68–85 record, in sixth place, 28½ games out of first; it was their worst season in 22 years.

Traynor was a professional to the end. At the end of the season he met with Frisch and Benswanger to talk about the team's future, and accompanied them to the minor league draft in New York. Others were less gracious. Frisch, never one of Traynor's favorite people to begin with, took oblique shots at his predecessor, boasting about the discipline and focus he would instill in the Pirates. Paul Waner added a sucker punch, telling a reporter, "Pie became rattled in the clinches."[51]

Traynor was a very smart baseball man; he knew the game as well as anyone. But his personality quirks hindered him as a manager. He sulked and grew deeply pessimistic when his team struggled, to the point where it became a drain on his own physical and emotional health and possibly affected his team's performance. He gave players the silent treatment and let problems fester rather than addressing issues directly and getting them resolved. Traynor hated it when people suggested he was too kind and soft-hearted to be a good manager, but in the end those critics might have had a point. In the *Pittsburgh Post-Gazette* Al Abrams contended, "Pie's tactics would have gone over great with a high school or college athlete where he would have been looked up to as a hero and leader, but with a gang of thoroughly hardened, grown-up men, driving leadership is sometimes required."[52] A writer in the *New York Times* offered that Traynor "treated his men a lot better than they treated him."[53]

That said, for all Frisch's bluster about changing the atmosphere in the clubhouse, his club lost 21 of its first 30 and was 15 games out by the end of June 1940. In seven years, Frisch's Pirates barely won more games than they lost. His best season was 1944, when the Pirates won 90 games but still finished 14½ games out of first place. As legendary *Chicago Tribune* writer Arch Ward suggested, "Maybe Pie Traynor wasn't such a bad manager after all."[54]

Nevertheless, for the first time in two decades, Traynor was out of uniform and it didn't feel right. He spent the next five years groping for the right path, struggling to figure out what came next. Eventually he found his way, but, like many, he found that transition from "athlete" to "regular person" to be emotionally wrenching, a kind of existential mid-life crisis. He was entering middle age and suddenly needed to construct a new identity for himself. Here he was with little formal education, not a whole lot of money in the bank, and not much on his resume that would qualify him for any kind of work outside of baseball. Even in baseball circles he was somewhat damaged goods, bearing the stigma of the 1938 pennant disaster. It must have been an empty, confusing, and somewhat terrifying feeling as he pondered his future.

13

At the Corner of Walk and Don't Walk

The scouting job, while it provided Traynor with a paycheck and some stability, was not really the answer. Pirate scout Joe Devine realized this and suggested that organized baseball create a job for Traynor. "In all my travels around the country I have found no player the fans are more interested in than Traynor.... A post could be created for him as a traveling ambassador of goodwill. His habits, his charming personality, everything about the man fit him for such a position."[1] But Devine was just talking to the wind; there were no such offers in the works.

Traynor did not seem to enjoy his work as a scout, nor does it appear he distinguished himself in the eyes of his employer. According to data compiled by the Society for American Baseball Research, Traynor signed one future major leaguer during this period, a good one in Andy Seminick, but the Pirates released Seminick after he hit just .156 in 19 games in the low minors.[2] When Traynor's boss, scouting director Joe Schultz, died in 1941, some expected Traynor would be promoted, but the Pirates passed him over.

Scouting just didn't seem to be the right place for Traynor to be at that point in his life.[3] He felt like he still belonged on the field. Although managing took a terrible toll on him, at least it kept him in the dugout, right in the thick of things. Pulling on that major league uniform just made him walk a little taller. "There's glamour to baseball," he once said.[4] As he fulfilled his scouting duties—watching, taking notes, and filing reports—he must have wondered where that glamour went. "I love the grief that goes with a manager's job," he declared in 1941. "Of course, I don't miss the daily headaches, the sleepless nights, but I loved it."[5]

There were plenty of on-field opportunities outside the Pirate organization; he just couldn't bring himself to make the leap. At the winter meetings in 1939, just weeks after he lost his job, the Detroit Tigers offered Traynor a spot on Del Baker's coaching staff. A friend encouraged him to go for it because "once you take off the uniform they forget you."[6] But Traynor claimed he was holding out for a managerial gig, spurned the offer, and missed out on a World Series share with the 1940 Tigers. Around the same time he turned down Leo Durocher's offer to become a coach in Brooklyn. Over the next few years, Traynor's name came up frequently whenever there was a minor league managerial opening. At various times, the press linked him to jobs in Seattle, Buffalo, and Albany, but Traynor was not particularly intrigued. "I'd take a job in the majors, but there is nothing for me in the minors," he said.[7]

For a while, Traynor remained sanguine about landing a major league job and tried to cast his situation in the best possible light. In May 1941 he said, "I think every manager should enjoy a sabbatical leave once every five years or so. I mean, take a long vacation, then come back refreshed and with a new viewpoint."[8] But a year later he seemed to have come to a reluctant acceptance that his time as a big league manager had come and gone, telling a friend wistfully, "The parade passes."[9]

The closest he came to managing in the majors again might have come several years later, in 1948. In Traynor's version of the story, Cincinnati's new manager Bucky Walters called Traynor asking for help. "I can't manage. You run the ballclub. And if anything should happen to me, you can take over," Walters reportedly told him. But again Traynor said no. "Nobody's going to say, if they let you go, that I stole your job. When you walk out, I walk out with you. Therefore, I'm going to stay in Pittsburgh."[10]

Traynor was at least partially to blame for his predicament. He could have helped resurrect himself and his reputation had he been willing to accept a coaching job or even a minor league managerial post, as many others in his position have done, but he was either too stubborn or too proud to go that route. Or maybe after more than 20 years, his emotional tie to the Pirates was simply too strong. "I'd feel strange in any other uniform. I guess I'm just a Pittsburgher and can't change," he said in 1943.[11]

In the early 1940s Traynor was seldom seen in the city. He and Eve decided to live year-round in Cincinnati and much of his scouting was done in the Midwest and West. When he attended a Pirates-Braves game in late August 1942, a reporter noted it was only the second time in three years he had watched the Pirates play.[12]

The 1942-43 offseason probably was the low point for Traynor. Unhappy with his work and looking for a physical and spiritual challenge, he signed up for the army in October 1942. "I had passed my physical and was ready to get a commission. And then before I was called, the ruling was made banning the 38-year-olds and over and they dropped me like a hot potato. It was one of the biggest disappointments of my life."[13]

Three months later, on January 10, came even worse news when Pie learned that his sister, Mary, had died. Mary, or "LuLu" as the family called her, was the second youngest of Traynor's siblings, almost eleven years Pie's junior, a petite woman who dressed stylishly. Her childhood was a little easier than that of Pie or any of her other older brothers. While they were forced to leave school in order to find jobs that would supplement the family income, Mary went to business school to learn typing and stenography. She later put her skills to use working for New England Telephone and Telegraph.

On New Year's Eve 1935, Mary married Don MacIsaac, a captain in the United States Air Corps.[14] After war broke out and her husband was dispatched to the Pacific theater, Mary contracted tuberculosis. At the time little could be done for t.b. patients beyond quarantining them, treating the symptoms, and crossing one's fingers. The use of antibiotics to treat the disease became possible after the war, but that was too late for Mary. After her diagnosis, she spent the rest of her life confined to the Somerville Contagious Hospital, where she died at the age of 33.[15]

It was while Traynor was grieving over the loss of his only sister that the Pirates completely severed ties with him. It was a strange parting. The team made no official announcement; the press caught on only after discovering Traynor's name was missing from the list of scouts on the 1943 roster. Chet Smith of the *Pittsburgh Press* called Traynor at home in Cincinnati to learn if he was still associated with the club.

"No, although I haven't been told officially," Traynor stated.

"Then how do you know you're not still with them?" Smith asked.

"Because they stopped paying me."[16]

The Pirates' side of the story was that Traynor had blown off a scheduled December meeting with them at the winter meetings in Chicago, and therefore they assumed that he was no longer interested in remaining with the organization. The Pirates obviously did not go out of their way to keep him in the fold. With the country in the midst of World War II and so many able-bodied young men in the armed services, there were not many young prospects for Traynor to scout. Once he was the face of the Pirate organization; now he was obsolete.

Out of organized baseball for the first time in nearly a quarter-century, Traynor told Smith he had no immediate plans. Since 1941 he had been moonlighting as a car salesman at a Cincinnati Lincoln-Mercury dealership owned by Johnny Dell, a former minor league ballplayer.[17] Traynor recognized it was a peculiar occupation for a man who had never been behind the wheel, but "[Dell] says I did all right."[18] He stayed on at that job until the autumn of 1943, when he signed on at the United States Playing Card Company, whose suburban Cincinnati plant had been converted for the manufacture of wartime materiel.[19]

The U.S. Playing Card Company was headquartered in a stout red brick building, distinguished by a four-story bell tower that stood atop its main entrance. "The company was deeply involved in several aspects of secret war work at that time.... We learned not to ask too many questions," said Ray Ostrander, who began working at the plant in 1938.[20] Among the wartime projects the U.S. Playing Card Company now publicly acknowledges: sewing parachutes for cluster bombs that were dropped on enemy troops, and manufacturing special playing cards for American prisoners of war in Germany. When submerged in water and peeled apart, the cards revealed maps of detailed escape routes from the Nazi camps.[21]

For all the fascinating things going on behind those brick walls, there was nothing intriguing or mysterious about Traynor's duties. He spent his days hunched over a lathe, grinding out parts for American war planes. It was hard, dirty work, but Traynor wasn't above that. "I just couldn't stand around and not do something to help win the war."[22] Eve contributed to the Allied cause in her own way by helping to run blood banks for the American Red Cross.[23]

At one time the Traynors had planned to build a home in the Queen City, but the war and resulting lack of building materials put the kibosh on those plans. After Pie took his new job, he and Eve moved to an apartment at 2356 Park Avenue in Norwood, Ohio, right up the street from the U.S. Playing Card factory; Pie's morning commute was a quick two-block walk. He kept his hand in baseball a little bit, too, joining former major leaguers Lew Fonseca and Leroy Parmelee as instructors at a series of baseball clinics for high school coaches in Illinois, Iowa, and Kansas.

Traynor was presented with an opportunity to return to Pittsburgh in late 1944. *Pittsburgh Post-Gazette* reporter Havey Boyle knew Traynor well and suggested to Jim Murray, the program director at KQV Radio, that someone as gregarious and smart as Traynor was a perfect fit for broadcasting. Murray was intrigued; no matter how Traynor sounded on the air, his name recognition alone was worth a lot. Following more than a month's worth of negotiations with Murray and KQV general manager Pete Wasser, Traynor agreed to leave Cincinnati to become a part of KQV's 6:00 P.M. newsblock and also to host a baseball school of the air on Saturday mornings during the summer. Ex-jocks were not nearly as prevalent behind the mic as they would become later, but even in the 1940s it was not unheard of. Traynor had high hopes. "I think it will work out all right. You see, I think radio is here to stay," he quipped.[24]

Traynor had established quite a social network in Cincinnati even though he only called the city home for five years. During the 1938-39 offseason, when he first rented an apartment in the city, he would hike three miles to the Cuvier Sports Club, plant himself on a sofa all afternoon, read a couple of newspapers, and shoot the breeze with anyone who happened by.[25] Over time, his circle of friends multiplied. On February 7, a few days before he left town, his buddies, including former Cincinnati Reds Rube Bressler and Larry Kopf, threw him a going-away party at Grammer's Café. "I really hate to leave Cincinnati. No place has been more hospitable."[26]

Nevertheless, Traynor was delighted to be in Pittsburgh again and the city was just as happy to have him back. On Sunday, February 18, the night before he was scheduled to make his radio debut, local sportswriters threw him a huge party that lasted long into the night. The diverse group of 80 attendees included Bill Benswanger, Art Rooney, two local judges, a county commissioner, and a city councilman. Each guest received a card, signed by the guest of honor, which read:

Dear Mrs. _____:

This will certify that your husband was at my party and behaved himself very well. I am sending you this card merely to prove he wasn't out with a babe, as you probably think.[27]

That was indicative of the jovial mood of the evening; it was a wild night. "No speaker, with the exception of Traynor ... was immune from the side remarks and general barrage of insults, thrown in fun, of course," observed Havey Boyle.[28] Traynor spoke last, said his thank yous and told a few funny stories, and then went home to get some rest before starting his new job.

At least one expert predicted big success for Traynor. "He has the perfect voice, with just enough of New England in it to make it smooth," wrote *Pittsburgh Press* media critic Si Steinhauser.[29] But Murray realized that Traynor, as a broadcasting novice, would need some help, so he teamed him with KQV news director Jack Henry, who was there to make Traynor look good and keep the program on track.

Henry was a native of Wales who came to the United States at around age ten, following the death of his mother. His accent stood out in his new home in western Pennsylvania, where schoolmates razzed him to "talk American." Henry wrote for United Press International and the *Pittsburgh Sun-Telegraph* before joining KQV, later becoming a stockbroker and a financial reporter for a local television station.[30] "He was not a great writer or anything like that but he was quite the humorist and was a bright guy and was funny as hell," recalled Pittsburgh sports historian Jim O'Brien.[31] "Jack was a small man, about half Pie's height. They were a funny pair together," said Chuck Reichblum, a Pittsburgh radio personality. "Jack was very literate and articulate; he was really the host of the show even though it was Pie's show."[32]

The Hot Corner, as KQV named Traynor's segment, began its life as a 15-minute program airing at 6:30 P.M. from Monday through Saturday. It was simple in concept and execution. Traynor would begin the program by reading the day's sports headlines, usually working off wire service copy. Then Henry would ask Traynor for his opinion about some hot topic in the world of sports, or he might simply invite Traynor to dip into his memory bank for a random anecdote about a famous personality or event. "Pie," Henry might say, "here's a letter asking you to tell a story about Casey Stengel when he managed the Toledo Mud Hens." And Traynor would promptly launch into some tale about Stengel in Toledo.[33] Sometimes a guest would stop by the studio and Traynor would be the one asking the questions.

The subject matter was pretty tame, but occasionally Traynor hit on more touchy issues. In 1946, Pirate players threatened to go on strike unless Bill Benswanger recognized the American Baseball Guild, a union organized by a young Boston lawyer named Robert Murphy. A June 6 United Press International story quoted Traynor as supporting the Guild. "It's here. Organization has had considerable success in other fields and baseball also will [benefit]."[34]

But the evening the comment hit the papers, Traynor went on the air and repudiated the story. "I not only did not support the Guild, but I turned down an offer made to me by Robert F. Murphy, the Guild organizer, to assist him," he told his listeners. "[A strike] would throw a harpoon into organized baseball."[35] UPI stood by its story and, frankly, Traynor's denial is hard to believe. It is theoretically possible that the reporter either fabricated the quote or completely misunderstood every word that came out of Traynor's mouth. More likely, though, Traynor simply spoke before thinking and, after seeing his words in print, became concerned about burning bridges within the Pirate organization.

That definitely seems to have been the reason he muted his rhetoric on the club's reluctance to sign African American players. Pittsburgh native Maurice Peatros, who was a promising young Negro League first baseman in the mid–1940s, told historian Brent Kelley that he appeared as a guest on Traynor's show three times and that Traynor was urging the Pirates, both publicly and behind the scenes, to integrate their organization by signing both him and fellow Pittsburgher Joe Atkins. But Traynor, who by this time was back on the Pirate payroll as a scout, told Peatros that Pirate management was pressuring him to back off, and he felt he had no choice but to let the issue drop.[36] Pittsburgh did not integrate at the major league level until 1954.

Late in 1957, ABC Radio purchased KQV and converted the station to a Top 40 music format. Arthur Godfrey and Edward R. Murrow were shoved aside in favor of Elvis Presley and Fats Domino. ABC knew what it was doing. The Pittsburgh music scene was really happening from the mid–1950s through the early 1960s; the city produced nationally known hit-makers like The Skyliners, The Vogues, The Del Vikings, Lou Christie, and Bobby Vinton. KQV became part of Pittsburgh's musical zeitgeist and turned itself into a ratings powerhouse, challenging and for a time edging out legendary heritage station KDKA, despite an inferior signal that dropped out at certain spots within the city.

In a moment of marketing inspiration, ABC decided to relocate the KQV studios from the 14th floor of the Chamber of Commerce building down to the building's ground floor at the corner of Seventh Avenue and Smithfield Street — "The corner of walk and don't walk" as the KQV disc jockeys called it. The new studios had huge picture windows facing the street and speakers mounted above the sidewalk so pedestrians could both see and hear the men behind the microphone (and they were all men in those days). People went nuts for this; there were crowds outside those windows constantly, and the staff had to wash the windows daily to get rid of the smudges. The jocks had the option of closing the blinds if the crowds proved a distraction, which they frequently did. "Sometimes at night it got pretty rowdy," said longtime KQV personality Chuck Brinkman.[37]

Though it was incongruous with the new format, KQV's evening newsblock remained. The station hung on to Traynor, although old colleagues like Jim Murray and Jack Henry exited. KQV moved Traynor's program to 5:55 P.M. and trimmed it to five minutes. In this shorter time slot Traynor, now without a co-host, mostly read scores and headlines, with less storytelling and fewer interviews.

It isn't clear how much Traynor really enjoyed his work, especially after the format change. "I think he worked at KQV because he needed the money," said Bob Gustine, the son of former Pirate third baseman Frank Gustine. "It was kind of a pain in the neck. We'd have him over for Christmas or Thanksgiving and he would say, 'I've got to get down there. I can't miss.' We'd have to take him down there. It took him all of five minutes and then we'd take him back with us."[38]

As a radio personality Traynor was distinctive if nothing else. First there was his thick Boston accent; no one else in Pittsburgh radio sounded remotely like him. But what also stood out were the ceaseless mispronunciations, malapropisms, and brain lapses. As Brinkman put it, "He had no radio skills at all."[39]

Traynor didn't like to adhere too closely to a script. "I always ad-lib," he once declared. "I think the fans like it when you speak straight from the heart."[40] But ad-libbing an interview, a news story, or even an anecdote is not easy when the broadcaster needs to get all the facts correct, remain coherent all the way through, manage his nerves, and keep his eye on a ticking clock. It is a skill that not everyone can master. Traynor certainly didn't. "You took your life in your hands [when] you gave him a live mic," said KQV newsman Keeve Berman.[41]

Pronouncing the names of people and places could be especially troublesome. "You didn't know if he was trying to be funny or just didn't know," said Roy McHugh.[42] It could have been a combination of both of those things; and sometimes even the smartest people find themselves with tangled tongues and frozen brains when a microphone is shoved in front of them. At least once Traynor referred to the great New York Yankee catcher from the 1950s as "Yoga Berry." The Niagara University basketball team became "Nicaragua." The University of Iowa was "Io-way." He turned Juniata College into "Juanita."[43]

"Anytime he had a name in front of him he didn't bother to ask anyone how to say it. He just gave it his own pronunciation," chuckled former KQV reporter Alan Boal. "He was kind of stubborn. He did things his own way."[44]

Live interviews also could be an adventure. One evening he was interviewing boxer Johnny Flynn about an upcoming fight in Pittsburgh. Flynn evidently was very nervous, unaccustomed to being on the air. Traynor was, well, Traynor.

"Johnny," Traynor began, "how do you think you'll do tonight in your fight against Bob Baker?"

Flynn, overcome by mic fright, swallowed his tongue. He couldn't say a word.

Unfazed, Traynor plowed on. "Johnny, how did you do in your last fight in Boston?"

Flynn remained frozen. And again Traynor, at a loss, just rolled into the next question. And the next one. And the next one. After five or six questions and no answers, Traynor wrapped up the segment with, "Ladies and gentlemen, you've just heard an interview with Johnny Flynn. Thank you, Johnny."[45]

"People were calling into the station saying, 'Something is wrong with my radio. I'm only hearing Pie Traynor's voice!'" laughed Boal. "He just went ahead with things like that when he didn't understand what was going on."[46]

During his program, Traynor was forced to read commercials live. This was unfortunate. "One of his sponsors was Monroe Super Load Levelers. They made load levelers for cars and trucks," recalled Berman. "He could never say it. It would come out as Monroe *Supler* Load Levelers. Always! It was horrible!"[47]

The American Heating Company was another sponsor. The commercial would begin with a recorded voice, saying, "Who can?" Traynor, live on the microphone, would respond, "Ameri-can!" and then read the rest of the commercial script. One night, the tape malfunctioned and the words "Who can?" were replayed four or five times in the span of about a minute. "Every time the thing said, 'Who can?' he'd stop in the middle of everything and go 'Amer-i-can' and he would start the whole damn commercial over again! It was ridiculously funny, but he didn't see anything wrong with it," roared Berman.[48]

Neither did most Pittsburghers. They ate it up. But Traynor's "style," if one can call it that, was an acquired taste for a lot of the trained radio professionals at KQV; not everyone there got it. One night, due to a scheduling conflict, he recorded his program and turned over the tape to a young studio engineer, Paul Carlson. Carlson's skin crawled listening to Traynor's "very frequent umms, ahhs, and other hems and haws. It seemed like every tenth syllable was excess baggage."[49]

Carlson promptly went to work on Traynor's reel with a razor blade and splicing tape, eliminating all of the pauses and stumbles. "He sounded one hundred percent better to my ear."[50] Not to Berman's, though. "I remember listening to it on the air and it was smooth. I couldn't believe what the hell I was listening to. Is that Pie?"

Berman exploded when Carlson told him of his well-intentioned deed. "I said, 'You killed Pie! That's not him. You can't do that!'"[51] Carlson threw up his hands. "I never again felt tempted to clean up a Pie Traynor broadcast.... The artistry belonged to the artists. Most engineers, myself included, don't know schtick."[52]

Another skeptic was John Rook, who at age 28 assumed program director duties at KQV in 1964. In his job, Rook was responsible for the overall sound of the station. He could hardly believe his ears the first time he heard Traynor. "As a new program director I tuned in one night and was listening to the station [driving] into the Liberty Tunnel. The station was sounding just fine. And then when I got to the other side of the tubes there was dead air and [Traynor's] meek little voice comes on. I came from Denver. What did I know about the Pirates? I listened to it and I thought, 'My God, this is just deplorable. What is this, a comedy show?' I made up my mind that this could not stay on the station."[53]

The next morning, Rook summoned Traynor for a meeting at which he planned to inform his sports director that his services were no longer needed. Traynor arrived around 11:00 in the morning, dressed immaculately as always in a suit and tie and perfectly shined shoes, and turned on the charm. "Mr. Rook, I'm Pie Traynor," he said as he reached across the desk to offer his hand to his new boss. "I felt so uncomfortable," said Rook. "Here was this man who was obviously 40 years older than me, calling me Mr. Rook. He was just a perfect gentleman with the softest voice. I wanted this guy as my grandfather."[54]

The two men walked to a nearby restaurant for lunch, and Rook learned first-hand just how popular Traynor was. "As we're walking along there is this traffic cop in the middle of the street who saw Pie and I approaching the corner and he stopped all traffic to let Pie and I across. So we got to the restaurant and there was a line of people waiting and the maitre d' saw us approaching and said, 'Right this way, Mr. Traynor.'"

Rook was sold. "When I walked back in [at KQV], the secretary had a look of horror on her face, thinking I had fired Pie. I said, 'Pie will do just fine.' KDKA carried the Pirates. He would have fit better on KDKA. But I sure as hell wasn't going to fire him."[55]

Listeners did not care that Traynor didn't sound as polished and professional as other broadcasters. In fact, it probably was a plus. "He was Pie Traynor, take him or leave him," said KQV news director Al Crouch. "That's a good thing, to be yourself. He didn't go on the air and pretend he was a sports announcer."[56] And so long as the audience liked what it was hearing, there was no reason for anyone at KQV to work with Traynor to help him sound better. "Never," insisted Rook. "The last thing I wanted to do was sit in front of him and tell him how to do anything."[57]

As Rook's story suggests, Traynor's KQV colleagues found him to be a delightful and interesting person. He might have loosened up a little more than usual around the radio guys, too. In radio the folks behind the microphones and the control boards are often hard-living, foul-mouthed, and a little bit twisted; in other words, fun people to be around. Maybe that's why Traynor felt free to give his male colleagues an occasional peek at a crude, teenage-boy sense of humor that he kept under wraps in more polite company.

For example, in 1949 American tennis star Gussie Moran shocked the All-England Lawn Tennis and Croquet Club by playing Wimbledon wearing a short tennis dress that revealed her ruffled, lacy panties underneath, which evolved into something of an international incident. Shortly thereafter, Traynor's guest was former tennis great Jack Kramer, who was in Pittsburgh promoting a professional tennis tournament. "Kramer was a real stiff, prissy, proper guy; part of the old tennis establishment," explained Chuck Reichblum.[58] In short, the perfect foil.

As Kramer entered the studio, Traynor pointed him to a chair, careful to make sure Kramer was seated with his back to the on-air light. Traynor situated himself, informed Kramer that they were about to go on, and began the ruse.

"The first question I have, Jack: You know all that controversy over Gussie Moran's lace panties?" asked Traynor, feigning seriousness.

"Yes," replied Kramer.

"Have you ever gotten into those panties?"

Kramer all but wet himself. He blushed, stammered, and gamely attempted some kind of dignified response, but within a few seconds Traynor cracked up and Kramer caught on to the gag — the microphones had been off the entire time. But, as Jim O'Brien heard it, Kramer never fully recovered. "He was so blown away by Traynor's question that he wasn't really any good the rest of the show."[59]

Traynor had mixed feelings about KQV's fishbowl studios. He seemed a bit uncomfortable with people standing on the sidewalk staring at him as he tried to read his copy. But the big window did have its benefits. "Pie would go on during the evening commute home, so we would stand there and look out over the street and watch all the babes go home," remembered Keeve Berman. "And in the summertime, of course, they were rather scantily dressed. He would stand there and say, 'Look at that broad over there.'" From there he would expound upon the wonders of the woman's beauty, frequently in PG-rated language peppered with pet names for various parts of the female anatomy.[60] "He talked about sex but it was more in a humorous way," Chuck Reichblum explained. "He grew up in the days when most baseball players were uneducated and talked about sex and swore all the time. He came out of that atmosphere. That's just what a lot of the old players did — talked about the girls."[61]

But Traynor revealed a more sober side, too. He kept up with the news and enjoyed sharing his perspective on current events with KQV's reporters. Berman recalls Traynor storming in one day in a particularly agitated mood. "He was disgusted. He said, 'Do you realize what a terrible man J. Edgar Hoover is? He's a dictator and is taking personal vengeance on politicians.' Now it's pretty general knowledge all the things Hoover did, but at that time nothing was known about it. I don't know where he got his information [but] he talked about it for days. He said, 'This guy is no good. They have to get rid of him.'"[62]

Traynor was not short on opinions. He traced many of America's problems in the 1960s back to the end of World War II. "Nations lost confidence in us when we dropped the atom bomb when Japan was beaten."[63] He also spoke of his loathing of Cuban leader Fidel Castro.[64] "Pie wasn't an ignorant person," Berman observed. "He was quite intelligent. He wasn't like a lot of sports personalities who live in their own world. He was quite concerned with the news and world affairs."[65]

All in all, for the crew at KQV, Traynor's buoyant personality and humanity far outweighed any on-air shortcomings. "He had a great spirit about him, a sweet, sweet person," Al Crouch gushed. "I'll never forget when he'd come into work in the afternoon, he'd say, 'Al, my boy, how are you?' It kind of made my day when he came in."[66]

One of the breaking stories Traynor covered occurred in February 1948 when he received the game's ultimate honor, election to the Baseball Hall of Fame. After falling two votes short of enshrinement the year before, he received 93 votes out of 121 ballots cast, placing him just above the 75 percent cutoff for election. Legend has it that Traynor first learned of his election when a newspaper photographer appeared at the KQV studios to snap his picture. ("I knew they weren't there to take my picture because I was a sports radio announcer," he quipped.[67]) He became just the second third baseman named to the Hall, and the first to be elected (Jimmy Collins was named by the Old-Timers' Committee in 1945).

The Baseball Hall of Fame did not begin hosting annual induction ceremonies until a few years later, so the Class of 1948 (Traynor and Herb Pennock) was officially enshrined along with the Class of 1949 — Mordecai "Three Finger" Brown, Kid Nichols, and Charlie Gehringer — on June 13, 1949, in Cooperstown, New York. Traynor and the 80-year-old Nichols (who brought his daughter, granddaughter, and great-grandson with him) were the only honorees in attendance. Brown and Pennock were dead while Gehringer irked a lot of people, including Traynor, by skipping the ceremony. He claimed he was too busy dealing with "the pressures of business."[68] That was a lie. In reality, Gehringer had a perfectly valid excuse had he chosen to use it; his wedding was that weekend.[69]

A crowd of 6,500, including Jewel Ens, Fred Clarke, and Pirate president Frank McKinney, sat in bright sunshine and watched Traynor, dressed sharply in a light-colored suit, make a very brief and simple acceptance speech.[70]

> This is a great honor and I am happy to be able to receive it. There are names of some great ballplayers in the shrine and I am indebted to those who made it possible for my name to be added. Thank you.[71]

The Traynors moved around constantly after returning to Pittsburgh, living in three different apartments from 1945 to 1950. But in 1951 they finally settled down at the Schenley Park Apartments at 4014 Fifth Avenue in the Oakland section of the city.[72] Pie and Eve furnished the place well. It was filled with books (Eve was a voracious reader), art, and personal memorabilia. "It was very

Traynor makes his Hall of Fame acceptance speech in Cooperstown, on June 13, 1949, while master of ceremonies Branch Rickey looks on (National Baseball Hall of Fame Library, Cooperstown, New York).

different than a run-of-the-mill home like I was brought up with," said the Traynors' nephew, Mike Helmer. "What they had in the home was very nice. And of course, they didn't have kids, so their things were all in place. And it had so much of a touch of them in it."[73] The apartment included a piece of artwork Eve had made when she was in fifth grade and a portrait of her done when she had visited Europe with a friend in 1952.[74]

The apartment building no longer exists; a University of Pittsburgh residence hall now sets on that ground. But when Traynor lived there, the location was, as Bob Gustine put it, "the center of the universe. The University of Pittsburgh was there, across the street from where he lived was Forbes Field, and across from that was where the hockey team played. And all the bars were around there. His world was within walking distance."[75]

Traynor defined the term "walking distance" differently than most. He never drove a car and apparently was never much interested in learning how. He would go anywhere, almost any distance, on foot. Once in the 1950s he was in New York City for a World Series game. After eating breakfast in his hotel on Thirty-fourth Street, he took off on foot up Eighth Avenue toward Yankee Stadium. He arrived 3½ hours later, just in time for the game. "The folks in Harlem must have thought I was nuts. Sure, I was tired when I got there, but I was loosened up and relaxed."[76]

Bob Gustine speculated that perhaps Traynor was a Luddite. "I don't think he liked mechanical things."[77] But Traynor's own explanation was much more straightforward. "I never learned to drive because I was afraid I'd find an excuse not to walk, which I've found so enjoyable, so relaxing and healthful."[78] In that sense, Traynor was ahead of his time. "It wasn't particularly an era like today when there is an emphasis on walking. It was really his particular thing," noted Helmer.[79]

Occasionally in bad weather or if he was in a hurry, he might accept a ride from a friend or from Eve. One time Chuck Reichblum's wife came by to pick up her husband from work and, since they were headed toward Oakland, they offered Traynor a ride, which he accepted. "As we were driving he said, 'You know, these cars are pretty good,'" Reichblum cackled. "As if cars had just been invented!"[80]

Traynor's home in Oakland was a three-mile walk from the KQV studios, and he made that walk virtually every day until he was almost 60 years old. In 1958, Pie and Eve moved downtown to Bigelow Square, much closer to the radio station, after Pie began showing signs of the chronic respiratory difficulties that eventually would kill him. But his illness didn't prevent him from walking. A chance encounter on the sidewalk with Pie Traynor remained part of everyday life in Pittsburgh. "He would stop everyplace and meet people and talk to them. It seemed kind of odd for a person of his stature," thought Pirate pitcher Nellie King.[81]

One day in 1955, Fred Remington of the *Pittsburgh Press* tailed Traynor as he made his rounds on his regular route from Oakland into the city. First, Traynor poked his head into a seamstress shop to inquire about the proprietor's husband, who was laid up with an illness.

"How is he?" asked Traynor.

"He's still up in bed, Pie," came the response from the pregnant woman. "He's feeling a little better. He'll be glad to know you were asking."

This prompted Remington to muse, "One wonders how many times over the years Pie has thrust his head in that doorway to inquire how things were going — not just to be pleasant but because he really cares — and how it must have brought a moment's brightness to some bleak days."

Next, Traynor dropped in on a businessman who had just invested $28,000 in upgrades to his shop. "How are you?" inquired Traynor. "How's business?" Kids called to him as he passed on the sidewalk beneath their school. Strangers rolled down their car windows to holler, "Hi, Pie!"[82]

What Remington observed that day was not unusual. This was Traynor's life. He was more than a public figure; he was almost public property. "Wherever he may be, Traynor has chain conversations, the other participants coming and going, new faces joining in the dialogue or one [making] room for another," wrote Roy McHugh in 1969.[83] Traynor mingled with the people of the city for hours at a time, day after day, for 25 years.

Few people could have handled that attention as gracefully as he did. "He was the friendliest celebrity I ever saw. He had no pretense at all. A little kid would come up to him and say, 'Hi Pie.' There was no 'Mr. Traynor,'" said Chuck Reichblum.[84]

"I don't think I ever saw him have a bad moment or brush off anybody," gushed Ed Kiely. "He'd stand and talk with him as if he knew them for a couple years."[85] Most people never would have guessed this was a man who years before had fled to the Wisconsin woods to avoid dinner invitations and speaking engagements.

One of the places Traynor frequently stopped on his hikes was the cramped, unprepossessing headquarters of the Pittsburgh Steelers, located at the Fort Pitt Hotel, on the corner of Tenth Street and Penn Avenue. The Steelers shared space with the Rooney-McGinley Boxing Club, founded in 1939, which promoted fights at Forbes Field, including the Jersey Joe Walcott–Ezzard Charles title bout in 1951.

The offices were in the back of the hotel, with huge windows facing out toward the parking lot. When a greenhorn visited the Steelers, he parked in the back, came around front, traipsed down a long corridor that ran the length of the hotel, and walked into the office like a normal human being. But people in the know, like Traynor, simply came in and out through the window. Legend has it that right after the Steelers relocated their offices to the eighth floor of the Union Trust Building, Traynor was absent for quite a while. When he finally showed up one afternoon, Steelers owner Art Rooney gave him the needle.

"We haven't seen you. Where have you been? Are you giving me the brush off?"

"Oh, I'm not coming here very often," Traynor deadpanned. "I might make a mistake and go out the window."[86]

Those offices probably are like no team offices one would encounter today, now that professional sports have become much more buttoned-down and corporate. Rooney ran his team on a shoestring, and the loose, gritty, lively office atmosphere reflected that. According to author Roy Blount, Jr., "There were stuffed chairs with worn edges ... and pictures randomly hung, and an old air conditioner which made a loud noise when it worked.... All sorts of sporting and charitable events were organized there, from prizefights to funerals for Irish paupers."[87] Want to meet the man who owns the Steelers? Come on by. "Art was very warm," said Ed Kiely, for many years the Steelers publicity director. "Newspaper guys would ask me if they could come and see him and I would say, 'Go back there. His door is open.'"[88]

If you stopped in at the right time, you probably would see Pie Traynor there, too, flopped down in one of those raggedy chairs, chewing the fat with a cigar-chomping Rooney, the two men enshrouded in a miasma of smoke. Traynor, who came by a couple times a week by one person's recollection, was just one member of a large and eclectic cast of characters. "The old Fort Pitt was a legendary place. They had racetrack guys and gamblers and all kinds of people hanging around," said Roy McHugh.[89]

"Did you ever see *Guys and Dolls*?" asked Art Rooney, Jr. "It was like that. It was a special, special time. Primo Carnera came in after he became a wrestler. Guys running for mayor. Guys running for governor. It went all the way from them to guys down to their last dollar looking for a handout. That was a daily situation."[90]

Boxer Billy Conn, who nearly upset Joe Louis for the heavyweight championship, was part of the fraternity. Pittsburgh mayor and future Pennsylvania governor David Lawrence would stop by. Priests were in and out all the time. One sight rarely seen in this inner sanctum: women. "You never saw wives around those guys," said Jack McGinley, whose grandfather was a partner of Rooney's in both the boxing club and the football team. "It was really a men's club."[91]

Traynor and the rest of the regulars had a genuine affection for one another. They gave each other colorful nicknames, like "The Senator" (Jim McGinley) or "The Chief" (Art Rooney). Some of the nicknames wouldn't pass muster a generation or so later — Traynor's pal Sam Leone was known as "Dago Sam." Someone once described them as Technicolor people. According to Jack McGinley, "They were smart, entrepreneurial, not venal in any way. It was the most remarkable group of men I think I ever knew."[92]

Keeping busy in retirement never was a problem for Traynor. He took on a grinding schedule of speaking engagements almost from the day he set foot back in Pittsburgh, routinely making three or four appearances a week. In 1927 he grumbled about all the "cold roast beef and potato salad" he had eaten the previous winter when the crush of the banquet circuit had worn him down. But after World War II, he probably ate more cold roast beef and potato salad than any man alive. Civic group meetings, fundraisers for charitable organizations, lodge dinners, high school sports awards banquets — he made the rounds.

Traynor was in constant demand as a public speaker after returning to Pittsburgh in 1945. For years he maintained a back-breaking schedule of appearances throughout western Pennsylvania, West Virginia, and Ohio. He is shown here speaking at a banquet around 1950 (Paul Traynor).

Of course, he was a given to speak at big events, like the annual Dapper Dan Dinner, but Art Rooney, Jr., believes Traynor put on a much better show at the smaller, more intimate affairs. "My uncle was a Franciscan missionary and they would have monthly meetings to raise money. He was a speaker there a number of times and he was phenomenal. He just got by at places like the Dapper Dan. But if you got him at these smaller affairs, he'd go on and on and not worry about things and just be himself. [At the bigger events] it was like it was all so structured."[93] By 1967, when he was consciously trying to cut back his schedule, Traynor estimated that he had made more than 5,000 public appearances.[94]

In the late 1940s, Ottie Cochran, a car dealer and former sandlot player, hired Traynor to coach the "Ottie Cochran All-Stars," which barnstormed around the Pittsburgh area. Traynor's team was an ensemble cast of local players, from kids in their late teens, to men in their 20s just back from war, and some reliable old hands who were pushing 40. They would meet downtown at the Point Church on the Boulevard of the Allies on Sunday morning and carpool to some tiny hamlet in western Pennsylvania. "At that time western Pennsylvania was as much a hotbed for baseball as it is now for football," said Jim Vanderlin, who was a batboy for a couple of games the Ottie Cochran team played in Armstrong County. "They would get about 150 people there, which was a good-sized crowd for a Sunday afternoon in a small town. They passed the hat and they probably got their beer money out of that."[95]

Traynor played occasionally, but mostly he was there as a drawing card, a role that suited him quite nicely, according to Jim Smith, one of the younger players on the Cochran roster. "It was a big, big deal for the people in some of those little towns for him to come in there. They would go crazy over him. He took his time, putting little kids on his knee, kidding around with them. He was so nice to them, just the nicest guy in the whole world. You couldn't imagine how much time he would spend with them. He didn't make their day; he made their year."[96]

The Cochran team played its first games in June 1946, the same month the Allegheny County commissioners named him recreation supervisor in the county parks department. Traynor's duties included organizing and operating free baseball clinics for kids age 10–14. These schools were modeled after a similar program that Rogers Hornsby directed in Chicago. Every Wednesday and Saturday during the summer, Traynor taught youngsters the fundamentals of baseball. After some instruction and practice, the group broke up into teams and played games.

Bob del Greco, who would go on to play nine years in the major leagues, was one of the local kids who participated. "[Traynor] was like the manager of the camp," according to del Greco. "We'd pick up teams and he would stop the game to tell us what we did wrong or what we did right."[97] Also under Traynor's aegis were the county's youth golf, tennis, and swimming programs. For all of this, he earned a pro-rated salary of $3,780 in 1946, which the county bumped up to just over $4,000 in 1947.[98] That was decent money (median family income in the United States was $3,000 in 1947), but it was paltry compared to the $15,000 the City of Chicago doled out to Hornsby for similar work.[99]

Traynor seemed to enjoy his work with the county and he certainly was proud of it. "We kept track of 300–400 kids and not one of them ever got into trouble," he once claimed.[100] But it wasn't major league baseball and it wasn't the Pittsburgh Pirates, and that was where his heart was. So when Pirate general manager Roy Hamey offered him a chance to rejoin the organization in late 1947, he jumped at the chance, resigning his post with the parks department and signing on to work as a scout and goodwill ambassador for the Bucs. Traynor's territory spanned a 100-mile radius around the city of Pittsburgh — fertile ground for a scout in those days. The area produced a bushel of fine major leaguers in the 1950s, including Dick Groat, Frank Thomas, Cal Abrams, Elroy Face, and Ron Kline.

The Pirates did not place tremendous demands on Traynor's shoulders. "He did it on his own pace, on his own time," according to Hamey's successor,

Joe L. Brown.[101] One of his main duties was conducting tryout camps and working out young prospects at Forbes Field. For quite a few years the organization provided him with a locker in the home clubhouse, where he would don a Pirates uniform before heading out to the field. Traynor was directly responsible for signing future Pirates Tony Bartirome and Bob del Greco, and also put

Traynor takes a cut during fielding practice at the Pittsburgh Pirates spring training in Fort Myers, Florida, in 1957. This was his first spring training in 19 years. He would be a regular in the Pirates' camp right up until his death in 1972 (Pittsburgh Pirates).

in a good word for Bill Mazeroski and Bob Purkey, who worked out under Traynor's exacting eye.

In 1957, Brown and manager Bobby Bragan invited Traynor to work as a guest instructor at the Pirates spring training site in Fort Myers, Florida. It was his first time in a training camp since 1939. "The biggest difference I can see now is the number of players," he told the *Pittsburgh Press'* Les Biederman. "We had only 30 or 35 players in camp in my day and never more than one field. The pitching machines and the batting cage are all new to me, too."[102] His primary duty was to work with the club's two third basemen, Frank Thomas and Gene Freese, both of whom were relatively new to the position. Traynor arrived the first weekend in March, accompanied by Eve, who immediately left her husband behind for a few days as she visited Miami, Havana, and Nassau.

Traynor thought he had some pretty good raw material with which to work. "Thomas has everything required of a good third baseman. He has a great pair of hands and a strong arm. He must learn to get the jump on the ball and then take the first step in the right direction.... He's a natural. I'd say whatever faults he has are only minor."[103] Regarding Freese, Traynor observed, "Last spring I thought Freese was the oldest-looking 22-year-old I ever saw. But he's quite a lot different today. He seems to have more pep and simply looks like a new man."[104]

It is debatable how much Thomas and Freese benefited from Traynor's words of wisdom. At the time, Thomas told reporters, "Pie Traynor has been a great help to me this spring. He's shown me two or three things I didn't know ... how to take a ball on throws to tag a runner, how not to go out and meet a ball thrown to me from the outfield, and how to straddle the bag. No one showed me these things before."[105] But asked to recall his experience a half-century later, Thomas wasn't nearly as effusive, saying, "He just told me to knock it down and throw it."[106]

Freese said Traynor was thorough and tried his best to help, but there weren't any groundbreaking flashes of insight. "He told us everything ... how to go to your left, go to your right, all the ordinary things you are supposed to do," Freese remembered. "You took his advice for the simple fact that you knew he was one of the greatest. But you got the same advice from just about everybody. Then you had to go out and work on it and it became your problem.... He was like all the other old timers. They'd say, 'Kid, go out and take 100 ground balls a day and you'll be all right.' I'd say, 'How about 50?'"[107]

The Freese-Thomas experiment ultimately didn't work out that well. Though both men enjoyed long, productive careers, neither ever was mistaken for a Gold Glove candidate. Nonetheless, the organization enjoyed having Traynor around, and his visits to spring training became an annual occurrence until, almost literally, the day he died. He got a kick out of working with young players. On one occasion, at a hotel in Sarasota, he buttonholed Bill Robinson, a Pittsburgh-area native who was getting a look at third base from the Chicago

White Sox. He gave Robinson an impromptu lesson in the intricacies of defense right there in the lobby, with the corner of a rug serving as the third base bag.[108] "They say you're a little crazy when you start doing things like this," Traynor quipped.[109]

As time went on, his official duties became less about hands-on teaching and more about just being Pie Traynor. "He probably instructed a little bit," remembered Rich Hebner, whose first spring training was in 1969. "But he would kind of hang around just to have a Hall of Famer around."[110] Traynor loved to pull on that Pirate uniform, walk around, and schmooze. He was like a pied piper for the geriatric set, surrounded by retirees and longtime fans for hours as he answered their questions and regaled them with his tales.[111] Traynor also rode along on the team bus to exhibition games, and even umpired some intrasquad games. "He would just kind of hang out in back of the pitcher and umpire the bases. He would say, 'Let's move it along lads, I've got to be at the dog track at 7:15,'" said pitcher Steve Blass.[112]

Of course, Traynor was always willing to provide the media in Florida with a detailed, usually sunny forecast of the Pirates' fortunes for the upcoming season. Casey Stengel had a reputation for butchering names and providing reporters with meandering, unintentionally funny answers to relatively simple questions, but Traynor could give the Ol' Perfessor a run for his money. Asked by WIIC sports director Red Donley in the spring of 1969 for his outlook on the Pirates, Traynor conjured up this gem:

> Well, they got some young fellas here like Heffner [Hebner] and also that boy from down in Cumberland, Maryland, [Bob] Robertson, the boy that's got power. He hits balls over the fence, 400 feet. So he's a long ball hitter and he's always hit. And once you get a fella that'll always hit, nobody's ever going to stop him, and this is the first year he's been healthy and he's 21 years old. Heffner's a young fella who's got power. Our catcher, Sangween [Manny Sanguillen], looks like a fella, too, that's got that added power.... We're trying to teach little Freddie Paytack [Patek] something. Freddie is a fella that used to hit bad balls, and a first ball hitter. Now he's changing his motive [sic]. Yesterday he got a hit with two strikes on him. That'll give him confidence.[113]

Despite the generation gap, Traynor ingratiated himself with the Pirate players. He brought a little life to the drudgery of spring training. "Pie had a lot of piss and vinegar," said Hebner. "He didn't just put on a uniform and mope around."[114] Nor did he come off as some kind of larger-than-life figure, like some former stars did. "I was scared of George Sisler," declared Blass. "I was 18 years old. He would sit in a lawn chair back of the batting cage during batting practice and say, 'OK, son, throw me 12 sliders down and away from this guy.' I was terrified. I was just trying to throw the ball in the cage!"[115]

As much as anything, Blass said, Traynor's presence helped instill respect for the great tradition of both the Pittsburgh Pirates and the game of baseball. "It was great just to know you were part of that kind of scenario. It gave you a little sense of professionalism that, hey, I'm involved in something that's pretty great here."[116]

Traynor was around the Pirates a lot during spring training and, to a lesser extent, during the season. He and the players grew pretty familiar with each other and, for the most part, genuinely enjoyed each other's company. Traynor and Hebner, both gregarious and slightly flaky third basemen from the Boston area who wore number 20, seemed to develop a particularly close relationship.

But there were exceptions, of course. During one training camp in the early 1960s, a snarky infield prospect responded to one of Traynor's suggestions by snapping, "You play third base your way and I'll play third base my way."[117]

Roberto Clemente evidently held Traynor in high regard; after breaking Traynor's team RBI record in 1972, he refused to acknowledge a standing ovation at Three Rivers Stadium because he believed such a gesture would be disrespectful. "The man whose record I broke was a great ballplayer, a great fellow. And he just died here a few months ago. That's why I didn't even tip my cap," said Clemente.[118] Though Traynor always admired Clemente's immense talent, he apparently did not care much for the Pirate right fielder as a person. As Traynor's friend Bruno Sammartino recalled, "He said Clemente was temperamental and sought special treatment and complained a lot. He was unsociable with some of the players. I got the impression that he saw a lot about Clemente that bothered him."[119] Whether those accusations were fair or not, Traynor was far from the only person who felt that way. As a young player, especially, Clemente was not a wildly popular man in the Pirate clubhouse.

Then there was Traynor's oddly strained relationship with Dick Groat. The two men had a dispute that stewed quietly, unaddressed, for many years. "Pie Traynor was not one of my favorite people."[120] Groat was a Pittsburgh native who was an All-American in baseball and basketball at Duke University. He signed with the Pirates a few days after graduation, bypassed the minor leagues, and immediately took over as the team's starting shortstop in June 1952. He acquitted himself well, batting .284 and finishing third in Rookie of the Year balloting. After two years of military service, Groat rejoined the Bucs and was a mainstay of their lineup until Joe L. Brown sent him to St. Louis in a highly unpopular deal following the 1962 season.

The Pirates were horrible during Groat's early years in the organization, losing more than 100 games from 1952 to 1954, then losing 94, 88, and 92 games from 1955 to 1957. As Groat tells it, Traynor saw him as the symbol of Bucco futility. "He used to make fun of our clubs when we played and I was one of the people who was the brunt of that—constantly."[121]

As Roy McHugh noted, "Everybody said [negative] things about the team. I don't think anyone was going around praising them."[122] But it was the personal nature of Traynor's comments that hurt Groat. "He used to call me 'the fair-haired boy,' always in a derogatory way, but never when I was around. And it came back to me. There are no secrets in your hometown."[123]

Could Traynor, who never had an opportunity to get much of an education, have been jealous of a "college boy" like Groat? Did he think everything came a little bit too easily for this very bright, athletically gifted young man who jumped straight from Duke to the majors? It's a mystery to Groat. "I have no idea what his problem was with me. I guess I just couldn't play."[124]

Groat got his vindication in 1960, when the Pirates defeated the New York Yankees in the World Series and Groat was named National League Most Valuable Player. "It's very easy to criticize a team that's finishing dead last. All of a sudden we learned how to win in '58. [Traynor] wasn't much of a factor then. When you're fighting for the pennant, people don't criticize much about a ball-club like that. And then when you win a world championship, it's over. You can't criticize then."[125]

The two men never even discussed their issues, much less resolved them. "I was a big Pie Traynor fan growing up. I had tremendous respect for him as a baseball player. Pie was a great, great, great player. I guess part of the resentment is the fact that I looked up to him so much. Pie was not fan of Dick Groat's. Don't ask me why."[126]

Traynor's long run at KQV finally came to an end in March 1966. Traynor no longer fit the station's format, and really hadn't since it flipped to Top 40 in 1958. By the mid–1960s, KQV was a phenomenon; it sounded incredible. Radio programmers from around the country visited Pittsburgh just to listen to the station and get some ideas to take back home with them. It was fast-paced, exciting, never a dull moment. In that context, it is remarkable that Traynor, with his awkward and hesitant style, lasted as long as he did. Chuck Brinkman doesn't recall much listener outcry when Traynor was let go. "He wasn't getting us that much" by the time he was fired, according to Brinkman.[127]

Traynor's health also was a factor. Respiratory problems, likely brought on by a lifetime of smoking and certainly not helped by Pittsburgh's horrific air quality, were catching up to him. When the weather was cold or snowy, he struggled to make the walk from his home into the station and was forced to call in sick a few more times than management would have liked. Besides, the bigwigs at ABC were anxious to get their new star, Howard Cosell, on the air in Pittsburgh. "They argued that Pie was limited mostly to Pirate and/or baseball information and Cosell covered the full gamut of sports," said John Rook.[128]

Finally, given the often brutal, bottom-line nature of corporate radio, it is unsurprising that dollars and cents played a role as well. It didn't really cost KQV anything to run Cosell's program, and that made Traynor vulnerable. "It was a shame," recalled Keeve Berman, who left KQV for ABC News in New York later that year. "They were also letting engineers go. I remember one engineer said, 'Let me be a courier, let me do anything. Don't let me go. I've been here for 20-some years.' But they didn't care."[129]

Traynor does not appear to have made any public comments about his departure, but his friend, Bill Cardille, suspected Traynor took it pretty hard. "He probably thought he was well received, which he was. But in radio and television, you can be let go for so many different reasons."[130] But Pie Traynor wasn't about to disappear. He was a guest in the living rooms of professional wrestling fans every Saturday night.

14

Live from Ringside

Although his KQV gig was over, Traynor was still all over the airwaves in Pittsburgh as a television pitchman. His popularity and common man's sensibilities made him a natural choice for advertisers looking for someone to sell their products. "Because he had such a feel for the people, people hustling tires or whatever felt that if Pie said it, people would believe it," said friend Ed Kiely.[1] Traynor did ads for a number of different companies in the 1950s and 1960s, but it was as the face of the American Heating Company that he left an indelible mark on the consciousness of a generation of Pittsburghers.

American Heating was founded by Pittsburgh native Max Berger, whose cousin gave him his start in the furnace business after Berger returned from fighting in Europe during World War II. Berger was an intelligent man and creative thinker who put home improvement projects within the financial reach of hundreds of working class families who otherwise would have been unable to afford them.[2] "Back in the '60s it wasn't real common to get a loan from a bank to get a roof fixed," according to Berger's son, Jack. "So my dad worked closely with Mellon Bank to let people buy things on credit."[3]

For a decade-and-a-half, American Heating sponsored WIIC-TV's locally produced professional wrestling program, *Studio Wrestling*, whose viewing audience was filled with kinds of workaday customers Berger hoped to reach. Every Saturday evening, from 6:00 to 7:30, fans across western Pennsylvania, Ohio, and West Virginia tuned in to Channel 11 to watch local heroes like Bruno Sammartino and Jumpin' Johnny DeFazio do battle with "evil villains" like George "The Animal" Steele, Baron Scicluna, and Gorilla Monsoon.

Wrestling still had a patina of legitimacy as a competitive sport in those days, so much so that it warranted coverage in Pittsburgh's major newspapers. Some fans recognized that the outcome of the matches was pre-determined; many other fans did not. But Traynor didn't see anything deceptive or dishonest about this. Even though everything was loosely scripted, Traynor appreciated that the men in the ring were hard-working entertainers. "Most [wrestlers] are fine athletes.... A lot of people say it's a show. It isn't a show — it's an exhibition, a crowd pleaser."[4]

Studio Wrestling was hugely popular. "When we had wrestling on, we outdrew the Steelers," boasted Bill Cardille, the show's host.[5] Matches held at Forbes Field and Pittsburgh's Civic Arena routinely drew 8,000–10,000 people during the 1960s. DeFazio, who later leveraged his name recognition to win a seat on the Allegheny County Board of Commissioners, says he and his cohorts became celebrities. "I could go anywhere in the country and for some reason people would recognize you. It was on every week and was the number one program in the area for a good while. Everyone knew you."[6]

Indeed, they did travel just about anywhere. Like many of the wrestlers, DeFazio held down a regular job during the week, toiling in a steel mill. But he spent his weekends on the road and in the ring. "On a Friday, I would leave at noon, go all the way up to Buffalo, wrestle up there, shower, and drive home. I'd be so tired I would be seeing things going across the road. I'd stop every so often to throw water on my face just to stay awake."[7]

Professional wrestling changed considerably after the 1970s, becoming a flashy, big-money, global entertainment industry. But in the 1950s and 1960s, most televised wrestling was locally produced, gritty, and no frills. "It wasn't as much show biz as it is now," according to DeFazio. "You just wrestled. Now they do crazy things."[8] Sammartino, who became disgusted with the direction professional wrestling took in the 1980s and 1990s, remembered those days fondly. "Guys didn't have bizarre gimmicks. There was no vulgarity or profanity or nudity like you see today. You didn't see skimpy clothes like today, where women are wearing a g-string and bra that barely covers their nipples. It was fairly clean entertainment."[9]

Nor did wrestlers resemble bodybuilders or cartoon characters; they were just strong, tough men usually with real-sounding (and often distinctly European) names who looked and spoke just like the guys who might work beside you at the mill or the buddies you might share a beer with down at the Sons of Italy or the Bavarian Hall. So it is not surprising that wrestling went over big in the Pittsburgh area, with its large blue-collar population and heightened sense of ethnic identity.

Cardille hosted *Studio Wrestling* almost from its inception. He came to Pittsburgh from Erie, where he cut his teeth in the television industry. "The government had a freeze on TV stations [in Pittsburgh]. The government lifted the freeze and there were six announcers hired and I was one of them," Cardille recalled.[10] He was one of the original announcers hired by WIIC, and his was the first voice heard when the station signed on in September 1957. He would become a Pittsburgh institution, and one of Traynor's closest friends.

The city's powerhouse station was KDKA, which signed on as WDTV in 1949. (Traynor did sports commentary on WDTV for a short time during the early 1950s.) KDKA and newcomer WTAE, which went on the air in 1958, both built strong reputations for news and public affairs programming. WIIC, though, took a different tack, with a news department that was bare bones compared to its competitors.[11] Instead, it focused its local production efforts on entertainment programming like *Studio Wrestling* and a late Saturday night double feature of old horror movies called *Chiller Theater*, which Cardille hosted for two decades.

Cardille turned down an offer to host *Studio Wrestling* when it debuted in 1959, but when the original host left the station after about two years, Cardille's boss convinced him to change his mind. He was a great choice, selling the matches with an over-the-top enthusiasm that was a perfect fit for the sport. He later was chosen to broadcast matches in Philadelphia, which were sanctioned by the Worldwide Wrestling Federation, later known as the WWF, which would launch pro wrestling onto the nation's pop culture radar in the mid–1980s. "There I worked for Vince McMahon, Sr., who was a terrific guy," Cardille remembered. "Nothing like his son, who is a [jerk]."[12]

Studio Wrestling's popularity contrasted with the low-budget nature of the production. The wrestling ring was surrounded by only a few rows of folding chairs, behind which stood a backdrop on which images of "fans" were painted in order to create the illusion of a much larger crowd. There weren't more than 200 people on hand, but on the screen it appeared that the rows of seats stretched endlessly into the darkness.

One of the most vociferous fans was a plump, middle-aged woman named Ann Buckalew, more familiarly known as "Ringside Rosie." Rosie was in the

Traynor and Bill Cardille on the set of WIIC-TV's *Chiller Theater* around 1970 (Bill Cardille).

front row every Saturday in her dark-framed glasses, screaming and wagging her finger at the bad guys, dressing down the bumbling referees, and wildly cheering for her favorites. "Everybody thought she was on the payroll, but she wasn't,"[13] said Traynor. Rosie became almost as big a star as the wrestlers. "I'm a real celebrity in my own right now. Everyone on the street stops me and talks about wrestling," she said in 1962.[14]

The few available seats were in high demand. Fans would start lining up outside the studios on "Television Hill" early Saturday afternoon, creating headaches for studio supervisor Lou Vlahos. "They'd be out there at 1:00 in the afternoon [even] in the middle of winter. Pie would come in and say, 'Lou, let them in. They're freezing!' I would say, 'Pie, let them freeze. They know what time they're supposed to be here.' We were still setting up the chairs and the ring and adjusting the lighting. There was a lot of stuff going on and you can't do that with people in the studios."[15]

The American Heating ads on *Studio Wrestling* were simple and straight-forward in concept, but frequently weird and unintentionally comical in execution. At the beginning of each spot (all done live, as many ads were in television's early days), Traynor stood in front of the ring and bellowed the tagline, "Who Can? Ameri-can! The American Heating Company!" The director then cut to a picture of the specific items being featured as Traynor voiced a description, whimsically assuring customers, "You can buy it now, but you won't have to pay for it until the birds chirp in the spring." (Or, if it was summertime, "You can buy it now, but you won't have to make the first payment until the snow falls in the winter.") The spots concluded with Traynor back on camera, wrapping up the spot. "Then Cardille would walk over. They would chat for a while [on camera] and have a couple of digs back and forth," Vlahos recalled.[16]

Traynor always looked exquisite, appearing in the ads wearing a suit and tie, his white hair combed perfectly. "He never put his eyeglasses on when he was on camera because he wanted to look good," remembered Berger. "But as soon as the camera cut off him, he would have to read the script and would immediately put the glasses back on. He couldn't read at all without his glasses but he didn't want to be seen with them on."[17]

Regrettably, almost no recordings of Traynor's American Heating ads are still around. ("We had a news director come in, I think in the early '80s, and he threw all those films away," lamented Cardille.[18]) One that does exist is uncomfortable to watch. Traynor stands alongside Cardille, his shoulders lifted up to give him a freakish, ramrod-straight posture. Traynor barks his lines, clearly reading from a TelePrompTer or cue cards, with an almost complete lack of intonation and inflection.[19]

As one watches it, it is remarkable to realize that this was a man who had been doing live television and radio for almost 25 years. "Bless his heart, he was such a wonderful storyteller, but as soon as he would get on camera he would be so stilted," said former WIIC news anchor and reporter Eleanor Schano.[20] For example, if an ad agency wanted on-air talent to include a pause in their delivery, they would insert the word "pause" in the copy. If they wanted a complete stop, they would insert the word "stop." Traynor couldn't deal with things like this. He would read the script verbatim, as if those cue words were there to be spoken. The result, of course, was ludicrous. "Hello, I'm Pie Traynor. Pause. And I'm batting for the American Heating Company. Stop."[21]

One time Schano tried to set him straight about why those cues were in the script. "Pie, that just means you're supposed to stop or pause."

But Traynor wouldn't budge. "No, no, no. You're wrong," he shot back. "When they put that on there you're supposed to say it exactly [as written]."

After seeing Traynor stumble through one reading after another, Schano felt embarrassed for him; she decided to call the advertising agency and see what could be done to give him a hand. "What happened was that after a while people were beginning to like him just the way he was. So they just let him go!"[22]

Cardille believes some of Traynor's trouble came from a familiar source — insecurity. "He was afraid to make a mistake. He wouldn't take his eyes of the TelePrompTer. If they wrote 'go fly a duck' on the prompter as a joke, he would have said, 'This is Pie Traynor. Who Can? Ameri-can! Go fly a duck!' He was determined. It was full steam ahead, damn the torpedoes."[23]

One wonders whether some of the bumbling might have been intentional. Traynor was no dummy, but some of his screw-ups were simply absurd. "The people we worked with would tease him good-naturedly and he went along with it. He never let on that his stumbles bothered him," said Cardille.[24] Could Traynor simply have been playing along, looking and sounding awkward in order to perpetuate the folksy image that people found endearing? It sounds plausible, but Cardille doesn't think that was the case. "He didn't do that on purpose. He was too proud."[25]

As strange as the ads were, they worked. Eventually, the Pittsburgh airwaves were fairly saturated with Traynor shilling for American Heating. "Television spots in those days were not nearly as expensive, especially in local TV," according to former *Pittsburgh Press* reporter Phil Musick. "Pie was on the tube about every five minutes."[26] The company eventually expanded its advertising to include local newspapers, which featured Traynor's visage and the familiar "Who Can? Ameri-can" catchphrase. Ask a Pittsburgher of a certain age about Pie Traynor and one of the first things they mention are the American Heating spots. Roy McHugh of the *Pittsburgh Post-Gazette* accompanied Traynor on a few of his long walks around the city and saw firsthand how that tagline had taken on a life of its own. "Almost everywhere he went someone would call out, 'Hey Pie, who can?' and he'd say, 'Ameri-can!'"[27]

Traynor had become a brand icon. American Heating's customer base consisted of regular, working class Joes. (As Jack Berger put it, "The Heinz family wasn't calling American Heating."[28]) Those were the kinds of people who enjoyed professional wrestling and could really appreciate Traynor's unpolished, everyman persona. "Those ads would routinely bring in quite a number of phone calls that would turn into leads," said Jack Berger.[29] Traynor was a major reason why Max Berger was able to grow his company into a 60-employee operation, one of the largest home-remodeling companies in the Pittsburgh area, before he sold it in the 1990s.

But some people believed the ads diminished Traynor, and that they were somewhat beneath him. "We dislike seeing Pie Traynor shoved slam bang into spots which are provokingly annoying," sniffed one anonymous TV columnist. "Pie is too fine a sportsman for anything tawdry, but those commercials he often has to report are strictly for the birds."[30] WIIC's Don Riggs felt like Traynor became "a caricature of himself."[31] Chuck Reichblum of WJAS Radio agreed. "In a way he became almost a clownish figure because of the American Heating ads and because of the way he had about him," contended Reichblum. "Kids who didn't know probably wouldn't have guessed that here was a Hall of Fame ballplayer ... [but] I think he was kind of oblivious to it."[32]

He might have been oblivious to what people thought; it's also possible that he didn't care. Some baseball purists clucked their tongues at a Hall of Famer like Traynor getting involved even peripherally in a business like pro wrestling, which had a shady reputation in some circles. But Traynor shrugged off those criticisms with a wink and a knowing grin. "Wrestling — that's the only real sport out there."[33]

Behind the scenes at *Studio Wrestling*, Traynor found himself in one of those enclaves of rough-hewn male camaraderie where he felt so much at home. He usually would show up around 4:30 P.M. and hold court in the announcer's booth, which Cardille describes as having been "as big as a kitchen, so there was room for everybody. He would tell us stories in there. I always got the first story and then the wrestlers would come in. Ninety-five percent of the time there were five to seven other people in the announcer's booth."[34]

Sammartino, who immigrated to the United States from battle-ravaged Abruzzo, Italy, as a boy following World War II, found Traynor particularly captivating. "When I first came to this country, I didn't know about baseball. I didn't know the history. So I was fascinated by all these stories he used to tell. He spoke very highly of Lou Gehrig, and how Gehrig was tight with a buck because he came from a very tough childhood with a lot of poverty and wanted to take care of his mother. He would smile and talk about what a wild man Babe Ruth was. I used to try to get to the studio early just to sit there and talk to him about these different things. I would talk to him for maybe an hour at a time. He was very open about his thoughts and feelings about different people. I felt a real honesty about him."[35]

DeFazio recalls hanging out while Traynor presided over intense discussions about horse racing and, especially, football. "I was a big football person, always talking football, and so was Pie," said DeFazio. "He would always know which team was good in the cold or which team would get tired in the heat. He'd always look at all these angles. I'd laugh to myself. I don't know if he bet on games or not, but he talked liked he did."[36]

Though the American Heating ads brought Traynor some income, financial concerns weighed on him and Eve in their golden years. They were hardly destitute, but by no means were they well-off either. "I guess we won't starve," Eve shrugged in 1967. "We'll get along."[37]

Like a lot of Americans his age, Traynor made some financial decisions as a young man that he came to regret. The Great Depression hit him with a one-two punch, wiping out much of his investment portfolio and dooming his sporting goods venture before it really even got off the ground.

Traynor enjoyed telling a story, perhaps apocryphal but nonetheless revealing, about an encounter he had with Ty Cobb during an exhibition game in the 1920s. Cobb, standing at third base, asked Traynor, "Do you have any money?"

"Yeah, I've got some back in the clubhouse," replied an unwitting Traynor.

"No!" Cobb growled. "Money for investing!"

Cobb supposedly advised Traynor to buy stock in Coca-Cola (a decision which eventually made Cobb millions). But Traynor didn't see the wisdom in that advice. "If I'm going to invest in a soft drink," he told Cobb, "I'm going to invest in Moxie."[38]

Then there was Traynor's aforementioned passivity in negotiating with the Pirates. "He never tried to make 10 cents for himself, but he helped a lot of other people get a job," Eve once griped. "Now that we're getting older I think it was a mistake, but I didn't think so then.... Maybe he could have made more, but he didn't care. He doesn't care about money."[39]

That remark was not literally true, of course. Anyone who has to buy food or pay bills cares about money to some extent. Traynor cared about money, too, especially in his later years when it was in relatively short supply. Still, Eve had a point. Even with some very real financial concerns looming over his head, Traynor couldn't bring himself to use his fame to make a few extra dollars. Worse, he probably allowed people to take advantage of his good nature.

"Pie could never say no," said Cardille. "He was just so benevolent. He never got paid much for his appearances and he did a lot of favors for people."[40] One Saturday, Traynor showed up later than usual for his *Studio Wrestling* appearance. He was looking unusually tired and a concerned Cardille asked what was wrong. Traynor informed him he had gone to Ohio to appear before a group of Little Leaguers.

"He had taken the bus to Steubenville, about 50 miles away," remembered Cardille. "He hit balls all day, worked with the kids, then came to the station around 5:00. He was dragging; he was too old to do that." Furthermore, he did it all for free. His "pay" for the afternoon consisted of two McDonald's hamburgers. Cardille was aghast. "I said, Pie, let us manage you. But he said, 'No, that's all right.' He'd give you the shirt off his back. That's probably why he had nothing."[41]

Eve admitted that she shared some of Pie's tendencies. "I'm just as bad as he is with giving money away and being generous."[42] Indeed. In the late 1930s, she loaned a friend $7,000, the equivalent of more than $100,000 in 2008 dollars. Unfortunately, she neglected to put anything in writing, so she and Pie had to sue the man to try to get the money back.[43]

The Pirates quietly helped Pie and Eve make ends meet, keeping him on the payroll until the end of his life. "They paid him under a scouting contract, but at Pie's age there wasn't really much scouting being done, although I'm sure in the earlier years there was. He just didn't have the health," said Douglas McCormick, a former member of the Pirates accounting department and later a financial advisor to Eve.[44] Joe L. Brown says it was the least the organization could do for a man who had been the team's most recognizable goodwill ambassador for almost a half-century. "Pie made friends wherever he went. Every club needs to be recognized and respected in their home territory, and everybody in Pittsburgh loved Pie."[45]

But Traynor was bitter that it had come to that, railing against the penuriousness of the Major League Baseball Players Association, which he felt had betrayed old-timers like him by refusing to include most of them in their pension system. He admired the audacity of Rogers Hornsby, whom Traynor said would insult the modern-day ballplayers to their faces. "He would say, 'We were the pioneers of baseball and made it possible for you fellows to get the pension and you don't include us.'"[46]

For Traynor, the pension was not just a money issue; it was about respect and gratitude. "We've never been included and it's never been brought up at any of their meetings. They're not going to include the old-timer at all," Traynor predicted in 1967. "There are fellows that should be included. Lefty Grove is one of the greatest pitchers who ever lived and he needs money. Lloyd Waner needed money badly. Max Carey is in bad shape financially. Zack Wheat is another one in bad shape financially. But you can't talk these present-day players about that because they have an idea that baseball started when they came in."[47]

Usually, though, Traynor didn't spend much time worrying about things—quite a contrast from his days on the baseball field. In retirement, his perspective on his life usually came from somewhere high up in the clouds. He was "naïve to a degree," according to Chet Smith of the *Pittsburgh Press*.[48] In a lot of ways, he remained a big, overgrown kid for most of his adult life, a trait that can be annoying in some people, but in Traynor's case most found it comical and endearing. Jack Henry described Traynor's general cluelessness in a light-hearted column penned in 1956.

> His reaction to everyday activities is at times exasperating. For example, several of us at KQV carefully save his mail. He just as promptly ignores all letters until

they become a fire hazard. Once we had to scurry through his mail backlog of two years to find a check that had been mailed to him. The check was there all right, but it leads us to wonder how many he has thrown away during a lifetime.... He has no idea of his social security number, nor the foggiest thought of where he can locate it. He forgets his wife's middle name. One of these days he will remember to pay his income tax BEFORE the deadline.[49]

Also lost in Traynor's mountain of unopened mail was an untold number of autograph requests. Catch Traynor on the street and he would sign autographs until his hand was sore. But he was unusual among living Hall of Famers in the 1950s and 1960s in that he almost never replied to fans or collectors through the mail. For a man like Traynor, who so passionately craved social interactions and physical activity, the thought of sitting alone at the kitchen table signing his name over and over must have seemed like the depths of soul-numbing tedium. He kept the letters and let them stack up in boxes, perhaps intending to respond sometime, but then he either forgot about it or just never got around to it.[50]

Nor was it especially unusual for Traynor to show up at the wrong location for something, schedule himself for public appearances in different towns at the same time, or forget an appointment altogether. One afternoon in the early days of his radio career, he encountered Chet Smith walking downtown. After an exchange of pleasantries, Traynor uncharacteristically cut the conversation short, saying he had to hustle to get ready for his daily radio show.

"You still have an hour to go, that's plenty of time," said a confused Smith.

"Yeah, but this is different," Traynor replied. "I forgot to tell the man I'm going to interview, so I have to go look for him."[51]

Fortunately, Eve was around to keep her husband's life pretty much on track most of the time. "She was a real caretaker for Pie in many ways, and not just in the latter part of his life," according to their nephew, Mike Helmer. "She took care of a lot details he wasn't interested in. He was bigger than life in terms of how he was viewed in Pittsburgh. He knew so many people of every walk of life. But I don't think he worried about the details of how the bills specifically got paid and things like that. She handled all of that. And I think whatever social life they had was through her."[52]

Eve was ambivalent about her husband's popularity and the role in which it cast her. While Pie relished the public's attention, Eve generally was much more private and reserved. "Sometimes I think she enjoyed [being a public figure], sometimes I think she didn't," said Frank Gustine, Jr.[53]

Eve carved out a life of her own, independent of Pie, by reading and attending the symphony, volunteering at Mercy Hospital and with the Pittsburgh Pinch Hitters, a group of Pirate players' wives and female front office employees who raised money for charity.[54] But she adored her husband, loved being with him, and was never fully comfortable sharing him with the rest of the city. "I'd have liked it if he'd spent more time at home, but if he's out talking baseball he'll stay all night. What are you going to do? You get used to it. If I didn't like to read, I'd have left him years ago."[55]

But let no one else insinuate that Pie was a less-than-ideal husband. One time Eve's sister, Jean, put her nose in where it didn't belong and suggested that Pie was being neglectful. At issue was a comparison between Jean's husband, an insurance executive who was always home in time for dinner, and Pie, who, of course, was always late.

"Jean, when Bill comes out of his office, is there anybody waiting for him on the street?"

"No," Jean muttered.

"Every place Pie has worked there [has been] a gang waiting for him," continued Eve. "And he never passes anyone up for an autograph. And I saw a lot of stars who did…. He's the nicest man to everyone he meets."[56]

Eve also was fiercely protective of Pie's reputation as a player. Pie was ostensibly humble and seldom discussed his own legacy. On the other hand, Eve, who wore her husband's Hall of Fame charm pendant on a gold chain around her neck, was almost obsessed with it. "I always detected a little jealousy when they talked about the great third basemen of all time and maybe mentioned Brooks Robinson or some of the great third basemen of the '60s or '70s," recalled Frank Gustine, Jr. "She didn't think Pie got enough credit. She'd be upset that they didn't remember Pie."[57]

Eve constantly was on alert for people who, in her mind, failed to pay proper respect. When she learned *Boston Globe* columnist Harold Kaese had referred to Pie as "the Brooks Robinson of another day," she phoned the paper with a correction. "Pie wasn't the Brooks Robinson of his day. Brooks Robinson is the Pie Traynor of *his* day."[58] After Robinson earned national acclaim for his stellar defensive play in Baltimore's World Series win over Cincinnati in 1970, Eve sneered, "Pie made those plays all the time…. Robinson couldn't carry Pie's glove."[59] Pie found Eve's hyper-vigilance kind of amusing. "I never think of things like getting credit," he said. "Just my wife."[60]

The Traynors never had children; a couple of their acquaintances recalled hearing whispers of fertility problems. But although they had no little ones of their own, Eve and Pie both retained a soft spot for kids. Eve's much-younger half-sister, Mary Jessop, remembered Pie playing games of "tickle" with her when she was small. "He just loved kids," Jessop said. "They wanted [children] but they never did have any."[61]

While Eve was sophisticated and image-conscious around adults, she let her guard down around children, becoming like a second mother or older sister to a lot of the kids she was close to. As far back as the 1930s, she took a pre-pubescent Bill Benswanger, Jr., to nightclubs, both during spring training and in Pittsburgh. "We had our favorite songs, our favorite places to go," he remembered.[62]

Bob Gustine had a similar experience a number of years later. "I was like

Mrs. Traynor's little boy. She would take me out to lunch and dinner and take me down to the [horse] races."[63] Once when he was seven or eight years old, Gustine insisted on paying Eve back by buying lunch for her. They went together to what, in a little boy's eyes, was the pinnacle of fine dining — the lunch counter at G.C. Murphy's. "I didn't know any better," Gustine laughed. "Here's this sophisticated lady and I'm sitting at a lunch counter at a five-and-ten-cent store ordering a grilled cheese sandwich and French fries, and I couldn't understand why she didn't want anything to eat. She just got a cup of coffee."[64]

Nephew Mike Helmer said when he was a child, Eve never seemed old, though she was pushing 60. "It was always fun when she was around. I remember her coming to our home when I was a 12-year-old kid and staying up very late with her. She liked to dance. She liked to listen to popular music. She was a big fan of Tom Jones and went to his concerts. It was kind of out of sync with what you would expect, but that was one of those things that made her fun to be around for a younger person because she seemed more with it. She was one of those relatives who makes a big impression on a kid."[65]

Among Eve's proudest moments came when her husband was named baseball's all-time third baseman, as a part of major league baseball's centennial celebration in 1969. "I'm so happy for Pie," she said. "Some of the writers today didn't see him play — some of the young writers. But they still voted for him."[66] Ceremonies were held in July in Washington, D.C., in conjunction with the All-Star Game. On July 22, Pie and Eve were among the guests of honor at a lavish $35-per-plate black-tie dinner at the Sheraton Park Hotel. The event was sold out weeks in advance and drew more than 2,000 guests, including members of President Richard Nixon's cabinet, Congress, and the Supreme Court; Archbishop of New York Terence Cardinal Cooke; and Apollo 8 commander Frank Borman, who Traynor acknowledged during his acceptance speech ("I was so proud of him for doing that," Eve said).[67] Traynor received two nearly identical trophies, a gold baseball mounted on a black base, for being named both the all-time third baseman and the greatest living third baseman.

The next afternoon, the president invited Traynor and the other honorees to the East Room of the White House. Nixon was a huge sports fan and appeared to be a bit star-struck. "I am awed by those who have made the team," the president remarked.[68] Nixon offered his personal congratulations to all of the players. He knew details about all of their careers, which impressed even Eve, a staunch Democrat who was enthralled with Nixon's political foes, the Kennedys. "I think because Nixon recognized Pie, that made her more positive toward him," chuckled Mike Helmer.[69]

The awards gave Eve another arrow to use against her husband's critics, both real and, in most cases, imagined. Several months later the Maryland Professional Baseball Players Association invited Traynor to its annual "Tops in Sports" banquet. The printed program included a photograph captioned, "Pie Traynor ... Great Third Baseman and Hall of Fame." The description sounds completely innocuous and perfectly appropriate, but Eve took quiet umbrage. In her copy she circled the word "great," jotted a question mark next to it, and scrawled a correction in the margin, "Voted July 1969 greatest living and greatest ever."[70]

Traynor had become a man who loved to be loved. He thrived on being in the spotlight, whether it was on TV every Saturday night or just kicking back

During baseball's centennial season, Traynor was named the greatest third baseman in baseball history and the greatest living third baseman. Here he accepts one of those awards in Washington, D.C., on July 22, 1969 (Paul Traynor).

and telling stories with a group of fans at a bar. This was not a man who could have been happy toiling away behind a desk before going home at night to eat a quiet dinner and watch TV. While he was never one to brag or draw attention to himself, there is no question that he enjoyed being visible.

In retirement, Traynor was fortunate not only to carve out a role perfectly suited to his personality, but also to have a wife who was patient and understanding enough to let him live the kind of life that he needed to live in order to find fulfillment. Unlike many athletes whose lives fall to pieces once they leave the playing field, Traynor found meaning in his post-baseball years. In many ways he seemed much more centered and content than he ever was as a player or manager, free from all of the self-imposed pressure to excel. By all indications it was a genuinely happy period in his life.

15

It Kind of Made Me Feel Like Crying

Early in his post-baseball life it seemed as if Traynor was in perpetual motion. His various jobs, his walking, and his public appearances kept him a very busy man. But over the last decade of his life, he slowly curtailed his activity as his health eroded.

Traynor was plagued by lung problems for many years. He was first hospitalized for breathing difficulties in the summer of 1958 when he spent four weeks at Pittsburgh's Mercy Hospital, receiving breathing treatments and also having a small benign tumor (unrelated to his respiratory ailment) removed from his chest. Sometime thereafter doctors diagnosed him with emphysema. Traynor was a smoker, which is the leading cause of emphysema. But it surely didn't help that he lived in Pittsburgh, where for so long the air quality was abominable.

Speaking about the effects of pollution on the lungs, Tony Gerber, a pulmonary specialist and assistant professor at the University of California, San Francisco, has stated, "Imagine putting acid right in your eye. It's that corrosive. This corrosiveness causes severe irritation and leads to problems like asthma attacks, coughing, wheezing, chest pain and even death."[1] Traynor's occupation as a baseball player and penchant for walking kept him outdoors for hours each day, where he breathed in all sorts of grime and toxins belched into the air by the city's factories.

By the early 1970s, Traynor was doctoring with John Shively, a young pulmonogist at Allegheny General Hospital. Shively recalled that by the time he began treating Traynor, his emphysema was in an advanced stage. "It's really an irreversible situation," said Shively. "You don't really treat it *per se*, but you treat the complications that develop. I'm sure we gave him everything we could at that point in time, but it didn't help too much. There's really not much therapeutic you can do. It's more or less just trying to keep him or any emphysema patient as comfortable as possible."[2]

It's hard to ascertain Traynor's thoughts and feelings about his illness because he didn't really talk about it. Up until the day he died, he never really looked ill. He wasn't hauling around an oxygen tank or visibly losing weight. Bob Gustine remembered that if someone judged Traynor by his handshake, he would have had no clue that this was a dying man. "He had a grip on him until the end, even when he was sick. I couldn't believe how strong he was. He was just a tough guy."[3]

Even some of Traynor's close friends failed to realize the severity of his illness, and that was fine with him. He was reluctant to admit to anyone, even himself, that he was nearing the end. A week before Traynor's death, reporter Bob Broeg asked him about his emphysema. "I don't have emphysema," he shot back.[4] Shively says even in the privacy of the hospital, Traynor's demeanor was unwavering. "He was a very stoic guy. He didn't complain even though he was in a fair amount of distress with his breathing. Some patients are complaining all the time, but I think he realized there wasn't much we could do about his condition. I'm sure if it wasn't for his wife, who dragged him to the doctor, he wouldn't have bothered to come."[5]

In 1964, as Traynor was beginning to come to terms with his own mortality, he was hit with the early deaths of his two youngest brothers within a three-month span. In March, cancer took the life of his 51-year-old brother Charles. Charley Traynor was born March 12, 1912, in Somerville, the sixth of the seven siblings and the only one to attend college, enrolling at Northeastern University in Boston. Like most students at Northeastern, Charley took five years to finish his degree, receiving his B.A. in industrial engineering in 1936.

Charley played baseball in college, a third baseman just like his brothers Pie and Art. Northeastern failed to maintain individual statistics from the early-to-mid 1930s, but according to sports information department records, Charley earned a varsity letter in baseball from 1933 to 35 after likely playing on the freshman squad in 1932.[6]

Though he enjoyed baseball, Charley harbored no illusions of following any further in Pie's footsteps. His talents lay elsewhere. After graduation he took a job with General Electric in Lynn, Massachusetts, just north of Boston. He apparently did well for himself at GE. He and wife Adelaide, whom he married in 1940, settled in the upscale community of Georgetown, Massachusetts, where they lived in an historic home that Charley liked to work on in his spare time.

Charley's life was quiet, low-key, happy. He had no children of his own but he got a kick out of driving down to his brother Bob's place in Narragansett, Rhode Island, frolicking with Bob's four kids and relaxing by the beach. He died three days shy of his 52nd birthday.

Then, just three months later, Pie lost his youngest sibling, John. John Wilson Traynor was born July 6, 1913.[7] He married Elma MacLean at age 20, fathered a daughter, Mary Lou, and eventually moved from Massachusetts to New Haven, Connecticut, where he worked as a construction foreman, first for the Maynard-Pyle Company and then for C.W. Blakeslee and Sons.[8] His work frequently took him away from his family, all over New England and even up into Canada.

John seemed to fit perfectly the stereotype of the New England male. He was devoted, quiet, and professed abhorrence for profanity. His family nicknamed him "The Silent Preacher." As a hobby he bred dogs, specifically Dalmatians and boxers. Like his brother, Charley, John was just 51 years old when he died in a nursing home on July 16, 1964, following a nine-month battle with lung cancer.[9]

Despite Pie's maladies, he and Eve remained an attractive, almost glamorous-looking couple. "For a man in his 70s, he cut a fairly imposing figure," said sportswriter Phil Musick.[10] He could have passed for an aging movie star, with pale green eyes and perfectly combed silver hair, carefully parted on the left side, which complemented his bronzed skin. From the neck down, he still resembled an athlete — as always, a solidly built, physically fit man. He dressed to the nines regardless of the occasion, always resplendent in a dark suit and tie. "He had the moves," said Bill Cardille. "He was elegant and he was a handsome guy."[11]

Eve, always alluring, became even more stunning with age. Like Pie, she took tremendous pride in her appearance and was always well put together. "She dressed very fashionably. She wore beautiful jewelry and had a large diamond ring. She was a very beautiful woman," observed Frank Gustine, Jr.[12] Sportswriter Bill Christine didn't disagree. "I remember she had knockout legs, legs of a woman 20 years younger," said Christine, who knew her when she was in her 60s.[13]

"Pie Traynor Night" at Three Rivers Stadium on August 30, 1971. On the left, Traynor chats with Pirate second baseman Bill Mazeroski while on the right, Eve Traynor has a friendly word with right fielder Roberto Clemente (copyright © 2009 *Pittsburgh Post-Gazette*; all rights reserved; reprinted with permission).

On April 26, 1971, Traynor fell ill after returning home from a speaking engagement in his birthplace of Framingham, Massachusetts. He was admitted to the hospital in Pittsburgh the next day. "I needed a lot of oxygen. My chest would become congested," he said upon his release ten days later. "I can't take my walks yet. I perspire when I move around. But I'll be back soon."[14]

Just five months before his death, Traynor prepares to throw out the first ball prior to Game Three of the World Series in Three Rivers Stadium on October 12, 1971. Standing to his left is major league baseball Commissioner Bowie Kuhn (Pittsburgh Pirates).

He was true to his word. During the late summer and fall of 1971, Traynor pushed himself hard, maybe too hard. In August he made what would be his final appearance at the Baseball Hall of Fame, accepting a plaque on behalf of new inductee Jake Beckley, a nineteenth century Pirate first baseman. Later that month the Pirates honored him at "Pie Traynor Night" at Three Rivers Stadium prior to a game against the Philadelphia Phillies. About six weeks after that, he was back at Three Rivers, receiving a rousing ovation as he stood alongside baseball commissioner Bowie Kuhn and threw out the ceremonial first pitch prior to Game Three of the 1971 World Series.

On November 20 the Baseball Writers Association of America honored Traynor at a banquet at the William Penn Hotel. The Pittsburgh chapter of the BBWAA had been a quiet organization; its new chairman, Bill Christine, thought a dinner honoring a local baseball legend, the kind of event that had been successful in other cities, could spark some excitement among the members and stir up good publicity in the process. Fans paid $20 per person or $35 per couple to spend "A Nite for Pie."

Christine insists that the banquet was by no means intended as a farewell, despite Traynor's poor health. "I don't think it was one of those things where we were rushing the grave to honor him," said Christine. "I think it was just that he was such a fixture in Pittsburgh and still lived there and had a lot of friends in baseball, so he seemed the obvious guy to throw a dinner for. He got pretty emotional about it and he even tried to talk me out of it. He said there were other guys who were more deserving. But I said we'll honor other guys later. I didn't have to twist his arm very much."[15]

Christine invited every living member of the Baseball Hall of Fame. Nine of them showed up. Casey Stengel, who appeared wearing a floppy hat emblazoned with a New York Mets logo, paid his own way, as did Bob Feller, who claimed his Volkswagen got such good gas mileage on the drive from Cleveland that no compensation was necessary. But Christine recalls former Cardinals slugger Joe Medwick being more difficult to handle. "I think he had been burned in one or two of these before where he incurred expenses upfront and then didn't get reimbursed. It was maybe minutes before the dinner and Medwick said he wouldn't go on and wouldn't sit on the dais unless our secretary-treasurer wrote him a check for his expenses. So we had to write Medwick a check as we were walking into the ballroom."[16]

Although the dinner failed to rake in the huge profits Christine was hoping for, those in attendance had a ball, with former Pirate slugger Ralph Kiner serving as the emcee and Stengel delighting the crowd with his imitations of Traynor's slump-shouldered batting stance and quick release. It was an emotional evening for Traynor, who surely recognized this could be the last time he saw many of his old friends. The sportswriters sent him a check from the proceeds of the event, but Traynor refused it. "That night alone," he said, "was a whole lot more than any person could have expected."[17]

Two weeks later, on December 5, Traynor's respiratory system broke down again. An ambulance rushed him from his apartment to the emergency room at Allegheny General Hospital, where he almost died. To save his life doctors performed a heart massage, breaking two of his ribs in the process. (Traynor later teased an apologetic physician, "That's all right. I've had some fastballs in the ribs that hurt worse than that."[18]) Newspaper reports downplayed the severity of his illness, labeling it as "a respiratory ailment" without much elaboration. It could have been a passing case of bronchitis for all anyone could gather from the papers, but the truth was he was in very bad shape. A few days into his stay, a Pittsburgh sportscaster, unaware of how sick Traynor was, called his hospital room for an interview. Forever accommodating, Traynor agreed. But as he spoke he began gasping for air and lost his grip on the receiver, sending it crashing to the floor.[19]

This was a wrenching time for Eve. Not only had Pie's health taken a decided turn for the worse, but also that December her younger brother, Dale, died after a year-long battle with pancreatic cancer. Eve had returned to Cincinnati several times during the preceding year to spend time with Dale. "She was torn. She had these two very significant people in her life very ill at the same time," said Mike Helmer, Dale's son. "Both of my aunts were just crazy about their brother. The two of them didn't always see eye-to-eye. Not that they didn't get along, but there was more of that sisterly rivalry. But the little brother was just kind of their pet and they both really doted on him a lot."[20]

Traynor's resilience and his will to live a normal life were admirable. He recovered from his hospitalization in time to attend the February 6 Dapper Dan Dinner, where he received a three-minute ovation.[21] By March 1972 he was feeling well enough to make his annual trip to Florida. A few years earlier the Bucs had moved their spring headquarters from Fort Myers to Bradenton. It was business as usual for him there, hanging out with fans, putting on a Pirates uniform, and tagging along on the team bus on road trips to exhibition games.

That spring, the Manatee County, Florida, Chamber of Commerce organized its ninth annual Hall of Fame dinner. When the evening's emcee, Frankie Frisch, was hit with pneumonia, they prevailed upon Traynor to pinch-hit. His performance, given the tenuous state of his own health, was nothing short of remarkable. Though he wheezed and sounded breathless at times, he was on top of his game that night — sharp, energetic, and funny. Bob Broeg of the *Sporting News* wrote, "The tempo of Traynor's remarks was quick, crackling, and, without the benefit of notes, generally factual and occasionally funny, including brief digressions that would have done justice to Casey Stengel." [22] When someone later complimented him on his work, he responded wryly, "I wasn't even bearing down."[23]

Traynor cut short his trip to Bradenton to return to Pittsburgh where, on March 11, he was to be inducted into the Fraternal Order of Eagles Hall of Fame. The night before departing he had dinner with Pirates equipment manager John

Hallahan, after which he moved over to join sportswriter Al Abrams, where he delighted the table with one tale after another, keeping them "laughing long and loud," as Abrams put it.[24] At the Eagles ceremony, Pat Livingston of the *Pittsburgh Press* thought Traynor looked "robustly well ... like he'd live forever."[25]

A few days later, on Thursday March 16, Traynor was visiting an acquaintance, Margaret O'Donnell, at her first floor apartment at 250 Melwood Avenue in Pittsburgh. At around 5:20 P.M., he collapsed. When police arrived, they found him sprawled unconscious on a living room sofa. Officers rushed Traynor to Shadyside Hospital, administering oxygen along the way, but when he arrived, emergency room doctors found him unresponsive with no breathing and no pulse.[26] They pronounced Traynor dead at 5:34 P.M., the cause of death listed as cardiac arrest due to severe pulmonary emphysema.[27]

Though he had been ill for a long time, the end came swiftly and without warning, which is not unusual with emphysema patients. "They seem like they are okay when they are quiet and not moving around [but] when you get that advanced state of emphysema, it doesn't take much to push you over the line," said Dr. Shively. "Their oxygen could bottom out and they could have a fatal heart arrhythmia. When you have an advanced disease like that, you're very fragile."[28]

Pittsburgh fans were stunned, as were the Pirates. The team learned of Traynor's death during the sixth inning of an exhibition game in Miami, when the stadium's public address announcer broke the news and asked for fans and players to stand and observe a moment of silence. "I just couldn't believe it when I heard that Pie died. I just couldn't believe it," the Pirates Willie Stargell told reporters.[29]

In the other clubhouse, the Orioles great third baseman Brooks Robinson expressed his shock. "I wrote to him when he was in the hospital over the winter and from the tone of his wife's reply, I thought he was going to be okay."[30] Rich Hebner probably took Traynor's death hardest of all the players. On the day of Traynor's burial, Hebner wore a black windbreaker during workouts in lieu of his usual uniform number 20 to honor his friend. "I wouldn't wear his number today even if we were playing a game. I told Pie they should have retired his number, but he seemed to want me to wear it."[31] (The Pirates retired Traynor's number a month later at a ceremony before the club's home opener.) Former teammates like Max Carey, Wilbur Cooper, and Lloyd Waner added their regrets. "When I heard tonight he had died, it kind of made me feel like crying," said Waner. "We lost Zack Wheat last week, you know. Maybe us Hall of Famers better watch out."[32]

Meanwhile, Eve, sensitive to what people might infer from her husband dying in another woman's apartment, was furious with how local newspapers reported on the circumstances of Pie's death. "We said he was found dead at the home of a friend. We didn't even say it was a woman. [But] Eve called me aside at the funeral and upbraided me for the article," remembered Bill Christine of the *Pittsburgh Press*. "I said, 'Eve, we had to acknowledge that he died someplace and he didn't die at home or at the hospital. And the way we put it in the paper, I don't think there was any room for anybody to read between the lines and think there was anything nefarious about this.' I think she kind of understood that. At least I'd like to think that she did because I didn't see her much after that."[33]

The viewing, which occurred on a rainy weekend in Pittsburgh, attracted hundreds of people from all walks of life to the Samson Funeral Home on Neville Street. "In the first few hours yesterday, a judge and a banker, a police chief and a television executive, a stock broker and an usher at Three Rivers Stadium paid their respects," wrote Roy McHugh in the *Pittsburgh Press*.[34] Eve held up well, though she still was coming to grips with her loss. "You expect him to wake up and tell a joke," she mused to a reporter. "He always complained that I didn't laugh at his jokes. I'd say, 'They're too corny.' And he'd answer, 'You don't understand them.' I'd say, 'I understand them all right but I heard those stories in grade school.' I never let him get ahead of me."[35]

Around 200 people attended the funeral the following Monday afternoon. The mourners included Traynor's six pallbearers—Cardille, former National League president Warren Giles, former Pirates manager Danny Murtaugh, Baseball Hall of Fame curator Ken Smith, Pittsburgh mayor Pete Flaherty, and Maury Splain of the Fraternal Order of Eagles.

Traynor's friend from his Cape Cod days, Reverend Nathaniel Moor, was unable to officiate so the honor went to retired Rabbi Solomon Freehof. "Pie and I are of different religions but ... death levels all barriers and makes the whole world kin."[36] During the eulogy, Freehof noted that "it was surprising that the newspaper articles printed since his death dealt mostly with the inner man and his friendliness."[37] Addressing Traynor, Freehof invoked a baseball metaphor. "Your name will appear in another lineup written in letters of light ... your human attainments written forever on the tablets of our hearts."[38] At the graveside, Eve chatted with Frank Gustine. Before leaving, she ducked under the black canopy that shielded Traynor's casket from the elements and plucked three red roses from the floral arrangement. "For third base. And we were married on the third."[39]

Eve handled Pie's death as well as could be expected. "Obviously, it was a big loss because that was all she had," according to her friend and financial advisor, Douglas McCormick. "But I don't think her personality would have allowed you to see any weaknesses she may have had. She was not one who was going to grieve openly with other people."[40] She did what she could to move forward after Pie's death. She apparently cut back on her volunteer work, but visited family in Cincinnati several times (including a trip for a nephew's wedding in 1974), went to a handful of Pirates games, even played the horses at a couple of local racetracks on occasion. But life was difficult without the man she had adored for more than 40 years. "She was a very kind lady, but also a very lonely lady," thought McCormick. "She was clearly more of a private person than Pie was. There were not a lot of people around she could confide in or trust."[41]

Eve was diagnosed with cancer in the mid–1970s. She moved in with her

Eve Traynor and Frank Gustine graveside during Pie Traynor's burial on March 20, 1972. His wife saved three roses from one of the floral arrangements. "For third base. And we were married on the third," she said, adding, "I hate to leave him" (copyright © 2009 *Pittsburgh Post-Gazette*; all rights reserved; reprinted with permission).

sister, Jean, in Cincinnati while recovering from cancer surgery, then returned
to Pittsburgh. McCormick recalls she was ill for about a year. "Near the end
she lost a lot of weight, lost her complexion, and looked terrible. Plus she lost
the desire to make herself look presentable. Toward the end those priorities
went by the wayside."[42] The ruinous effects of cancer on Eve's physical appearance must have been particularly devastating for this beautiful woman who
always had been so meticulous about how she looked.

Eve conveyed to those around her a sense that she had accepted her fate,
according to Patti Mistick, a Pirate front office employee who knew her from
the Pittsburgh Pinch Hitters.[43] Curiously, though, she waited until a week before
her death, after she had suffered a stroke, to have a last will and testament
drawn up; by that time she was so ill that she could only manage to mark a
shaky "x" in place of her signature.[44]

Eve clutches the jersey of the man closest and dearest to her heart during a ceremony
to retire his number 20 at the Pirates home opener on April 17, 1972 (Bettmann/Cor-
bis).

Eve died at Allegheny General Hospital early in the morning of May 11, 1977, at the age of 72. She left behind an estate valued at $42,332, roughly equivalent to $150,000 in 2008 dollars. She and Pie were cautious with their investments after being crushed by the stock market in the 1930s. Jewelry accounted for about 15 percent of the value of the estate, with almost all of the remainder in U.S. savings bonds, a savings account, and a checking account.[45]

What of the legacy of Pie Traynor? One could argue that he was the most popular athlete in the history of Pittsburgh sports. He was the face of the Pirates during an era when the team was an annual pennant contender and when baseball was far and away America's most culturally relevant sport. But he grew into an even more beloved figure after his retirement, with his appearances on radio, on television, and on the streets.

"He became what Art Rooney would call a 'Pittsburgh guy,'" said historian Jim O'Brien.[46] Pittsburgh guys are down-to-earth, hard-working, unpretentious; people like Rooney himself, Arnold Palmer, Bill Mazeroski, Hines Ward, and Traynor. It is not a town that tolerates self-aggrandizing, prima donna nonsense. *Newsweek* columnist Howard Fineman put it well. "Ultimately, no one in Pittsburgh was or is allowed to pull rank. It's a civic crime. More than that, it's impossible. If you are a Pittsburgher, well, that's what you are, whether you are a Mellon or [a] guy who sells them."[47]

O'Brien thinks that attitude is rooted in the city's DNA. "Pittsburgh was definitely a working man's town in [Traynor's] days. Nobody thought they were a big shot because they were reminded every day when they came home dirty. Even the white-collar workers came home with soot on their white shirts."[48] Although Traynor was a national celebrity who was on a first-name basis with politicians and entertainers, he never lost touch with his own humble working-class roots.

Figuring out Traynor's place in the hearts and minds of Pittsburghers is easy. Sorting out where he belongs among the pantheon of the greatest baseball players of all time is a more formidable task. In the opinion of the great Baltimore Orioles third baseman Brooks Robinson, "Pie Traynor would be in the Hall of Fame today. If a ballplayer is good enough to be in the Hall of Fame in one era, he would be good enough ... in any era."[49] But not everyone sees it that way. Although the rules of baseball have changed little since the 1880s, the way the game is played has varied from one generation to the next, even from one ballpark to the next. For example, it was nothing particularly special for a player to hit .300 in the 1930s, a prolific offensive era. But in 1968, a season in which pitching ruled the game, a .300 average would have put a man in the running for a batting championship. Hitting 20 home runs in the cavernous Houston Astrodome was a much more impressive accomplishment than popping 20 home runs out of Philadelphia's itsy-bitsy Baker Bowl. In sum, comparing players across history requires some fairly sophisticated statistical analysis—and even then it's not an exact science.

For many, many years—until at least the 1970s—Traynor generally was regarded as the greatest third baseman in history. Even while he was still an active player, experts tended to limit the discussion of all-time third baseman to Traynor and Jimmy Collins, who played for the Red Sox and Boston Beaneaters around the turn of the twentieth century. By the late 1930s, most people who had seen Collins in his prime were either very old or dead, and he gradually fell out of the discussion, leaving the crown to Traynor.

But in the 1990s and certainly into the twenty-first century, Traynor's reputation as a player took a pummeling. With the advent of advanced statistical metrics, his career suddenly looked rather ordinary in a lot of ways. ESPN's Jayson Stark ruminated, "The more you look back on Traynor's career, the more you wonder if this guy was the elite player he was ... cooked up to be."[50] The website baseballthinkfactory.org was the site of an informative and spirited back-and-forth about Traynor's merits or lack thereof. One detractor wrote of him, "mediocre hitter, fielding was not that special."[51] In his list of the top third basemen of all time, seminal baseball researcher Bill James ranked Traynor only 15th.[52]

Stark points to a statistic known as OPS+ which, as he explains, "adjusts a player's OPS for both his home ballpark and the era he played in, then stacks it up against his peers."[53] The OPS+ of an "average" major league hitter is always 100; the higher the OPS+, the better the hitter. A player with an OPS+ of 150 has enjoyed an MVP–caliber season, while a player with an OPS+ of 70 might want to begin exploring alternate career paths. Traynor's career OPS+ was 107, which is good, but beneath that of most Hall of Famers, and lower than one might expect from someone who was long considered the standard bearer at his position.

Traynor's career defensive numbers do not leap off the page, either. Although his career range factor (in essence, the number of plays he made per game) was exemplary, his fielding percentage definitely was not; his lifetime mark of .947 was only about average when stacked up against that of his third base contemporaries.

Other statistics, however, cast Traynor's career in a more positive light. Bill James created a tool called the Gray Ink Test, which assigns a player points based upon how many times he finished in the top ten of his league in important offensive categories. Traynor's Gray Ink score puts him slightly above Jimmy Collins and just about in the middle of the pack among players enshrined in Cooperstown.[54] What Traynor had going for him as a hitter was consistency. He never had what one would consider a great offensive season. Instead, he had a decade's worth of very good years.

The Gray Ink Test, of course, does not take defense into consideration. Traynor accumulated a mountain of errors in the early 1930s, when he was playing with a dead arm, and those seasons are a drag on his career numbers. But at his best, he was a brilliant defensive player, leading National League third basemen in double plays four times and assists three times. Over the course of his career he was not as consistent on defense as he was at the plate, but his peak performance was higher —from about 1923 to 1928, he was a dominant defensive third baseman.

Traynor also led the National League in putouts seven times, although the significance of that achievement is unclear. A widely accepted theory among researchers who study baseball statistics is that, for third basemen, putouts have little to do with ability; instead, they are said to be almost exclusively a byproduct of a player's home ballpark.[55] For instance, a third baseman in a stadium with a vast area of foul territory obviously is likely to catch many more foul pops than if he played somewhere with less foul ground.

Forbes Field did have a decent amount of foul territory along the third base line; plus, with its spacious outfield, there might have been more plays at third base than in other parks, as players tried to stretch doubles into triples. On the other hand, it appears Traynor worked with less foul territory in Forbes than third basemen at the Polo Grounds or Ebbets Field (although exact measurements are impossible to determine).[56] Also, outside of the Traynor years, Forbes Field third basemen only led the league in putouts four times in 47 seasons. Traynor did it seven times in 13 years of full-time play. In no way does this disprove the theory, but it does lead one to wonder whether skill might have played *some* part in Traynor's putout numbers.

Traynor appears to have suffered largely because his statistics tell an inconclusive story. Some of his numbers look great, but others are rather pedestrian. Plus, importantly, by the turn of the twenty-first century, the statistics were all anyone had to go by. Nearly everyone who had watched Traynor play was dead, and there exist almost no films or photographs of the man in action. Most diehard baseball fans have seen a photo of Brooks Robinson making a diving play at third base or video of Ozzie Smith scampering deep into the hole at shortstop, leaping into the air, and throwing out a hapless runner. There are no such iconic images of Traynor that would make people say, "Wow!" and thereby cement his legacy in their minds.

But perhaps the most critical issue to consider is that third basemen aren't what they used to be. Throughout most of Traynor's career, it was primarily a defensive-oriented position; any kind of offense received from that spot typically was considered a bonus. Traynor certainly was not the first modern-era third baseman to combine slick glove work with a dangerous bat, but he was among the first.

Over the second half of the twentieth century, the emphasis at third shifted toward offense. It is telling that on Bill James' 2001 list of the top third basemen, the only pre–1930 player ahead of Traynor was Frank Baker. Baker probably was a better player, but it's a close call. For a long time those who thought Traynor was the greatest third baseman ever could build a very compelling case. However, that is no longer true. Traynor's numbers at the plate simply don't stand up next to those of more recent third basemen like Eddie Mathews, Mike Schmidt, and George Brett, who not only excelled defensively, but who also were among the most feared sluggers of their eras.

In the end, though, perhaps it is best to judge Traynor within the context of his time. To use an analogy, if Ford Motor Company had rolled out a Model T in 2008, no one would have bought one. Why would a modern consumer want to drive a car with a top speed of 40 miles per hour, no power steering, and a hand crank? Times change. But that doesn't mean the Model T was a bad car. It was a fine car in its day and marked a great leap forward in transportation. Similarly, given what was expected of third basemen in the 1920s and 1930s, Pie Traynor was a fantastic player.

In 1965, when discussing whether Traynor was a better third baseman than Jimmy Collins, Lee Allen and Tom Meany wrote, "Perhaps it is enough to say that Collins revolutionized third base play and Traynor, coming along a generation later, developed the art of the position to near perfection."[57] And perhaps now it is enough to say that those who came along after Traynor built on what he did and perfected the position even further.

The press, right from the start of Traynor's career, depicted him as an All-American boy. Indeed, there was a large element of truth in that framing — he was kind, conscientious, intelligent, and strikingly handsome. On top of all that, of course, he was a richly gifted athlete. But the All-American boy archetype that we see so often in sports is really just a shortcut that, even when largely accurate, only provides a two-dimensional understanding of a person. It both reveals and conceals. Traynor had feet of clay, just like every other human being. He had his vices — he drank, smoked, played the horses, enjoyed a dirty joke from time to time. He also had personality traits that many would consider flaws — he was stubborn, neurotic, nursed grudges, and was kind of careless about his finances.

We tend to be of two minds when confronted with people who seem faultless. We admire them, but we also look at them with a little resentment or, at best, a healthy degree of skepticism, and rightfully so. Idols often are best revered from afar. Politicians, entertainers and sports figures usually take great pains to cultivate an appealing public persona. But when we peer behind the curtain, what we see is not always pretty.

Pie Traynor, on the other hand, never put on any kind of mask. There was no need. He was imperfect, but imperfections are what make people real; and, anyway, his kindness and fundamental humanity far outweighed his foibles. Anyone with Traynor's body of work on the baseball field is destined to have countless fans. But in Pittsburgh, three decades after he stripped off his uniform for the final time, Traynor had more than fans. He had a city full of friends — people who admired him as much for what he did as a player as for who he was as a man.

Appendix 1: Funeral Service

Funeral Services for Harold J. "Pie" Traynor
Pittsburgh, Pennsylvania
March 20, 1972
by
Dr. Solomon B. Freehof
Rabbi Emeritus, Rodef Shalom Temple
Pittsburgh, Pennsylvania

The Eulogy

Friends and dear ones of Harold Joseph Traynor. You will pardon a personal reference. When my dear friend "Bill" Benswanger died, I was recuperating in Florida and could not be present at his funeral service. Now that Pie Traynor has died, his own dear friend, the emeritus dean of the Episcopal Cathedral, Dean Moor, is also recuperating down south and cannot be here. Eve Traynor has asked me to officiate. The fact that Pie Traynor and I belonged to different religions seemed to her to be no drawback and certainly it was no drawback to me, for death levels all barriers and makes the whole world kin.

Knowing now that I needed to speak in honor of Pie Traynor, I returned to the many articles that had been written in his memory in the Pittsburgh papers. Re-reading them I realized there was something unusual about them. They were speaking of the greatest third baseman in baseball history. And one would expect that the article would be filled with descriptions of his skills, his record, and some of the famous plays that he made. But curiously enough, except for one brief statement about his lifetime batting average, and another sentence about his fielding, all of the many articles spoke of other matters entirely. They told of his love of telling stories to people, about the baseball characters he had known and reflected his pride in his great contemporaries, his respect for the younger players of today, and what is after all an acid test of a man, his wonderful ability to talk to children.

Why all this emphasis on a great athlete's amiability and friendliness? Should it not be taken for granted that a decent man can get along with people and is friendly? Evidently the newspapermen felt that this open-hearted friendliness of Pie Traynor's was something exceptional. They knew well that

231

there were some great players who were just baseball machines, skilled and strong, able to work superbly day after day. But off the field some of them were miserable human beings, coarse, selfish, and bitter. What all these articles wanted to say about Pie Traynor was that he was not primarily an efficient baseball machine, but that he was a lovable human being who was also a great baseball player.

Since the writers understood that it was his personality that was worth their emphasis, we will ask, how is it that this man came to be such a friendly person? This has become a real question nowadays when we are living in a world of bitterness. Between the generations today there is a gap of misunderstanding, between the races, a spark of hate, and between nations, the danger of war. In our world now so embittered, how can any man keep himself in a mood of such an open-hearted friendliness to his fellow man?

An answer to this question is provided by the French essayist and philosopher, Montaigne. He said that a man must first be a friend to himself before he can be a friend to others. This saying can best be understood from the other side of the coin. It means that if a man is hateful to other people, it is because without knowing it, he is really hating himself. If, for example, a man is a failure in life, he has to bolster his self-respect by boasting and by tearing down others. If he has done evil in his life, he conceals the pangs of conscience by striking out in all directions. But Pie Traynor never needed those negative reactions. He was a great success and therefore did not need to boast or deprecate others. He never stepped on the heads of others while climbing up the ladder. His conscience was clear. Thus all his human goodness was the result of inner health. His outer amiability was the reflection of his inner serenity.

But we really do not need the guidance of the French philosopher. Pie Traynor was an Episcopalian and he must frequently have heard the phrase in the *Episcopal Book of Common Prayer*, which explains the relationship between the inner mood and outer actions. The *Episcopal Book of Common Prayer* describes a sacrament as follows: "It is the outward and visible form of an inner and spiritual grace." Pie Traynor's friendship to all was an outgoing radiance that shone from within.

And so we are all bereaved at his passing. May God console Eve Traynor and his mourning brothers and grant them strength. May God console us all. His passing is a cloud across the light of our life.

As for you, Pie Traynor, you began in Framingham, Massachusetts. You earned your first living in baseball in Portsmouth; and your great career was here in Pittsburgh. Now, at the age of 72, you are released. But your name will appear in another lineup written in letters of light. Here among us, your baseball achievements are recorded in the record books. But your human attainments are written forever on the tablets of our hearts.

Appendix 2:
Major League Statistics

Harold Joseph "Pie" Traynor

Height: 6'0" Weight: 170 Batted: Right Threw: Right
Born: November 11, 1898, in Framingham, Massachusetts
Died: March 16, 1972, in Pittsburgh, Pennsylvania

BATTING

Year	G	AB	R	H	2B	3B	HR	RBI	SB	BB	SO	BA	OBP	SLG	OPS+*
1920	17	52	6	11	3	1	0	2	1	3	6	.212	.268	.308	63
1921	7	19	0	5	0	0	0	2	0	1	2	.263	.300	.263	48
1922	142	571	89	161	17	12	4	81	17	27	28	.282	.319	.375	78
1923	153	616	108	208	19	19	12	101	28	34	19	.338	.377	.489	125
1924	142	545	86	160	26	13	5	82	24	37	26	.294	.340	.417	100
1925	150	591	114	189	39	14	6	106	15	52	19	.320	.377	.464	108
1926	152	574	83	182	25	17	3	92	8	38	14	.317	.361	.436	109
1927	149	573	93	196	32	9	5	106	11	22	11	.342	.370	.455	114
1928	144	569	91	192	38	12	3	124	12	28	10	.337	.370	.462	113
1929	130	540	94	192	27	12	4	108	13	30	7	.356	.393	.472	111
1930	130	497	90	182	22	11	9	119	7	48	19	.366	.423	.509	124
1931	155	615	81	183	37	15	2	103	6	54	28	.298	.354	.416	107
1932	135	513	74	169	27	10	2	68	6	32	20	.329	.373	.433	118
1933	154	624	85	190	27	6	1	82	5	35	24	.304	.342	.372	104
1934	119	444	62	139	22	10	1	61	3	21	27	.309	.341	.410	98
1935	57	204	24	57	10	3	1	36	2	10	17	.279	.323	.373	84
1937	5	12	3	2	0	0	0	0	0	0	1	.167	.167	.167	-9
Career	1,941	7,559	1,183	2,416	371	164	58	1,273	158	472	278	.320	.362	.435	107

*OPS+ is calculated by adding on-base percentage and slugging percentage, then measuring that total against the league average and adjusting for ballpark factors. An OPS+ of 100 is considered to be "average."

FIELDING

Year	POS	G	E	FP	lgFP	RF	lgRF
1920	SS	17	12	.860	.941	4.35	5.47
1921	3B	3	1	.917	.940	3.67	2.97
	SS	1	0	1.000	.952	2.00	5.60
1922	3B	124	21	.945	.948	2.93	2.93

Year	POS	G	E	FP	lgFP	RF	lgRF
	SS	18	10	.910	.945	5.61	5.46
1923	3B	152	26	.950	.947	3.26	2.95
	SS	1	0	1.000	.938	6.00	5.40
1924	3B	141	15	.968	.956	3.17	2.81
1925	3B	150	24	.957	.939	3.53	2.85
	SS	1	0	1.000	.952	4.00	5.20
1926	3B	148	23	.952	.953	3.11	2.81
	SS	3	1	.960	.949	8.00	5.30
1927	3B	143	19	.962	.945	3.34	2.82
	SS	9	1	.976	.945	4.56	5.18
1928	3B	144	27	.946	.943	3.27	2.96
1929	3B	130	20	.951	.953	2.97	2.79
1930	3B	130	25	.941	.950	3.06	2.71
1931	3B	155	37	.925	.944	2.94	2.72
1932	3B	127	27	.936	.945	3.11	2.74
1933	3B	154	27	.946	.949	3.09	2.89
1934	3B	110	14	.954	.945	2.65	2.73
1935	3B	49	18	.888	.941	2.92	2.71
	1B	1	0	n/a	n/a	0.00	9.60
1937	3B	3	0	1.000	.952	3.33	2.73
Career	**3B**	**1,863**	**324**	**.947**	**.947**	**3.12**	**2.82**
	SS	**50**	**24**	**.913**	**.944**	**5.04**	**5.40**
	1B	**1**	**0**	**n/a**	**n/a**	**0.00**	**9.60**

FP: fielding percentage
lgFP: league average fielding percentage
RF: range factor [(assists + putouts) / games]
lgRF: league average range factor

Chapter Notes

Chapter 1

1. Draft registration card for James Henry Traynor, September 12, 1918; death certificate for James Henry Traynor, Massachusetts Department of Vital Statistics.

2. 1901 Census of Canada.

3. 1891 Census of Canada.

4. Marriage slip for James Traynor and Lydia Matthews, Nova Scotia Archives and Records Management.

5. United States Census, 1900–1930.

6. Bruno Ramirez, *Crossing the 49th Parallel* (Ithaca, NY: Cornell University Press, 2001), 13.

7. Colin Howell, *Northern Sandlots: A Social History of Maritime Baseball* (Toronto: University of Toronto Press, 1995), 128–129.

8. Framingham, MA, Historical Society archives; Framingham, MA, street listings.

9. Laurie Evans-Daly and David C. Gordon, *Images of America: Framingham* (Mount Pleasant, SC: Arcadia Publishing, 1997), 69–70; Stephen W. Herring, *Framingham: An American Town* (Framingham, MA: Framingham Historical Society, 2000), 212–214.

10. Videotaped lecture by Sol Gittleman, Somerville Community Access Television, April 4, 1995.

11. Ibid.

12. Annual Report of the Massachusetts State Board of Conciliation and Arbitration (January 1904), 60–61.

13. Social Security Online, the official website of the U.S. Social Security Administration, http://ssa.gov/history/pdf/hr35report5.pdf (February 26, 2009).

14. Patrick D. Reagan, *Designing a New America: The Origins of New Deal Planning, 1890–1943* (Amherst: University of Massachusetts Press, 1999), 115.

15. United States Census, 1900 and 1910; Draft registration card for Harold Joseph Traynor, September 11, 1918; Application for unskilled labor from Harold Traynor, United States Civil Service Commission, January 17, 1918; Birth certificate for Harold Joseph Traynor, Massachusetts Department of Vital Statistics.

16. 1891 Census of Canada; Paul Traynor family archives.

17. *Pittsburgh Press*, June 21, 1934.

18. Framingham, MA, School Department archives.

19. Carole Zellie, *Beyond the Neck: The Architecture and Development of Somerville, MA* (Cambridge, MA: Landscape Research, 1982), 46.

20. Ibid., 42.

21. Ibid.

22. *Pittsburgh Press*, June 20, 1934.

23. *The Somerville Journal and Somerville Press*, March 4, 1948.

24. Ibid.

25. *Sporting News*, April 1, 1972.

26. Bob Broeg, *Super Stars of Baseball* (St. Louis: Sporting News, 1971), 256–257.

27. Lee Greene, "At Third Base, Pie Traynor," *Sport*, July 1962.

28. *Pittsburgh Post-Gazette*, June 22, 1981.

29. *Somerville, MA, City Directory, 1899–1901* (Boston: W.A. Greenough).

30. *Pittsburgh Press*, June 21, 1934.

31. St. Bonaventure University archives, Olean, New York.

32. *Pittsburgh Press*, June 21, 1934.

33. *New York Times*, April 26, 1945.

34. *Pittsburgh Press*, April 22, 1956.

35. *Pittsburgh Post-Gazette*, June 7, 1928; United States Census, 1920.

36. *Somerville Journal*, January 15, 1915.

37. Somerville, MA, School Department archives.

38. *Boston Globe*, February 25, 1923.

39. *Pittsburgh Press*, June 21, 1934.

40. *Somerville Journal*, March 23, 1972.

41. *Boston Globe*, June 17, 1918.

42. Ibid.

43. *Boston Globe*, August 20, 1918.

44. *Somerville (MA) Press*, May 23, 1913.

45. Military records of James Edward Traynor, United States National Archives and Records Administration.

46. *Pittsburgh Press*, June 22, 1934.

47. Paul Traynor, interview with author, November 16, 2008.

48. Military records of James Edward Traynor, National Archives and Records Administration.

49. Paul Traynor, interview with author, November 16, 2008.

50. *Lowell (MA) Sun*, January 11, 1949 and January 21, 1953.

51. *Woburn (MA) Daily Times*, February 14, 1975.

52. Social Security Death Index.

53. *Somerville Press*, August 11, 1916.

54. *Somerville Press*, September 8, 1916.

Chapter 2

1. Harold Traynor, application for unskilled labor, United States Civil Service Commission, January 17, 1918.

2. Trade and record card, General Correspondence, 1909–1969. Boston Navy Yard, National Archives and Records Administration, Northeast Region (Boston).

3. *Somerville (MA) Journal*, May 17, 1918.

4. *Pittsburgh Press*, June 22, 1934.

5. West Virginia Division of culture and history website, www.wvculture.org/history/military/nitro01.html (February 13, 2009).

6. William D. Wintz, *Nitro: The World War I Boom Town* (Charleston, WV: Pictorial Histories Publishing, 1985), 59.

7. *Pittsburgh Press*, June 22, 1934.

8. Ibid.

9. Ibid.

10. Ibid.

11. Draft registration card for Harold Joseph Traynor, September 11, 1918.

12. *Somerville (MA) Journal*, March 27, 1972 and October 2, 1975.

13. Malden (MA) Historical Society archives.

14. *Bates Student*, January 17, 1986.

15. *Boston Globe*, July 15, 1913; *Malden (MA) Evening News*, March 20, 1963.

16. *Malden (MA) Evening News*, March 20, 1963.

17. Obituary, *Bates Alumni Magazine*, May 1986, 71.

18. Undated article, Edmund S. Muskie Archives and Special Collections Library at Bates College.

19. Arthur Railton, *The History of Martha's Vineyard: How We Got to Where We Are* (Beverly, MA: Commonwealth Editions, 2006), 274.

20. *Falmouth (MA) Enterprise*, June 30, 1917.

21. *Pittsburgh Press*, December 12, 1971.

22. Helen L. Harriss, *Trinity and Pittsburgh* (Greensburg, PA: Charles M. Henry, 1999), 139–140.

23. John Garner, email to author, February 25, 2009.

24. *Falmouth (MA) Enterprise*, July 13, 1918.

25. Christopher Price, *Baseball by the Beach* (Yarmouth Port, MA: On Cape Publications, 1998), 175.

26. Ibid., 9.

27. Dan Crowley, *Baseball on Cape Cod* (Mount Pleasant, SC: Arcadia Publishing, 2004), 13.

28. *New Bedford (MA) Times*, July 9, 1919.

29. *Boston Globe*, September 6, 1919.

Chapter 3

1. *Boston Globe*, March 17, 1972.

2. *Pittsburgh Post*, January 13, 1924.

3. *Somerville Press*, October 16, 1914.

4. Harold Kaese, *Boston Braves 1871–1953* (Boston: Northeastern University Press, 2004), 137.

5. Ibid., 136–137.

6. *Pittsburgh Press*, May 13, 1929.

7. *New York Times*, July 12, 1934.

8. Ibid.

9. Frank Graham, "On Seeing Pie Traynor Again," *Baseball Digest*, October 1954, 80.

10. Roy McHugh, telephone interview with author, February 15, 2006.

11. Graham, "On Seeing Pie Traynor Again," 80.

12. *New York Journal American*, December 16, 1947.

13. *Pittsburgh Press*, May 13, 1929.

14. *Chicago Tribune*, April 12, 1930.

15. *Sporting News*, January 19, 1947; *Pittsburgh Press*, June 22, 1934.

16. *Pittsburgh Press*, May 13, 1929.

17. *Sporting News*, January 28, 1967.

18. Derek Gentile, *The Complete Boston Red Sox* (New York: Black Dog and Leventhal Publishers, 2003), 299–300.

19. Ed Barrow and James Kahn, *My Fifty Years in Baseball* (New York: Loward-McCann, 1951), 112.

20. *Pittsburgh Press*, May 13, 1929.

21. Ibid.

22. *Virginian-Pilot and Norfolk Landmark*, July 22, 1920.

23. *Boston Globe*, February 25, 1923.

24. *Virginian-Pilot and Norfolk Landmark*, July 24, 1920.

25. Joan Estienne, telephone interview with author, January 27, 2009; *Virginian-Pilot and Norfolk Landmark*, July 22, 1920.

26. Clay Shampoe and Thomas R. Garrett, *Baseball in Portsmouth, Virginia* (Mount Pleasant, SC: Arcadia Publishing, 2004), 16.

27. Ibid., 21.

28. *Virginian-Pilot and Norfolk Landmark*, July 22, 1920.

29. Barrow, *My Fifty Years in Baseball*, 113.

30. Undated article (circa 1937), Paul Traynor family archives.

31. *Pittsburgh Press*, June 22, 1934.

32. *Portsmouth Star*, May 23, 1920.

33. *Portsmouth Star*, June 21, 1921.

34. *Portsmouth Star*, June 17, 1920.

35. *Portsmouth Star*, June 22, 1920.

36. *Portsmouth Star*, June 13, 1920.

37. *Virginian-Pilot and Norfolk Landmark*, July 9, 1920.

38. *Virginian-Pilot and Norfolk Landmark*, July 16, 1920.

39. *Pittsburgh Press*, June 23, 1934.

40. *Virginian-Pilot and Norfolk Landmark*, July 17, 1920.

41. *Pittsburgh Post*, June 22, 1923.

42. Fred Lieb, *The Pittsburgh Pirates* (Carbondale and Edwardsville, IL: Southern Illinois University Press, 2003), 46.

43. Ibid.

44. Ibid.

45. Harold Seymour, *Baseball: The Golden Age* (New York: Oxford University Press, 1971), 34.

46. Barrow, *My Fifty Years in Baseball*, 113.

47. *Virginian-Pilot and Norfolk Landmark*, July 22, 1920.

48. Ibid.

49. Daniel R. Levitt, *Ed Barrow: The Bulldog Who Built the Yankees First Dynasty* (Lincoln: University of Nebraska Press, 2008), 172.

50. *Washington Post*, March 25, 1947.

51. *Washington Post*, March 1, 1939.

52. *Virginian-Pilot and Norfolk Landmark*, August 1, 1920.

53. *Pittsburgh Press*, June 10, 1926.

54. *Pittsburgh Press*, March 22, 1939.

55. www.retrosheet.org; review of game play-by-play accounts from 1922 to 1924 in the *Pittsburgh Times-Gazette*.

56. *Pittsburgh Post-Gazette*, October 7, 1937; *Pittsburgh Post-Gazette*, October 8, 1937; Tom Simon, ed., *Baseball Stars of the National League* (Dulles, VA: Brassey's, 2004), 180.

57. Ibid.

58. Art McKennan, interviewed by Rob Roberts for the Society for American Baseball Research Oral History Committee, July 14, 1994.

59. Ibid.

60. *Sporting News*, November 4, 1937.

Chapter 4

1. Lee Gutkind, *Lessons in Persuasion* (Pittsburgh: University of Pittsburgh Press, 2000), 286.

2. David Cicotello and Angelo Louisa, eds., *Forbes Field: Essays and Memories of the Pirates' Historic Ballpark, 1909–1971* (Jefferson, NC: McFarland, 2007), 15.

3. Ibid., 16

4. Philip Lowry, *Green Cathedrals* (New York: Walker, 2006), 187.

5. *Pittsburgh Post-Gazette*, May 27, 1933.

6. Research by Ronald Selter, Society for American Baseball Research, emailed to author, January 22, 2009.

7. *SABR Baseball Encyclopedia: The Home Run Log*, www.members.sabr.org/members.cfm?a=rtl&rtl=enc (February 1, 2009).

8. David Finoli and Bill Ranier, *The Pittsburgh Pirates Encyclopedia* (Champaign, IL: Sports Publishing, 2003), 489.

9. Steve Blass, telephone interview with author, January 11, 2007.

10. Pie Traynor, "Silent Movies Only Break," *A Nite for Pie Program*, November 20, 1971.

11. Anonymous account of a conversation with Pie Traynor, Pittsburgh Pirates archives.

12. Ibid.

13. *Pittsburgh Gazette-Times*, September 1, 1921.

14. *Pittsburgh Sun-Telegraph*, January 2, 1943.

15. Ibid., *Sporting News*, January 5, 1922.

16. *Pittsburgh Gazette-Times*, September 1, 1921.

17. *New York Times*, April 17, 1921.

18. United States Census, 1920.

19. Don Rogosin, *Invisible Men: Life in Baseball's Negro Leagues* (Lincoln: University of Nebraska Press, 2007), 50–51.

20. Beverley Gooch, telephone interview with author, August 22, 2006.

21. *Pittsburgh Press*, January 23, 1937.

22. *Birmingham Barons: About*, http://Birmingham.barons.milb.com (March 23, 2009).

23. *Birmingham News*, April 19, 1921.

24. *Birmingham News*, April 20, 1921.

25. *Birmingham News*, April 23, 1921.

26. *Birmingham News*, June 19, 1921.

27. Tony Bartirome, telephone interview with author, February 27, 2007.

28. *Birmingham News*, June 19, 1921.

29. *Birmingham News*, July 1, 1921.

30. *Brooklyn Eagle*, July 19, 1921.

31. Ibid.

32. *Birmingham News*, August 27, 1921.

33. Timothy Whitt, *Bases Loaded with History: The Story of Rickwood Field, America's*

Oldest Baseball Park (Birmingham, AL: R. Boozer Press, 1995), 35.

34. *Pittsburgh Press*, February 27, 1957.

35. Art McKennan, interviewed by Rob Roberts for the Society for American Baseball Research Oral History Committee, July 14, 1994.

36. *Pittsburgh Press*, June 6, 1936.

37. Graham, "On Seeing Pie Traynor Again," 80.

38. Bill Veeck and Ed Linn, *Veeck as in Wreck* (Chicago: University of Chicago Press, 2001), 30.

39. Ibid., 31.

40. Bill James, *The New Bill James Historical Baseball Abstract* (New York: Free Press, 2001), 617.

41. David Pietrusza, Matthew Silverman and Michael Gershman, eds., *Baseball: The Biographical Encyclopedia* (Kingston, NY: Total Sports Publishing, 2000), 707.

42. Personal correspondence from the archives of Bill Christine; Roger Birtwell, "Pie Traynor: Best of All Third Basemen," *Baseball Digest*, September 1969.

43. *Pittsburgh Post-Gazette*, March 12, 1957.

44. James, *The New Bill James Historical Baseball Abstract*, 130.

45. Broeg, *Super Stars of Baseball*, 257.

46. Cait Murphy, *Crazy '08* (New York: Smithsonian Books, 2008), 17.

47. Charles Alexander, *John McGraw* (Lincoln: University of Nebraska Press, 1995), 104.

48. Harold Seymour, *Baseball: The Golden Age* (New York: Oxford University Press, 1971), 25.

49. Frank Graham, *McGraw of the Giants: An Informal Biography* (New York: Putnam's, 1944), 143.

50. Art McKennan, interviewed by Rob Roberts for the Society for American Baseball Research Oral History Committee, July 14, 1994; Dick Bartell and Norman Macht, *Rowdy Richard: The Story of Dick Bartell* (Berkeley, CA: North Atlantic Books, 1993), 57.

51. Steven Goldman, *Forging Genius: The Making of Casey Stengel* (Dulles, VA: Brassey's, 2005), 77.

52. Lee Greene, "At Third Base, Pie Traynor," *Sport*, July 1962.

53. Recorded deed, Middlesex County (MA) Book of Deeds, September 24, 1921.

Chapter 5

1. *Sporting News*, January 5, 1922.

2. *Pittsburgh Press*, July 6, 1959.

3. United States Census, 1920.

4. *Pittsburgh Post-Gazette*, November 19, 2003.

5. H.L. Mencken, *Prejudices, Sixth Series* (New York: Knopf, 1927), 187–188.

6. *Pittsburgh Press*, April 21, 1922.

7. *Pittsburgh Post*, April 21, 1922.

8. Tom Murray, ed., *Sport Magazine's All-Time All-Stars* (New York: Atheneum, 1977).

9. *Boston Evening Transcript*, August 24, 1925.

10. *Pittsburgh Press*, August 9, 1927.

11. *Pittsburgh Press*, March 3, 1943.

12. Greene, "At Third Base, Pie Traynor."

13. *Pittsburgh Post*, April 30, 1922.

14. *Pittsburgh Press*, May 16, 1922.

15. *Pittsburgh Press*, April 1, 1924.

16. *Pittsburgh Press*, July 1, 1922.

17. *Pittsburgh Post*, July 1, 1922.

18. Talmadge Boston, *1939: Baseball's Tipping Point* (Albany, TX: Bright Sky Press, 2005), 80.

19. *Pittsburgh Post*, April 5, 1923.

20. Broeg, *Super Stars of Baseball*, 255.

21. *Pittsburgh Post*, May 19, 1923.

22. *Pittsburgh Press*, May 13, 1923.

23. *Pittsburgh Post*, June 6, 1923.

24. Jack McGinley, telephone interview with author, May 9, 2007.

25. Art McKennan, interviewed by Rob Roberts for the Society for American Baseball Research Oral History Committee, July 14, 1994; Broeg, *Super Stars of Baseball*, 255; Peter Golenbock, *Wrigleyville* (New York: St. Martin's Press, 1999), 185.

26. Broeg, *Super Stars of Baseball*, 255.

27. Art McKennan, interviewed by Rob Roberts for the Society for American Baseball Research Oral History Collection, July 14, 1994.

28. Clifton Blue Parker, *Big and Little Poison* (Jefferson, NC: McFarland, 2003), 163.

29. Bartell, *Rowdy Richard*, 71.

30. *Pittsburgh Post*, July 12, 1923.

31. *Pittsburgh Post*, July 31, 1923.

32. Ibid.

33. *Pittsburgh Post-Gazette*, March 6, 1948.

34. *Pittsburgh Post*, November 14, 1923.

35. *Pittsburgh Post*, September 3, 1923.

36. *Pittsburgh Press*, March 20, 1972.

37. Bob McGee, *The Greatest Ballpark Ever: Ebbets Field and the Story of the Brooklyn Dodgers* (New Brunswick, NJ, and London: Rivergate Books, 2005), 109.

38. Ibid.

39. *Sporting News*, September 27, 1923.

40. *Pittsburgh Post*, December 2, 1923; *Sporting News*, December 13, 1923; *Pittsburgh Post*, January 13, 1924; *Pittsburgh Post-Gazette*, April 3, 1930; *Pittsburgh Press*, June 25, 1934.

41. Karl Haueser, interview with author, February 3, 2007.

42. Ibid.
43. Ibid.
44. *Sporting News*, February 20, 1950.
45. Pete Cava, *Tales From the Cubs Dugout* (Chicago: Sports Masters, 2000), 69.
46. Ibid., 67.
47. *Pittsburgh Press*, May 23, 1924.
48. *Pittsburgh Press*, June 10, 1924.
49. *Pittsburgh Post*, June 16, 1924.
50. *Sporting News*, March 19, 1925.
51. *Pittsburgh Press*, March 2, 1925.
52. *Sporting News*, July 3, 1924.
53. *Pittsburgh Post*, June 19, 1924.
54. *Pittsburgh Press*, June 24, 1924.
55. *Pittsburgh Press*, February 27, 1939.
56. Robert W. Creamer, *Stengel: His Life and Times* (New York: Dell Publishing, 1984), 157.
57. *Pittsburgh Post*, August 3, 1924.
58. *Pittsburgh Post*, August 18, 1924.
59. Martin Appel and Burt Goldblatt, *Baseball's Best* (New York: McGraw-Hill, 1977), 367.
60. Kaese, "Pie Traynor: Greatest of the Third Basemen."
61. *Pittsburgh Gazette Times*, September 24, 1924.
62. *Pittsburgh Post*, September 26, 1924.
63. *Sporting News*, October 2, 1924.

Chapter 6

1. Daniel Ginsburg, *The Fix Is In* (Jefferson, NC: McFarland, 2004), 186.
2. *Pittsburgh Post*, October 3, 1924.
3. *Washington Post*, October 3, 1924.
4. *Sporting News*, October 16, 1924.
5. *Pittsburgh Press*, October 3, 1924.
6. *Pittsburgh Post-Gazette*, June 28, 2005.
7. *Pittsburgh Press*, March 2, 1925.
8. Art McKennan, interviewed by Rob Roberts for the Society for American Baseball Research Oral History Committee, July 14, 1994.
9. *Pittsburgh Press*, June 10, 1926.
10. William R. Denslow, *10,000 Famous Freemasons from K to Z Part Two* (Whitefish, MT: Kessinger Publishing, 2004), 252.
11. *New York Times*, June 17, 1925.
12. A.R. Cratty, "Fred Clarke, the Ex-Manager, Believed to Be Worth One Million Dollars as the Result of Luck Discoveries in Oil," *Sporting Life*, January 13, 1917.
13. *Pittsburgh Post*, August 22, 1925.
14. *Somerville* (MA) *Journal*, August 21, 1925; Marilyn Lenick family archives.
15. *Boston Globe*, August 26, 1925.
16. *Pittsburgh Press*, October 2, 1925.
17. *Pittsburgh Press*, September 18, 1925.
18. Pietrusza, *Baseball: The Biographical Encyclopedia*, 569.
19. Eugene Murdock, *Baseball Players and Their Times: Oral Histories of the Game, 1920–1940* (Westport, CT: Meckler Publishing, 1991), 177.
20. Reed Browning, *1924* (Amherst and Boston: University of Massachusetts Press, 2003), 121.
21. Henry W. Thomas, *Walter Johnson: Baseball's Big Train* (Washington, D.C.: Phenom Press, 1995), 275.
22. Ibid., 274.
23. *Washington Post*, November 5, 1974.
24. Ibid.
25. *Pittsburgh Press*, July 19, 1960.
26. Jeff Carroll, *Sam Rice* (Jefferson, NC: McFarland, 2007), 131.
27. *Pittsburgh Press*, October 11, 1925.
28. Carroll, *Sam Rice*, 129.
29. Ibid.
30. Ibid., 130.
31. Ibid.
32. *Washington Post*, November 5, 1974.
33. *Pittsburgh Post-Gazette*, July 27, 1934.
34. Carroll, *Sam Rice*, 136.
35. *Washington Post*, October 13, 1925.
36. *New York Times*, October 15, 1925.
37. *Pittsburgh Press*, July 19, 1960.
38. *Washington Post*, October 14, 1925.
39. Tom DeVeaux, *The Washington Senators* (Jefferson, NC: McFarland, 2001), 92.
40. *New York Times*, October 15, 1925.
41. Lawrence S. Ritter, *The Glory of Their Times* (New York: William Morrow, 1984), 285.
42. *Pittsburgh Press*, July 19, 1960.
43. Ibid.
44. *Pittsburgh Post*, October 16, 1925.
45. *Boston Record American*, March 18, 1972.
46. Curt Smith, *Storied Stadiums: Baseball History Through Its Ballparks* (New York: Carroll & Graf, 2001), 76.
47. *Washington Post*, October 16, 1925.
48. *Sporting News*, October 22, 1925.
49. *Pittsburgh Press*, October 15, 1925.
50. Thomas, *Walter Johnson*, 284.
51. *New York Times*, October 17, 1925.
52. *Los Angeles Times*, September 13, 1925.
53. *New York Times*, October 16, 1925.
54. *Sporting News*, October 22, 1925.
55. *Pittsburgh Press*, September 29, 1926.

Chapter 7

1. *SABR Minor Leagues Database*, http://minors.sabrwebs.com/cgi-bin/index.php (November 4, 2008).

2. Jack McGinley, telephone interview with author, May 9, 2007.

3. *Pittsburgh Post*, March 14, 1926.

4. Ibid.

5. *Pittsburgh Press*, March 23, 1926.

6. Ibid.

7. *SABR Minor Leagues Database*, http://minors.sabrwebs.com/cgi-bin/index.php (November 4, 2008).

8. United States Coast Guard National Maritime Center archives.

9. Paul Traynor, interview with author, November 16, 2008.

10. Undated photograph, Marilyn Lenick family archives.

11. Ritter *The Glory of Their Times*, 334.

12. *Pittsburgh Post*, March 3, 1926.

13. Nellie King, interview with author, February 22, 2006.

14. Wint Capel, *Fiery Fast-Baller: The Life of Johnny Allen, World Series Pitcher* (Lincoln, NE: Writer's Showcase, 2001), 51.

15. *Pittsburgh Post*, March 26, 1926.

16. *Pittsburgh Press*, September 29, 1926.

17. *Pittsburgh Post*, September 15, 1926.

18. *Pittsburgh Press*, September 13, 1926.

19. Ibid.

20. *Pittsburgh Press*, July 11, 1937.

21. *Pittsburgh Press*, August 13, 1926.

22. Frederick G. Lieb, *The Pittsburgh Pirates* (Carbondale, IL: Southern Illinois University Press, 2003), 223.

23. *Pittsburgh Press*, August 13, 1926.

24. Ibid.

25. *Pittsburgh Press*, September 29, 1926.

26. *Pittsburgh Press*, August 14, 1926.

27. *Pittsburgh Press*, August 15, 1926.

28. *Pittsburgh Press*, August 18, 1926.

29. *Pittsburgh Press*, September 29, 1937.

30. *Pittsburgh Press*, December 1, 1937.

31. Bartell, *Rowdy Richard*, 43.

32. *Pittsburgh Press*, August 20, 1926.

33. Brian Mulligan, *The 1940 Cincinnati Reds* (Jefferson, NC: McFarland, 2005), 28–30; *Pittsburgh Press*, September 25, 1938.

34. Burnett County (WI) Historical Society archives.

35. *Pittsburgh Post*, January 21, 1927.

36. *Los Angeles Times*, October 20, 1927.

37. *Pittsburgh Post-Gazette*, February 20, 1929.

38. Broeg, *Super Stars of Baseball*, 258.

39. Burnett County (WI) Historical Society archives.

40. F.C. Lane, "The Ace of National League Hurlers," *Baseball Magazine*, October 1929.

41. *Pittsburgh Post-Gazette*, February 20, 1929.

42. Opal Larson, telephone interview with author, January 4, 2007.

43. Ritter, *The Glory of Their Times*, 338.

44. Bill James, *Whatever Happened to the Hall of Fame* (New York: Fireside, 1995), 178.

45. Randy Roberts, *Pittsburgh Sports: Stories from the Steel City* (Pittsburgh, University of Pittsburgh Press, 2002), 80.

46. *Pittsburgh Post-Gazette*, May 29, 1927.

47. Jack Berger, telephone interview with author, June 10, 2007.

48. Al Crouch, telephone interview with author, August 7, 2006.

49. Jim O'Brien, telephone interview with author, September 25, 2006.

50. *Pie*, Narr. Red Donley, WIIC-TV, Pittsburgh, PA, August 1967.

51. *Pittsburgh Post-Gazette*, June 25, 1927.

52. John Drebinger, "Two 'Nice Guys' Receive Their Reward," *Baseball Magazine*, June 1948.

53. *Pittsburgh Post-Gazette*, July 29, 1927.

54. *Sporting News*, April 1, 1972.

55. *Pittsburgh Press*, August 10, 1927; *Pittsburgh Post-Gazette*, August 12, 1927.

56. *Pittsburgh Press*, July 20, 1960.

57. *Pittsburgh Press*, September 1, 1938.

58. Jonathan Eig, *Luckiest Man: The Life and Death of Lou Gehrig* (New York: Simon & Schuster, 2005), 92.

59. *New York Times*, October 4, 1927.

60. Eig, *Luckiest Man*, 94.

61. *Pittsburgh Post-Gazette*, October 4, 1927.

62. Parker, *Big and Little Poison*, 88.

63. *New York Times*, October 5, 1960.

64. Donald Honig, *The October Heroes* (Lincoln: University of Nebraska Press, 1996), 124.

65. *New York Times*, October 5, 1960.

66. Dean Sullivan, *Middle Innings: A Documentary History of Baseball, 1900–1948* (Lincoln: University of Nebraska Press, 1998), 130–131.

67. *Pittsburgh Press*, October 8, 1927.

68. Donald Honig, *Baseball When the Grass Was Real* (New York: Berkley Publishing, 1975), 116.

69. Honig, *The October Heroes*, 127.

70. Harvey Frommer, *Five O' Clock Lightning: Babe Ruth, Lou Gehrig, and the Greatest Baseball Team in History, the 1927 New York Yankees* (New York: Wiley, 2007), 171.

71. *Pittsburgh Press*, February 24, 1928.

72. Honig, *The October Heroes*, 128.

73. *New York World-Telegram*, October 3, 1960.

74. *Pittsburgh Press*, September 1, 1938.

75. *Pittsburgh Post-Gazette*, October 11, 1927.

76. Bill Cardille, telephone interview with author, February 5, 2007.

77. Don Riggs, telephone interview with author, November 19, 2007.

78. Marilyn Lenick, interview with author, September 16, 2006.

79. *Pittsburgh Post-Gazette*, May 5, 1938.

80. *Toronto Star*, September 18, 1928.

81. *Pittsburgh Press*, July 8, 1928.

Chapter 8

1. Bob Gustine, telephone interview with author, March 6, 2006.

2. *Pittsburgh Press*, March 10, 1929.

3. *Sporting News*, February 28, 1929.

4. *SABR Minor Leagues Database*, http://minors.sabrwebs.com/cgi-bin/index.php (November 4, 2008).

5. *Pittsburgh Post-Gazette*, March 21, 1929.

6. Bartell, *Rowdy Richard*, 70.

7. Clayton Woody, "Dick Bartell Remembers '27 Yankees— With Awe!" *Baseball Digest*, July 1981.

8. Les Biederman, "Man with a Magnet," *A Nite for Pie Program*, November 20, 1971.

9. Bartell, *Rowdy Richard*, 70.

10. Ibid.

11. Ibid.

12. *Los Angeles Times*, December 16, 1931; *Pittsburgh Post-Gazette*, May 27, 1933; Undated article from Paul Traynor family archives.

13. *Los Angeles Times*, December 16, 1931.

14. Harry Keck, "Stolen Bats Sweetest: Traynor," *Baseball Digest*, July 1945.

15. Ibid.

16. Ibid.

17. *Pittsburgh Press*, July 6, 1959.

18. David Falkner, *Nine Sides of the Diamond* (New York: Times Books, 1990), 112–113.

19. *Pittsburgh Post-Gazette*, September 2, 1929.

20. *Sporting News*, October 31, 1929.

21. *Pittsburgh Press*, March 3, 1943.

22. *Pittsburgh Post-Gazette*, December 11, 1929.

23. *Mansfield (OH) News Journal*, September 3, 1971.

24. *Pittsburgh Post-Gazette*, February 21, 1930.

25. Ibid.

26. *Pittsburgh Post-Gazette*, April 4, 1930.

27. *Pittsburgh Press*, April 10, 1930.

28. *Pittsburgh Press*, April 11, 1930.

29. *Pittsburgh Post-Gazette*, April 3, 1930.

30. *Chicago Tribune*, March 21, 1930; *Sporting News*, April 10, 1930.

31. *Pittsburgh Post-Gazette*, April 12, 1930.

32. *Pittsburgh Post-Gazette*, April 3, 1930.

33. *Pittsburgh Post-Gazette*, April 5, 1930.

34. *Pittsburgh Post*, January 13, 1924; *Pittsburgh Post-Gazette*, April 3, 1930; *Pittsburgh Press*, June 25, 1934.

35. *Pittsburgh Press*, May 7, 1930.

36. Ibid.

37. *Pittsburgh Press*, May 11, 1930.

38. *Pittsburgh Post-Gazette*, June 29, 1930.

39. *Pittsburgh Post-Gazette*, August 18, 1930.

40. *Pittsburgh Press*, June 12, 1933.

41. United States Census, 1920 and 1930.

42. Divorce Decree, Adelia Helmer vs. Jacob Helmer, Franklin County, Indiana, December 28, 1923; United States Census, 1930.

43. Mike Helmer, telephone interview with author, April 3, 2007.

44. Ibid.

45. Mike Helmer, telephone interview with author, April 3, 2007; Brookville, Indiana property records complied by Wilhelm Law Office, Brookville, IN.

46. Reed Browning, *1924* (Amherst and Boston: University of Massachusetts Press, 2003), 61–62.

47. *Sporting News*, January 8, 1931.

48. *Sporting News*, July 14, 1932; Mike Helmer, telephone interview with author, April 3, 2007.

49. *Pittsburgh Press*, June 12, 1933.

50. Mike Helmer, telephone interview with author, April 3, 2007.

51. Ibid.; *Pittsburgh Press*, June 12, 1933.

52. Bill Nowlin and Kit Krieger, "La Tropical Park, Then and Now," *The National Pastime*, Number 25, 2005.

53. Ibid., 5.

54. *Uniontown* (PA) *Daily News Standard*, January 5, 1933.

55. *Pittsburgh Post-Gazette*, March 17, 1936.

56. Laura Hillenbrand, *Seabiscuit: An American Legend* (New York: Ballantine Books, 2003), 16.

57. Art Rooney, Jr., telephone interview with author, July 9, 2007.

58. Ibid.

59. *Pittsburgh Post-Gazette*, April 15, 1934.

60. *Pittsburgh Press*, April 22, 1934.

61. *Pittsburgh Press*, August 26, 1931.

62. *Pittsburgh Press*, September 22, 1931.

63. John F. Bowman and Edward K. Muller, *Before Renaissance: Planning in Pittsburgh 1889–1943* (Pittsburgh, PA: University of Pittsburgh Press, 2006), 195.

64. *Sporting News*, November 12, 1954; Dennis DeValeria and Jeanne Burke DeValeria, *Honus Wagner* (New York: Henry Holt, 1995), 299; Pete Castiglione, telephone interview with author, December 6, 2007.

65. *Lowell* (MA) *Sun*, October 4, 1950.

Chapter 9

1. *New York Times*, January 17, 1972.
2. *Pittsburgh Post-Gazette*, June 23, 1969.
3. John McCollister, *The Good, the Bad, and the Ugly: Heart-Pounding, Jaw-Dropping, and Gut-Wrenching Moments from Pittsburgh Pirates History* (Chicago: Triumph Books, 2008), 167; David Finoli and Bill Ranier, *The Pittsburgh Pirates Encyclopedia* (Champaign, IL: Sports Publishing, 2003), 473.
4. *Pittsburgh Press*, June 28, 1934.
5. *Sporting News*, January 29, 1972.
6. Bill James, *The New Bill James Historical Baseball Abstract* (New York: Free Press, 2001), 546.
7. Ibid., 592–594.
8. *Pittsburgh Gazette Times*, June 3, 1923.
9. *Nebraska State Journal*, October 6, 1940.
10. *Pittsburgh Post-Gazette*, September 9, 1932.
11. *Pittsburgh Post-Gazette*, July 7, 1932.
12. *Pittsburgh Press*, June 12, 1933.
13. *Pittsburgh Press*, April 11, 1971.
14. *Chicago Tribune*, May 24, 1939.
15. *Pittsburgh Press*, April 22, 1956.
16. *Pittsburgh Post-Gazette*, July 28, 1932.
17. *Pittsburgh Press*, August 11, 1932.
18. *Pittsburgh Press*, August 25, 1932.
19. Transcribed Massachusetts Death Record, James Henry Traynor, Mass Document Retrieval Services.
20. *Pittsburgh Press*, August 4, 1933.
21. Charles C. Alexander, *Breaking the Slump* (New York: Columbia University Press, 2002), 62.
22. *Sporting News*, February 9, 1933.
23. Ibid.
24. *Washington Post*, August 31, 1971.
25. Albert Theodore Powers, *The Business of Baseball* (Jefferson, NC: McFarland, 2003), 64; Paul D. Staudohar and J.A. Mangan, eds., *The Business of Professional Sports* (Urbana and Chicago: University of Illinois Press, 1991), 111.
26. *Washington Post*, August 31, 1971.
27. Marilyn Lenick, interview with author, September 16, 2006.
28. *Narragansett* (RI) *Times*, January 5, 1984.
29. *Pittsburgh Press*, March 3, 1933.
30. *Pittsburgh Press*, June 6, 1933.
31. *Pittsburgh Post-Gazette*, February 15, 1937.
32. *Pittsburgh Press*, April 15, 1934.
33. *Pittsburgh Press*, July 6, 1933.
34. *Philadelphia Inquirer*, July 1, 1996.
35. *Washington Post*, July 7, 1933.
36. *Pittsburgh Press*, September 30, 1939.
37. *Pittsburgh Press*, July 11, 1933.
38. *Pittsburgh Press*, July 10, 1933.
39. *Pittsburgh Press*, July 6, 1959.
40. *Pittsburgh Press*, July 25, 1969.
41. Roy McHugh, telephone interview with author, February 15, 2006.
42. Ibid.
43. *Pittsburgh Press*, July 25, 1969.
44. *Pittsburgh Post-Gazette*, August 29, 1933.
45. *Pittsburgh Press*, April 15, 1934.
46. *Pittsburgh Post-Gazette*, April 19, 1934.
47. *Pittsburgh Press*, April 23, 1934.
48. *Pittsburgh Press*, May 8, 1934.
49. Ibid.
50. *Pittsburgh Press*, June 20, 1934.
51. *Pittsburgh Press*, June 19, 1934; *Pittsburgh Press*, February 22, 1935.
52. *Washington Post*, June 20, 1934; *Sporting News*, June 28, 1934.
53. *Pittsburgh Press*, June 19, 1934.
54. *Pittsburgh Post-Gazette*, January 2, 1935.
55. *Sporting News*, June 28, 1934.
56. Ibid.
57. *Pittsburgh Press*, June 21, 1934.
58. William A. Cook, *Waite Hoyt: A Biography of the Yankees' Schoolboy Wonder* (Jefferson, NC: McFarland, 2004), 126.
59. Lieb, *The Pittsburgh Pirates*, 252.
60. *Pittsburgh Press*, July 21, 1934.
61. *Pittsburgh Post-Gazette*, July 25, 1934.
62. *Sporting News*, August 9, 1934.
63. *Sporting News*, November 15, 1934.

Chapter 10

1. Pie Traynor file, National Baseball Hall of Fame and Museum Library.
2. *New York World-Telegram*, September 21, 1938.
3. *Philadelphia Record*, June 20, 1936.
4. *Pittsburgh Press*, September 8, 1938.
5. *New York World-Telegram*, March 6, 1936.
6. *Pittsburgh Press*, March 2, 1948.
7. *Sporting News*, March 29, 1969.
8. Les Biederman, "Man with a Magnet," *A Nite for Pie Program*, November 20, 1971.
9. Bartell, *Rowdy Richard*, 55.
10. Martha Shea, email correspondence with author, March 18, 2009.
11. *Brookville Democrat*, September 9, 1998.
12. Ibid.
13. Pie Traynor player contract, Pie Traynor files, National Baseball Hall of Fame and Museum Library.
14. *Washington Post*, January 27, 1934.
15. *Washington Post*, November 17, 1934; *Pittsburgh Post-Gazette*, December 7, 1934; *Sporting News*, December 6, 1934.
16. *Sporting News*, December 6, 1934.

17. *Pittsburgh Post-Gazette*, March 17, 1935.

18. Harpo Marx with Roland Barber, *Harpo Speaks* (New York: Limelight Editions, 1961, printed in 1988), 210.

19. Bill Cardille, telephone interview with author, February 28, 2006; Joe L. Brown, telephone interview with author, August 20, 2006; Lou Vlahos, telephone interview with author, October 22, 2007.

20. *The Ballplayers — Babe Herman.* Baseballlibrary.com, http://www.baseballlibrary.com/player.php?name=Babe_Herman_1903 (December 30, 2008).

21. *Pittsburgh Press*, November 26, 1934.

22. Ibid.

23. Bill James and Rob Neyer, *The Neyer/James Guide to Pitchers* (New York: Fireside, 2004), 136; *Pittsburgh Post-Gazette*, March 5, 1936.

24. *Pittsburgh Press*, May 24, 1935.

25. *Pittsburgh Press*, May 22, 1935.

26. Robert W. Creamer, *Babe: The Legend Comes to Life* (New York: Simon & Schuster, 1992), 397.

27. William A. Cook, *Waite Hoyt: A Biography of the Yankees' Schoolboy Wonder* (Jefferson, NC: McFarland, 2004), 128.

28. *Pittsburgh Press*, July 5, 1935.

29. *Pittsburgh Post-Gazette*, May 10, 2006.

30. Robert W. Creamer, *Babe: The Legend Comes to Life* (New York: Simon & Schuster, 1992), 397.

31. *Sporting News*, April 1, 1972.

32. *Pittsburgh Post-Gazette*, May 27, 1935.

33. *Pittsburgh Post-Gazette*, May 10, 2006.

34. Milton Berle, *B.S. I Love You. Sixty Years with the Famous and Infamous* (New York: McGraw-Hill, 1988), 182.

35. Cook, *Waite Hoyt*, 130.

36. *Pittsburgh Post-Gazette*, June 28, 1935.

37. *Pittsburgh Post-Gazette*, July 30, 1935.

38. *Pittsburgh Post-Gazette*, April 7, 1936.

39. *Pittsburgh Press*, September 3, 1935.

40. *Pittsburgh Sun-Telegraph*, September 6, 1935.

41. *New York World-Telegram*, September 6, 1935.

42. *Pittsburgh Press*, September 5, 1935.

43. *Pittsburgh Press*, November 8, 1935.

44. *Chicago Tribune*, October 16, 1935.

45. *Pittsburgh Post-Gazette*, December 4, 1935.

46. *Pittsburgh Post-Gazette*, December 28, 1935.

47. *Pittsburgh Press*, November 30, 1935.

48. Ibid.

49. John G. Skipper, *Take Me Out to the Cubs Game* (Jefferson, NC: McFarland, 2002), 16.

50. *Pittsburgh Press*, August 4, 1938.

51. *Pittsburgh Press*, June 15, 1937.

52. *Sporting News*, April 7, 1938.

53. *Pittsburgh Post-Gazette*, January 6, 1937.

54. *Cincinnati Post*, November 22, 1935.

55. *Sporting News*, December 2, 1936.

56. *Pittsburgh Post-Gazette*, December 28, 1935.

57. Ibid.

58. *Pittsburgh Post-Gazette*, February 5, 1936.

59. *Pittsburgh Press*, April 9, 1936.

60. *Pittsburgh Post-Gazette*, February 20, 1936.

61. *Sporting News*, February 27, 1936.

62. *Pittsburgh Press*, March 13, 1936.

63. *Pittsburgh Press*, April 21, 1936.

64. *Pittsburgh Press*, April 7, 1937.

65. *Pittsburgh Tribune-Review*, March 18, 2008; *OnQ OnDemand: Flood of 1936*, http://www.wqed.org/ondemand/onq/php?cat=6&id=19 (January 12, 2009).

66. *Pittsburgh Tribune-Review*, March 18, 2008; John F. Bowman and Edward K. Muller, *Before Renaissance: Planning in Pittsburgh 1889–1943* (Pittsburgh: University of Pittsburgh Press, 2006), 227.

67. *Pittsburgh Press*, April 15, 1936.

68. *Pittsburgh Press*, June 1, 1936.

69. *Pittsburgh Press*, July 9, 1936.

70. *Pittsburgh Press*, March 3, 1943.

71. *Pittsburgh Post-Gazette*, July 16, 1936.

72. *Pittsburgh Post-Gazette*, January 6, 1938.

73. *Pittsburgh Post-Gazette*, October 18, 1938.

74. *Pittsburgh Press*, July 30, 1936.

75. Ibid.

76. *Pittsburgh Press*, September 17, 1936.

77. *Pittsburgh Press*, October 30, 1936.

78. *Pittsburgh Press*, December 10, 1936.

79. *Pittsburgh Press*, December 5, 1936.

80. *Pittsburgh Post-Gazette*, February 3, 1937; *Brookville* (IN) *Democrat*, January 28, 1937.

81. *Chicago Tribune*, April 10, 1937.

82. *Pittsburgh Press*, March 28, 1937.

83. *Pittsburgh Post-Gazette*, March 4, 1937.

84. *Pittsburgh Press*, March 12, 1937.

85. *Pittsburgh Press*, March 4, 1937.

86. *Pittsburgh Press*, March 28, 1937.

87. Ibid.

88. *Pittsburgh Post-Gazette*, April 12, 1937.

89. *Pittsburgh Press*, March 31, 1937.

90. *New York Times*, March 14, 1937.

91. *Pittsburgh Press*, June 15, 1937.

92. *Pittsburgh Post-Gazette*, July 13, 1937.

93. *Pittsburgh Press*, September 20, 1937.

94. *Pittsburgh Press*, July 21, 1937.

95. *Sporting News*, July 29, 1937.

96. Ibid.

97. *Los Angeles Times*, October 1, 1938.

Chapter 11

1. *Pittsburgh Post-Gazette*, October 15, 1937.

2. *Pittsburgh Press*, October 6, 1937.

3. *Pittsburgh Press*, December 3, 1937.

4. John Holway, *Josh and Satch* (Westport, CT, and London: Meckler Publishing, 1991), 103–104.

5. Ibid.; "5th Inning — Shadow Ball," *Baseball*, Dir. Ken Burns, PBS, Arlington, VA, 1994.

6. *Pittsburgh Courier*, September 2, 1939.

7. Ibid.

8. Brent Kelley, *The Negro Leagues Revisited* (Jefferson, NC: McFarland, 2000), 184–185.

9. Mark Ribowsky, *A Complete History of the Negro Leagues 1884–1955* (New York: Carol Publishing Group, 1995), 252.

10. Lawrence D. Hogan, *Shades of Glory* (Washington, D.C.: National Geographic, 2006), 328–329.

11. Ibid.

12. Ibid.

13. Neil Lanctot, *Negro League Baseball* (Philadelphia: University of Pennsylvania Press, 2004), 223.

14. *Pittsburgh Press*, January 9, 1938.

15. *Pittsburgh Post-Gazette*, January 10, 1938.

16. *Pittsburgh Post-Gazette*, January 11, 1938.

17. *Pittsburgh Press*, January 9, 1938.

18. *Pittsburgh Press*, January 9, 1938; *Pittsburgh Post-Gazette*, January 11, 1938.

19. *Pittsburgh Post-Gazette*, January 12, 1938.

20. *Pittsburgh Post-Gazette*, January 18, 1938.

21. *Sporting News*, May 5, 1938.

22. *Pittsburgh Press*, April 6, 1938.

23. Ibid.

24. *Pittsburgh Post-Gazette*, April 5, 1938.

25. *Pittsburgh Press*, September 28, 1938.

26. *Pittsburgh Post-Gazette*, September 3, 1938.

27. *Pittsburgh Post-Gazette*, April 6, 1938.

28. *Pittsburgh Post-Gazette*, April 19, 1938.

29. Vince Staten, *Ol' Diz* (New York: HarperCollins, 1992), 191.

30. *Pittsburgh Post-Gazette*, April 18, 1938.

31. *Pittsburgh Post-Gazette*, April 27, 1938.

32. Les Biederman, "Man with a Magnet," *A Nite for Pie Program*, November 20, 1971; Broeg, *Super Stars of Baseball*, 266.

33. *Pittsburgh Press*, May 25, 1938.

34. *Pittsburgh Post-Gazette*, August 30, 1938.

35. *Pittsburgh Press*, June 4, 1938.

36. Peter Golenbock, *The Spirit of St. Louis* (New York: Avon Books, 2000), 237–238.

37. *Sporting News*, October 30, 1946.

38. *Pittsburgh Post-Gazette*, July 25, 1938.

39. *Pittsburgh Press*, August 8, 1938.

40. *Pittsburgh Post-Gazette*, August 8, 1938.

41. *Washington Post*, January 7, 1939.

42. *Pittsburgh Post-Gazette*, August 11, 1938.

43. *New York Times*, September 15, 1938.

44. *Pittsburgh Post-Gazette*, September 7, 1938.

45. *Pittsburgh Post-Gazette*, August 29, 1938.

46. *Pittsburgh Press*, September 1, 1938.

47. Ibid.

48. *Pittsburgh Press*, September 9, 1938.

49. *Pittsburgh Post-Gazette*, September 10, 1938.

50. *Los Angeles Times*, September 10, 1938.

51. Glenn Stout and Richard A. Johnson, *The Cubs* (New York: Houghton Mifflin, 2007), 169.

52. *Pittsburgh Press*, September 15, 1938.

53. Ibid.

54. *Pittsburgh Press*, September 18, 1938.

55. *Pittsburgh Press*, March 17, 1939.

56. *Pittsburgh Press*, November 20, 1938.

57. *Washington Post*, September 21, 1938.

58. *New York Times*, September 22, 1938.

59. *Chicago Tribune*, September 22, 1938.

60. *Pittsburgh Press*, July 21, 1960.

61. *Chicago Tribune*, September 27, 1938.

62. *Chicago Daily News*, September 27, 1938.

63. Staten, *Ol' Diz*, 194.

64. Robert Gregory, *Diz* (New York: Viking, 1992), 348.

65. *Pittsburgh Post-Gazette*, September 28, 1938.

66. Gregory, *Diz*, 351.

67. *Pittsburgh Press*, September 29, 1938.

68. *Chicago Daily News*, September 29, 1938.

69. *Connellsville* (PA) *Daily Courier*, September 23, 1958.

70. Bob Smizik, *The Pittsburgh Pirates: An Illustrated History* (New York: Walker, 1990), 57.

71. *Pittsburgh Press*, September 29, 1938.

72. Jim Enright, *Chicago Cubs* (New York: Macmillan, 1975), 80–81.

73. *Pittsburgh Press*, September 29, 1938.

74. *Pittsburgh Press*, January 4, 1939.

75. Ritter, *The Glory of Their Times*, 343.

76. Smizik, *The Pittsburgh Pirates*, 58.

77. Ritter, *The Glory of Their Times*, 344.

78. *Pittsburgh Press*, December 25, 1945.

79. *Pittsburgh Press*, April 27, 1942.

80. Honig, *Baseball When the Grass Was Real*, 137.

81. *Pittsburgh Post-Gazette*, September 30, 1938.

82. *Pittsburgh Post-Gazette*, August 18, 1939.

83. *Pittsburgh Press*, October 3, 1938.

84. Ibid.

85. *Pittsburgh Press*, October 6, 1938.

86. Smizik, *The Pittsburgh Pirates*, 58.

87. Lawrence S. Ritter, *The Glory of Their Times* (New York: William Morrow, 1984), 344.

88. *Pittsburgh Press*, December 25, 1945.

89. Chuck Reichblum, telephone interview with author, September 28, 2006.

90. Bill James, *Bill James' Guide to Baseball Managers* (New York: Scribner's, 1997), 99; Jeff Angus, *Management by Baseball* (New York: Collins, 2006), 51–52.

91. *Sporting News*, November 30, 1949.

92. *Pittsburgh Post-Gazette*, February 14, 1939.

93. *Pittsburgh Post-Gazette*, April 9, 1939.

94. *Sporting News*, October 20, 1938.

95. Sigal G. Barsade, Arthur P. Brief and Sandra E. Spataro, "The Affective Revolution in Organizational Behavior: The Emergence of a Paradigm." In Jerry Greenberg, ed., *OB: The State of the Science, Second Edition* (Hillsdale, NJ: L. Erlbaum Associates, 2003), 3–52.

96. *Chicago Tribune*, December 20, 1938.

Chapter 12

1. *Pittsburgh Press*, October 18, 1938.

2. *Pittsburgh Press*, November 22, 1938.

3. *Pittsburgh Press*, July 21, 1960.

4. *Los Angeles Times*, March 26, 1939.

5. *Pittsburgh Post-Gazette*, January 13, 1939.

6. *Pittsburgh Press*, January 10, 1939.

7. *Pittsburgh Post-Gazette*, December 14, 1939.

8. *Pittsburgh Press*, January 9, 1939.

9. Ibid.

10. *Pittsburgh Press*, August 29, 1939.

11. *Pittsburgh Post-Gazette*, April 19, 1939.

12. *Pittsburgh Press*, January 10, 1939; *Los Angeles Times*, March 9, 1939.

13. Honig, *Baseball When the Grass Was Real*, 51.

14. *Pittsburgh Post-Gazette*, February 21, 1939.

15. *Pittsburgh Press*, March 4, 1939.

16. *Pittsburgh Post-Gazette*, March 8, 1939.

17. *Pittsburgh Post-Gazette*, March 18, 1939.

18. Roy McHugh, telephone interview with author, February 15, 2006.

19. Pie, Narr. Red Donley, WIIC-TV, Pittsburgh, PA, August 1967.

20. *Pittsburgh Post-Gazette*, March 18, 1939.

21. *Pittsburgh Post-Gazette*, March 24, 1939.

22. *Sporting News*, March 20, 1939.

23. *Pittsburgh Press*, April 5, 1948.

24. Ibid.

25. Ibid.

26. Lieb, *The Pittsburgh Pirates*, 256.

27. *Pittsburgh Press*, May 27, 1939.

28. *Pittsburgh Press*, June 5, 1939.

29. Jim Reisler, *A Great Day in Cooperstown* (New York: Carroll & Graf, 2006), 9.

30. *Pittsburgh Press*, July 18, 1939.

31. *Pittsburgh Press*, July 20, 1939.

32. *Pittsburgh Press*, July 16, 1939.

33. *Pittsburgh Press*, July 30, 1939.

34. *Pittsburgh Press*, August 16, 1939.

35. *Pittsburgh Press*, August 31, 1939.

36. *Washington Post*, February 22, 1940.

37. *Pittsburgh Press*, August 25, 1939.

38. Ibid.

39. *Newport Daily News*, March 31, 1960.

40. *Pittsburgh Post-Gazette*, March 17, 1972.

41. *Sporting News*, June 27, 1940.

42. *Pittsburgh Post-Gazette*, March 17, 1972.

43. Bob Gustine, telephone interview with author, March 6, 2006.

44. *Pittsburgh Press*, September 24, 1939.

45. Ibid.

46. *Pittsburgh Press*, September 29, 1939.

47. *Sporting News*, October 12, 1939.

48. *Washington Post*, September 29, 1939.

49. *Pittsburgh Sun-Telegraph*, September 29, 1939.

50. *Washington Post*, September 30, 1939.

51. *Austin (TX) American*, April 15, 1940.

52. *Pittsburgh Post-Gazette*, October 2, 1939.

53. *New York Times*, March 26, 1940.

54. *Chicago Tribune*, June 19, 1940.

Chapter 13

1. "Editorial Comment," *Baseball Magazine*, February 1940.

2. "SABR Baseball Encyclopedia," Society for American Baseball Research Website, http://members.sabr.org/members.cfm?a=rtl&rtl=enc&enc=crd&crd=sct&pid=14330 (June 22, 2008).

3. *Pittsburgh Post-Gazette*, August 26, 1942.

4. *Pittsburgh Sun-Telegraph*, September 29, 1939.

5. *Pittsburgh Press*, May 5, 1941.

6. *Pittsburgh Press*, March 7, 1957.

7. *Pittsburgh Press*, May 5, 1941.

8. Ibid.

9. *Charleroi (PA) Daily Mail*, June 9, 1942.

10. Pie, Narr. Red Donley, WIIC-TV, Pittsburgh, PA, August 1967.

11. *Pittsburgh Press*, March 3, 1943.

12. *Pittsburgh Press*, August 27, 1942.

13. *Pittsburgh Press*, March 3, 1943.

14. Marriage certificate for Donald MacIsaac and Mary Traynor, Massachusetts Department of Vital Statistics.

15. Death certificate for Mary MacIsaac, Massachusetts Department of Vital Statistics.

16. *Pittsburgh Press*, March 3, 1943.

17. *Cincinnati Enquirer*, November 9, 1941.

18. *Cincinnati Enquirer*, February 9, 1945.

19. Pie Traynor files at National Baseball Hall of Fame Library, Cooperstown, NY; *Sporting News*, May 4, 1944.

20. Lloyd Shoemaker, *The Escape Factory* (New York: St. Martin's Press, 1990), 111.

21. Ibid.; The United States Playing Card Company Website, http://www.usaplaying-card.com/history.html (January 18, 2009).

22. *Cincinnati Enquirer*, October 28, 1943.

23. Undated article, Paul Traynor family archives.

24. *Monesson* (PA) *Daily Independent*, January 13, 1945.

25. *Cincinnati Post*, January 27, 1939.

26. *Cincinnati Enquirer*, February 9, 1945.

27. *Toronto Star*, February 24, 1945

28. *Pittsburgh Post-Gazette*, February 19, 1945.

29. *Pittsburgh Press*, February 19, 1945.

30. Account of Jack Henry's life courtesy of his widow, Jean Henry, telephone interview with author, November 5, 2006.

31. Jim O'Brien, telephone interview with author, September 25, 2006.

32. Chuck Reichblum, telephone interview with author, September 28, 2006.

33. *Pittsburgh Press*, March 3, 1957.

34. *Pittsburgh Press*, June 6, 1946.

35. *Pittsburgh Press*, June 7, 1946.

36. Brent Kelley, *The Negro Leagues Revisited* (Jefferson, NC: McFarland, 2000), 184–185.

37. Chuck Brinkman, telephone interview with author, August 16, 2006.

38. Robert Gustine, telephone interview with author, March 6, 2006.

39. Ibid.

40. Pie Traynor files at National Baseball Hall of Fame Library, Cooperstown, NY.

41. Keeve Berman, telephone interview with author, July 27, 2006.

42. *Pittsburgh Post-Gazette*, February 23, 2000.

43. Roy McHugh, telephone interview with author, February 15, 2006; Smizik, *The Pittsburgh Pirates*, 43.

44. Alan Boal, telephone interview with author, February 28, 2006.

45. Ibid.; Roy McHugh, telephone interview with author, February 15, 2006.

46. Alan Boal, telephone interview with author, February 28, 2006.

47. Keeve Berman, telephone interview with author, July 27, 2006.

48. Ibid.

49. Jeff Roteman's KQV Web Site, http://user.pa.net/~ejjeff/jeffkqv2.html (December 30, 2007).

50. Ibid.

51. Keeve Berman, telephone interview with author, July 27, 2006.

52. Jeff Roteman's KQV Web Site, http://user.pa.net/~ejjeff/jeffkqv2.html (December 30, 2007).

53. John Rook, telephone interview with author, February 18, 2006.

54. Ibid.

55. Ibid.

56. Al Crouch, telephone interview with author, August 7, 2006.

57. John Rook, telephone interview with author, February 18, 2006.

58. Chuck Reichblum, telephone interview with author, September 28, 2006.

59. Jim O'Brien, telephone interview with author, September 25, 2006.

60. Keeve Berman, telephone interview with author, July 27, 2006.

61. Chuck Reichblum, telephone interview with author, September 28, 2006.

62. Keeve Berman, telephone interview with author, July 27, 2006.

63. *Boston Globe*, March 19, 1972.

64. Keeve Berman, telephone interview with author, July 27, 2006; Bruno Sammartino, telephone interview with author, February 9, 2007.

65. Keeve Berman, telephone interview with author, July 27, 2006.

66. Al Crouch, telephone interview with author, August 7, 2006.

67. *Pittsburgh Post-Gazette*, February 28, 1948.

68. *Sporting News*, June 22, 1949.

69. Richard Bak, *Cobb Would Have Caught It* (Detroit: Wayne State University Press, 1991), 190; John Skipper, Charlie Gehringer biographer, email to author, January 22, 2009.

70. *Pittsburgh Press*, June 14, 1949.

71. *Pittsburgh Post-Gazette*, June 14, 1949.

72. *Pittsburgh City Directory, 1946–1964 and 1970* (Pittsburgh: R.L. Polk).

73. Mike Helmer, telephone interview with author, April 3, 2007.

74. *Pittsburgh Post-Gazette*, July 28, 1969.

75. Robert Gustine, telephone interview with author, March 6, 2006.

76. *Sporting News*, August 2, 1969.

77. Robert Gustine, telephone interview with author, March 6, 2006.

78. *Sporting News*, August 2, 1969.

79. Mike Helmer, telephone interview with author, April 3, 2007.

80. Chuck Reichblum, telephone interview with author, September 28, 2006.

81. Nellie King, telephone interview with author, February 22, 2006.

82. *Pittsburgh Press*, November 14, 1955.

83. *Pittsburgh Press*, November 19, 1971.

84. Chuck Reichblum, telephone interview with author, September 28, 2006.

85. Ed Kiely, telephone interview with author, May 4, 2007.

86. Ibid.

87. Roy Blount, Jr., *About Three Bricks Shy ... and the Load Filled Up* (Pittsburgh: University of Pittsburgh Press, 2004), 132.

88. Ibid.

89. Roy McHugh, telephone interview with author, August 7, 2007.

90. Art Rooney, Jr., telephone interview with author, July 9, 2007.

91. Jack McGinley, telephone interview with author, May 9, 2007.

92. Ibid.

93. Art Rooney, Jr., telephone interview with author, July 9, 2007.

94. *Pie*, Narr. Red Donley, WIIC-TV, Pittsburgh, PA, August 1967.

95. Jim Vanderlin, telephone interview with author, August 21, 2006.

96. Jim Smith, telephone interview with author, January 26, 2008.

97. Bob del Greco, telephone interview with author, May 23, 2006.

98. *Controller's 86th Annual Report of the Fiscal Affairs of Allegheny County for the Year Ending December 31, 1946*, 18; *Controller's 87th Annual Report of the Fiscal Affairs of Allegheny County for the Year Ending December 31, 1947*, 20.

99. Charles C. Alexander, *Rogers Hornsby* (New York: Henry Holt, 2005), 285.

100. *Pie*, Narr. Red Donley, WIIC-TV, Pittsburgh, PA, August 1967.

101. Joe L. Brown, telephone interview with author, August 20, 2006.

102. *Pittsburgh Press*, March 7, 1957.

103. *Pittsburgh Press*, March 3, 1957.

104. Ibid.

105. *Pittsburgh Post-Gazette*, March 13, 1957.

106. Frank Thomas, telephone interview with author, May 21, 2006.

107. Gene Freese, telephone interview with author, August 3, 2007.

108. *Pittsburgh Press*, March 22, 1972.

109. *Cincinnati Post and Times-Star*, February 21, 1966.

110. Rich Hebner, telephone interview with author, May 23, 2006.

111. *Valley News Dispatch*, March 16, 1972.

112. Steve Blass, telephone interview with author, January 11, 2007.

113. "Pie Traynor Talks About Ringside Rosie," YouTube, http://www.youtube.com/watch?v=pbsnmPJtaHU (May 22, 2008).

114. Rich Hebner, telephone interview with author, May 23, 2006.

115. Steve Blass, telephone interview with author, January 11, 2007.

116. Ibid.

117. *Pittsburgh Press*, April 18, 1965.

118. Bruce Markusen, *The Great One* (Champaign, IL: Sports Publishing, 2001), 293–294.

119. Bruno Sammartino, telephone interview with author, February 9, 2007.

120. Dick Groat, telephone interview with author, July 12, 2007.

121. Ibid.

122. Roy McHugh, telephone interview with author, August 11, 2007.

123. Dick Groat, telephone interview with author, July 12, 2007.

124. Ibid.

125. Ibid.

126. Ibid.

127. Chuck Brinkman, telephone interview with author, August 16, 2006.

128. John Rook, email with author, April 23, 2005.

129. Keeve Berman, telephone interview with author, July 27, 2006.

130. Bill Cardille, telephone interview with author, February 28, 2006.

Chapter 14

1. Ed Kiely, telephone interview with author, May 4, 2007.

2. *Pittsburgh Post-Gazette*, November 1, 2006.

3. Jack Berger, telephone interview with author, June 10, 2007.

4. Robert D. Willis, "Wrestlers Are Underrated as Athletes, Says Former Baseball Star," *Wrestling Confidential*, November 1964.

5. Bill Cardille, telephone interview with author, February 28, 2006.

6. John DeFazio, telephone interview with author, August 15, 2006.

7. Ibid.

8. Ibid.

9. Bruno Sammartino, telephone interview with author, February 9, 2007.

10. Bill Cardille, telephone interview with author, February 28, 2006.

11. Lynn Boyd Hinds, *Broadcasting the Local News: The Early Years of KDKA-TV* (University Park, PA: Penn State University Press, 1995).

12. Bill Cardille, telephone interview with author, February 28, 2006.

13. "Pie Traynor Talks About Ringside Rosie," YouTube, http://www.youtube.com/watch?v=pbsnmPJtaHU (May 22, 2008).

14. "The Eyes Have It in Pittsburgh," Chiller Theater Memories, http://chillertheatermemories.com/WestlingArticle.htm (June 27, 2008).

15. Lou Vlahos, telephone interview with author, October 22, 2007.

16. Ibid.

17. Berger, Jack, telephone interview with author, June 10, 2007.

18. Cardille, Bill, telephone interview with author, February 28, 2006.

19. "Chiller Theater — Chilly Billy — American Heating Commercial," *YouTube*, http:www.youtube.com/watch?v=6Jk8HO4FNhk&feature=related (May 22, 2008).

20. Eleanor Schano, telephone interview with author, September 18, 2006.

21. Ibid.

22. Ibid.

23. Bill Cardille, telephone interview with author, February 5, 2007.

24. Ibid.

25. Ibid.

26. Phil Musick, telephone interview with author, February 14, 2007.

27. Roy McHugh, telephone interview with author, February 15, 2006.

28. Jack Berger, telephone interview with author, June 10, 2007.

29. Ibid.

30. *Charleroi* (PA) *Daily Mail*, August 16, 1956.

31. Don Riggs, telephone interview with author, November 19, 2007.

32. Chuck Reichblum, telephone interview with author, September 28, 2006.

33. *Sporting News*, August 2, 1969.

34. Bill Cardille, telephone interview with author, February 28, 2006.

35. Bruno Sammartino, telephone interview with author, February 9, 2007.

36. John DeFazio, telephone interview with author, August 15, 2006.

37. *Pie*, Narr. Red Donley, WIIC-TV, Pittsburgh, PA, August 1967.

38. Tom McDonough, telephone interview with author, March 31, 2006.

39. *Pie*, Narr. Red Donley, WIIC-TV, Pittsburgh, PA, August 1967.

40. Bill Cardille, telephone interview with author, February 28, 2006.

41. Ibid.

42. *Pie*, Narr. Red Donley, WIIC-TV, Pittsburgh, PA, August 1967.

43. *Cincinnati Times-Star*, January 19, 1938.

44. Douglas McCormick, interview with author, August 14, 2006.

45. Joe L. Brown, interview with author, August 20, 2006.

46. *Pie*, Narr. Red Donley, WIIC-TV, Pittsburgh, PA, August 1967.

47. Ibid.

48. *Pittsburgh Press*, March 3, 1943.

49. *Pittsburgh Press*, April 22, 1956.

50. John Bennett, email with author, May 26, 2006; Richard Simon, email with author, May 25, 2006; Jack Smalling, email with author, May 25, 2006.

51. *Pittsburgh Press*, August 17, 1948.

52. Mike Helmer, telephone interview with author, April 3, 2007.

53. Frank Gustine, Jr., telephone interview with author, June 1, 2006.

54. *Pittsburgh Post-Gazette*, July 28, 1969; Patti Mistick, telephone interview with author, January 17, 2007.

55. *Pie*, Narr. Red Donley, WIIC-TV, Pittsburgh, PA, August 1967.

56. Ibid.

57. Frank Gustine, Jr., telephone interview with author, June 1, 2006.

58. *Pittsburgh Press*, March 22, 1972.

59. *Boston Globe*, March 19, 1972.

60. *Pittsburgh Press*, April 11, 1971.

61. *Brookville Democrat*, September 9, 1998.

62. William Benswanger, Jr., telephone message left for author, October 17, 2007.

63. Gustine, Robert, telephone interview with author, March 6, 2006.

64. Ibid.

65. Mike Helmer, telephone interview with author, April 3, 2007.

66. *Pittsburgh Post-Gazette*, July 28, 1969.

67. Ibid.

68. *Sporting News*, August 2, 1969.

69. Mike Helmer, telephone interview with author, April 3, 2007.

70. Paul Traynor family archives.

Chapter 15

1. "Report Names the 'Burgh Nation's Sootiest City," KDKA.com, http://kdka.com/health/sootiest.city.pittsburgh.2.713291.html (July 5, 2008).

2. John Shively, telephone interview with author, April 17, 2007.

3. Bob Gustine, telephone interview with author, March 6, 2006.

4. *Sporting News*, April 1, 1972.

5. John Shively, telephone interview with author, April 17, 2007.

6. Northeastern University Sports Information Department archives.

7. Birth certificate for John Traynor, Massachusetts Department of Vital Statistics.

8. Marriage certificate for John Traynor and Elma MacLean, Massachusetts Department of Vital Statistics.

9. *Hartford Courant*, July 18, 1964; Death certificate for John Traynor, Connecticut State Department of Health.

10. Phil Musick, telephone interview with author, February 14, 2007.

11. Bill Cardille, telephone interview with author, February 28, 2006.

12. Frank Gustine, Jr., telephone interview with author, June 1, 2006.

13. Bill Christine, telephone interview with author, March 8, 2007.

14. *Connellsville* (PA) *Daily Courier*, May 12, 1971.

15. Bill Christine, telephone interview with author, March 8, 2007.

16. Ibid.

17. *Pittsburgh Press*, March 22, 1972.

18. *Pittsburgh Press*, March 22, 1972.

19. Ibid.

20. Mike Helmer, telephone interview with author, April 3, 2007.

21. *Pittsburgh Post-Gazette*, March 18, 1972.

22. *Sporting News*, March 18, 1972.

23. *Pittsburgh Press*, March 11, 1972.

24. *Pittsburgh Post-Gazette*, March 18, 1972.

25. *Pittsburgh Press*, March 17, 1972.

26. Aided-Injury Animal Bite Report, Harold Traynor, Pittsburgh Bureau of Police, March 16, 1972.

27. Certificate of death, Harold Joseph Traynor, Pennsylvania Department of Health.

28. John Shively, telephone interview with author, April 17, 2007.

29. *Pittsburgh Post-Gazette*, March 21, 1972.

30. *Pittsburgh Post-Gazette*, March 17, 1972.

31. *Pittsburgh Post-Gazette*, March 21, 1972.

32. *Pittsburgh Post-Gazette*, March 17, 1972.

33. Bill Christine, telephone interview with author, March 8, 2007.

34. *Pittsburgh Press*, March 19, 1972.

35. Ibid.

36. *Pittsburgh Post-Gazette*, March 21, 1972.

37. Ibid.

38. Paul Traynor family archives.

39. Ibid.

40. Douglas McCormick, interview with author, August 14, 2006.

41. Ibid.

42. Ibid.

43. Patti Mistick, telephone interview with author, January 17, 2007.

44. Will of Eve Traynor, Vol. 553, Pg. 967, May 20, 1977.

45. Inventory of Estate of Eve Traynor, Vol. 335, Pg. 553, February 23, 1978.

46. Jim O'Brien, telephone interview with author, September 25, 2006.

47. "Fineman: The Pennsylvania Polka," www.newsweek.com/id/120170 (March 9, 2007).

48. Jim O'Brien, telephone interview with author, September 25, 2006.

49. Brooks Robinson, telephone interview with author, April 12, 2009.

50. Jayson Stark, *The Stark Truth: The Most Overrated and Underrated Players in Baseball History* (Chicago: Triumph Books, 2007), 114.

51. Baseball Think Factory website, www.Baseballthinkfactory.org/files/hall_of_merit/discussion/pie_traynor (March 7, 2009).

52. Bill James, *The New Bill James Historical Baseball Abstract* (New York: Free Press, 2001), 588–590.

53. Stark, *The Stark Truth*, Pg. 53.

54. www.baseball-reference.com (March 7, 2009).

55. Clay Davenport, Joseph Sheehan, and Chris Kahrl, *Baseball Prospectus 2002* (Dulles, VA: Potomac Books, 2002), 8.

56. Ron Selter, email to author, January 15, 2009.

57. Lee Allen and Tom Meany, *Kings of the Diamond* (New York: Putnam's, 1965), 139.

Bibliography

Archival Resources

Allegheny County, PA, Register of Wills.
Bill Christine personal archives.
Burnett County (WI) Historical Society archives.
Connecticut Department of Public Health.
Edmund S. Muskie Archives and Special Collections Library at Bates College.
Framingham, MA, School Department archives.
Franklin County, IN, Clerk's Office.
Franklin County, IN, Recorder's Office.
Helen Zimmerman family archives.
Malden, MA, Historical Society archives.
Marilyn Lenick family archives.
Massachusetts Department of Vital Statistics.
National Archives and Records Administration.
National Baseball Hall of Fame Library.
Northeastern University Sports Information Department archives.
Nova Scotia Archives and Records Management.
Paul Traynor family archives.
Pennsylvania Department of Health.
Pittsburgh Bureau of Police.
Pittsburgh Pirates archives.
St. Bonaventure University archives.
Society for American Baseball Research Oral History Collection.
Somerville, MA, School Department archives.
United States Coast Guard National Maritime Center archives.

Government Documents

Annual Report of the Massachusetts State Board of Conciliation and Arbitration, January 1904.
Census of Canada, 1891 and 1901.
Controller's 86th Annual Report of the Fiscal Affairs of Allegheny County for the Year Ending December 31, 1946.
Controller's 87th Annual Report of the Fiscal Affairs of Allegheny County for the Year Ending December 31, 1947.
United States Census, 1900, 1910, 1920, 1930.

Newspapers

Austin (TX) *American*
Bates (ME) *Student*
Boston Evening Transcript
Boston Globe
Boston Record American
Brooklyn Eagle
Brookville (IN) *Democrat*
Charleroi (PA) *Daily Mail*
Chicago Daily News
Chicago Tribune
Cincinnati Enquirer
Cincinnati Post
Cincinnati Times-Star
Connellsville (PA) *Daily Courier*
Falmouth (MA) *Enterprise*
Hartford Courant
Los Angeles Times
Lowell (MA) *Sun*
Malden (MA) *Evening News*
Mansfield (OH) *News Journal*
Monesson (PA) *Daily Independent*
Narragansett (RI) *Times*

Nebraska State Journal
New Bedford (MA) *Times*
New York Times
New York World-Telegram
Newport (VA) *Daily News*
Philadelphia Inquirer
Philadelphia Record
Pittsburgh Courier
Pittsburgh Gazette-Times
Pittsburgh Post
Pittsburgh Post-Gazette
Pittsburgh Press
Pittsburgh Sun-Telegraph
Pittsburgh Tribune-Review
Portsmouth (VA) *Star*
Somerville (MA) *Journal*
Somerville (MA) *Press*
Sporting News
Toronto Star
Uniontown (PA) *Daily News Standard*
Valley News Dispatch (PA)
Virginian-Pilot and Norfolk Landmark
Washington Post
Woburn (MA) *Daily Times*

Personal Communication

Bartirome, Tony, former Pittsburgh Pirate player and trainer. Telephone interview, February 27, 2007.

Bennett, John, baseball historian. Email message, May 26, 2006.

Benswanger, Bill, Jr. Telephone message, October 17, 2007.

Berger, Jack, son of founder of American Heating. Telephone interview on June 10, 2007.

Berman, Keeve, former KQV employee. Telephone interview on July 27, 2006.

Blass, Steve, former Pittsburgh Pirate player. Telephone interview on January 11, 2007.

Boal, Alan, former KQV employee. Telephone interview on February 18, 2006.

Brinkman, Chuck, former KQV employee. Telephone interview on August 16, 2006.

Brown, Joe L., former Pittsburgh Pirates general manager. Telephone interview on August 20, 2006.

Cardille, Bill, friend of Traynor and former WIIC employee. telephone interviews on February 28, 2006, and February 5, 2007.

Castiglione, Pete, former Pittsburgh Pirate. Telephone interview, December 6, 2007.

Christine, Bill, former newspaper reporter. Telephone interview, March 8, 2007.

Crouch, Al, former KQV employee. Telephone interview, August 7, 2006.

DeFazio, John, former professional wrestler. Telephone interview, August 15, 2006.

del Greco, Bob, former Pittsburgh Pirate. Telephone interview, May 23, 2006.

Estienne, Joan, daughter of Portsmouth teammate Lester Bangs. Telephone interview with author, January 27, 2009.

Freese, Gene, former Pittsburgh Pirate. Telephone interview, August 3, 2007.

Friend, Bob, former Pittsburgh Pirate. Telephone interview, July 17, 2007.

Garner, John, Cape Cod League historian. Email message, February 25, 2009.

Gooch, Beverley, son of Traynor teammate Johnny Gooch. Telephone interview, August 22, 2006.

Groat, Dick, former Pittsburgh Pirate. Telephone interview, July 12, 2007.

Gustine, Bob, friend of Traynor. Telephone interview, March 6, 2006.

Gustine, Frank, Jr., friend of Traynor. Telephone interview, June 1, 2006.

Haeuser, Karl, resident of Paso Robles, CA. Telephone interview, February 3, 2007.

Hebner, Rich, former Pittsburgh Pirate. Telephone interview, May 23, 2006.

Helmer, Dale, nephew of Traynor. Telephone interview, April 3, 2007.

Henry, Jean, friend of Traynor. Telephone interview, November 5, 2006.

Kiely, Ed, friend of Traynor. Telephone interview, May 4, 2007.

King, Nellie, former Pittsburgh Pirate. Telephone interview, February 22, 2006.

Larson, Opal, resident of Webster, WI. Telephone interview, January 4, 2007.

Lenick, Marilyn, niece of Traynor. In-person interview, September 16, 2006.

McCormick, Doug, former Pittsburgh Pirate employee. Telephone interview, August 14, 2006.

McDonough, Tom friend of Traynor. Telephone interview, March 31, 2006.

McGinley, Jack, Jr., friend of Traynor. Telephone interview, May 9, 2007.

McHugh, Roy, former newspaper reporter. Telephone interviews, February 15, 2006 and August 7, 2007.

Mistick, Patti, Pittsburgh Pirates employee. Telephone interview, January 17, 2007.

Musick, Phil, former newspaper reporter. Telephone interview, February 14, 2007.

O'Brien, Jim, Pittsburgh sports historian. Telephone interview, September 25, 2006.

Penn, Virgil, III, Masonic historian. Email message, October 14, 2006.

Reichblum, Chuck, former Pittsburgh radio personality. Telephone interview, September 28, 2006.

Riggs, Don, former WIIC employee. Telephone interview, November 19, 2007.

Robinson, Brooks, Baltimore Orioles Hall of Famer. Telephone interview, April 12, 2009.

Rook, John, former KQV employee. Email message, April 23, 2005; telephone interview, February 18, 2006.

Rooney, Art, Jr., former Pittsburgh Steelers employee. Telephone interview, July 9, 2007.

Sammartino, Bruno, former professional wrestler. Telephone interview, February 9, 2007.

Schano, Eleanor, former WIIC employee. Telephone interview, September 18, 2006.

Selter, Ron, baseball researcher. Email messages, January 15, 2009 and January 20, 2009.

Shea, Martha, owner of the Hermitage. Email message, March 18, 2009.

Shively, John, Traynor's physician. Telephone interview, April 17, 2007.

Simon, Richard, autograph collector. Email message, May 25, 2006.

Skipper, John, baseball historian. Email message, March 3, 2009.

Smalling, Jack, autograph collector. Email message, May 25, 2006.

Tabbert, Mark, Director of Collections at George Washington Masonic. Email message, September 13, 2006.

Thomas, Frank, former Pittsburgh Pirate. Telephone interview, May 21, 2006.

Traynor, Paul, great nephew of Traynor. In-person interview, November 16, 2008.

Vanderlin, Jim, former batboy for semipro games. Telephone interview, August 21, 2006.

Vlahos, Lou, friend and former WIIC employee. Telephone interview, October 22, 2007.

Books

Alexander, Charles C. *Breaking the Slump.* New York: Columbia University Press, 2002.

_____. *John McGraw.* Lincoln: University of Nebraska Press, 1995.

_____. *Rogers Hornsby.* New York: Henry Holt, 2005.

Allen, Lee, and Tom Meany. *Kings of the Diamond.* New York: Putnam's, 1965.

Angus, Jeff. *Management by Baseball.* New York: Collins, 2006.

Appel, Martin, and Burt Goldblatt. *Baseball's Best.* New York: McGraw-Hill, 1977.

Bak, Richard. *Cobb Would Have Caught It.* Detroit: Wayne State University Press, 1991.

Barrow, Ed, and James Kahn. *My Fifty Years in Baseball.* New York: Coward-McCann, 1951.

Bartell, Dick, and Norman Macht. *Rowdy Richard: The Story of Dick Bartell.* Berkeley, CA: North Atlantic Books, 1993.

Berle, Milton. *B.S. I Love You: Sixty Years with the Famous and Infamous.* New York: McGraw-Hill, 1988.

Blount, Roy, Jr. *About Three Bricks Shy ... and the Load Filled Up.* Pittsburgh: University of Pittsburgh Press, 2004.

Boston, Talmadge. *1939: Baseball's Tipping Point.* Albany, TX: Bright Sky Press, 2005.

Bowman, John F., and Edward K. Muller. *Before Renaissance: Planning in Pitts-*

burgh 1889–1943. Pittsburgh: University of Pittsburgh Press, 2006.

Broeg, Bob. *My Baseball Scrapbook*. St. Louis: Rivercity Publishers, 1983.

_____. *Super Stars of Baseball*. St. Louis: Sporting News, 1971.

Browning, Reed. *1924*. Amherst and Boston: University of Massachusetts Press, 2003.

Capel, Wint. *Fiery Fast-Baller: The Life of Johnny Allen, World Series Pitcher*. Lincoln, NE: Writer's Showcase, 2001.

Carroll, Jeff. *Sam Rice*. Jefferson, NC: McFarland, 2007.

Cava, Pete. *Tales from the Cubs Dugout*. Chicago: Sports Masters, 2000.

Cicotello, David, and Angelo Louisa, ed. *Forbes Field: Essays and Memories of the Pirates' Historic Ballpark, 1909–1971*. Jefferson, NC: McFarland, 2007.

Cook, William A. *Waite Hoyt: A Biography of the Yankees' Schoolboy Wonder*. Jefferson, NC: McFarland, 2004.

Creamer, Robert W. *Stengel: His Life and Times*. New York: Dell Publishing, 1984.

_____. *Babe: The Legend Comes to Life*. New York: Simon & Schuster, 1992.

Crowley, Dan. *Baseball on Cape Cod*. Mount Pleasant, SC: Arcadia Publishing, 2004.

Davenport, Clay, Joseph Sheehan and Chris Kahrl. *Baseball Prospectus 2002*. Dulles, VA: Potomac Books, 2002.

Denslow, William R. *10,000 Famous Freemasons from K to Z Part Two*. Whitefish, MT: Kessinger Publishing, 2004.

DeValeria, Dennis, and Jeanne Burke DeValeria. *Honus Wagner*. New York: Henry Holt, 1995.

DeVeaux, Tom. *The Washington Senators*. Jefferson, NC: McFarland, 2001.

Eig, Jonathan. *Luckiest Man: The Life and Death of Lou Gehrig*. New York: Simon & Schuster, 2005.

Enright, Jim. *Chicago Cubs*. New York: Macmillan, 1975.

Evans-Daly, Laurie, and David C. Gordon. *Images of America: Framingham*. Mount Pleasant, SC: Arcadia Publishing, 1997.

Falkner, David. *Nine Sides of the Diamond*. New York: Times Books, 1990.

Finoli, David, and Bill Ranier. *The Pittsburgh Pirates Encyclopedia*. Champaign, IL: Sports Publishing, 2003.

Frommer, Harvey. *Five O' Clock Lightning: Babe Ruth, Lou Gehrig, and the Greatest Baseball Team in History, the 1927 New York Yankees*. New York: Wiley, 2007.

Gentile, Derek. *The Complete Boston Red Sox*. New York: Black Dog and Leventhal Publishers, 2003.

Ginsburg, Daniel. *The Fix Is In*. Jefferson, NC: McFarland, 2004.

Goldman, Steven. *Forging Genius: The Making of Casey Stengel*. Dulles, VA: Brassey's, 2005.

Golenbock, Peter. *The Spirit of St. Louis*. New York: Avon Books, 2000.

_____. *Wrigleyville*. New York: St. Martin's Press, 1999.

Graham, Frank. *McGraw of the Giants: An Informal Biography*. New York: Putnam's, 1944.

Gregory, Robert. *Diz*. New York: Viking, 1992.

Gutkind, Lee. *Lessons in Persuasion*. Pittsburgh: University of Pittsburgh Press, 2000.

Harriss, Helen L. *Trinity and Pittsburgh*. Greensburg, PA: Charles M. Henry, 1999.

Herring, Stephen W. *Framingham: An American Town*. Framingham, MA: Framingham Historical Society, 2000.

Hillenbrand, Laura. *Seabiscuit: An American Legend*. New York: Ballantine Books, 2003.

Hinds, Lynn Boyd. *Broadcasting the Local News: The Early Years of KDKA-TV*. University Park: Penn State University Press, 1995.

Hogan, Lawrence D. *Shades of Glory*. Washington, D.C.: National Geographic, 2006.

Holway, John. *Josh and Satch*. Westport, CT: Meckler Publishing, 1991.

Honig, Donald. *Baseball When the Grass Was Real*. New York: Berkley Publishing, 1974.

_____. *The October Heroes*. Lincoln: University of Nebraska Press, 1996.

Howell, Colin. *Northern Sandlots: A Social History of Maritime Baseball*. Toronto: University of Toronto Press, 1995.

James, Bill. *Bill James' Guide to Baseball Managers*. New York: Scribner's, 1997.

_____. *The New Bill James Historical Baseball Abstract*. New York: Free Press, 2001.

_____. *Whatever Happened to the Hall of Fame*. New York: Fireside, 1995.

James, Bill, and Rob Neyer. *The Neyer/James Guide to Pitchers*. New York: Fireside, 2004.

Kaese, Harold. *Boston Braves 1871–1953*. Boston: Northeastern University Press, 2004.

Kelley, Brent. *The Negro Leagues Revisited*, Jefferson, NC: McFarland, 2000.

Lanctot, Neil. *Negro League Baseball*. Philadelphia: University of Pennsylvania Press, 2004.

Levitt, Daniel R. *Ed Barrow: The Bulldog Who Built the Yankees' First Dynasty*. Lincoln: University of Nebraska Press, 2008.

Lieb, Frederick G. *The Pittsburgh Pirates*. Carbondale: Southern Illinois University Press, 2003.

Lorant, Stefan. *Pittsburgh: The Story of an American City*. Pittsburgh: Derrydale Press, 1999.

Lowry, Philip. *Green Cathedrals*. New York: Walker, 2006.

Lubove, Roy. *Twentieth Century Pittsburgh*. New York: John Wiley, 1969.

Markusen, Bruce. *The Great One*. Champaign, IL: Sports Publishing, 2001.

Marx, Harpo, with Roland Barber. *Harpo Speaks*. New York: Limelight Editions, 1961 (printed in 1988).

McCollister, John. *The Good, the Bad, and the Ugly: Heart-Pounding, Jaw-Dropping, and Gut-Wrenching Moments from Pittsburgh Pirates History*. Chicago: Triumph Books, 2008.

McGee, Bob. *The Greatest Ballpark Ever: Ebbets Field and the Story of the Brooklyn Dodgers*. New Brunswick, NJ: Rivergate Books, 2005.

Mencken, H.L. *Prejudices, Sixth Series*. New York: Knopf, 1927.

Mulligan, Brian. *The 1940 Cincinnati Reds*. Jefferson, NC: McFarland, 2005.

Murdock, Eugene. *Baseball Players and Their Times: Oral Histories of the Game, 1920–1940*. Westport, CT: Meckler Publishing, 1991.

Murphy, Cait. *Crazy '08*. New York: Smithsonian Books, 2008.

Murray, Tom, ed. *Sport Magazine's All-Time All-Stars*. New York: Atheneum, 1977.

Parker, Clifton Blue. *Big and Little Poison*. Jefferson, NC: McFarland, 2003.

Pietrusza, David, Matthew Silverman and Michael Gershman, eds. *Baseball: The Biographical Encyclopedia*. Kingston, NY: Total Sports Publishing, 2000.

Pittsburgh City Directory, 1946–1964 and 1970. Pittsburgh: R.L. Polk.

Powers, Albert Theodore. *The Business of Baseball*. Jefferson, NC: McFarland, 2003.

Price, Christopher. *Baseball by the Beach*. Yarmouth Port, MA: On Cape Publications, 1998.

Railton, Arthur. *The History of Martha's Vineyard: How We Got to Where We Are*. Beverly, MA: Commonwealth Editions, 2006.

Ramirez, Bruno. *Crossing the 49th Parallel*. Ithaca, NY: Cornell University Press, 2001.

Reagan, Patrick D. *Designing a New America: The Origins of New Deal Planning, 1890–1943*. Amherst: University of Massachusetts Press, 1999.

Reisler, Jim. *A Great Day in Cooperstown*. New York: Carroll & Graf, 2006.

Ribowsky, Mark. *A Complete History of the Negro Leagues 1884–1955*. New York: Carol Publishing, 1995.

Ritter, Lawrence S. *The Glory of Their Times*. New York: William Morrow, 1984.

Roberts, Randy. *Pittsburgh Sports: Stories from the Steel City*. Pittsburgh: University of Pittsburgh Press, 2002.

Rogosin, Donn. *Invisible Men: Life in Baseball's Negro Leagues*. Lincoln: University of Nebraska Press, 2007.

Seymour, Harold. *Baseball: The Golden*

Age. New York: Oxford University Press, 1971.

Shampoe, Clay, and Thomas R. Garrett. *Baseball in Portsmouth, Virginia.* Mount Pleasant, SC: Arcadia Publishing, 2004.

Shoemaker, Lloyd. *The Escape Factory.* New York: St. Martin's Press, 1990.

Simon, Tom, ed. *Baseball Stars of the National League.* Dulles, VA: Brassey's, 2004.

Skipper, John G. *Take Me Out to the Cubs Game.* Jefferson, NC: McFarland, 2002.

Smith, Curt. *Storied Stadiums: Baseball History Through Its Ballparks.* New York: Carroll & Graf, 2001.

Smizik, Bob. *The Pittsburgh Pirates: An Illustrated History.* New York: Walker, 1990.

Somerville, MA, City Directory, 1899–1901. Boston: W.A. Greenough.

Stark, Jayson. *The Stark Truth: The Most Overrated and Underrated Players in Baseball History.* Chicago: Triumph Books, 2007.

Staten, Vince. *Ol' Diz.* New York: HarperCollins, 1992.

Staudohar, Paul D., and J.A. Mangan, eds. *The Business of Professional Sports.* Urbana: University of Illinois Press, 1991.

Stout, Glenn, and Richard A. Johnson. *The Cubs.* New York: Houghton Mifflin, 2007.

Sullivan, Dean. *Middle Innings: A Documentary History of Baseball, 1900–1948.* Lincoln: University of Nebraska Press, 1998.

Thomas, Henry W. *Walter Johnson: Baseball's Big Train.* Washington, D.C.: Phenom Press, 1995.

Veeck, Bill, and Ed Linn. *Veeck as in Wreck.* Chicago: University of Chicago Press, 2001.

Whitt, Timothy. *Bases Loaded with History: The Story of Rickwood Field. America's Oldest Baseball Park.* Birmingham, AL: R. Boozer Press, 1995.

Wintz, William D. *Nitro: The World War I Boom Town.* Charleston, WV: Pictorial Histories Publishing, 1985.

Zellie, Carole. *Beyond the Neck: The Architecture and Development of Somerville, MA.* Cambridge, MA: Landscape Research, 1982.

Journals and Magazines

Baseball Digest
Baseball Magazine
Bates Alumni Magazine
The National Pastime
OB: The State of the Science, Second Edition
Sporting Life
Wrestling Confidential

Miscellany

A Nite for Pie Program, November 20, 1971.

Television Programs

"5th Inning — Shadow Ball." *Baseball,* Dir. Ken Burns, PBS, Arlington, VA, 1994.

Pie. Narr. Red Donley, WIIC-TV, Pittsburgh, PA, August 1967.

Videotaped lecture by Sol Gittleman, Somerville (MA) Community Access Television, April 4, 1995.

Internet Resources

Baseballlibrary.com
Baseball-reference.com
Baseballthinkfactory.org
ChillerTheaterMemories.com
KDKA.com
Newsweek.com
Retrosheet.org
Jeff Rotemann's KQV website (http://user.pa.net/~ejjeff/jeffkqv2.html)
Social Security Online (www.ssa.gov)
Society for American Baseball Research Baseball Encyclopedia
Society for American Baseball Research Minor Leagues Database
United States Playing Card Company website (www.usaplayingcard.com)
West Virginia Division of Culture and History website (www.wvculture.org)
WQED.org
YouTube.com

Index

Numbers in **_bold italics_** indicate pages with photographs.